J. (John) Perry

A Full Course Of Instructions For The Use Of Catechists

J. (John) Perry

A Full Course Of Instructions For The Use Of Catechists

ISBN/EAN: 9783743686663

Printed in Europe, USA, Canada, Australia, Japan

Cover: Foto ©Thomas Meinert / pixelio.de

More available books at **www.hansebooks.com**

A FULL COURSE OF INSTRUCTIONS FOR THE USE OF CATECHISTS;

BEING AN EXPLANATION OF THE CATECHISM,

ENTITLED

AN ABRIDGMENT OF CHRISTIAN DOCTRINE.

BY

THE REV. JOHN PERRY.

"They that instruct many to justice, shall shine as stars for all eternity."—*Dan.* xii., 3.

Fifth Edition.

DUBLIN:
JAMES DUFFY & SONS, 15 WELLINGTON QUAY,
AND
1A PATERNOSTER ROW, LONDON.

PRINTED BY
EDMUND BURKE & Co.,
61 & 62 GREAT STRAND STREET, DUBLIN.

APPROBATION

OF THE

RIGHT REV. DR. WAREING.

"HAVING attentively perused the Work of the REV. JOHN PERRY, entitled '*A full Course of Instructions for the Use of Catechists*,' I have great pleasure in recommending the same, as an orthodox and useful exposition of Catholic doctrine, and well calculated to assist, as well those who seek for instruction, as those who are employed in giving catechetical discourses.

"✠ WILLIAM, BISHOP OF ARIOPOLIS,
Vicar Apostolic of the Eastern District.

"NORTHAMPTON,
December 15th, 1847."

✠

"Meditate upon these things: be wholly in these things: that thy profiting may be manifest to all. Take heed to thyself, and to doctrine; be earnest in them: for in doing this, thou shalt both save thyself, and them that hear thee."—1 Tim. iv., 15, 16.

PREFACE.

THE duty of imparting Religious Instruction to others is, for all these upon whom it devolves, a very serious and important duty; and highly advantageous, when properly discharged, both to the Instructor and the Instructed. How very desirable, therefore, it is, that all who undertake this important and responsible duty should fit themselves for discharging it in a proper manner! And it is with the view of assisting them in this that the following "*Full Course of Instructions for the Use of Catechists*" is presented to them.

It claims not, indeed, to be entirely the original composition of him who presents it;

but professes to be, in a great measure, selected and compiled from various Authors.

The Instructions are drawn up in a condensed form, with the design of rendering them more useful to those, for whose assistance they are mainly intended. For, thereby, preparation for instructing becomes more easy; and, moreover, something is left to be drawn out by the Catechist.

INTRODUCTION.

MAN was created for a most important end—"*to love and serve God in this world, and to be happy with him for ever in the next;*" and the main business of our life consists in labouring for the attainment of this end. That we may not wander, or be led astray in this important work, but may arrive securely at the end for which we were created; God has established a Church upon earth, and appointed it to be, in all nations, throughout all ages, our Teacher and our Guide. In order to serve God, as he wishes to be served by us; that is to say, in order to please God in this life, so as to enjoy him in the next, we must believe *the teaching*, and follow *the guidance*, of his Church; because she teaches and guides the Faithful authoritatively, by his express commission, and under his promised direction.

We must *believe* whatever Christ teaches, as proposed and expounded to us by the Church: and the chief things which we are thus required to believe, we learn from the exposition of *the Apostles' Creed.*

But, belief is not sufficient, without practice—*faith will not save us without good works:* we must keep, therefore, the laws or *Commandments* of God; both those which were at first delivered to man by his own mouth, and also those which, by an authority received from him, are delivered to us by the mouth of his Church.

But we cannot *practise* our faith, or keep the Commandments, *without the help of God's grace;* and hence, the Catechism introduces the Commandments by a short exposition of *Prayer*, which is a *means of grace*, indispensably necessary for all persons—is the easiest for us to have recourse to—is, at all times and in all places, completely within our power--and the use of which requires not the outward administration of the Church.

II. To prayer must be added the use of *the Sacraments*, which Christ has instituted in his Church; which are also *efficacious means of grace*—the *most* efficacious means wherewith he has furnished us; and without the use of which prayer will become ineffectual. It is very important, therefore, that every one should be acquainted with these means of grace, and should know how to make a good and profitable use of them: for, a *proper use of the Sacraments* may be said to be *the* practice of Religion; because thereby we shall infallibly obtain such graces as will secure the practice of all the rest.

For, by making a *proper* use of the Sacraments, we shall not merely believe what God has taught, and keep his commandments; but we shall effectually root out our *Vices*, and acquire all necessary *Virtues:* we shall advance rapidly in the practice of *the Three Theological Virtues*—our *Faith* will become every day more lively, our *Hope* and confidence in God more firm, and our *Charity* more pure and ardent; our souls will be adorned with *the Gifts*, and enriched with *the Fruits of the Holy Ghost:* we shall be enabled to be constantly laying up abundant stores of merits for the next life, by the performance of *the Works of Mercy* both *corporal and spiritual*—and by the practice of *the Three eminent good Works;* and thus shall we become entitled to the inestimable *Blessings* promised in the *Eight Beatitudes*.

In a word, the proper use of the Sacraments will enable us to reduce to practice *the Christian's Rule of Life*, by leading us to a constant and faithful performance of *the Christian's Daily Exercise:* or, in other words, by means of the Sacraments, we shall be enabled to acquire *the perfection* which God expects from us; and to arrive securely at our last end—the possession of our God in a happy eternity.

CONTENTS.

A FULL COURSE OF

INSTRUCTIONS

FOR THE USE OF CATECHISTS.

PRELIMINARY INSTRUCTION.

On the Obligation and Advantages of being instructed; and the lamentable consequences arising from Ignorance.

SINCE God has made us "to *know him*, love him, and serve him in this world; and to be happy with him for ever in the next;" it follows, as a necessary consequence, that we are bound to take the means of accomplishing this end of our creation. But, as we cannot take means of which we are ignorant, it also follows that we are bound to *learn* what those means are, and how to employ them. Now, we acquire this necessary knowledge, by acquiring a knowledge of our Religion; and, therefore, as attending Catechetical Instructions is the chief means by which people generally come to know their Religion, I will show, 1st, the Necessity of each one learning his Religion, or the Obligation of attending to Religious Instruction; 2ndly, The great Advantages of being well instructed; and 3rdly, The lamentable Evils arising from ignorance. After this I will point out the Means of becoming instructed.

I. The OBLIGATION of learning our Religion arises, in the first place, from the express command of Almighty God:—In the Old Law, God commanded his people to be careful to learn his precepts and ordinances; the ceremonies of Religion; and what he had done for them; and to teach these things to their children: "Lay up these my words in your hearts and minds, and hang them for a sign on your hands, and place them between your eyes; teach your children that they may meditate on them."[1] Are *Christians* to be less diligent in learning their Religion?

In the New Law, Christ requires his Apostles (and their successors) to "teach all nations;"[2] to "preach the Gospel to every creature:"[3] Now, this implies a necessity in the people to learn. And we may judge of the importance of being instructed, by the diligence with which the Apostles fulfilled this duty of teaching—and also by the express declaration of Christ: "He that believeth not," i.e., he who receives not what you teach, "shall be condemned."[4] And again: "He that heareth you, heareth me; and he that despiseth you, despiseth me;"[5] i.e., he who refuses or neglects to hear *you*, is as guilty as if he refused or neglected to hear me; because you teach in my name, and by my authority.

But, if God had given no express command on this subject, still you would be obliged to get instructed; because a knowledge of Religion is necessary for being saved. Now, this knowledge consists in knowing God—his Perfections—the wonders of his works—and what he has done for *us;* in knowing the end of our creation—the homage we owe to our Creator, and how we are to pay it—the commandments we have to observe—and the rewards we have to gain; and in knowing *the means* of gaining those rewards. And can you be well acquainted with these important truths, without taking means to learn them?

1. Instruction, then, teaches us to know God—his Perfections; what he has done for us as Creator—what as Redeemer; and the other articles of Christian belief. All these we *must* believe, for "without faith it is

(1) Deut. xi., 18, 19, 20. (2) Matt. xxviii., 19. (3) Mark xvi., 15. (4) Mark xvi., 16. (5) Luke x., 16.

impossible to please God;"[6] and "he that believeth not shall be condemned."[7] But how can we *believe* without knowing? and how can we *know*, without getting instructed? "How shall they believe *him*, of whom they have not heard? and how shall they hear without a preacher? Faith then cometh by hearing."[8] *(Example of the Eunuch of Queen Candace:—* "Philip said: Thinkest thou that thou understandest what thou readest? who said: And how can I, unless some man show me?"[9])

2. We are placed in this world for a particular end; viz., to worship God and keep his commandments in this life; and to be rewarded in the next. Now, we worship God and keep his commandments, by practising the Religion of Christ. But how can we practise it, unless we are instructed in what the Christian Religion teaches? Persons ignorant of their duty are answerable for their ignorance, if, through their own fault, they have neglected Instructions. You *hardly can* be ignorant, except through your own fault; because public instructions are regularly given; and by attending to them, *every one* MAY know all that is necessary for salvation—all the necessary means of being saved.

3. Amongst these means of salvation, the most effectual are the *Sacraments.* By a good use of them, we receive grace (without which we can do nothing); for they are the *channels of grace.* How important then it is, to be instructed in the *nature* and *effects* of the Sacraments, and in the *dispositions* necessary for worthily receiving them! For, without knowing these, we cannot make a good use of the Sacraments; and thus, without Instruction, the means of salvation become useless.

(6) Heb. xi., 6.
(7) Mark xvi., 16.
(8) Rom. x., 14, 17.
(9) Acts viii., 30, 31.

[*Apply in a similar manner any other important duties.*]

II. There are very GREAT ADVANTAGES to be derived from attending religious Instructions. For Religion is the science of salvation; by learning what it teaches, you learn how to save your soul: what advantages, then, in attending Instructions! Salvation is a difficult work—beset with temptations and snares; the enemy is always seeking your ruin: now, Instruction enables us to pass uninjured through all these difficulties, dangers, and temptations.

We cannot be too well instructed. Good instruction is a seed, which, sooner or later, will produce fruit. Well instructed persons are more firm in their faith—can withstand greater assaults, &c.; because they know how to cast themselves on God, and to seek his assistance: therefore they are not so liable to fall off. And if they do fall, they *more easily* rise, because they know the means; and they *sooner* rise, because their remorse is greater—they cannot still the voice of their conscience. What advantages, then, in being well instructed!

III. But, on the other hand, most LAMENTABLE ARE THE CONSEQUENCES arising from ignorance! it is impossible to enumerate them. Ignorance is the cause of heresies, and of persecutions: "For if they *had known*, they would never have crucified the Lord of glory."[10] Whence proceeds such a general forgetfulness of God? what is the cause of that indifference for Religion, which is so common in the world? *Ignorance.* For no wonder that Religion is so little practised by those who are ignorant of what it teaches. It will be found, at the last day, that many have been lost through ignorance, who, had they attended to instructions would have been saved. For, as St.

(10) 1 Cor. ii., 8.

Augustin says, "Ignorance, when avoidable, is a sin." And, as it is a sin attended with such *lamentable Consequences*, take care not to become guilty of it; with this view, resolve to be attentive in future to religious Instructions.

PRELIMINARY INSTRUCTION CONTINUED.

On the Means of acquiring Instruction.

Having shown the *Obligation* and *Advantages* of attending to religious Instruction, and also the great *Evils arising from Ignorance*, I will now point out *the Means*, which you should employ, of becoming instructed. You have abundant means, if you will but make use of them.

1. The first means is by Private Instruction: i.e., by such as is derived from Parents or Friends, or from one's own reading.

They who *can* read *ought;* for, the being able to read is a talent to be returned with interest;—they who *cannot* read, may easily *get others* to read for them; and they *would*, if truly zealous, and anxious to be instructed. (*Example:* When persons are deficient in the knowledge of their trade, do they not take every means and opportunity of gaining more information?)

They who are able to instruct the ignorant, cannot perform a more meritorious work: it is a great charity; it is one of the spiritual works of mercy—it is what Christ came from heaven to do, and to set us an example of. "They who instruct many to justice, shall shine as stars for all eternity."[11] It is a work most pleasing to God; highly beneficial to our neighbours, and also to ourselves; for it will draw down blessings on both.

(11) Dan. xii., 3.

But fathers, mothers, and all heads of families, are more particularly called upon to perform this office of instruotion: "If any man have not care of his own, and especially those of his house; he hath denied the faith, and is worse than an infidel.'"[12]—Some parents imagine themselves excused from the obligation of instructing, thinking it is their Pastor's duty. It is *his* duty; but they are not excused on that account: they are more strictly bound, with regard to their own children, than their Pastor; yet, how generally is this duty neglected! How many parents will have reason to weep and tremble, when they stand before the judgment seat of God? for they will have a severe account to give!

It follows, therefore, that ill-instructed parents are under a double obligation of attending Instructions, in order that, by becoming instructed themselves, they may be able to teach their children. Every parent *can* and *ought* to teach his children who God is—to say their prayers—to avoid sin—to fear hell—to desire heaven, &c.

2. THE SECOND MEANS IS BY PUBLIC INSTRUCTION: that is, by attending regularly at the Instructions which are given publicly by their pastor. This is a means of Divine institution: "The lips of the Priest shall keep knowledge, and they shall seek the law at his mouth."[13] "Go and teach all nations,...teaching them to observe all things whatsoever I have commanded you; and behold I am with you all days, even to the end of the world;"[14] and therefore, "he that heareth you, heareth me."[15] Thus, it is Christ himself who teaches by his ministers: "For Christ therefore we are ambassadors, God as it were exhorting by us."[16] The opportunity of receiving Instruction from those who

(12) 1 Tim. v., 8.
(13) Mal. ii 7
(14) Matt. xxviii., 19, 20.
(15) Luke x., 16.
(16) 2 Cor. v., 20.

are duly appointed to teach, is a special grace . . to be accounted for hereafter. How many neglect this grace! and allow those under their charge to neglect it also!

There are some who think it a matter of little consequence to neglect the explanation of the Catechism; imagining themselves sufficiently instructed—a sure sign they are ignorant. In the affair of Religion and salvation, even the most learned have always something more to learn. [*The parable of the talents*[17] *shows that the more persons have, the more they are expected to gain; and that if they do not improve their talent, it will be taken away.*]

These person, who imagine themselves to be sufficiently instructed, may perhaps know their Prayers—the Articles of the Creed—the Commandments—the Sacraments. But is nothing more required of them? Do they know how to *defend* the articles of their belief? Are they "always ready to satisfy every one that asketh them a reason of that hope which is in them?"[18]—Do they know what particular actions are forbidden by each Commandment? and how to make the *best use* of the Sacraments?—Do they know how to escape the dangers of the world —the snares, delusions, and temptations of the devil—the allurements of self-love, and of their passions?—Do they know the best means of becoming daily more and more perfect? Until you know *all these*, you are not so sufficiently instructed, as to be at liberty to neglect the public instructions of your Pastor: unless distance, or some other great inconvenience, excuse you. For these public instructions are not for children *only*, but for all.

Persons will sometimes excuse themselves from attending, by saying *they have no time*. No time! Why are they forbidden to work on Sundays and Holidays?

(17) Matt. xxv., 14 to 30 (18) 1 Peter iii., 15.

Why are they sent into this world? What is time given them for? Is it *really* want of *time*, or want of zeal and diligence? Could they not find time, by a little forecast and contrivance?—And after all, what employment is so important as learning how to save one's soul? "What doth it profit a man, if he gain the whole world, and lose his own soul?"[19] Be diligent, therefore, and regular, in attending instructions.

3. I will now say a few words, in conclusion, on the dispositions necessary for profiting by instructions:—You should ask God to enlighten your *mind* to understand, and to dispose your *heart* to receive and practise, what you are about to hear.[20]—"Our words, when we instruct, (says St. Augustin,) are like the labours of a gardener, when he cultivates: they cannot produce any fruit, unless God give it." For it is "God that giveth the increase."[21] To God then we must apply: the Pastor before he instructs—the people before they hear: the Pastor, also, after he has instructed, should ask a blessing on what he has said—the people on what they have heard.

During the time of instruction, you should of course be very attentive; when you hear anything which is particularly applicable to yourselves, you should try to remember it; and should resolve there and then to put it in practice. For, the chief end of instruction is to know *what* to practise, and *how* to practise it. In order to be "blessed," you must not only "*hear* the word of God," but you must also "*keep* it."[22] "My word shall not return to me *void*."[23]

Lament the little profit which you may have hitherto derived from instruction; and the loss of so many instructions which you have neglected to attend to; resolve to be more diligent and regular in future; and

(19) Matt. xvi., 26. (20) Acts xvi., 11. (21) 1 Cor. iii., 7. (22) Luke xi., 28. (23) Isais lv., 11.

endeavour henceforth to profit by every opportunity of instruction, which shall be offered you.

EXPLANATION

OF THE

INTRODUCTORY CHAPTER OF THE CATHECHISM.

INSTRUCTION I.

On the Existence of God—the End of our Creation—the Immortality of the soul—and Free-will.

Who made you?—God.

Why did God make you?—To know him, love him, and serve him in this world; and to be happy with him for ever in the next.

To whose likeness did God make you?—God made me to his own image and likeness.

Is this likeness in your body or in your soul?—In my soul.

In what is your soul like to God?—In this, that my soul is a spirit, has understanding, and free-will, and is immortal.

What do you mean, when you say your soul is immortal?—I mean that my soul can never die.

In what else is your soul like to God?—In this, that as in one God, there are three Persons; so in my one soul there are three powers.

Which are these three powers?—My will, my memory, and my understanding.

I. Existence of God:—The Catechism very properly commences by pointing out the existence of a God, *as our Creator;* and that we are bound, *as his creatures*, to know, love, and serve him.

How do you *know* that there is a God?

1. The very fact of our own existence proves it for, if we ask ourselves this question: "*Who made*

me?" we can find no reasonable answer, except this: "*A self-existent Being.*" Again, if we ask the different things around us, their answer must be the same. From this self-existence of God, all his other perfections flow.

2. The magnificence and harmony of the creation prove it: all nature proclaims the existence of a God.

3. There is another argument which comes more home: Conscience makes us feel there is a God—that there is an all-seeing witness............For, whence comes that pleasure which we experience after performing good works? consolation in patient suffering? confidence in death?—whence that remorse after secret crimes? terrors at death? &c. Hence, there cannot be *really* a positive *Atheist.*

II. End of our Creation:—*Knowing*, then, that there *is a God*, (and we are bound to know this, for God made us *to know him*,) we must, as a necessary consequence of this knowledge, *love and serve him.* For *why* did God make you?

St. Paul teaches us that we cannot "come to God," or be eternally happy with him, "without believing that he is, and that he is a rewarder to them that seek him."[24] But if we content ourselves with *knowing and believing only*, we fall far short, &c. For God commands us to *love him* also—and to love him *above all things:* i.e., with a love of *preference:* "For he that loveth father or mother more than me is not worthy of me."[25] *(Example of Abraham*, in being ready to sacrifice his only son;[26] *and also of the Apostles*, in being able to say: "Who shall separate us from the love of Christ? shall tribulation? or persecution? or the sword?...I am sure that neither life nor death, nor things present, nor things to come...nor any other creature, shall be able to separate us from the love of

(24) Heb. xi., 6. (25) Matt. x., 37. (26) Gen. xxii.

God, which is in Christ Jesus our Lord."[27] *Every one of us* should be able to say the same.)

How are you to *show* that you love God? By faithfully *serving* him: "If you love me, keep my commandments."[28] Like the Martyrs, we must be ready to suffer all—to sacrifice all, rather than disobey the law of God.

This knowing, loving, and serving God, is the way by which we are to arrive at the great end for which we were created—the enjoyment of God in a happy eternity. For,

Why did God make you?—To know him, love him, and serve him in this world; and TO BE HAPPY with him for ever in the next.

The happiness provided for us in the next life cannot be conceived, much less described: it consists in the *beatific vision.* *(Example:* How enraptured with delight the three Apostles were, when they beheld our Blessed Lord transfigured before them![29]) The happiness of heaven is to be given to us, as a reward we are placed here for a short time, in a state of trial. to merit it. Therefore, be diligent in loving and serving God; and he will be liberal in rewarding you—he will make you happy with himself in heaven; because that is the end for which he created you.

III. IMMORTALITY OF THE SOUL:—*To whose likeness did God make you?*—God made me to his own image and likeness.

Is this likeness in your body or in your soul?—In my soul.

After having created heaven and earth, God held a council within himself, "and he said: Let us make

(27) Rom. viii., 35 38, 39. (28) John xiv., 15. (29) Matt. xvii., 1 to 9.

man to our own image and likeness...and God created man to his own image."[30]——*The whole business of our life consists in labouring to perfect this image of God in our soul.*

In making man, God formed his body "of the slime of the earth; and breathed into his face the breath of life, and man became a living soul;"[31] i.e., God gave him a soul, which is *spiritual and immortal*, like himself.

What do you mean when you say your soul is immortal?—I mean that my soul can never die.

When the body dies, the soul does not. How do we know this? We know it—

1. From reason:—The soul is a spirit; and reason shows that it is not the nature of a spirit to die; because, being a simple immaterial substance, it contains in itself no principle of dissolution.

2. From the Divine justice:—For, being infinitely just, God will reward virtue, and punish vice. Now, it very often happens, that, during life, the wicked prosper . . . ; whilst the good are afflicted, oppressed, persecuted unto death . . . But, if there were no future life, where would be the justice of God?—This consideration made the Psalmist say: "Behold these are sinners; and yet abounding in the world *they* have obtained riches . . and *I* have been scourged all the day. I studied that I might know this thing; it is labour in my sight until I go into the Sanctuary of God, and understand concerning their last ends."[32]

3. From Divine Revelation:[33]—"God created man incorruptible."[34] "The souls of the just are in the hand of God, and the torment of death shall not

(30) Gen. i., 26, 27. (32) Ps. lxxii., 12 to 17.
(31) Gen. ii., 7. (33) 3 Kings xvii., 21, 22; Luke xvi., 22 to 31.
(34) Wisd ii., 23; Mt. xxii., 32.

touch them. In the sight of the *unwise* they *seemed* to die; and their going away from us was taken for utter destruction: but they are in peace; . . their hope is full of immortality."[35]

IV. FREE-WILL:—What is meant by *free-will?* It is that power or faculty of the soul, by which we are enabled to choose either to do good, or to do evil. Free-will is necessary in a state of trial: for without it, there would be no merit. "Before man is life and death, good and evil; that which he shall choose shall be given him."[36] "God will render to every man according to his works."[37]

INSTRUCTION II.

On the Folly of neglecting Salvation; on worshipping God by Faith, Hope, and Charity; and on the Happiness of attending to this Worship of God.

Which must you take most care of—your body or your soul?—Of my soul.

Why so?—Because Christ has said, "What doth it profit a man, if he gain the whole world, and lose his own soul?"

What must you do to save your soul?—I must worship God by faith, hope, and charity; that is, I must believe in him, hope in him, and love him with my whole heart.

1. FOLLY OF NEGLECTING SALVATION:—These words, "What doth it profit a man, if he gain the whole world, and lose his own soul,"[38] . . deserve our most serious attention; yet, alas! how few reflect, &c. To judge from the general conduct of mankind, we might suppose that riches and earthly enjoyments are the sole objects of their pursuit. . . Yet, how little do these things profit, &c.? . . .

(35) Wisd. iii., 1 to 4.
(36) Eccli. xv., 18; Deut. xxx., 15, 19.
(37) Rom. ii., 6.
(38) Matt. xvi., 26.

Example of Solomon:—"He *surpassed* in riches all that were before him in Jerusalem;" and he said: "Whatsoever my eyes desired, I refused them not; and I withheld not my heart from enjoying every pleasure, and delighting itself in the things which I had prepared. And when I turned myself to the labours wherein I had laboured in vain, I saw in all things vanity and vexation of mind."[39]

Example of the rich man who was summoned out of life in the very act of exulting in his wealth:—Rejoicing in his abundance, he said: "Soul, thou hast much goods laid up for many years: take thy rest; eat, drink, and make good cheer. But God said to him: Thou fool! this night do they require thy soul of thee and whose shall those things be, which thou hast provided? So is he that layeth up treasure for himself, and is not rich towards God."[40]

Example of Dives and Lazarus:—"There was a certain rich man who was clothed in purple and fine linen, and feasted sumptuously every day. And there was a certain beggar, named Lazarus, who lay at his gate, full of sores; desiring to be filled with the crumbs that fell from the rich man's table, and no man did give him. And it came to pass that the beggar died, and was carried by angels into Abraham's bosom. And the rich man also died; and he was buried in hell. And lifting up his eyes when he was in torments, he saw Abraham afar off, and Lazarus in his bosom. And he cried, and said: Father Abraham, have mercy on me; and send Lazarus that he may dip the tip of his finger in water to cool my tongue; for I am tormented in this flame. And Abraham said to him: Son, remember that thou didst receive good things in thy lifetime, and likewise Lazarus evil things: but now he is comforted, and thou art tormented."[41]

(39) Ec. ii., 1 to 11. (40) Luke xii., 16 to 31. (41) Luke xvi., 19 to 31.

What a folly it is, thus to condemn one's self to endless misery, for the sake of a few momentary enjoyments! What doth it profit a man to have gained the whole world, when his soul is lost? lost irrecoverably! . . .

II. Faith, Hope, and Charity:—*What must you do to save your soul?*—I must worship God by faith hope, and charity; that is, I must believe in him, hope in him, and love him with my whole heart.

Faith, Hope, and Charity are virtues that relate immediately to God. They are not *acquired* but *infused:* we should pray for them, and make Acts of them; because they are necessary for salvation. It is by these virtues (which include every other), that we must worship God.

How do we worship God by *Faith?* When we believe all he has revealed, *because* he is the very truth, and believe it whether we comprehend it or not; we *then* give him the homage of our reason—we pay homage to his eternal truth.

How do we worship God by *Hope?* When we serve him with full assurance of obtaining whatever is necessary for us, resting that assurance on the reflection that God is infinitely *good, merciful, powerful, and faithful;* we *then* give him the homage of our confidence—we pay homage to his goodness, power, and promises. This perfect confidence is a homage very pleasing to him.

How do we worship God by *Charity?* When we love him above all things, *because* he is infinitely deserving of our love; i.e., when we love him *for his own sake*, and, on this account, obey his will; we *then* give him the homage of our heart or affections—we pay homage to *all* his Divine perfections, by which he is infinitely good in himself, and infinitely deserving of our love. This is the most pleasing homage we can pay him.

III. HAPPINESS OF SERVING God:—To worship God, by exercising these three virtues; or, in other words, to worship him by leading a truly virtuous life, is a sure means of becoming happy, not only in heaven, but even in this life. There can be no true happiness without peace and contentment of mind: now, earthly enjoyments, and sinful gratifications, can never produce this; but they have a contrary effect: "For the wicked are like a raging sea, which can never rest... There is no peace for the wicked, said the Lord God."[42]

It is *in the service of God only*, that true peace or content of heart can be found; because this is the gift of God—a gift which he promises to his servants: "Peace I leave you, my peace I give unto you; not as the world giveth, do I give unto you."[43] Here is promised a peace far superior to the false peace of the world—even "the peace of God, which surpasseth all understanding"[44]—"a joy which no man shall take from you."[45] This is that hundred-fold, which God gives to those, who, for his sake, renounce earthly attachments.[46]

What greater happiness can there be than the testimony of a *good conscience?* "For our glory is this, the testimony of our conscience."[47] This is a source of the greatest comfort; and draws down every grace and blessing: "If our heart reprehend us not, we have confidence towards God; and whatever we shall ask, we shall receive of him."[48]

It is this confidence towards God that makes the virtuous man happy in life, and happy in death; "The fear of the Lord shall delight the heart, and shall give joy and gladness, and length of days. With

(42) Is. lvii., 20, 21. (43) John xiv., 27. (44) Phil. iv., 7. (45) John xvi., 22. (46) Mark x., 29, 30. (47) 2 Cor. i., 12. (48) 1 John iii. 21.

him that feareth the Lord it shall go well in the latter end; and in the day of his death he shall be blessed."[49]

Enter, therefore, in good earnest, upon the practice of virtue; serve God diligently, and with a willing heart; and your reward will be very great, not only in heaven, but even in this life.

INSTRUCTION III.

The Rule of Faith.

What is Faith?—It is to believe, without doubting whatever God teaches.

Why must you believe whatever God teaches?—Because God is the very truth, and cannot deceive nor be deceived.

How are you to know what the things are which God teaches?—By the testimony of the Catholic Church, which God has appointed to teach all nations, all those things which he has revealed.

Faith, as applied to revealed truths, is a complete certainty—"it is the evidence of things that appears not."[50] To have faith, therefore, is to be *quite certain* of the truths we profess: for, if there be any doubt or misgiving, it is not *Faith*, but only, at most, a strong *opinion*. Divine faith is distinguished from mere human belief, by the authority on which it is grounded. That which makes faith *divine* is this—believing revealed truths *because* God, who is truth itself, has declared them: for what He has said *must* be true, whether we comprehend it or not.

But has God left us any *certain* means or *rule*, whereby we can know *with certainty* what he has said or revealed? He has: the Catechism says, we are to learn this from the Church—from *that very Church*

(49) Eccli. I., 12, 13. (50) Heb. xi., 1.

which God has established, and "appointed to teach all nations all those things which he has revealed."[51]

As there is but "*one Lord*," so there can be but "*one faith*"[52]—but one *true* Church: for Christ could not teach contradictory doctrines. Now, it is by the belief and practice of what he *did* teach, that we are to be saved: "He that believeth and is baptized, shall be saved; but he that believeth not, shall be condemned."[53] Therefore, it is a matter of the greatest consequence to know *those very doctrines*, which we are thus required to believe: and all *can* know them with certainty, because we have sufficient means of coming to the certain knowledge of them.

Indeed, as Christ requires us all to believe, *under pain of eternal death*, it follows that he must have given us the means of coming to a certain knowledge of the truth; since it would be inconsistent to require *belief*, without giving the means of coming to a certain knowledge of what he thus requires us to believe. Therefore, by following the means which he has given, (i.e., by following the appointed *Rule of Faith*,) we can come to know, with certainty, the true doctrines.

The appointed *Rule of Faith*, to be sufficient to bring mankind to this certain knowledge; and indeed to be consistent with the wisdom and goodness of God, must be, 1st, *Plain*, or suited to the capacity of mankind generally; 2ndly, *Universal*, or containing all the truths revealed; 3rdly, *Certain*, both in itself and in its application to us. No Rule of Faith can be the true one, unless it has these three qualities.

What, then, *is* the Rule appointed by Christ? Protestants say: "*It is the Bible only*—the WRITTEN WORD *is the entire Rule for all*." Catholics say: "*It is the whole word of God, both written and unwritten;*

(51) Matt. xxviii., 19, 20.
(52) Eph. iv., 5.
(53) Mark xvi., 16.

and this as taught and explained by the Church: it is the teaching of the Church."

To know which is the true Rule, we must see which has the necessary qualities:—

1. The Protestant Rule of taking the *Scripture alone*, is not *plain*, nor suited to the capacity of mankind generally. It is most *unsuited* to those who *cannot read:* how many such were there, especially in the earlier ages? for there was no printing till more than 1400 years after Christ. It is *not suited* to those who *can* read, but have not judgment to understand the true sense of what they read. And how many are there, who cannot understand the sense of the Scriptures! That the number of such is vastly great is evident from plain fact; for we see, that those who have not the Catholic Church to guide them, disagree about the meaning of Scripture. The Scripture itself says, it is "hard to be understood," and is "wrested by the unlearned and unstable to their own destruction."[54] Therefore, the Protestant Rule is not plain; but it is a most difficult and dangerous rule.

On the other hand, nothing can be more plain, more easy, and more suited to the capacity of mankind generally, than the Catholic Rule. Those who cannot read, can listen to instructions—those who can read, but have not capacity to judge of the sense, can understand what they are to believe, when it is expounded to them. This rule is in accordance with the words of Christ: "Go and *teach* all nations......*teaching* them to observe all things, whatsoever I have commanded you."[55]

2. The Protestant Rule of taking the *Scripture alone*, is not a *universal* Rule—it does not contain *all* revealed truths. For, 1st, It commands not the first, but the seventh day of the week, to be kept holy;[56]—

(54) 2 Pet. iii., 15. (55) Matt. xxviii., 19.
(56) Gen. ii., 2, 3; Exod. xx., 8 to 11

2ndly, It forbids the eating of blood, &c.;[57]—3rdly, The authenticity, integrity, truth, and inspiration of Scripture, are the very foundation of the Protestant Rule—the faith of Protestants rests entirely upon these facts; and yet they cannot be learned from Scripture alone. Therefore, Scripture alone is not a universal Rule.

The Catholic Rule, on the contrary, teaches the *whole* Word of God. Christ taught his Apostles all the truths of his Religion—they taught their disciples—and thus the religion of Christ has been handed down from generation to generation, according to that commission which he gave to his Apostles, saying: "Go and teach all nations; . . . . teaching them to observe all things, whatsoever I have commanded you; and behold I am with you all days, even to the end of the world."[58] It is by this means alone, that we can know the lawfulness of keeping the Sunday holy, instead of the Saturday; and of eating blood; the inspiration of the Scripture, &c.

3. The Protestant Rule of taking the *Scripture alone*, is not a *certain Rule*. The *true sense* is, as far as it goes: but, 1st, "The unlearned wrest it to their own destruction"[59]—2ndly, The most learned disagree about the sense of it—3rdly, Even the same persons alter their opinions; being "carried to and fro by every wind of doctrine"[60]—4thly, The whole Catholic Church is against their interpretation! What security, then, can they have in their Rule? For, in its application, it is attended with nothing but difficulty, uncertainty, and doubt.

But, on the other hand, the Rule of the Catholic Church is completely secure—it is perfectly *certain:* and it is in this certainty, that the beauty and excel-

(57) Acts xv., 28, 29.
(58) Matt. xxviii., 19, 20.
(59) 2 Pet. iii., 16.
(60) Eph. iv., 14.

lency of the Catholic Rule chiefly consists. That it *is* certain is clear—

First, from the very nature of the Rule itself; not consisting in the private opinions of a few, &c., but in the authoritative decision of multitudes of every age, and of every nation; differing, indeed, in all other things, but all agreeing in the Articles of their Faith. What but an overruling Providence could produce and maintain, throughout all ages and all nations, this perfect agreement in the doctrines of Faith? Amongst Protestants, scarcely can two persons agree in their belief, which shows the uncertainty of their Rule—

Secondly, from the method observed in delivering the truths, &c. For the Pastors of the Catholic Church deliver the truths which they teach, not as their own private opinions, but as received from their forefathers. Thus, the Apostles taught what they had received from Christ—the second generation what they had received from the Apostles—and so on. Thus was handed down, and is still handed down, "the faith once delivered to the saints."[61]

Thirdly, and above all, from the sacred character of INFALLIBILITY, *promised* (and therefore given) by Christ to his Church. For, if the Church is secured, by the express promises of Christ, from ever teaching anything but truth, then the teaching of the Church is a *certain and secure Rule of Faith*. And the proofs that it is so secured, I will bring forward and explain in the next Instruction.

INSTRUCTION IV.

The Proofs of Infallibility.

What is Faith?—It is to believe, without doubting, whatever God teaches.

Why must you believe whatever God teaches?—Because

(61) Jude.

God is the very truth, and cannot deceive, nor be deceived.

How are you to know what the things are which God teaches?—By the testimony of the Catholic Church, which God has appointed to teach all nations, all those things which he has revealed.

In the last Instruction, I explained how there can but be one *true* Church—but one Faith—how Christ has left sure means of coming to the *certain* knowledge of this one Faith—how that means is the *Rule of Faith*, which all must follow—and how this Rule must be plain, &c. I showed that these qualities belong, not to the Protestant, but to the Catholic Rule—and that what especially renders the Catholic Rule *certain* and *secure*, is the sacred character of INFALLIBILITY, *promised* (and therefore *given*) by Christ to his Church. I will now show you what those promises are:—

1. I will first quote a passage of the Old Testament, where God says: "There shall come a Redeemer to Sion . . . . This is my covenant with them, saith the Lord: my Spirit that is in thee, and my words that I have put in thy mouth, shall not depart out of thy mouth, nor out of the mouth of thy seed, nor out of the mouth of thy seed's seed, saith the Lord, from henceforth and for ever."[62] Here are promised two things: 1st, That the *Spirit* of God (i.e., the Spirit of Truth) shall never depart from the Church; and, 2ndly, That the *Words* of God (i.e., the words of Truth) shall never depart from *the mouth* (i.e., from the *teaching part*) of the Church. And the promise of these two things is to continue in force through all future generations, "from henceforth and for ever, saith the Lord."

2. When the "Redeemer *did* come to Sion" to es-

(62) Is. lix., 20, 21.

tablish the Christian Religion, he confirmed and renewed the promise of these two things: "I will ask the Father, and he shall give you another *Paraclete*, that he may *abide with you for ever;* the *Spirit of Truth*, whom the world cannot receive;...but he *shall* ABIDE *with you*, and shall be in you."[63] "But the Paraclete, the Holy Ghost, whom the Father will send in my name, he will teach you all things, and bring all things to your mind, whatsoever I shall have said to you."[64] For, "when he, the Spirit of Truth, is come, he will teach you *all truth*."[65]

Here is promised, in the first place, the *perpetual* PRESENCE of the Spirit of Truth. And this promise *began* to be accomplished on the day of Pentecost, when "*they were all filled with the Holy Ghost*, and they began to speak with divers tongues, according as the Holy Ghost gave them to speak."[66] And here are promised also, in the second place, the words of truth, or the *perpetual* TEACHING of the Spirit of Truth: "He will teach you all things"—"all truth." And this part of the promise *began* ilkewise to have its fulfilment at Pentecost: "They began *to speak*......according as the *Holy Ghost* gave them to speak." Besides, Christ said to the Father: "The words which thou *gavest to me*, I *have given* TO THEM."[67] The words of truth, here *given* to the Apostles, were evidently to remain in them, and in their successors, till the end of time; for Christ commissions them to teach his truths to all nations *till the end of the world;* promising, at the same time, that he himself will be perpetually with them in that teaching: "Go and teach all nations;......teaching them to observe all things whatsoever I have commanded you: and behold *I am with you all days even to the end of the world*."[68]

(63) John xiv., 16, 17. (64) John xiv., 26. (65) John xvi., 13. (66) Acts ii., 4. (67) John xvii., 8. (68) Mat. xxviii., 19, 20.

Christ promises infallibility to his Church still more explicitly, in these words: I say to thee, that thou art *Peter*, and upon *this rock* I will build my Church, and the gates of hell *shall not prevail* against it."[69] The meaning of this promise is evident from another passage: "Every one that heareth these my words, and doth them, shall be likened to a *wise man, that built his house* UPON A ROCK; and the rain fell, and the floods came, and the winds blew, and they beat upon that house, and it fell *not*, FOR it was founded *upon a rock*. And every one that heareth these my words, and doth them not, shall be like a foolish man, that built his house upon the sand; and the rain fell, and the floods came, and the winds blew, and they beat upon that house, and *it fell*."[70] Therefore by building his Church *upon a rock*, Christ evidently meant, building it so as that it should *never* fall. And hence St. Paul gives the Church this glorious title: "The Church of the living God, which is the pillar and ground of the truth."[71]

I have now explained the *Rule of Faith;* and have proved, that the teaching of the Catholic Church has all those qualities which a Rule of Faith must necessarily have. And, that it is the true and appointed Rule, which all must follow, is still further confirmed by Scripture:—

1. The Apostles were commissioned to *preach* and *teach;* not to *write*.

2. The world was converted, not by the distributing or the *reading* of the *Bible*, but *by preaching*, as is related in Scripture, especially in the Acts of the Apostles. So likewise, in after times, the Church has been continued and extended *by teaching*, as Ecclesiastical History clearly shows.

3. Scripture itself directs us to the *teaching* of the

(69) Matt. xvi., 18. (70) Matt. vii., 24 to 27. (71) 1 Tim. iii., 15

Pastors of the Church; and not to the learning of our faith from the *Bible alone:* "No prophecy of Scripture is of private interpretation."[72]—"He that heareth you, heareth me."[73]—"If he will not hear the Church, let him be to thee as the heathen and the publican."[74] "Remember your prelates, who have spoken the word of God to you; *whose faith follow.*"[75]

4. The Pastors of the Church have been appointed and commissioned for the purpose of teaching, directing, and guiding the people: "For the lips of the Priest shall keep knowledge, and they shall seek the law at his mouth; because he is the Angel of the Lord of Hosts."[76] "And he gave some Apostles, and other some Pastors, and Doctors; for the perfecting of the Saints, for the work of the Ministry, for the edifying of the body of Christ; until we all meet into the unity of faith;......that henceforth we be no more children tossed to and fro', and carried about with every wind of doctrine."[77]

From all these clear and positive and repeated declarations of God, it is evident that *the teaching of the Church* is the true, appointed, and secure Rule of Faith, and is the one which Scripture points out to us.

INSTRUCTION V.

On Tradition.

What is Faith?—It is to believe, without doubting, whatever God teaches.

Why must you believe whatever God teaches?—Because God is the very truth, and cannot deceive, nor be deceived.

How are you to know what the things are which God teaches?—By the testimony of the Catholic Church,

(72) 2 Pet. i., 20. (74) Matt. xviii., 17. (76) Mal. ii., 7.
(73) Luke x., 16. (75) Heb. xiii., 7, 17. (77) Eph. iv., 11 to 14.

which God has appointed to teach all nations, all those things which he has revealed.

In the two last Instructions, I have explained the *Rule of Faith*, and shown that the *teaching of the Church* is the true Rule; i.e., the entire Word of God, as taught and explained by the Church, is the Rule of Faith appointed by Christ.

The Word of God consists of *all those truths which he has revealed to man*, whether written in Scripture or not. What the Apostles taught by writing, is *Scripture;* what they taught without writing, is called *Tradition.* What then is Tradition?

I. TRADITION is *the handing down of revealed truths not contained, or not clearly contained in Scripture.* Do not the Scriptures, then, contain *all* that Christ taught? No. After his last supper, Christ said: "I have yet *many things* to say unto you, but you cannot bear them *now.* But when he the Spirit of Truth is come, he will teach you all truth. For he shall not speak of himself; because he shall receive of mine, and shall show it to you."[78] Here we see, that many things were to be taught by the Holy Ghost, after his coming on the day of Pentecost.——It is related of Christ, that, after his resurrection, he taught many things concerning the kingdom of God, i.e., the kingdom of his Church: "To whom (i.e., to the Apostles) Christ showed himself alive, after his passion, by many proofs, for forty days appearing to them, and speaking of the kingdom of God."[79] Now, where is all this written?——St. John concludes his Gospel thus: "But there are also many other things, which Jesus did; which if they were all written every one, the world itself, I think, would not be able to contain the books that should be written."[80] Therefore, all is not

(78) John xvi., 12, 13, 14. (79) Acts i., 3. (80) John xxi., 25.

written in Scripture.——Indeed, Protestants themselves believe many traditionary doctrines; as, for example, the lawfulness of keeping holy the Sunday, instead of Saturday—of eating blood, and things strangled—of Infant baptism—the inspiration and canon of the Scriptures.

II. What is THE PRINCIPLE OF TRADITION? It is this: An invariable rule, that every generation adhere firmly to the doctrines received from the preceding, and carefully commit *the very same doctrines* to the succeeding generation. The Apostles established this principle, and also efficacious means to preserve it. Thus, they commanded the *Pastors* whom they ordained, and the *faithful* at large, to preserve and hand down the doctrines committed to them: "O Timothy, keep that which is committed to thy trust, avoiding the profane novelties of words."[81] "Hold the form of sound words, which thou hast *heard* of me in faith... Keep the good things committed to thy trust by the Holy Ghost who dwelleth in us."[82]......" Continue thou in those things which thou hast learned, and which have been committed to thee, knowing of whom thou hast learned them."[83]—What strict commands *to preserve* the doctrines which they had received.

He also commands *that the doctrines be handed down;* and that *means be taken* for their being still further handed down to succeeding generations: "And the things which thou *hast heard of me* by many witnesses, THE SAME *commend* to faithful men, who shall be fit to teach others also."[84]

So far the Apostle's instructions lay an obligation upon *Pastors* of adhering to, and of handing down, the doctrines committed to them; but the same obligation of adhering to the doctrines delivered, he also

(81) 1 Tim. vi., 20.
(82) 2 Tim. i., 13, 14.
(83) 2 Tim. iii., 14.
(84) 2 Tim. ii., 2.

lays upon the faithful at large: "Therefore, brethren, stand fast; and *hold the traditions* which you have learned, *whether by word* or by our Epistle."[85] St. Jude tells us, he wrote his Epistle purposely to enforce this duty on the faithful: "I was under a necessity to write to you, to beseech you to contend earnestly for the faith once delivered to the saints."[86]

Not content with these strict and positive commands, the Apostles were very earnest, moreover, in warning the faithful against all *new doctrines* and the *teachers of them:* "Be not led away with various and *strange* doctrines.[87]" "Avoid the profane *novelties* of words."[88] "Now, I beseech you, brethren, to mark them who cause dissensions, . . . contrary to the doctrines you have learned; and to *avoid them.*"[89] "A man that is a *heretic*, after the first and second admonition, *avoid;* knowing that he, that is such a one, is subverted, and sinneth, being condemned by his own judgment."[90]——And St. Paul goes so far as to *pronounce anathema* against any one, even against an angel from heaven, who should attempt to teach any other Gospel, except that which he had taught."[91] The principle of Tradition could not be laid down *more clearly*, or *more strongly*, than in the texts which I have quoted.

From these texts, then, it is evident, that the rule of *traditionary teaching* WAS established by the Apostles, as a means of preserving and handing down the deposit of faith.

III. ADHERENCE OF THE CHURCH TO THIS PRINCIPLE:—But has the Church always adhered to this rule? Yes: for, 1st, Scripture, in the above texts, proves this fact, for the Apostolic age; 2ndly, The

(85) 2 Thess. ii., 14. (87) Heb. xiii., 9. (89) Rom. xvi., 17.
(86) Jude 3. (88) 1 Tim. vi., 20. (90) Tit. iii., 10.
(91) Gal. i., 8, 9.

writings of the Fathers, and the Acts and Professions of Councils, for the succeeding ages;[92] 3rdly, The Church universally teaches and acts upon it, in the present age: No trace can be found of there ever having been any change on this point; indeed, it is by this rule—by this Apostolic principle, that the Church has always condemned new doctrines.

But has the Church never altered or corrupted the Apostolic Traditions? No; for, 1st, The writings of he Fathers show, that the Church has *always* been *the same*, as at the present time; 2ndly, Because the very principle of the Church has always been, and is now, never to alter, add to, or take from, the body of doctrines received; but always "to contend earnestly for the faith once delivered to the Saints;"[93] 3rdly, Because it is the universal character of the Catholic Church, that she has been always utterly averse to novelties; always solicitous in detecting, and firm in condemning, all new doctrines. Her enemies have even made it a charge against her, that she *cannot* alter—'There is no hope or possibility of reforming her, (they say), because she *cannot* change;' 4thly, Because such vast multitudes, and so many nations, are concerned; 5thly, Because she is secured by the promised assistance of Christ: "I am with you all days, even to the end of the world;"[94] and also by the promised assistance of the Holy Spirit: "But the Holy Ghost, whom the Father will send in my name, he will teach you all things, and bring all things to your mind, whatsoever I shall have said to you."[95]

Hence, when difficulties or disputes about doctrine arise, which call for the decision of the Church, she assembles her chief Pastors or Bishops in Council, has recourse to revelation, both written and unwritten;

(92) *See* Wiseman's Lectures on the Doctrines and Practices of the Catholic Church; *Vol.* 1, *Lecture* 5, p. 140 to 147, *first Edition*.
(93) Jude 3. (94) Matt. xxviii., 20. (95) John xiv., 26.

and, having carefully and diligently examined, she then decides by virtue of her divinely authorized commission: "Go and teach all nations."[96] "The Holy Ghost hath appointed you Bishops to rule the Church of God."[97] Now, in this decision, by virtue of the express promises of Christ, the Church is divinely assisted. Thus, in the first Council, held at Jerusalem, the Apostles began their decision in these words: "It hath seemed good to the Holy Ghost and to us."[98] Hence, how perfectly *secure* are Catholics, in relying on the authoritative teaching of the Church! Nothing *can* be more secure; for God has pledged his word for it; and though "heaven and earth may pass away," he declares that "his word shall not pass away."[99] "God is not as man, that he should lie; nor, as the son of man, that he should be changed. Hath he said, then, and will he not do? hath he spoken, and will he not fulfil?"[100]

EXPLANATION
OF THE
APOSTLES' CREED.

INSTRUCTION VI.

FIRST ARTICLE OF THE CREED.

On the Apostles' Creed—and on the Attributes of God.

What are the Chief things which God teaches?—They are contained in the Apostles' Creed.

What is the First article of the Apostles' Creed?—I believe in God the Father Almighty, Creator of heaven and earth.

(96) Matt. xxviii., 19, 20. (98) Acts xv., 28. (100) Numb. xxiii., 19.
(97) Acts xx., 28. (99) Mark xiii., 31.

What is God?—God is a Spirit; the Creator and Sovereign Lord of all things.

Why is he called Almighty?—Because he can do all things whatever he pleases, and nothing is impossible or difficult to him.

Why is he called Creator of heaven and earth?—Because he made heaven and earth, and all things out of nothing, by his only word.

Had God any beginning?—No; he always was, is, and always will be.

Where is God?—God is everywhere.

Does God know and see all things?—Yes; God does know and see all things.

Has God any body?—No; God has no body; he is a pure Spirit.

I. Apostles' Creed:—The Apostles' Creed contains the leading Articles of Faith. It is divided into three principal parts; and is again subdivided into twelve Articles.——Before the Apostles separated to "go into the whole world and preach the Gospel to every creature,"[1] they composed this creed, that it might be some means of enabling all the Faithful to think and speak the same things. Tertullian, in the second age, calls it: "A rule of Faith descending from the tradition of the Apostles."——It is *short*, that every one may be able to learn it: and it is very *comprehensive;* therefore we should say it with reflection.

What is the First Article of the Apostles' Creed?—I believe in God the Father Almighty, Creator of heaven and earth.

By these words, "*I believe,*" is meant (not *I think—I suppose—I am of opinion*, but) I hold for certain—with full conviction—without the least doubt or misgiving: And this certainty rests on a Divine authority,

(1) Mark xvi., 15.

viz., on the authority of God's word, as proposed to us by his Church: it rests, therefore on an infallible authority.

II. Attributes of God:—*What is God?*—God is a Spirit; the Creator and Soveveign Lord of all things.

What is a Spirit? It is an active, intellectual, immaterial being. God is an *infinitely perfect* Spirit.

What is meant when we say: *God is infinitely perfect?* We mean, that God possesses in himself all Perfections without limitation.

Can you name some of God's Perfections or Attributes? Yes; God is omnipresent—infinitely wise, holy, just, and powerful; infinitely good, merciful, and true—infinitely amiable, incomprehensible, eternal, and unchangeable.

We should frequently think on these Divine Perfections: for, such reflection will lead us to *fear God;* and will thus be a check to vice: it will also excite us to *love and serve God;* and will thus be an inducement to virtue. Indeed, what greater check, &c., than to consider, that,

1. *God is everywhere?* He is always present, wherever we are: "For in him we live and move and be."[2] "Whither shall I go from thy Spirit? or whither shall I flee from thy face? If I ascend into heaven thou art there; if I descend into hell, thou art present. If I take my wings early in the morning, and dwell in the uttermost parts of the sea; even there also shall thy hand lead me, and thy right hand shall hold me."[3]

Then *does God know and see all things?*—Yes; God does know and see all things; because,

2. *God is infinitely wise:* He knows the past, the

(2) Acts xvii., 28. (3) Ps. cxxxviii., 7 to 12.

present, and the future; even our secret thoughts and intentions: "For the eyes of the Lord are far brighter than the sun, beholding round about all the ways of men; . . . and looking into the hearts of men, into the most hidden parts. For he beholdeth all things."[4] "The works of all flesh are before him; and there is nothing hidden from his eyes; he seeth from eternity to eternity."[5] ——And as,

3. *God is infinitely Holy* so he loves virtue, wherever he sees it; and cannot endure iniquity: "Thy eyes are too pure to behold evil."[6] "The way of the wicked is an abomination to the Lord."[7] With reason, therefore, does the Wise Man say: "To God the wicked and his wickedness are hateful alike."[8]

Not only does God *see* and *hate* our iniquities, but he will also *punish* them, if we die in the guilt of them;——because,

4. *God is infinitely Just:* He will execute strict and impartial justice upon all mankind, without respect of persons. For, "God will render to every man according to his works; to them, indeed, who seek glory, and honour, and incorruption; eternal life: but to them who are contentious, and who obey not the truth, but give credit to iniquity; wrath and indignation. Tribulation and anguish upon every soul of man, that worketh evil; . . . but glory, and honour, and peace to every one that worketh good . . . For there is no respect of persons with God."[9]

God then knows all our ways—his "eyes behold both the good and the evil;"[10] and he will deal with us according to strict justice. The rewards of virtue will be "exceedingly great;"[11] and the punishments of sin will be most terrible;——because,

5. *God is infinitely Powerful:* He is able to reward

(4) Eccl. xxiii., 28. 29.
(5) Eccl. xxxix., 24, 25.
(6) Hab. i., 13.
(7) Prov. xv., 9, 26.
(8) Wisd. xiv., 9.
(9) Rom. ii., 5 to 11.
(10) Prov. xv., 3.
(11) Matt. v., 11, 12.

most abundantly; and to execute his vengeance with inconceivable severity: "All things are in his power, and there is none that can resist his will."[12] "Out of his mouth proceedeth a sharp two-edged sword; that with it he may strike the nations:"[13] for "He only is mighty—the King of kings, and Lord of lords."[14]

Were we to consider these Divine Attributes—were we to reflect seriously and frequently upon them, how afraid should we be of offending a God, who is so terrible in his vengeance! What a horror should we have of sin, and how careful should we be in avoiding it, if we thus considered what "a fearful thing it is to fall into the hands of the living God!"[15]

Were these the only Attributes of God, we should have *reason indeed to fear*. But, besides these which are of such a terrifying nature, there are others which are calculated to raise us to the highest degree of hope and confidence; and which we can never reflect upon without the greatest consolation. For God is *infinitely good and merciful;* and *true* to his promises, &c. These (wherever man is concerned), are the dearest of his Attributes: For "his tender mercies are above all his works."[16] These I will explain in the next Instruction.

INSTRUCTION VII.

FIRST ARTICLE CONTINUED.

The Attributes of God (continued.)

What is God?—God is a Spirit; the Creator and Sovereign Lord of all things.

Why is he called Almighty?—Because he can do all things whatever he pleases, and nothing is impossible or difficult to him.

Why is he called Creator of heaven and earth?—Be-

(12) Esther xiii., 9
(13) Apoc. xix., 15.
(14) 1 Tim. vi., 15.
(15) Heb. x., 31.
(16) Ps. cxliv., 9.

cause he made heaven and earth, and all things out of nothing, by his only word.

Had God any beginning?—No; He always was, is, and always will be.

Where is God?—God is everywhere.

Does God know and see all things?—Yes; God does know and see all things.

Has God any body?—No; God has no body: he is a pure Spirit.

In the last Instruction, I explained some of the attributes or perfections of God—those which tend chiefly to excite our fears—I showed that he is *everywhere*, and sees and *knows all things;* that he is *infinitely holy*, and hates iniquity—*infinitely just*, and will punish it, and that, being *infinitely powerful*, he can, and will punish impenitent sinners with inconceivabl severity. "Were these (I said) the only attributes of God, we should have reason indeed to fear. But, besides these, which are of such a terrifying nature, there are others which are calculated to raise us to the highest degree of hope and confidence; and which we can never reflect upon without the greatest consolation For God is *infinitely good*, and *merciful*, and *true*, *infinitely amiable*, *incomprehensible*, *eternal*, and *unchangeable*.

1. *God is infinitely good:* His infinite goodness appears in his great love for us: "I have loved thee with an everlasting love, taking pity on thee."[17] "God so loved the world, as to give his only begotten Son."[18] Happy in himself, in the possession of his infinite perfections, his goodness makes him desirous of communicating this happiness, &c. With this view, he created us; with the same view, he is continually heaping favours, &c.: "Thou openest thy hand, and fillest with blessing every living creature."[19] "What

(17) Jer. xxxi., 3. (18) John iii., 16. (19) Ps. cxliv., 16.

is there (he says) that I ought to do more to my vineyard, that I have not done to it?"[20] And if we offend him, he is ready to pardon——because,

2. *God is infinitely merciful:* "His tender mercies are above all his works."[21] He assures us, saying: "I desire not the death of the wicked, but that the wicked turn from his way and live. The wickedness of the wicked shall not hurt him, in what day soever he shall turn from his wickedness."[22] For, "the Lord is gracious and merciful, patient and plenteous in mercy." And "his mercy endureth for ever."[23]——Even "when thou art angry thou wilt remember mercy."[24] For, "as a father hath compassion on his children, so hath the Lord compassion on them that fear him."[25]

How consoling are these reflection! how cheering How they serve to inspire confidence—to raise our hopes! And more especially when we go on to consider the immense promises of God in our favour—promises which are sure to be fulfilled on his part——because,

3. *God is infinitely true:* He is truth itself: "God is not as man, that he should lie......Hath he then said, and will he not do? hath he spoken, and will he not fulfil?"[26] Now he *has* spoken great things in our favour: "He hath given us great and precious promises:"[27]——For,

As to the present life, 1st, In all our trials and temptations, he promises us *protection and victory*: "God is faithful, who will not suffer you to be tempted above what you are able."[28]——2ndly, If we unhappily fall, he promises us *mercy and pardon*: "As I live, saith the Lord, I desire not the death of the wicked, but

(20) Is. v., 4.
(21) Ps. cxliv., 9.
(22) Ezech. xxxiii., 11, 12.
(23) Ps. cxliv., 8; cv., 1.
(24) Hab. iii., 2.
(25) Ps. cii., 13.
(26) Nm. xxiii., 19.
(27) 2 Pet. i., 4.
(28) 1 Cor. x., 13.

that the wicked turn from his way and live."[29] "Take away the evil of your devices from my eyes; cease to do perversely, learn to do well.....And then come and accuse me, saith the Lord: If your sins be as scarlet, they shall be made as white as snow."[30]——3rdly, In our troubles and afflictions, he promises us *relief and consolation:* "Come to me, all you that labour, and are burdened, and I will refresh you."[31] "To him that overcometh, I will give the hidden Manna."[32]——4thly, In all our wants he promises to bestow upon us *whatever is necessary*, if only we will serve him: "Seek ye first the kingdom of God, and his justice; and ALL *these things* SHALL be added unto you." "Ask, and it *shall* be given unto you."[33]

And, *as to the next life*, he promises to reward his faithful servants with eternal happiness: "Amen, I say to you, there is no man who hath left house, or lands, or kindred for my sake, and for the Gospel, who shall not receive a hundred times as much, now in this time; and in the world to come, life everlasting."[34]—Consider also the great and precious promises contained in the Eight Beatitudes.

Now, as the Psalmist says, "God is faithful in all his words;"[35] and he declares that, though "heaven and earth shall pass away; yet *his word* shall not pass away."[36]

If, then, we love and serve him, (and what powerful motives!) our reward is certain: and it is no less a reward than *God himself*[37]—a God infinitely good, and amiable, incomprehensible, eternal, and unchangeable.

4. *God is infinitely Amiable:* All that is *amiable* in creatures, is but as a drop to an ocean, when compared with the infinite *Amiability of God.* He is so lovely

(29) Ezech. xxxiii., 11. (32) Apoc. ii., 17. (35) Ps. cxliv., 13.
(30) Is. i., 16, 17, 18. (33) Matt. vi., 33; vii., 7. (36) Mark xiii., 31.
(31) Matt. xi., 28. (34) Mark x., 29. (37) Gen. xv., 1.

and enchanting, that all the blessed, in beholding him, are enraptured with delight: *to see* God is their essential happiness. O how great is the multitude of thy sweetness, O Lord, which thou hast hidden for them that fear thee!"[38] "They shall be inebriated with the plenty of thy house; and thou shalt make them drink of the torrent of thy pleasure: for with thee is the fountain of life."[39] The greatness of this happiness cannot be conceived——because,

5. *God is Incomprehensible:* "Behold, God is great, exceeding our knowledge."[40] "Glorify him as much as ever you can, for he will yet far exceed............ exalt him as much as you can, for he is above all praise."[41] With reason, then, does Christ encourage us, in our trials and difficulties, by the prospect of this reward: "Be glad and rejoice, for your reward is very great in heaven."[42] And this reward will last for ever——because,

6. *God is Eternal* and *Unchangeable:* He is the High and the Eminent, who inhabiteth *eternity.*"[43] "Behold I live for ever and ever"—"and I change not."[44]

Such is the God whom we are commanded to serve! These are some of his attributes or perfections. And can we have a more powerful incitement to virtue, than to consider them attentively? I entreat you, therefore, to make them frequently the subject of your serious reflections. For such reflections cannot fail to have a powerful influence in leading you to *avoid evil and do good.*

(38) Ps. xxx., 20.
(39) Ps. xxxv., 9.
(40) Job xxxvi., 26.
(41) Ec. xliii., 32, 33.
(42) Matt. v., 12.
(43) Is. lvii., 15.
(44) Ap. i., 18; Mal. iii., 6.

INSTRUCTION VIII.

FIRST ARTICLE CONTINUED.

On the Work of Creation.

What is the First Article of the Apostles' Creed?—I believe in God the Father Almighty, Creator of heaven and earth.

What is God?—God is a Spirit; the Creator and Sovereign Lord of all things.

Why is he called Almighty?—Because he can do all things whatever he pleases, and nothing is impossible or difficult to him.

Why is he called Creator of heaven and earth?—Because he made heaven and earth, and all things out of nothing, by his only word.

The two last Instructions were on the Divine Attributes or Perfections. It was there shown, how an attentive consideration of them would influence us to "avoid evil, and do good"—how God's Justice, together with his Wisdom and Power, inspire a salutary fear; and how his Goodness and Mercy excite confidence and love.——I have now to explain how he has *exercised and manifested* his Attributes, in the great work of *Creation.*

In the next Instruction, I shall have to explain how he still *continues* to exercise and manifest them, in the watchful *Providence*, by which he preserves governs, and directs all things, for the good of his creatures, especially man. This will supply additional motives to love and serve him with gratitude and confidence.

I. God, the Creator:—What means "*Creator?*" It means one who produces things out of nothing: it is only God who can *create.*

What is a *creature?* It is that which is produced out of nothing: All beings, except God, are creatures

"In the beginning God *created* heaven and earth."[45] "All things were made by him."[46] "He *spoke*, and they were made; he *commanded*, and they were created."[47]

Why did God create......? For his own greater honour and glory; and for the good of his creatures: "The Lord hath made all things for himself."[48]

II. The Six Days of Creation:—Why did he employ six days? Because such was his will: he could as easily have done it *all at once*, if such had been his will.

1st day of Creation: On this day, God created heaven and earth—and the light—and divided the light from darkness.

2nd day: He made the firmament, and divided the waters that were under the firmament, from those that were above the firmament.

3rd day: He collected the waters that were under the firmament, and caused the dry land to appear; and he made the earth bring forth green herbs and fruit-trees.

4th day: He made lights in the firmament of heaven: a greater light to rule the day; and a less light to rule the night; and the stars. And he set them in the firmament of heaven to serve for signs, and for seasons, and for days, and years.

5th day: He made the birds and fishes—and commanded them to increase and multiply.

6th day: He made the animals, and reptiles; and, lastly, man and woman; and he commanded these also to "increase and multiply."[49]

It was in the course of these six days, that God created the *Angels*.[50] The Scriptures do not say on which day the Angels were created; but they say,

(45) Gen. i., 1. (46) John i., 3. (47) Ps. cxlviii., 5. (48) Prov. xvi., 4. (49) Gen. i., 1 to 31. (50) 4th Council of Lateran.

"*In six days* the Lord made HEAVEN and earth, and *all things* that are *in them*."[51]

7th day: God rested on the seventh day; and he blessed it, and sanctified it.

III. THE PRINCIPAL CREATURES:—What are the *principal* creatures which God made; or those in which he has most displayed his Attributes, and over which he exercises a more especial Providence? *Angels and Men.* (These are the principal, because endowed with reason, understanding, and free will.)

1. What do you mean by *Angels?* Pure spirits who surround God's throne—"his ministers who do his will."[52] Their number is very great: "Thousands of thousands ministered to him, and ten thousand times a hundred thousand stood before him."[53]

They were created in a state of *grace*—and of *happiness*—but yet in a state of *trial.*——Lucifer, the brightest, and many others with him, fell by pride—were cast out of heaven—and changed into devils: "God spared not his angels that sinned."[54] Those fallen angels tempt mankind: "Your adversary, the devil, as a roaring lion, goeth about seeking whom he may devour; whom resist ye, strong in faith."[55]——The greater part of the Angels persevered in grace; these were immediately admitted to the beatific vision, and they were thereby secured in eternal happiness.——They assist us; and pray for us: For "they are all ministering spirits, sent to minister for them, who shall receive the inheritance of salvation."[56] They are appointed to be our Guardians: "The Angel of the Lord shall encamp round about them that fear him, and shall deliver them."[57]

2. What is *man?* A being composed of a body and a soul; endowed with reason, understanding, and free-

(51) Exod. xx., 11.
(52) Ps. cii., 21.
(53) Dan. vii., 10.
(54) 2 Pet. ii., 4.
(55) 1 Pet. v., 8, 9.
(56) Heb. i, 14.
(57) Ps. xxxiii., 8.

will; only "a little less than the Angels;"[58] created to fill up the place of the fallen Angels in heaven.

In making man, God formed his body of the earth; and created his soul out of nothing: "And the Lord God formed man of the slime of the earth; and he breathed into his face the breath of life; and man became a living soul......Then the Lord God cast a deep sleep upon Adam; and he took one of his ribs; and he built it into a women; and brought her to Adam."[59]

Our first Parents were created (like the Angels) in a state of innocence, grace, and happiness, and also in a state of trial. "And the Lord God put man into the Paradise of pleasure, to dress it, and to keep it."[60] They were not subject to sickness or pains; and were never to have died; but they were to have remained in the paradise of pleasure, till they were translated to heaven.

Did they continue in this happy state? No; they soon lost their innocence, by transgressing the only precept which God had given them to try their obedience. For God had "commanded them, saying: Of every tree of Paradise thou shalt eat; but of the tree of knowledge of good and evil, thou shalt not eat; for, in what day soever thou shalt eat of it, thou shalt die the death."[61] The devil tempted Eve......"And the serpent said to the woman: Why hath God commanded you, that you should not eat of every tree of Paradise? And the woman answered him, saying: Of the fruit of the trees that are in Paradise we do eat: but of the fruit of the tree which is in the midst of Paradise, God hath commanded us that we should not eat, lest perhaps we die. And the serpent said to the woman: No; you shall not die the death. For God doth know, that in what day soever you shall eat

(58) Ps. viii., 6; Heb. ii., 7.
(59) Gen. ii., 7, 21, 22.
(60) Gen. ii., 15.
(61) Gen. ii., 16, 17.

thereof, your eyes shall be opened; and you shall be as gods, knowing good and evil. And the woman saw that the tree was good to eat, and fair to the eyes, and delightful to behold: and she took the fruit thereof, and did eat, and gave it to her husband, who did eat."[62]

They then lost their innocence, and happiness: their understanding was darkened—their reason blinded—their inclinations became prone to evil—they were doomed to labour, pains, sickness, and death. For God said to the woman: "I will multiply thy sorrows, and thy conceptions; in sorrow thou shalt bring forth children; and thou shalt be under thy husband's power." And to Adam he said: "Cursed is the earth in thy work. In the sweat of thy brow shalt thou eat thy bread; till thou return to the earth, out of which thou wast taken: for dust thou art, and into dust thou shalt return."[63]

In consequence of Adam's fall, we are all born in sin.——If we had been left to ourselves, we must have been all lost for ever; because incapable of making atonement for our guilt.——But the infinite Goodness and Mercy of God promised a Redeemer...

INSTRUCTION IX.

FIRST ARTICLE CONTINUED.

On the Providence of God.

What is God?—God is a Spirit; the Creator and Sovereign Lord of all things.

Why is he called Almighty?—Because he can do all things whatever he pleases, and nothing is impossible or difficult to him.

Why is he called Creator of heaven and earth?—Because

(62) Gen. iii., 1 to 6. (63) Gen. iii., 16 to 19.

he made heaven and earth, and all things out of nothing, by his only word.

I have shown how God has displayed his divine Attributes, particularly his Wisdom, Power, and Goodness, in the great work of the Creation. I will now explain the *Providence of God;* because it is a continued exercise of the same Attributes, for the preservation and good of his creatures, particularly man. For, we cannot exist of ourselves; but we need God's continual preservation: "He upholds all things by the word of his power."[64]

I. PROVIDENCE OF GOD.—What is meant by "*the Providence of God?*" His eternal Will, by which he preserves, governs, and disposes all things. It consists chiefly in the exercise of three of his Divine Attributes, viz.:—

1. *His Wisdom*, by which he knows all his creatures—their ends (which are always some good)—the means of obtaining those ends—and the impediments which would prevent the obtaining of them;—

2. *His Goodness*, which inclines him to forward those ends by furnishing the proper means for that purpose, and by removing the impediments or obstacles;—

3. *His Power*, by which he *can* and *does* execute these beneficent designs in our favour, unless we prevent him by wickedness. The Scripture declares, that "all things are in his power, and there is none that can resist his will;"[65]—that "in his hands are both we, and our works;"[66]—and that "his wisdom ordereth all things sweetly:"[67]—"Wherefore, give not thy mouth to cause thy flesh to sin; and say not before the angel, there is *no providence:* lest God be

(64) Heb., i. 3.
(65) Esther xiii., 9.
(66) Wisd. vii., 16.
(67) Wisd. viii., 1.

angry at thy words, and destroy all the works of thy hands."[68]

Can we disappoint God's Providence? No; because we can neither deceive his *wisdom*, nor resist his *power*. "There is no wisdom, there is no prudence, there is no counsel against the Lord."[69] "All things are in his power; and there is none that can resist his will."[70]

Does any thing happen really *by chance?* A thing *is said* to happen by chance, when WE see no cause why it should have happened—had no foresight that it would happen—nor any intention to cause it. Now, *to us* many things happen so; but *to God* nothing for, his Providence rules and directs all things.—— Sin he foresees; and he *suffers* it to be committed by us, because he has given us free-will. If we avoid it, he will reward us; but if we commit it he will punish us.

II. PROVIDENCE REGULATES FOR OUR GOOD:— Does Providence exert itself for our good? Yes; and hence the Scriptures admonish us, saying: "Cast all your care upon him, for he hath care of you."[71] He exercises his goodness, and providential care, in three ways:—

1. *In providing* everything necessary for our good: "The eyes of all hope in thee, O Lord, and thou givest them meat in due season. Thou openest thy hand, and fillest with blessing every living creature."[72] "Behold the birds of the air; for they neither sow, nor do they reap, nor gather into barns, and your Heavenly Father feedeth them...how much more you, O ye of little faith? Therefore, be not solicitous, saying: What shall we eat, or what shall we drink, or wherewith shall we be clothed? For your Heavenly Father *knoweth* that you have need of

(68) Eccles. v., 5. (70) Esther xiii., 9. (72) Ps. cxliv., 15, 16
(69) Prov. xxi., 30. (71) 1 Pet. v., 7; Ps. liv., 23.

all these things. Seek ye therefore first the kingdom of God, and his justice; and all these things shall be added unto you."[73]

2. *In preserving and delivering* us from evils; and in turning to our good such temporal evils, as he permits for our trial: "There shall no evil come to thee; for he hath given his Angels charge over thee, to keep thee in all thy ways. In their hands they shall bear thee up, lest thou dash thy foot against a stone."[74] "The Lord is the protector of my life, of whom shall I be afraid?"[75] Therefore, in all difficulties and temptations, have recourse to him with confidence of *deliverance*, or of *support*.

3. *In ruling and ordering* all things for the good of his servants: "In all thy ways think on God, and he will direct thy steps."[76] For "his wisdom ordereth all things sweetly:" Hence, "to them that love God, all things work together unto good."[77]

How is it, then, that there is so much sin and misery in the world? As to *sin*, God forbids it—gives us abundant helps to avoid it—deters us from it by threats; and then leaves us to follow our free-will: he merely *permits* sin to happen.——But as to human miseries—misfortunes, afflictions, persecutions—these God absolutely *ordains* for our good: "Good things and evil, life and death, poverty and riches, *are from God*."[78] Even when the affliction comes to us immediately from the wickedness of men; it is equally the will of God, as far as regards *our suffering* and *our* good.

Example of Joseph:—Joseph said to his brethren: "Not by your counsel was I sent hither; but by the will of God;"—"You thought evil against me; but God turned it into good."[79]

Example of Christ:—He was crucified by the

(73) Matt. vi., 26 to 33. (74) Ps. xc., 10, 11, 12. (75) Ps. xxvi., 1. (76) Prov. III., 6. (77) Rom. viii., 28. (78) Eccli. xi., 14. (79) Gen. xlv., 8; l, 20.

wickedness of the Jews; yet he suffered it as being ordained by his Heavenly Father: "Father, if it be possible, let this chalice pass from me; nevertheless, not as I will, but as thou wilt."[80] "Put up thy sword into its scabbard; the cup which *my Father hath given* me to drink, shall I not drink it?"[81]

Therefore, consider men as merely executing, in your regard, what the Providence of God ordains for your good; and receive it with patience, resignation, and even thanksgiving. "When men shall revile you, and persecute you;" do not fret and show impatience, but "be glad and rejoice; because your reward is very great in heaven."[82] For it is *God himself* who sends the afflictions and persecutions *for your good*. For,

He sends them in order to bring you to a sense of your duty—to teach you penance, patience, and resignation—to purify your affections, and wean them from the world—to increase your merits and future glory. It is for this reason, that St. Paul says; "Whom the Lord loveth, he chastiseth; and he scourgeth every son whom he receiveth."[83] "For *that* which is at present momentary and light of our tribulation, worketh for us above measure, exceedingly, an eternal weight of glory."[84] Receive your crosses, therefore, not only with patience and resignation, but also with thanksgiving; like holy Job, when he said: "The Lord gave, and the Lord hath taken away: as it hath pleased the Lord, so it is done; blessed be the name of the Lord."[85]

Think frequently on the Providence of God—on the tender care and solicitude with which he provides for your welfare. Thank him for the blessings received—and pray for a continuance of them; thank him even for his very chastisements, as being the effects of his

(80) Matt. xxvi., 39. (81) John xviii., 11. (82) Matt. v., 12. (83) Heb. xii. 6. (84) 2 Cor. iv., 17. (85) Job i., 21.

love; throw yourself on his Providence in the spirit of resignation, and with an entire confidence in his mercy and goodness, through the infinite merits of Christ.

INSTRUCTION X.

FIRST ARTICLE *concluded.*—SECOND ARTICLE.

On the Trinity—and the Incarnation.

How many Gods are there?—There is but one God.

Are there not more Persons than one in God?—Yes; in God there are three Persons.

Which are they?—God the Father, God the Son, and God the Holy Ghost.

Are not these three Gods?—No; the Father, the Son, and the Holy Ghost, are all but one and the same God.

What is the Second Article of the Creed?—And in Jesus Christ, his only Son, our Lord.

Who is Jesus Christ?—He is God the Son, made man for us.

Is Jesus Christ truly God?—Yes; Jesus Christ is truly God.

Why is Jesus Christ truly God?—Because he has the self-same Divine nature with God the Father, being equal to him in all perfections.

Was Jesus Christ always God?—Yes; Jesus Christ was always God, born of the Father from all eternity.

Which Person of the Blessed Trinity is Jesus Christ?—He is the second Person of the Blessed Trinity.

Is Jesus Christ truly Man?—Yes; Jesus Christ is truly man.

Why is Jesus Christ truly man?—Because he has the nature of man, having a body and a soul like ours.

Was Jesus Christ always Man?—No; he has been man only from the time of his Incarnation.

What do you mean by his Incarnation?—I mean his assuming human nature, when he was conceived and made man, in the womb of the Blessed Virgin Mary.

How many natures then are there in Jesus Christ?—There are two natures in Jesus Christ; the nature of God, and the nature of man.

How many Persons are there in Jesus Christ?—In Jesus Christ there is only one Person; which is the Person of God the Son.

Why was God the Son made man?—To save us from sin and hell.

The Power, Wisdom, and Goodness of God, as displayed in his works, give an exalted idea of his infinite greatness: For "the heavens show forth the glory of God:"[86] and "his work is praise and magnificence."[87]

But his infinite Perfections, considered in themselves, give a more exalted, and more sublime idea of the greatness of his infinite Majesty! It is in the very *possession* of these Attributes, that his greatness essentially consists: "For the Almighty *himself* is above all his works."[88] In each attribute he is infinite and incomprehensible; but in none more so, than in his mysterious and incomprehensible *mode of existence*; which I will now explain:

God exists *one* in ESSENCE, *three* in PERSONS: This is a mystery, and is expressed by "*Unity* and *Trinity* of God." And God, the Son, exists as having *two* NATURES in *one* Divine PERSON; the same Person, (viz., the Person of God the Son) being both God and man. This mystery was accomplished by what is called the "*Incarnation* of the Son of God;" and is the greatest display of his love for man.— —These are the two greatest and most important truths in Religion.

I. THE UNITY AND TRINITY OF GOD:—What is meant by the *Unity* of God? That the Divine nature or substance, or the Divinity, is but *one*. Reason teaches that there cannot be more than one Divine

(86) Ps. xviii., 2. (87) Ps. cx., 3. (88) Eccli. xliii., 30.

nature; Revelation also teaches it: "Hear, O Israel, the Lord our God is one Lord."[89]

What is meant by the *Trinity* of God? That in the one Divine nature, there are three Persons. This truth may be shown from the Old Testament: "*God* said: *Let us* make man to *our* own image." "*God* said: Lo, Adam is become as *one of us*."[90] "By the *Word* of the *Lord* the heavens were established, and all the powers of them by the *Spirit* of his mouth."[91]——It is proved much more clearly from the New Testament: "*I* will ask *the Father*, and he will give you *another* Comforter, *the Spirit of Truth*."[92] "Go and teach all nations, baptizing them in the name of *the Father*, and of *the Son*, and of *the Holy Ghost*."[93] There are THREE who give testimony in heaven, the Father, the Word, and the Holy Ghost; and these three are one."[94]

Are the Three Persons in God really *distinct* Persons? Yes; for in the text: "*I* will ask the *Father*, and he will give you *another Comforter*, *the Spirit of Truth*," he who asks, is a person really distinct from him to whom the request is made; and he who is asked for is distinct from both. Each of the three Persons has certain personal properties, which cannot be attributed to the others. Thus, the Father is the first Person, and proceeds from no one: this cannot be said of the Son, nor of the Holy Ghost. The Son is the second Person, is begotten, and has assumed our human nature: this cannot be said of the Father, nor of the Holy Ghost. The Holy Ghost is the third Person, and proceeds from the Father and the Son; this cannot be said of the first and second Persons.

Is each Person God? and equal God? Yes; "To us there is but one *God*, THE FATHER, of whom are all things."[95] "In the beginning was the Word, and

(89) Deut. v., 4. (90) Gen. i., 26; iii., 21, 22. (91) Ps. xxxii. 6. (92) John xiv., 16. (93) Mat. xxviii., 19. (94) 1 John v., 7. (95) 1 Cor. viii., 6.

the Word was with God, and THE WORD was *God*."[96] "Why hath Satan tempted thy heart, that thou shouldst lie to THE HOLY GHOST?.........Thou hast not lied to men, but to *God*."[97] "And THESE THREE are *one*."[98]

Can we comprehend this mystery? No; God alone can comprehend himself; because *he* is infinite, *we* finite. The mystery of the Trinity has been revealed; and therefore we must believe it; we should rest satisfied with our measure of knowledge; for "He that is a searcher of majesty, shall be overwhelmed by glory."[99]

II. THE SECOND ARTICLE OF THE CREED.

The Second Article teaches that *the Word*, or Second Person of the Trinity, besides being "GOD, having the self-same nature with God the Father," is also "MAN, having a body and soul like ours." For,

Who is Jesus Christ?—He is GOD the Son, made MAN for us.

Is he then *truly God?* Yes; St. Paul says, that Jesus Christ "is over all things, *God* blessed for ever."[100] "*The Word* was *God*."[1] "*I* am the Alpha and Omega, the beginning and the end, saith *the Lord God*, who is, and who was, and who is to come, THE ALMIGHTY......I am the first and the last, and am alive and *was dead;* and behold I am living for ever and ever, and have the keys of death and of hell."[2]

[*See also* Rom. xiv., 11, *and* Philip. ii., 10, *compared with* Is. xlv., 21 to 25; *also* Heb. i., 5, 6, 8, 9, *compared with* Ps. xliv., 7, 8; *also* Heb. i., 6, *compared with* Ps. xcvi., 7.]

(96) John i., 1.
(97) Acts v., 4.
(98) 1 John v., 7.
(99) Prov. xxv., 27.
(100) Rom. ix., 5.
(1) John i., 1.
(2) Apoc. i., 8, compared with verses 17, 18.

Is Jesus Christ also *truly Man* as well as *God?* Yes; because God the Son assumed our human nature and united it to his Divine nature, so as to form but one person. This is what is meant by his *Incarnation.* Thus, St. Paul says, that Christ Jesus "being in the *form of God* thought it not robbery to be equal with God; but emptied himself, taking the *form of a servant*, being made in the likeness of men."[3] "In the beginning was the Word and *the Word was God*... And *the Word* WAS MADE FLESH."[4] Therefore, he is both God and man.

Are there, then, *two natures* in Jesus Christ? Yes; but the nature of God, and the nature of Man, are so united as to form but *one Person.* "As soul and body is one man, so God and man is one Christ."[5] "*I* and the Father are ONE."[6] Again: "The Father is GREATER than *I.*"[7] Here, the same person, "*I,*" speaks of himself both as God and as man.

Has he *always* been both God and Man? No; before his Incarnation, the Son of God existed in the nature of God only; from that time, he exists in two natures, the same Person being both God and man.

Will he now always exist in two natures? Yes; 1st, because he is called "a *Priest* for ever."[8] 2ndly because St. Paul says: "JESUS CHRIST yesterday and to-day, *he is the same for ever.*"[9]

Why was God the Son made man?—To save us from sin and hell.

In order to save us, it was necessary he should be able to suffer: as God he could not; hence he became man, and, as such, he was subject to human sufferings—hunger, fatigue, grief, temptations, pain, death

(3) Phil. ii., 6, 7.
(4) John i., 1, 14.
(5) Athanasian Creed.
(6) John x., 30.
(7) John xiv., 28.
(8) Heb. v., 6.
(9) Heb. xiii., 8.

—to all our infirmities, except our sins; and these he undertook to cancel. What an excess of love! how we should thank him for it! how it should encourage us to have recourse to him, under all difficulties and temptations, with an entire confidence! "For we have not a High Priest who cannot have compassion on our infirmiteis; but one tempted in all things like as we are, without sin. Let us go, therefore, with confidence, to the throne of grace; that we may obtain mercy, and find grace in seasonable aid."[10]

INSTRUCTION XI.

SECOND ARTICLE CONCLUDED.

A Short History of Religion, from the first promise of a Redeemer to its Fulfilment.

Who is Jesus Christ?—He is God the Son, made man for us.

Why was God the Son made man?—To save us from sin and hell.

Man was created *in innocence*—and *for heaven*. He fell by sin; and so lost both. Being unable of himself to make atonement, he had nothing before him but the sad prospect of misery, both here and hereafter. Upon his repentance, God took compassion on him, and promised him a Redeemer; but this promise was not fulfilled till after 4,000 years; yet, in the meantime, it was frequently renewed.——This promise raised, and its renewal kept up, in the ancient people, a most longing desire for the coming of their Redeemer; and formed a great part of their religion. "Amen, I say to you, that many prophets and just men have desired to see the things that you see, and

(10) Heb iv., 15, 16.

have not seen them."[11] "Abraham, your father, rejoiced that he might see my day; he saw it, and was glad."[12]

I will now run through a short History of Religion, from the first promise of a Redeemer to its fulfilment

This promise was first made, when God said: "*I will put enmities between thee and the Woman, and thy seed and* HER SEED: SHE SHALL CRUSH THY HEAD, *and thou shalt lie in wait for her heel.*"[13] Thus, the Redeemer was to be born of her posterity.

Adam and Eve transgressed the Divine command; and were driven out of Paradise; their first children were Cain and Abel; Cain killed his brother Abel, through envy; Seth was born in the place of Abel; Seth and his race were good; Cain and his race were bad: hence we see the consequences of the good or bad example of parents. The descendants of Seth intermarried with those of Cain; and thereby became corrupted. And "God seeing that the wickedness of men was great upon the earth, said: I will destroy man whom I have created, from the face of the earth; . . for it repenteth me that I have made them. But Noe found grace before the Lord."[14] This threat of the Almighty was executed by a universal Deluge; but Noe and his family were saved in the Ark, which God had commanded him to make. [*Anno Mundi*, 1656].

After the Deluge, "God blessed Noe and his sons," viz., Sem, Cham, and Japhet; "and he said to them: Increase and multiply, and fill the earth."[15] Cham brought a curse upon himself, by an act of disrespect towards his father; and this curse descended to his posterity.——The descendants of Noe having multiplied after the flood, began to build the tower of

(11) Matt. xiii., 17.
(12) John viii., 56.
(13) Gen. iii., 15.
(14) Gen. vi., 5, 7, 8.
(15) Gen. ix., 1.

Babel, &c.; but God confounded their language. Men soon became wicked as before; and the knowledge of the true God was *almost* lost.

To preserve at least *some* knowledge of himself, God called *Abraham*, of the race of Sem. [*Anno Mundi*, 2,008.] And the promise of a Redeemer was renewed to him: "*In thy seed all the nations of the earth shall be blessed.*"[16] God conducted him into the land of Canaan, which was *then* inhabited by the wicked race of Cham, but which was now promised to Abraham; for it was to be taken from *them* in consequence of their crimes; but this promise was not fulfilled till after 400 years.

God made a covenant with Abraham, and ordained circumcision to be a sign to that covenant. When Abraham and Sarah were almost a hundred years old, Isaac was promised them; and when Isaac was grown up, God commanded Abraham to sacrifice him.[17]

The promise of a Redeemer was renewed to Isaac: "*I will be with thee, and I will bless thee; . . . And in thy seed shall all the nations of the earth be blessed.*"[18] ——Isaac had two sons, Jacob and Esau. Esau, the first-born, sold his birthright; and so lost his Father's blessing, which was conferred upon Jacob.

Jacob had twelve sons—the twelve Patriarchs. Before the birth of Benjamin, Joseph, who was the eleventh, received marks of his Father's particular affection: for this his brothers envied him—sold him to the Ismaelites—they to Putiphar in Egypt, an officer of Pharao; Joseph was favoured by his Master—tempted by his Mistress—cast unjustly into prison, &c.—made ruler of Egypt, in consequence of having foretold the seven years' famine. The Brethren of Joseph go from the land of Canaan, to buy corn in Egypt—Joseph makes himself known to them: and

(16) Gen. xxii., 18. (17) Gen. xxii., 1, &c. (18) Gen. xxvi., 3, 4.

sends for his Father, Jacob, who, with his whole family, goes to dwell in Egypt. The Hebrews (*i.e.*, the family of Jacob) multiply exceedingly, and prosper; but are oppressed after Joseph's death.

MOSES, of the tribe of Levi, was born in the year of the World, 2,433, and before Christ, 1,571. At "the Mountain of God, Horeb," in the land of Madian, "God appeared to him in a flame of fire out of the midst of a bush; and he saw that the bush was on fire, and was not burnt."[19]

God sent him to Pharao. to deliver the Hebrews from slavery. Pharao would not release the people; for which God afflicted Egypt with ten plagues; viz., 1, he turned the waters into blood; 2, sent frogs; 3, gnats; 4, flies; 5, death of cattle; 6, ulcers in men and beasts; 7, hail and fire: 8, locusts; 9, darkness; 10, death of the first-born.[20] By these plagues, Pharao was compelled to let the people go; and they departed out of Egypt with 600,000 fighting men. The Red Sea dividing, they passed through on dry land—they sojourned forty years in the Desert; during which period, they received the Ten Commandments—adored the golden calf—were fed with manna from heaven—frequently rebelled against God—and were punished for their rebellion. By Divine appointment, Aaron was made high priest; and the priesthood was to descend in his family. Contrary to this appointment, Core, Dathan, and Abiron, assumed the office of the priesthood; for this crime, both they, and their families, were swallowed down alive into hell, by the earth opening beneath their feet; and all those persons who joined in their schismatical worship, were likewise destroyed. The Jewish sacrifices, ceremonies, and festivals were figurative, having a reference to the promised Redeemer; "For there is no other name

(19) Exod. iii., 2. (20) Exod. from chap. vii. to xii.

under heaven given to men, whereby we must be saved."[21]——Moses and Aaron both died, without entering the promised land. Of all that left Egypt, only two (Josue and Caleb) entered it.

Josue succeeded Moses, as the leader of Israel. Under him, the Israelites settled in the land of Promise, after having conquered their way. After Josue, the people were governed by Judges, of whom there were fourteen during about 300 years. During this period, they were frequently taken captive, in punishment of their sins; and, on their repentance, were delivered. Rejecting the government of Judges, the people *will* have a King; and God, condescending to their wish, directs Samuel, the last of the Judges, to give them a King.

The first King was Saul, chosen for them by God himself, but he was afterwards rejected for his conduct; and God directed Samuel to anoint David in his place.

David, being anointed King, slew Goliah, the Champion of the Philistines, in single combat; having fallen into the two grievous crimes of Adultery and Murder, he was brought to sincere repentence by the admonition of the Prophet Nathan;[22] when David had sinned again, by numbering the people through vanity; God punished him severely, but offered him his choice of three chastisements, viz., either three years' famine; or to be vanquished in war, during three months; or to have the sword of the Lord and pestilence in the land, during three days. "And David said: It is better for me to fall into the hands of the Lord (for his mercies are many), than into the hands of men. So the Lord sent a pestilence upon Israel; and there fell of Israel 70,000 men."[23] David composed a number

(21) Acts iv., 12. (22) 2 Kings xii., 1 to 15.
(23) 1 Paral. xxi., 11 to 17.

of Psalms, which breathe a spirit of devotion and of penance, and in which he foretells Christ and his Passion. The promise of the Redeemer was renewed to him: "*God hath sworn to him with an oath, that, of the fruit of his loins, one should sit upon his throne.*"[24]

Solomon, his Son, who succeeded him, was the wisest of men, and his reign was happy and prosperous. He built the temple of Jerusalem, 1,004 years before Christ. Towards the end of his life, Solomon fell from God by an inordinate love of women, and even became an idolater. In punishment of these crimes, God divided the Kingdom, after Solomon's death. For Roboam, his son, retained only the tribes of Juda and Benjamin, with that of Levi; and Jeroboam, his servant, was made King of the other ten tribes.

Elias began to prophesy in the reign of the wicked king Achab; and was taken up into the heavens alive, about 895 years before Christ. After this, there were more than 400 years of Prophets; during which, Salmanasar, King of Assyria, took the ten tribes (which formed the kingdom of Israel) captive to Ninive. [A.C. 721.) More than 100 years after this event, Nabuchodonosor, King of Babylon, took the Jews also (i.e., those who formed the kingdom of Juda) captive to Babylon, and destroyed the city and temple of Jerusalem. The Jews remained in the Babylonish captivity seventy years; during which period, Daniel foretold *the time* of Christ's coming, saying: "That, *from the going forth of the word to build up Jerusalem again, unto Christ the Prince, there shall be seven weeks, and sixty-two weeks; and after sixty-two weeks, Christ shall be slain.*"[25] By each week in his prophecy, is meant seven years. Cyrus, King of Persia, (who had been foretold by Isaias 200 years before his birth,) delivered the Jews from their captivity, 536 years before

(24) Acts ii., 30; Ps. cxxxi., 11. (25) Dan. ix., 25, 26.

Christ. Soon after this, (in the time of Malachy, the last of the Prophets,) the temple of Jerusalem was rebuilt, and also the walls and the city; and the Jews lived in peace 300 years, at the end of which period a terrible persecution was raised against them.

For Antiochus Epiphanes, King of Syria, "went up against Israel: and he went up to Jerusalem with a great multitude: and he proudly entered into the Sanctuary, and he took away the golden altar;...... and he took the silver and gold, and the precious vessels, and the hidden treasures which he found;...... and he made a great slaughter of men, and spoke very proudly. And there was great mourning in Israel."[26] For Antiochus took Jerusalem—plundered and profaned the Temple—forbade the exercise of the Jewish Religion—introduced idolatry in its place—and persecuted the people most furiously, putting all recusants to death. During these persecutions of Antiochus, the Jews gave glorious examples of fidelity to the Law of God. Eleazer, at the age of ninety, suffered death, rather than eat swine's flesh; and seven brothers, (called the seven Machabees,) with their mother, endured most excruciating deaths for the same cause.[27] ——The Jews at length recovered Jerusalem, and restored the exercise of their Religion; and they enjoyed peace till Jerusalem was again taken by the Romans under Pompey, A.C. 69; and 32 years afterwards, Herod was declared by them King of Judea.

The world now enjoyed *universal peace;* but was buried in idolatory, crimes, and the grossest ignorance of religion: and it was in this state of things, that CHRIST WAS BORN. He came both to *Redeem*, and to *Teach:* For he came "to *save* his people from their sins;"[28] and also "to *enlighten* them that sit in dark-

(26) 1 Mac. i., 21, &c. (27) 2 Mac. vi.; and vii.
(28) Matt. i., 21.

ness, and in the shadow of death; to direct our feet into the way of peace."[29]

INSTRUCTION XII.

THIRD ARTICLE.

History of the Incarnation, and Birth of Christ—and of his Life, to the Commencement of his Passion.

What is the Third Article of the Creed?—Who was conceived by the Holy Ghost, born of the Virgin Mary.

How was Christ made man?—He was conceived and made man, by the power of the Holy Ghost, in the womb of the Virgin Mary, without having any man for his father.

Where was our Saviour born?—In a stable at Bethlehem.

Upon what day was he born?—Upon Christmas-day.

The *First Article* of the Creed has been explained, by Instructions on what has been revealed concering the nature of Almighty God—on the Greatness of his Divine Attributes, which constitute his infinite Perfection, and render him infinitely amiable, and deserving of our love and service—on the Manifestation of these Attributes in the great work of the creation; particularly in the creation of man—and on the infinite love, by which God promised a Redeemer to man, after his fall.

The *Second Article* also has been explained, by Instructions showing who this promised Redeemer is; that is to say, on God the Son, who assumed the nature of man to save us from sin and hell.

We come now to the *Third Article*, which contains the *Fulfilment* of that promise, in the INCARNATION and BIRTH OF CHRIST.

(29) Luke i., 79

What is the Third Article of the Creed?—Who was conceived by the Holy Ghost, born of the Virgin Mary.

How was Christ made man?—He was conceived and made man, by the power of the Holy Ghost, in the womb of the Virgin Mary, without having any man for his father.

I. The B.V.M. is the Mother of God:—Is, then, the Blessed Virgin the *Mother of God?* Yes; for it cannot be denied, that she who brings forth *a person* is truly his mother, although she does not produce his soul: and, therefore, in bringing forth Jesus Christ, who is the *Person of God the Son*, the Blessed Virgin is truly his Mother, although she did not produce his Divinity; i.e., she is truly the Mother of Him who is the *Person* of God the Son: "The Holy One, who shall be *born of thee*, shall be called *the Son of God*. . . . Whence is this to me, that the Mother of my Lord should come to me?"[30]

I will now give a short account of the *Incarnation and birth* of Christ; and also of his *Life* up to the commencement of his Passion, as contained in the Gospel.

The Prophet Isaias had long foretold, that Christ should be born of a Virgin: "Behold a Virgin shall conceive, and bear a Son, and his name shall be called Emmanuel:"[31] "Which, being interpreted, is God with us."[32]

II. The Incarnation Accomplished:—St. Luke describes the manner in which this prophecy was fulfilled: "The Angel Gabriel was sent from God into a city of Galilee, called Nazareth, to a Virgin espoused to a man whose name was Joseph, of the house of David; and the Virgin's name was Mary. And the Angel being come in, said unto her: Hail, full of grace, the Lord is with thee; blessed art thou among women.

(30) Luke i., 35, 43. (31) Is. vii., 14. (32) Matt. i., 23.

Who, having heard, was troubled at his saying, and thought with herself what manner of salutation this should be. And the Angel said to her: Fear not, Mary, for thou hast found grace with God: Behold thou shalt conceive in thy womb, and shalt bring forth a Son; and thou shalt call his name JESUS: He shall be great, and shall be called the Son of the Most High; and the Lord God shall give unto him the throne of David his father; and he shall reign in the house of Jacob for ever; and of his kingdom there shall be no end. And Mary said to the Angel: How shall this be done, because I know not man? And the Angel answering, said to her: The Holy Ghost shall come upon thee, and the power of the Most High shall overshadow thee: and therefore also the Holy One which shall be born of thee, shall be called the Son of God. . . . And Mary said: "Behold the handmaid of the Lord; be it done to me according to thy word. And the Angel departed from her."[33]

So far the Evangelist relates how the mystery of the *Incarnation* was accomplished.

He then goes on to relate how the other part of the prophecy of Isaias was fulfilled; viz.,

III. THE BIRTH OF CHRIST:—"And it came to pass, that, in those days, there went out a decree from Cæsar Augustus, that the whole world should be enrolled. . . . And all went to be enrolled, every one into his own city. And Joseph also went up from Galilee, out of the city of Nazareth, into Judea, to the city of David, which is called Bethelehem, (because he was of the house and family of David,) to be enrolled with Mary, his espoused wife, who was with child. And it came to pass, that, when they were there, her days were accomplished that she should be delivered. And she brought forth her first-born Son, and wrapped him

(33) Luke i, 26 to 38.

up in swaddling clothes, and laid him in a manger; because there was no room for them in the inn. And there were in the same country, shepherds watching, and keeping the night-watches over their flock. And behold an Angel of the Lord stood by them, . . . and said to them: Fear not; for behold I bring you good tidings of great joy, that shall be to all the people; for this day is born to you a SAVIOUR, who is CHRIST THE LORD, in the city of David. And this shall be a sign unto you: You shall find THE INFANT wrapped in swaddling clothes, and laid in a manger. . . . And after the Angels departed from them into heaven, the shepherds said one to another: Let us go over to Bethlehem, and let us see this word that is come to pass, which the Lord hath showed to us. And they came with haste; and they found Mary and Joseph, and THE INFANT lying in a manger. And seeing, they understood of the word that had been spoken to them concerning THIS CHILD . . . And the shepherds returned, glorifying and praising God for all the things they had heard and seen, as it was told unto them."[34]

In this account of our Redeemer's Birth, two things are to be observed by us:—1st, An overruling Providence, by which Christ's Birth and all the circumstances of it were brought about, in accordance with the ancient Prophecies; and 2ndly, Christ's infinite love, in beginning so soon to suffer for us, and to give us examples of poverty, humility, mortification; . . . thus destroying the three great hinderances to our salvation.

IV. THE LIFE OF CHRIST:—The Birth of Christ was made known first to the Jews, in the persons of the poor shepherds; and afterwards to the Gentiles, in the persons of the three Wise Men, who came from the east to adore him. He was circumcised on the

(34) Luke ii., 1 to 20.

eighth day after his Birth; was persecuted by Herod; fled into Egypt; and, after Herod's death, returned to Nazareth; at the age of twelve years, he went up to the Temple of Jerusalem, with his Blessed Mother and St. Joseph. And "when they returned, the Child Jesus remained in the Temple; and his parents knew it not. And thinking that he was in the company, they came a day's journey, and sought him among their kinsfolks and acquaintance: and not finding him, they returned into Jerusalem, seeking him. And it came to pass, that, after three days, they found him in the Temple, sitting in the midst of the Doctors, hearing them, and asking them questions. And all that heard him were astonished at his wisdom and his answers. And his Mother said to him: Son, why hast thou done so to us? behold thy father and I have sought thee sorrowing. And he said to them: How is it that you sought me? did you not know, that I must be about my Father's business? . . And he went down with them, and came to Nazareth, and was subject to them. . . . And Jesus advanced in wisdom, and age, and grace with God and men."[35] ——No more is related of him till the age of thirty.

Who was John the Baptist? He was the Son of Zachary and Elizabeth—"the voice of one crying in the wilderness: Prepare ye the way of the Lord; make straight his paths."[36] At the age of thirty, Christ, having been baptized by him in the Jordan, began his public ministry, by preaching, doing good to all, curing all kinds of diseases among the people, —casting out devils—and working the most astonishing miracles, to prove that he was the Messias. Thus, when John the Baptist sent to ask him, saying: "Art thou he that art to come, or look we for another? Jesus said to them: Go and relate to John what you

(35) Luke ii., 41 to 52. (36) Luke iii., 4.

have heard and seen; the blind see, the lame walk, the lepers are cleansed, the deaf hear, the dead rise again, and the poor have the Gospel preached to them."[37] "And Jesus went about all Galilee, preaching the gospel of the kingdom; and healing all manner of sickness, and every infirmity among the people."[38] Soon after he had begun his public mission, he chose his twelve apostles, who were to teach all nations all things whatsoever he commanded them.[39]

Beside the miracles already mentioned, he changed water into wine[40]—raised the dead to life: "And he said: Young man, I say to thee arise; and he that was dead, rose up."[41] "He cried out with a loud voice: Lazarus, come forth; and presently he that had been been dead came forth."[42] He fed five thousand men with five loaves and two fishes, and they took up twelve baskets full of what remained of the fragments."[43] He also fed four thousand with seven loaves and a few fishes, and there remained seven baskets full of fragments."[44] When the storm arose at sea, which put the apostles in fear of perishing, "he commanded the winds and the sea, and there came a great calm."[45]

He appealed to his miracles as proofs, &c.: "If you will not believe me, *believe my works*...(for) the works that I do in the name of my Father, they give testimony of me."[46] "Believe for the very works, sake."[47] "If I had not done among them the works that no other man hath done, they would not have sin,"[48] Yet, notwithstanding his great miracles, and his unwearied charity in doing good to all, the Jews were continually seeking opportunities to kill him: but "no

(37) Matt. xi., 3, 4, 5. (38) Matt. iv., 23. (39) Luke vi., 13 to 16. Matt. xxviii., 19, 20 (40) John ii., 1 to 10. (41) Luke vii., 14.15. (42) John xi., 43, 44. (43) John vi., 5 to 14. (44) Mat. xv., 32 to 28. (45) Matt. viii., 23 to 27. (46) John x., 38. (47) John xiv., 12 (48) John xv., 24.

man laid hands on him, *because* his hour was not yet come."[49]

After having spent three years in his public ministry—in preaching, and teaching, and doing good to all, he at length gave us the greatest testimony of his love, in the institution of the Blessed Eucharist. After this he permitted himself to be betrayed by his own disciple—to be apprehended by his own chosen people—to be cruelly treated by them, and put to death.——But of his sufferings and death, I will give a more particular account in the next instruction.

The Life of Christ should be the frequent subject of your meditation. Reflect, therefore, occasionally on the chief events of his life—on his examples of fraternal charity (for his miracles were to do good); on his examples of patience under contradiction, of poverty of spirit, of humility, of zeal, of obedience, of conformity to God's will, and of other great virtues.

INSTRUCTION XIII.

FOURTH ARTICLE.

Christ's Passion and Death.

What is the Fourth Article of the Creed?—Suffered under Pontius Pilate, was crucified, dead and buried.

What did Christ suffer?—A bloody sweat, scourging at the pillar, crowning with thorns, and the carriage of his cross.

What else?—He was nailed to a cross, and died upon it between two thieves.

Why did he suffer?—For our sins.

Upon what day did he suffer?—On Good-Friday.

Where did he suffer?—On Mount Calvary.

In the last Instruction I explained the Third Article

(49) John vii., 30; viii., 20.

of the Creed, by giving the Scriptural account of the *Incarnation* and *Birth* of Christ; and I gave also a short history of his *Life*. We come now to the Fourth Article, which makes mention of his *Passion* and *Death*.——And, as the sufferings which he endured for our sake, are a striking proof of his great love for us, it is very important that you should *know well* the history of his passion and death; that the consideration of what he has suffered for your sake may inflame your hearts with a return of love.

"Jesus knowing that his hour was come, that he should pass out of this world to the Father; having loved his own who were in the world, he loved them unto the end."[50] And it was *then* (at the end of his life) that he gave us the greatest and tenderest proofs of his love....

Going up to Jerusalem, he entered the city in triumph, amidst the acclamations of the people. For "they took branches of palm trees, and went forth to meet him, and cried: Hosanna, blessed is he that cometh in the name of the Lord, the King of Israel."[51] *(These same people, a few days after, cried out: "Crucify him, Crucify him;" which shows what little account is to be made of the esteem or disesteem of men!)*

"Now the feast of unleavened bread, which is called the Pasch, was at hand. And the chief priests, and the scribes sought how they might put JESUS to death."[52] "Then went out one of the twelve, who was called Judas Iscariot, to the chief priests, and he said to them: What will you give me, and I will deliver him unto you? But they appointed him thirty pieces of silver. And from thenceforth he sought opportunity to betray him."[53] And Jesus "sent Peter and John, saying: Go and prepare for us the Pasch, that we may

(53) Matt. xxvi., 14, 15, 16. (51) John xii., 12, 13.
(52) Luke xxii., 1, 2. (50) John xiii., 1.

eat....And when the hour was come, he sat down, and the twelve apostles with him."[54]

"And whilst they were at supper, JESUS took bread, and blessed, and broke, and gave to his apostles, and said: "Take ye and eat: This is my body. And taking the chalice, he gave thanks; and gave to them, saying: Drink ye all of this. For this is my blood of the New Testament, which shall be shed for many unto remission of sins."[55]

Having thus instituted the Blessed Sacrament of the Altar, JESUS went into the Garden of Gethsemani with Peter, James, and John. "Then he saith to them: My soul is sorrowful even unto death. And going a little further, he fell upon his face and prayed, saying: Father, if thou wilt, remove this chalice from me: But yet not my will, but thine, be done. And being in an agony, he prayed the longer. And his sweat became as drops of blood trickling down upon the ground."[56] (*Example of having recourse to God in our troubles; and of praying with great reverence, with perseverance, and with complete submission to the Divine will.*)

"Then he cometh to his disciples, and saith to them:...Rise, let us go: behold he is at hand that will betray me." Scarcely had he said this, when Judas, at the head of a great multitude, came and betrayed him with a kiss."[57]

"And they took JESUS, and bound him; and they led him away to Annas first." And here they examined Jesus concerning his disciples and his doctrine. Answering, he said: "I have spoken openly to the world...and in secret I have said nothing...Ask them who have heard me." Then "one of the servants, standing by, gave JESUS a blow, saying: Answerest

(54) Luke xxii., 8, 14. (55) Matt. xxvi., 26, 27, 28.
(56) Matt. xxvi., 38, 39; Luke xxii., 42, 43, 44.
(57) Matt. xxvi., 46 to 50.

thou the high priest so? And Jesus answered him: If I have spoken evil, give testimony of the evil; but if well, why strikest thou me?"[58] *(Example of mildness and forbearance under injuries, provocations, and insults.)*

"And Annas sent him bound to Caiphas the high priest."[59] And here they "sought false witness against JESUS, that they might put him to death...And the high priest rising up, said to him: Answerest thou nothing to the things which these witness against thee? But JESUS held his peace. And the high priest said to him: I adjure thee by the living God, that thou tell us if thou be the Christ, the Son of God? JESUS saith to him: Thou hast said it. Then the high priest rent his garments, saying: He hath blasphemed; what further need have we of witnesses? Behold, now you have heard the blasphemy; what think you: But they answered and said: He is guilty of death. Then did they spit in his face, and buffeted him, and struck his face with the palms of their hands" and bid him prophesy who it was that struck him.[60]

Notwithstanding the admonition of his Divine Master, and his own protestations, Peter denied his Lord three times; and even confirmed his denial with an oath.[61] *(Example of the fatal consequences of presumption or self-confidence, which leads to grievous falls; and of immediate correspondence with the grace of repentance, which leads to pardon.——Judas also repented of his treason; but without hope of pardon—he joined despair with his repentance: and therefore he died in his sin.)*

"And when morning was come (i.e., on the morning of Good Friday), they took counsel against JESUS, that they might put him to death. And they brought

(58) John xviii., 12 to 23.
(59) John xviii., 24.
(60) Matt. xxvi., 57 to 68.
(61) Matt. xxvi., 69 to 75.

him bound to *Pontius Pilate* the Governor."[62] And here "they began to accuse him" of being seditious, "of stirring up the people" to rebellion, "of perverting the nation," &c. But Pilate said to them: "I find no cause in him." And he sent him to *Herod* Antipas, son of that Herod who killed the Innocents. "And Herod, with his army, set him at nought; and mocked him, putting on him a white garment; and sent him back to Pilate."[63]

Pilate, wishing to deliver Jesus out of the hands of the Jews, (for "of necessity he was to release unto them one upon the feast-day,") proposed to them two, viz., Barabbas, a murderer: and Jesus. But the whole multitude together cried out, saying: Away with this man, and release unto us Barabbas. And Pilate again spoke to them, desiring to release Jesus. But they cried out again, saying: Crucify him, Crucify him. And he said to them the third time: "Why, what evil hath this man done? I find no cause of death in him: I will chastise him therefore, and let him go. But they were instant with loud voices requiring that he might be crucified, and their voices prevailed." And he released unto them Barabbas.[64]

"Then Pilate took JESUS, and scourged him.—— And the soldiers, platting a crown of thorns, put it upon his head; and they put on him a purple garment; and they came to him and said: Hail, King of the Jews; and they gave him blows. Pilate therefore went forth again, and saith to them: Behold I bring him forth unto you, that you may know that I find no cause in him. (Jesus therefore came forth, bearing the crown of thorns and the purple garment.) And he saith to them: *Behold the Man.*" But "they cried out, saying: Crucify him: Crucify him...If thou

(62) Matt. xxvii., 1, 2.
(63) Luke xxiii., 1 to 12.
(64) Luke xxiii., 13 to 25.

release this man, thou art not Cæsar's friend...Then, therefore, he delivered him to them to be crucified."[65] (*Example of the fatal consequences of loving the friendship of the world.*)

"And they took JESUS, and led him forth. And bearing his own cross, he went forth to that place which is called Calvary."[66] Having arrived at Calvary, he was stripped of his clothes, nailed to the Cross, and crucified upon it between two thieves; and while he was hanging on the Cross, he was reproached, reviled, and blasphemed by the surrounding multitude. He lived three hours on the Cross, enduring the most excruciating tortures; during which time the sun was darkened.[67]

The seven last words on the Cross:—

1. "Father, forgive them; for they know not what they do."[68]

2. "Amen, I say to thee, this day thou shalt be with me in Paradise."[69]

3. "Woman, behold thy Son;—Behold thy Mother."[70]

4. "My God, my God, why hast thou forsaken me?"[71]

5. "I thirst."[72]

6. "It is consummated."[73]

7. "Father, into thy hands I commend my spirit. And saying this, he gave up the Ghost."[74]

When he "yielded up the Ghost," all nature proclaimed his Divinity: "The veil of the Temple was rent in two, from the top even to the bottom; and the earth quaked; and the rocks were rent; and the graves were opened; and many bodies of the saints that had slept, arose; and coming out of the tombs

(65) John xix., 1 to 16.
(66) John xix., 16, 17.
(67) Matt. xxvii, 39 to 45; Luke xxiii., 35 to 45.
(68) Luke xxiii., 34.
(69) Luke xxiii., 43.
(70) Jn. xix., 26, 27.
(71) Mat. xxvii., 46.
(72) John xix., 28.
(73) John xix., 30.
(74) Luke xxiii., 46.

after his resurrection, came into the holy city, and appeared to many." And some of them that witnessed his crucifixion, "having seen the earthquake, and the things that were done, said: Indeed, this was the Son of God."[75] "And all the multitude of them that were come together to that sight, and saw the things that were done, returned striking their breasts."[76]

And when it was evening, Joseph of Arimathea "went to Pilate, and asked the body of JESUS; and Pilate commanded that it should be delivered to him. And Joseph taking the body, . . . laid it in his own new monument, which was hewed out of a rock; and he rolled a great stone to the door of the monument, and went his way. . . . And the chief priests and Pharisees made the sepulchre sure, sealing the stone and setting guards."[77]

The death of Christ was not forced, but *voluntary:* "I lay down my life that I may take it up again. . . No man taketh it away from me; but I lay it down of myself."[78]

Fruits of his Death:—1. He has delivered us by it from sin; and from the slavery of the devil: "He hath washed us from our sins in his own blood;"[79]—2, He has reconciled us to God: "For God indeed was in Christ, reconciling the world to himself;"[80] 3, He has re-opened to us the gates of heaven, which had been so long closed against all mankind: "For, "being consummated he became the cause of eternal salvation to all that obey him."[81]

EXHORTATION:—Frequently reflect on the sufferings of Jesus Christ—consider who is it that suffers? for whom does he suffer? from whom? how much? in what manner? He suffers with patience: with per-

(75) Matt. xxvii., 50, 54. (76) Luke xxiii., 48. (77) Matt. xxvii., 57 to 66. (78) John x., 17, 18. (79) Apoc. i., 5. (80) 2 Cor. v., 19. (81) Heb. v., 9.

fect resignation; with charity; praying for his very persecutors, and pleading their excuse to his Heavenly Father.

INSTRUCTION XIV.

FOURTH ARTICLE *concluded.*—FIFTH ARTICLE.

On the Sign of the Cross; the Descent of Christ into Limbo; and his Resurrection.

Why do we make the Sign of the Cross?—For two reasons: First, to put us in mind of the Blessed Trinity, and, secondly, to put us in mind that God the Son became man, and died upon a Cross for us.

What puts us in mind of the Blessed Trinity, when we make the Sign of the Cross?—These words: In the name of the Father, and of the Son, and of the Holy Ghost.

What puts us in mind that Christ became man, and suffered on a Cross?—The very making or signing ourselves with the Sign of the Cross.

What is the Fifth Article of the Creed?—He descended into hell; the third day he rose again from the dead.

Whither did the soul of our Saviour go after his death?—His soul went down into that part of hell called Limbo.

What do you mean by Limbo?—I mean a place of rest, where the souls of the saints who died before Christ were detained.

Who were those Saints?—Those who had faithfully observed the laws of God.

Did none go up to Heaven before our Saviour?—No they expected him to carry them up thither.

What means the third day he rose again from the dead?—It means, that after Christ had been dead and buried, part of three days, he raised his blessed body to life again on the third day.

On what day did Christ rise again from the Dead?—On Easter-day.

I. SIGN OF THE CROSS:—As the Sufferings and

Death of Christ are a most striking proof of his great love for us, we cannot think of them too often. The frequent reflection . . inflames, &c. ; and is very pleasing to Christ. For this reason it is, that we make such frequent use of the Sign of the Cross in all our prayers and ceremonies.——For,

1. As the Catechism teaches, the Sign of the Cross serves to remind us of two most important truths of religion—of those two truths which contain the *sum* of all Christian knowledge : for it reminds us of our last end, viz., the Blessed Trinity ; and also of the means of attaining that end, viz., Jesus Christ, who is "the way, the truth, and the life."[82]

2. When we begin and end our prayers with the Sign of the Cross, it is as much as to say : We pray through the merits of Christ.

3. It is a powerful defence in temptation. As the blood of the Paschal Lamb, sprinkled on the door-posts, was a preservative against the destroying Angel ; so the sign of the Cross, or of Christ's blood being shed for us, preserves us from falling into the destructive hands of the angels of darkness. The Fathers of the Church speak of it as such.

4. The use of it is most ancient in the Church :—Tertullian says : "At every step, at our coming in, and going out, when we sit down to table, when we go to bed, we imprint on our foreheads the Sign of the Cross."

When we make the Sign of the Cross, we should accompany the act with proper dispositions. As "circumcision profiteth indeed, if thou keep the law ; but if thou be a transgressor of the law, thy circumcision is made uncircumcision,"[83] so likewise the Sign of the Cross profiteth indeed, if, &c . . In order to derive ad-

(82) John xiv., 6. (83) Rom. ii., 25.

vantage from it, it should be made *correctly*, *deliberately*, *and devoutly.*

II. DESCENT INTO LIMBO:—*What is the Fifth Article of the Creed?*—**He descended into hell; the third day he rose again from the dead.**

Whither did the soul of our Saviour go after his death?—**His soul went down into that part of hell called Limbo.**

When Christ died upon the Cross, his soul separated from his body; but did the Divinity also separate from it? No; the Divinity remained united with the body, and also with the soul.

Christ being dead, Joseph of Arimathea took down the *body* of Jesus, and laid it in his own new monument, to the door of which he rolled a large stone; and the Jews, having sealed the stone, set guards round the sepulchre. But whither did the *soul* of Jesus go? His soul went into Limbo. The Apostles' Creed says: "He descended into Hell:" by which is meant, not into hell where the wicked are punished, but into "the heart of the earth:"[84] "He descended into the lower parts of the earth"[85]—into that place where Lazarus was seen "in Abraham's bosom;[86] which place Catholics call "*Limbo*."

Why did he go thither? 1st: To communicate the happy tidings of Redemption, &c.; "He went and preached to those spirits that were in prison;"[87] 2nd: To deliver the saints who were there detained, and to take them to heaven at his ascension: "Ascending on high, he led captivity captive."[88]

Had none gone to heaven before our Saviour? No; for he says: "No man hath ascended into heaven, but the Son of Man who is in heaven."[89] Enoch and Elias were taken up: but only to the lower heavens: they

(84) Matt. xii., 40. (85) Eph. iv., 9. (86) Luke xvi., 23. (87) 1 Pet. iii., 19. (88) Eph. iv., 8. (89) John iii., 13.

do not enjoy the *beatific vision;* Adam's sin had shut the gates of heaven against all mankind. . .

Did Christ's presence occasion great joy to the souls in Limbo? Yes; it was the great object of their desires: And, as, "hope that is deferred, afflicteth the soul;"[90] so the presence of Christ, by removing that afflicting delay, changed Limbo into a Paradise of delight; and hence he said to the penitent thief "This day thou shalt be with me in *Paradise.*"[91]

How long did the soul of Christ remain there? From three o'clock on Friday afternoon, till early on Sunday morning.

III. Resurrection of Christ.—*What means the third day he rose again from the dead?*—It means that after Christ had been dead and buried, part of three days, he raised his blessed body to life again on the third day.

On what day did Christ rise again from the dead?—On Easter-day.

How did he raise himself to life again? By his own Divine power, his soul returned to the body, &c.; "I lay down my life, that I may take it again....And I have power to lay it down, and I have power to take it up again."[92] "Destroy this temple, and in three days I will raise it up......but he spoke of the temple of his body."[93]

"And when it began *to dawn* towards the first day of the week, came Mary Magdalen and the other Mary to see the sepulchre: and behold there was a great earthquake. For an Angel of the Lord descended from heaven, and coming, rolled back the stone, and sat upon it. And the guards were struck with terror, and became as dead men."[94] For a guard of soldiers had been set round the sepulchre, to prevent the body

(90) Prov. xiii., 12. (92) John x., 17, 18. (94) Matt. xxviii., 1 to 4.
(91) Luke xxiii., 43. (93) John ii., 19, 21.

from being taken away, till after the third day; and they did this with the view of proving Christ to be a deceiver: "And the chief priests and Pharisees came together to Pilot, saying: Sir, we have remembered that that seducer said, while he was yet alive: 'After three days I will rise again.' Command, therefore, the sepulchre be guarded until the third day; lest, perhaps, his disciples come and steal him away, and say to the people: 'He is risen from the dead;' and the last error shall be worse than the first."[95]

When the guards, who had been stationed round the sepulchre, had seen the Angel roll away the stone and sit upon it, "some of them came into the city, and told the chief priest all things that had been done." But they "gave a great sum of money to the soldiers, saying: Say you, His disciples came by night, and stole him away when we were asleep."[96] "They give us *sleeping* witnesses," says St. Augustin. The Apostles would not dare to attempt to steal him away—they were too timid. Christ gave demonstrative proofs that he had risen again; for he frequently appeared to many, during forty days; he showed them his hands and feet; and he even commanded Thomas to touch the wounds which had been made in his hands and sides.[97]

The *Resurrection* of Christ is a most important Article of Christian Faith; it is a fundamental Article. For, this *fact* being proved, proves the *truth* of Christianity:—

1. Because it was foretold: "And Jesus said to them: The Son of man shall be betrayed into the hands of men; and they shall kill him; and *the third day he shall rise again.*"[98] Hence, the Jews guarded the sepulchre to prove him a deceiver.

(95) Matt. xxvii., 62 to 66.
(96) Matt. xxviii., 11 to 15.
(97) Luke xxiv., 39, 40; John xx, 20, 27.
(98) Matt. xvii., 21, 22.

2. Because, when the Jews asked a sign of his being the Messias, he gave them this very sign: "As Jonas was in the whale's belly three days and three nights; so shall the Son of Man be in the heart of the earth three days and three nights."[99]

3. Because the Apostles made this fact the *groundwork* of their preaching. Thus St. Paul says: "If Christ be not risen again, then is our preaching vain, and your faith is also vain...But now Christ *is* risen from the dead, the first fruits of them that sleep."[100]

INSTRUCTION XV.

SIXTH ARTICLE.

The Ascension of Jesus Christ—Satisfaction, Redemption, and Impetration.

What is the Sixth Article of the Creed?—He ascended into heaven, sits at the right hand of God the Father Almighty.

When did our Saviour go up to heaven?—Forty days after he rose again.

Why is he said to sit at the right hand of God the Father: Has God the Father any hands?—No; God the Father has no hands, because he is a pure spirit; but the meaning of these words is, that Christ, as man, occupies the next place to God in heaven; being, as God, equal to his Father in all things.

On what day did our Saviour go up to heaven?—On Ascension-day.

I. THE ASCENSION:—After his Resurrection from the dead, our Blessed Lord frequently appeared to his Apostles: "To whom he showed himself alive after his passion, by many proofs, for forty days appearing to them, and speaking of the kingdom of God."[1]

(99) Matt. xii., 40. (100) 1 Cor. xv., 14 to 20. (1) Acts i., 3.

After having instructed his Apostles in all the mysteries of the kingdom, and "opened their understanding that they might understand the Scriptures ;"[2] he gave them commission to go and teach all nations; and promised to be with them in their teaching till the end of the world; and he empowered them to confirm their preaching with miracles: "Go ye into the whole world, and preach the Gospel to every creature. He that believeth and is baptized, shall be saved; but he that believeth not, shall be condemned. And these signs shall follow them that believe: In my name they shall cast out devils; they shall speak with new tongues; they shall take up serpents; and if they shall drink any deadly thing, it shall not hurt them; they shall lay their hands upon the sick, and they shall recover."[3]

On the fortieth day, "he led them out as far as Bethania (to Mount Olivet); and lifting up his hands, he blessed them: and it came to pass, whilst he blessed them, he departed from them, and was carried up to heaven."[4] "And whilst they were beholding him going up to heaven, behold two men stood by them, in white garments; who also said to them: Ye men of Galilee, why stand ye looking up to heaven? This Jesus who is taken up from you into heaven, shall so come as you have seen him going up into heaven."[5]

Where is Jesus Christ *now?* He "sitteth at the right hand of God the Father Almighty."[6] ——He ascended, 1, To take possession of that seat of glory for himself, as man: "Ought not Christ to have suffered these things, and so to enter into his glory?"[7]—and, 2, To prepare a place for us, to draw our hearts after him—and to be our Mediator with the

(2) Luke xxiv., 45.
(3) Matt. xxviii., 19, 20.
Mark xvi., 15 to 19.
(4) Luke xxiv., 50, 51.
(5) Acts i., 9, 10, 11, 12.
(6) Apostles' Creed
Mark xvi., 19.
(7) Luke xxiv., 26.

Father: "Let not your hearts be troubled;...in my Father's house, there are many mansions; and if I go, and prepare a place for you, I will come again, and will take you to myself; that where I am, you also may be."[8] Christ "is at the right hand of God," says St. Paul, "always living to make intercession for us." "If any man sin, we have an advocate with the Father, Jesus Christ, the just."[10]

II. SATISFACTION, REDEMPTION, IMPETRATION.

Having been taught, in the preceding Articles, *who* Christ is; his Incarnation; his Birth; his Life; his Passion, and Death; his Resurrection; and, lastly, his Ascension into heaven; we should now pause to consider the great blessings we receive, through what he did and suffered for us while on earth. These blessings are, 1, The *Satisfaction* which he has made for us to the Divine Justice; 2, The *Redemption* which he has purchased for us; and, 3, His *Impetration*, or the continual application of his merits for obtaining special blessings for us.

1. What is SATISFACTION? It is offering the offended or injured party a compensation equal to the offence; so as to appease him, and render him propitious and merciful. Now this is what Christ has done for us, by offering the infinite merits of his Passion and death, in *satisfaction* for our sins. Our sins had offended the *infinite* Majesty of God: Christ offered an *infinite* atonement.——Are the merits of Christ, then, of INFINITE value? Yes; 1, Because the dignity of his Person, being infinite, gave an infinite value to whatever *He* offered for us: His actions were the *actions of God;* and therefore, of infinite value—of infinite merit; 2, Because the perfection of charity, also, with which he suffered for us, gave infinite value to

(8) John xiv., 1, 2, 3. (9) Rom. viii., 34; Heb. vii., 25. (10) John ii. 1.

his sufferings. For this charity was no less than the infinite love of the Son of God for his eternal Father "My *meat* is to do the will of him that sent me, that I may perfect his work." "For I do always the things that please him."[11]

2. What is REDEMPTION? It is buying from slavery one who had once been free. Man was free at first; then he became enslaved to sin and Satan; and now he is redeemed from both, and from eternal death: "In Jesus Christ we have redemption through his blood, the remission of sins:"[12] For he hath "washed us from our sins in his own blood."[13]——By sin we had brought upon ourselves, not only temporal, but *eternal death*: "Thou shalt die *the* death."[14] Jesus Christ, having taken upon himself our sins, suffered death in atonement for them; and he offered his death to *redeem us* from that eternal death, to which we had been doomed; and thus he purchased our freedom.

3. What is the Benefit of Christ's IMPETRATION? By his merits, which are *infinite*, Christ has purchased for us *all the graces and helps* we can stand in need of. He has not only cancelled the decree of our eternal condemnation, and restored our title to the kingdom of heaven; but he has purchased for us all the means, which will enable us to arrive at that kingdom. Now, it is *through Christ's Impetration*, that we obtain these graces, and all the spiritual blessings which we receive: we obtain them, by his presenting his merits to the Father in our behalf. Thus it is, that, "sitting at the right hand of God, he maketh intercession for us;"[15] thus it is, that, when we have sinned, he is our "Advocate with the Father;"[16] that he is our only Mediator, who can offer his own independent merits in our favour.

(11) John iv., 34; viii. 29. (12) Colos. i., 14. (13) Apoc. i., 5. (14) Gen. ii., 17. (15) Rom. viii., 34. (16) 1 John ii., 1

Since Christ has redeemed *all* men FULLY, will *all* therefore be saved? No; certain conditions are required, on our part, for applying the merits of his Redemption to our souls; for we must *believe* and *practise* what he teaches, i.e., we must have "*faith* working by *charity*."[17] There are but few, comparatively, who comply with *both* these conditions: and hence, though *all* are redeemed, yet but few are saved. The far greater part imitate the slothful servant, who having a talent in his possession, buried it, instead of making a profitable use of it.[18] Do not imitate them; but employ the means of salvation, which Christ has purchased for you. Take every opportunity, which Religion and your circumstances afford, of applying his merits to your souls. For this purpose, frequent the Sacraments, which are the appointed means of obtaining this application of his merits—Hear Mass, which is another appointed and powerful means—Be diligent and fervent in your prayers, offering them up *through Christ's merits:* "Amen I say to you, if you ask the Father anything *in my name*, he will give it you."[19] By thus making use of the means appointed for applying the merits of Christ to your soul, you will obtain such graces, as will enable you to join *good works* to your *faith*, and so to secure your salvation.

INSTRUCTION XVI.

SEVENTH ARTICLE.

On the Day of Judgment.

What is the Seventh Article of the Creed?—From thence he shall come to judge the living and the dead.

Will Christ ever come again?—Yes; he will come down from heaven at the last day, to judge all men.

(17) Gal. v., 6. (18) Matt. xxv., 14 to 30. (19) John xvi., 23.

What are the things he will judge?—All our thoughts, words, and works.

What will he say to the wicked?—Go, ye cursed, into everlasting fire.

What will he say to the just?—Come, ye blessed of my Father, receive ye the kingdom which is prepared for you.

Shall not every man be judged at his death, as well as at the last day?—Yes; he shall.

In the preceding Articles of the Creed, we have considered Jesus Christ in the quality of our *Redeemer*, but, in this Seventh Article, we have to consider him as our *Judge*.

When will he judge us? He will judge us, first, at our death; and, secondly, at the last day.

I. AT OUR DEATH:—For "it is appointed unto men once to die; and, after this, the judgment."[20] [*Example of Dives and Lazarus.*[21]]

What need then is there of the General Judgment?

1. To vindicate the ways of God's Providence and to justify the conduct of his saints. Providence so ordains, that the virtuous often live in adversity, affliction, and oppression—that, during life, they are publicly treated with contempt and scorn—that their piety is looked upon as folly, and their virtues as hypocrisy: whereas, the wicked are frequently allowed to prosper in this world—to live at their ease, in the enjoyment of wealth and earthly comforts.——The Psalmist, considering the earthly prosperity of the wicked, says: "Doth God know? Behold these are sinners; and yet abounding in the world, they have obtained riches! And I said: then have I in vain justified my heart, and washed my hands among the innocent; and *I have been scourged* all the day . . . I studied that I might know this thing; it is labour

(20) Heb. ix., 27 (21) Luke xvi., 19 to 21

in my sight; until I go into the sanctuary of God, and understand concerning their last ends."[22] For *then* the scale will be turned. When the wicked shall behold the Elect raised to honour, *then* repenting and groaning for anguish of spirit, they will say: "These are they whom we had heretofore in derision, and for a parable of reproach. We fools esteemed their life madness, and their end without honour: behold how they are now numbered among the children of God, and their lot is among the saints."[23]

2. To do justice to Jesus Christ as man. On earth he was publicly dishonoured by the world: "He became a worm and no man, the reproach of men, and the outcast of the people; and all they that saw him, laughed him to scorn."[24] He was falsely accused, and unjustly condemned; and was executed in ignominy, as if he had been a malefactor. But, at the last day, he will be glorified before all; he will sit to judge all the nations of the earth.

3. To judge the *whole man*, body as well as soul.

II. At the last Day:—For, "when the Son of Man shall come in his majesty, all nations shall be gathered together before him: and he shall separate them one from another, as the shepherd separateth the sheep from the goats: and he shall set the sheep on his right hand, but the goats on his left. Then shall the King say to them that shall be on his right hand: Come, ye blessed of my Father, possess ye the kingdom prepared for you from the foundation of the world . . . Then he shall say to them also that shall be on his left hand: Depart from me, ye cursed, into everlasting fire, which was prepared for the devil and his angels. . . . And these shall go into everlasting punishment; but the just into life everlasting."[25]

(22) Ps. lxxii., 12 to 17.
(23) Wisd. v., 1 to 5.
(24) Ps. xxi., 7, 8.
(25) Matt. xxv., 31 to 46.

1. *Signs that will precede the General Judgment:*—There shall be "wars and rumours of wars; nation shall rise up against nation; and there shall be pestilences, and famines, and earthquakes in places. Now all these are the beginnings of sorrows."[26]— -After these things, "there shall be signs in the sun, and in the moon, and in the stars; and upon the earth distress of nations, by reason of the roaring of the sea and of the waves; men withering away for fear and expectation of what shall come upon the whole world: for the powers of heaven shall be moved."[27]

2. *Universal Destruction:*—After these signs, will come the *general Destruction.* Torments of devouring fire will pour down, and consume all earthly things—cottages and palaces alike: *then* there will be an end of all worldly greatness. Our *good works*, and *evil deeds*, will alone remain of all that we possessed on earth: these will accompany us to the judgment-seat of God.

3. *Description of the General Judgment:*—After the universal Destruction, an Archangel will summon all mankind, saying: "Arise ye dead; and come to judgment." Then, in a moment, the whole human race will be assembled into the valley of Josaphat, which is in sight of Mount Calvary: "I will gather together all nations, and will bring them down to the Valley of Josaphat; . . for there will I sit to judge all nations round about."[28]

"And then shall appear the *Sign of the Son of Man* in heaven; and then shall all tribes of the earth mourn: and they shall see the Son of Man *coming* in the clouds of heaven, with much power and majesty."[29] How different is *this*, from his *first coming!* Not now to seek and to save; not to console; but to *Judge!*

(26) Matt. xxiv., 6, 7, 8.
(27) Luke xxi., 25, 26.
(28) Joel iii., 2, 3.
(29) Matt. xxiv., 30.

What a terror to the wicked! what a consolation to the good!

The Judge being come, "and all the angels with him; then shall he sit upon the seat of his Majesty; and all nations shall be gathered together before him; and he shall *separate* them one from another, as the shepherd separateth the sheep from the goats, and he shall set the sheep on his right hand, but the goats on his left."[30] In this separation, there will be no distinction, except of virtue and vice—the chaff will then be separated from the wheat.

All mankind standing, in awful silence, before the judgment-seat of God, the conscience of every one will be *laid open* to public view—*secret sins* will be made known: "For the Lord will both bring to light the hidden things of darkness, and will make manifest the counsels of hearts."[31] What a terror and confusion this will be to sinners! and especially to *Christian* sinners! But the *just* shall then "lift up their heads and rejoice:"[32] their private virtues, and all their good works, will be made known, and will contribute to their honour and happiness: they will not then repent of having served God!

The Sentence which will close the General Judgment:—All mankind seeing now the true state of their consciences, the Judge will turn to the just,. . .and will pronounce their consoling sentence: "Come, *ye blessed* of my Father, possess ye the kingdom prepared for you from the foundation of the world." There wil *then* be an end of all their crosses, afflictions, trials, mortifications!——But, turning to the wicked, he will doom them to endless misery: "Depart from me, *ye cursed*, into everlasting fire, which was prepared for the devil and his angels."[33] This, then, is the end of the criminal pleasures and sinful vanities of this world—

(30) Matt. xxv., 31, 32, 33.
(31) 1 Cor. iv., 5.
(32) Luke xxi., 28.
(33) Matt, xxv., 34, 41.

eternal misery in the flames of hell!!!——For, the wicked will *then* be swallowed down into the bottomless abyss, to remain there for ever. But the just will ascend with Christ and his Angels into everlasting happiness.

How this last Judgment shows the importance of serving God, and of saving our souls! You may have which sentence you please . . . You only have to make good use of the talents, &c.; and then, like the good and faithful servants, you will receive that consoling sentence, which will put you in possession of eternal happiness.

INSTRUCTION XVII.

EIGHTH ARTICLE.

The Descent of the Holy Ghost—and the Establishment of the Church.

What is the Eighth Article of the Creed?—I believe in the Holy Ghost.

Who is the Holy Ghost?—He is the Third Person of the Blessed Trinity.

From whom doth he proceed?—From the Father and the Son.

Is he equal to them?—Yes; he is the same Lord and God as they are.

When did the Holy Ghost come down on the Apostles in fiery tongues?—On Whit-Sunday.

Why did he come down upon them?—To enable them to preach the Gospel, and to plant the Church.

As, in the first Article of the Creed, we profess our belief in God the Father; and, in the six following Articles, in God the Son, and the mysteries of Redemption; so, in the Eighth Article, we profess our belief in God the Holy Ghost.

I. Descent of the Holy Ghost:—The Athanasian Creed shows the necessity and importance of knowing what we are to believe, concerning the three Divine Persons; and, consequently, concerning the Holy Ghost. It teaches us that He is the same Nature, and same God, as the Father and the Son; and equal to them in all Perfections.

He PROCEEDS from the Father and the Son; and is one God with them: "There are three who give testimony in heaven; the Father, the Word, and the Holy Ghost, and these three are one."[34]——The manner of his PROCESSION is a mystery; and, therefore, we cannot comprehend it.[35]

When did the Holy Ghost come down on the Apostles in fiery tongues?—On Whit-Sunday.

How long was this after the Ascenion? Ten days.——After Christ had ascended into heaven, the Apostles retired to Jerusalem, and spent the ten days in silence and prayer. This shows how we are to prepare for receiving the Holy Ghost; or for receiving his grace in any of the Sacraments: it shows that we should spend some time in *retirement and prayer*.

On the day of *Pentecost* the Holy Ghost descended upon the Apostles: And when the days of Pentecost were accomplished, they were all together in one place: and suddenly there came a sound from heaven, as of a mighty wind coming, and it filled the whole house where they were sitting; and there appeared to them parted tongues, as it were of fire: and it sat upon every one of them: and they were all filled with the Holy Ghost, and they began to speak with divers tongues, according as the Holy Ghost gave them to speak."[36]——At the baptism of our Saviour, the Holy Ghost appeared "*as a dove*," to denote *innocence:*

(34) 1 John v., 7.
(35) John xv., 26; xvi., 14, 15.
(36) Acts ii., 1 to 4.

but, at Pentecost he appeared as "*parted tongues*," to denote *universal preaching:* and the tongues seemed to be "*of fire*," to denote the *charity*, *zeal*, and *success* of that preaching.

Effects of the Descent of the Holy Ghost:—The Apostles were changed into quite other men. *Before* they received the Holy Ghost, they were weak, timid, hid themselves for fear of the Jews: but *now*, they are inflamed with divine love, zeal, and courage; they bodly preach in public. *Before*, they were dull, could hardly understand his doctrines: *now*, they are enlightened; the Holy Ghost "teaching them all things, and bringing all things to their mind, whatsoever Christ had said to them;"[37] and giving them the gift of tongues, and power to confirm their preaching by miracles.[38] These miraculous manifestations of the Divine power were necessary in the first establishment of the Church: the first missionaries to any infidel nation have, in like manner, worked miracles.

II. The Establishment of the Church, by the Preaching of the Apostles; and the Success of their Preaching:—The Apostles preached the Gospel first to the Jews; then to the Samaritans; and after that to the Gentiles.

1. *To the Jews first*, because they were the chosen people, the children of Abraham, to whom the promises were more immediately made.

Their preaching to the Jews was attended with great success: "The Lord working withal, and confirming the word with signs that followed."[39] At St. Peter's first sermon, 3,000 were converted; and at the second, 5,000. The other Apostles preached with the like success: "The Lord increased daily together such as should be saved."[40]

(37) John xiv., 26.
(38) Mark xvi., 17, 18.
(39) Mark xvi., 20.
(40) Acts ii., 47.

Exemplary Life of the first Christians.—The first Christians were all of one heart—they were detached from earthly things—they sold their possessions to be distributed as each man had need—they lived in common—and assembled daily to prayer—and they esteemed themselves happy in suffering for Christ, like the Apostles, who "went from the presence of the Council, rejoicing that they were accounted worthy to suffer reproach for the name of Jesus."[41] For the Christians were persecuted by the unconverted Jews: for, though many of the Jews were converted, yet the great body of the Jewish nation remained hardened in their unbelief.

The judgments of God at length fell upon that unhappy people, for their crimes and abuse of grace; for they were given up to a reprobate sense; their city was besieged and destroyed, under the Emperor Vespasian; and more than a million of the inhabitants perished by famine, or the sword.

2. The Jewish *nation* not receiving the faith, the Apostles turned *next to the Samaritans.* Philip, the Deacon, converted great numbers of them; and Peter and John were sent to confirm them; "And there was great joy in the city;" for the Samaritans received the faith with gladness.[42]

3. After this, God made known to Peter, that it was now time to preach *to the Gentiles.* Cornelius was the first of them who received the faith.[43] In order to "teach all nations," the Apostles dispersed; and they converted great multitudes in the different countries to which the went. St. Paul was called to the Apostleship, when on his way to Damascus; and none preached more successfully. Thus, the Apostles established the Christian Religion with great *rapidity and success*, in a world buried in idolatry and every kind

(41) Acts v., 41. (42) Acts viii., 8. (43) Acts x., 1, &c.

of crime, in spite of persecutions raised by the devil, God rendering their preaching efficacious by his grace, and by miracles.

The Apostles sealed, with their blood, the Faith which they had taught; leaving other appointed ministers to continue the same work. Thousands also of the Christians suffered death for the faith, in the violent persecutions which were raised against them. The constancy and example of the Martyrs served very much to extend the faith, for which they thus suffered and died.

INSTRUCTION XVIII.

NINTH ARTICLE.

The Pastor's Authority to teach and govern; and the People's Obligation to hear and obey.

What is the Ninth Article of the Creed?—The Holy Catholic Church: the Communion of Saints.

What is the Catholic Church?—All the faithful under one head.

The Catholic Church consists of all those throughout the whole world, who, being baptized, believe (at least implicitly), and profess the true doctrines of Christ; and are in communion with his Vicegerent on earth, the Pope. These are composed of Pastors and People: the Pastors are the *teaching part* of the Church, commissioned to this office by Christ.

I. *The Pastors' Authority*, AS TEACHERS, *proved:*—

1. Christ declares, that HE himself *was* "*sent* to preach the Gospel;"[44] and this office he fulfilled: "All things whatsoever I have heard of my Father, I have made known to you."[45] Now, he sent the Apostles

(44) Luke iv., 18. (45) John xv., 15.

with full commission to teach the same: "*As* the Father hath sent me, I also send you:"[46] "Going, therefore, teach all nations . . . . . teaching them to observe all things whatsoever I have commanded you."[47]

2. This commission was *to continue.* Thus, it was communicated afterwards to Matthias; to Paul; by him to Timothy: "The things which thou hast heard of me by many witnesses, the same commend to faithful men, who shall be fit to teach others also."[48] It was communicated likewise to Titus; and was to be still further handed down: "For this cause I left thee in Crete, that thou shouldst ordain Priests in every city, as I also appointed thee."[49]

3. This authority is further confirmed, by the light in which Pastors are represented in Scripture: For, 1, They are spoken of as *Ambassadors of Christ.* "For Christ, therefore, we are Ambassadors, God as it were exhorting by us;"[50] 2, As *acting in the person of Christ:* "He that heareth you, heareth me."[51] 3, As *messengers sent from God:* "The lips of the Priest shall keep knowledge, and they shall seek the law at his mouth; because he is the Angel of the Lord of Hosts."[52]

Thus, nothing can be more clear than this Authority of the Pastors to teach. . . And the *Obligation of the people to receive their faith* from them can be shown to be equally clear.

II. *The People's Obligation to* HEAR *and* RECEIVE *the Teaching of the Church:—*

1. The Pastors are commanded to "preach the Gospel to every creature;"[53] and this command is accompanied with the declaration of Christ, that "they who will not believe, shall be condemned."[53]

(46) John xx., 21.
(47) Matt. xxviii., 19, 20.
(48) 2 Tim. ii., 2.
(49) Tit. i., 5.
(50) 2 Cor. v., 20.
(51) Luke x., 16.
(52) Mal. ii., 7.
(53) Mark xvi., 15, 16.

Therefore, the people are obliged to believe and follow their teaching; and to do so, under pain of eternal condemnation.

2. The Pastors were instituted to keep the people "in unity of faith;"[54] therefore, the people *must* receive their faith from them; otherwise that object could not be obtained.

3. Christ says of himself: "All power is given to me in heaven and on earth."[55] Now, this power he communicated to his Apostles; for he adds: "Going, therefore, teach all nations;[55] for, "as the Father hath sent *me*, I also *send you;* "[56] i.e., invested with the same power and authority. Now, all mankind are obliged to hear the teaching of *Christ;* therefore, all are obliged to hear *those Pastors*, who teach by his commission.

4. He explains this still more clearly, when he says: "He that *heareth you*, heareth *me;* and he that *despiseth you*, despiseth *me;*"[57] thus requiring the same submission to the Pastors of the Church, as to himself.

5. Our Lord condemns all those who *will not* hear the Church, as being no better than heathens and publicans.[58] This shows the strictness of the obligation, &c. . .

6. St. Paul says: "Remember your prelates, who have spoken the word of God to you; *whose* faith FOLLOW."[59]

7. St. John, speaking of himself and the other Pastors of the Church, gives the following rule, as a sure means of distinguishing truth from error, saying: "We are of God, he that knoweth God, heareth us; he that is not of God, heareth not us, *in this* we know the spirit of truth and the spirit of error."[60]

(54) Eph. iv., 11, 12, 13.
(55) Matt. xxviii., 18, 19.
(56) John xx., 21.
(57) Luke x., 16.
(58) Matt. xviii., 17.
(59) Heb. xiii., 7.
(60) 1 John iv., 6.

Thus, then, you see how great is the teaching authority of the Pastors of the Church; how *strict* also the *obligation of the people* to attend to their teaching.

III. *The Pastors' Authority* TO RULE AND GOVERN *the Church proved*:—

What other powers, besides that of teaching, has Christ given to the Pastors? To *rule* and *govern* the Church; the *full powers* of the Priesthood are communicated to them for this purpose: "Take heed to yourselves and to the whole flock, wherein the holy Ghost hath appointed *you Bishops*, to RULE THE CHURCH OF GOD."[61]

This *ruling* comprises three general heads, mentioned by St Paul.[62] He say they are appointed—

1. "For the perfecting of the saints;" i.e., for conducting the faithful to perfection, by directing, ... prescribing rules, . . . giving advice,...and imploring the necessary graces.

2. "For the work of the ministry;" i.e., for instructing, preaching, administering the Sacraments, offering Sacrifice, and performing the other services of the Church.

3. "For the edifying of the body of Christ;" i.e., for regulating the exterior of Religion—for preventing scandals—and for maintaining the discipline of the Church.

IV. *The Peoples' Obligation to obey the Pastors of the Church proved*:—

Are the people *obliged* in conscience *to obey* their Pastors? Most certainly they are: "Let every soul be subject to higher powers; for there is no power but from God; and those that are, are ordained of God: therefore he that resisteth the power, resisteth the ordinance of God; and they that resist, purchase to themselves damnation."[63] "Obey your prelates, and be

(61) Acts xx., 23. (62) Eph. iv., 12, 13. (63) Rom. xiii., 1, 2

subject to them; for they watch, as being to render an account of your souls."[64]

In what are you to obey your Pastors? In spiritual things—in all such as regard Religion and conscience. Therefore, when you disobey the Commandments of the Church, which regard religion and conscience, you sin—you despise a Divine authority; and you despise *the whole* of that authority; for the precepts of the Church are given by the united sanction of the entire body of Pastors. And when you disregard the instructions, admonitions, exhortations, and advice of your own Pastor, you transgress likewise against an authority appointed by God: "He that heareth you, heareth me; and he that *despiseth you*, despiseth me."[65]

INSTRUCTION XIX.

NINTH ARTICLE CONTINUED.

The Supremacy of Saint Peter—The Church cannot err.

What is the Ninth Article of the Creed?—The Holy Catholic Church; the Communion of Saints.

What is the Catholic Church?—All the faithful under one head.

Who is that head?—Christ Jesus our Lord.

Has the Church any visible head on earth?—Yes; the Bishop of Rome.

Why is the Bishop of Rome the head of the Church?—Because he is the successor of St. Peter, whom Christ appointed to be the head of his Church.

What is the Bishop of Rome called?—He is called the Pope, which word Pope signifies Father.

Is, then, the Bishop of Rome our Spiritual Father?—Yes; he is the Spiritual Father of all the faithful.

Can the Church err in what she teaches?—No; she can not err in matters of faith.

(64) Heb. xiii. 17. (65) Luke x. 16.

Why so?—Because Christ has promised that hell's gates shall not prevail against his Church; that the Holy Ghost shall teach her all truths; and that he himself will abide with her for ever.

The Church is the Congregation of *all* who believe and profess the true doctrines of Christ. These form one united body: "We *being many* are *one body* in Christ."[66] "And there shall be one fold, and one shepherd."[67]

I. THE CHURCH, then, IS ONE UNITED BODY:—In what are the Faithful united, so as to form but "one fold"—but "one body in Christ?" They are united in these three things, viz.:—

1. In the same faith: the Pastors teach, and all believe and profess, those very same truths which were taught by Christ and promulgated by his Apostles: For, as there is but "one Lord," so there is but "one faith."[68]

2. In the participation of the same Sacraments—those very Sacraments instituted by Christ—thus, of Baptism it is said: "In one spirit were we all baptized into one body."[69] And of the Blessed Eucharist: "All we being many, are one body, who partake of that one bread."[70]

3. In being all governed by one head: thus literally forming "one fold, under one shepherd."

II. SUPREMACY OF PETER:—*The Church*, then, *is governed by one head.* Who is that head? The Bishop of Rome, as the successor of St. Peter. The chief head is Jesus Christ: for God "hath subjected all things under his feet; and hath made him head over all the Church, which is his body."[71] But Christ being the *invisible* head, has appointed one under him to be the *visible* head—to act as his vicegerent on earth.

(66) Rom. xii. 5. (67) John x., 16. (68) Eph. iv., 5. (69) 1 Cor xii., 13. (70) 1 Cor. x., 17. (71) Eph. i., 22. 23.

Whom has he appointed to this office? St. Peter, and his successors.

Proofs from Scripture that St. Peter was appointed to be the Head:—

1. Christ changed his name to Peter, i.e., *a rock* and declared that he built his whole Church upon him, as its solid foundation: thus he put Peter in place of himself.[72]

2. Christ gave the power of *the keys* to him, but not to the others. Now, the power of the *keys* denotes supreme authority. Thus: "I will lay the key of the house of David upon his shoulder; and *he* shall open, and none shall shut; and he shall shut, and none shall open."[73]. This was prophesied of Christ, who says of himself: "Thus saith the Holy One and the True One; he that hath the key of David; he that openeth, and no man shutteth; shutteth, and no man openeth."[74] Consequently, when he said to Peter: "To thee I will give the keys of the kingdom of heaven, and whatsoever thou shalt bind up on earth, it shall be bound also in heaven; and whatsoever thou shalt loose upon earth it shall be loosed also in heaven;"[75] he evidently communicated to him this supreme authority in "the house of David," i.e., in the Church; appointing him his vicegerent on earth.

3. When Satan desired to have the Apostles in his power, in order to prevent the overthrow of his kingdom, our Lord said to Peter: "Simon, Simon, Satan hath desired to have *you*, that he may sift you as wheat; but I have prayed for *thee*, that thy faith fail not: and thou being once converted, confirm thy brethren."[76] Why thus secure *Peter only?* and why leave and commission *him* to confirm the rest?

4. Again, after his Resurrection, our Lord said to

(72) Matt. xvi., 18. (73) Is. xxii., 22. (74) Apoc. iii., 7. (75) Matt. xvi., 19. (76) Luke xxii., 31, 32.

the same Apostle: "Simon, son of John, lovest thou me *more* than these? He saith to him: Yea, Lord, thou knowest that I love thee. He saith to him: Feed my lambs. He saith to him again: Simon, son of John, lovest thou me? He saith to him: Yea, Lord, thou knowest that I love thee. He saith to him: Feed my lambs." He asked Peter the same question a third time; and, having received the same answer, "he said to him: Feed my sheep."[77] Why was *greater* love exacted from Peter than from the rest? Because a greater responsibility was entrusted; for Christ made him the shepherd of his entire flock—of both sheep and lambs, i.e., of both Clergy and Laity; he made him the "one shepherd" of his "one fold," i.e., the chief Pastor of his Church.

5. In the lists of the Apostles given in the Gospel, Peter is always put *first;* and he is expressly styled THE *first:* "The names of the twelve Apostles are these: THE FIRST, Simon who is called Peter."[78]

6. Peter acted as the head, in the assembly to choose St. Matthias;[79] and in opening the first Council at Jerusalem, saying: "Men brethren, you know that, in former days, God made choice among us, that by *my* mouth the Gentiles should hear the word of the Gospel, and believe."[80]

7. The Councils and ancient Writers attest this doctrine...

8. Peter's successors have invariably exercised this office from his time to the present day.

Why did Christ appoint a *visible* Head? Because the Church is a *visible body*—a body composed of many members, and to be spread over all nations, differing in language, laws, customs, and political views; and yet to be *one body.* Now, it would be impossible to

(77) John xxi., 15, 16, 17.
(78) Matt. x., 2.
(79) Acts i., 15 to 22.
(80) Acts xv., 7.

preserve unity, &c., without a visible head......(We have an example of this impossibility in the Reformation......)

The pope's supremacy consists in his primacy, both of honour and of jurisdiction, over all the Bishops and Churches of the whole world.

III. THE CHURCH CANNOT ERR:—As the power of teaching is given to the Pastors, do Christ's promises of preserving the true doctrines belong to them? Yes; they belong to the body of Pastors united with their head. This is what is meant by "*the teaching authority of the Church.*" This teaching authority cannot lead us into false doctrines; "because Christ has promised that hell's gates shall not prevail against his Church," i.e., against the teaching authority of his Church: "Thou art Peter, and upon this rock I will build my Church, and the gates of hell shall not prevail against it."[81]——"There shall come a Redeemer to Sion, and to them that return from iniquity in Jacob. This is my covenant with them, saith the Lord: My spirit that is in thee, and my words that I have put in thy mouth, shall not depart out of thy mouth, nor out of the mouth of thy seed, nor out of the mouth of thy seed's seed, saith the Lord, from henceforth and for ever."[82]——"Going, therefore, teach all nations......and behold I am with you all days, even to the end of the world."[83]——"I will ask the Father, and he shall give you another Paraclete, that he may abide with you for ever, the Spirit of Truth......He shall abide with you, and shall be in you."[84]——"But when he, the Spirit of Truth, is come, he will teach you all truth."[85] Hence, St. Paul gives the Church this glorious title: "The Church of the living God, the pillar and ground of the truth."[86]

(81) Matt. xvi., 18. (83) Matt. xxviii., 19, 20. (85) John xvi., 13.
(82) Is. lix., 20, 21. (84) John xiv., 16, 17. (86) Tim. iii., 15.

Since, then, we are to receive our faith from the teaching of the pastors of the Church, what are the doctrines which they do teach? The Catechism is a summary of them; and hence, it should be well learnt, and the Explanation of it should be well attended to; parents should teach it to their children, and should send them to their Pastor for instruction. If parents are culpably negligent in this duty, will they not have to answer for the consequences of their children's ignorance?

INSTRUCTION XX.

NINTH ARTICLE CONTINUED.

The Four Marks of the Church.

Has the Church of Christ any marks by which you may know her?—Yes; she has these four marks: she is One, she is Holy, she is Catholic—she is Apostolical.

How is the Church One?—Because all her members agree in one faith, are all in one Communion, and are all under one head.

How is the Church Holy?—Because she teaches a holy doctrine, invites all to a holy life, and is distinguished by the eminent holiness of so many thousands of her children.

How is the Church Catholic or Universal?—Because she subsists in all ages, teaches all nations, and maintains all truths.

How is the Church Apostolical?—Beoause she comes down by perpetual succession, from the Apostles of Christ; and has her doctrine, her orders, and her mission from them.

Seeing that Christ has established a Church, which can never fail; that he has appointed Pastors in it, whom he requires us to hear *cs himself;* and from whom he commands us to receive our faith, under pain of eternal condemnation ; the great question is, *Which is that Church?* and, *Who are those Pastors?* A most important inquiry! for it decides at once all religious controversies. "This (says St. Augustin) is a very short way—it requires no labour."[87*]

Which, then, is the true Church? This is easily discovered by those who *seek sincerely*. For the true Church has certain MARKS, which are sufficiently plain to lead any person to embrace it. The true Church has these four marks: she is *One*—she is *Holy*—she is *Catholic*—she is *Apostolical*. The Church of Christ has, and must have, these four Marks. Reason tells us so;...the Fathers also tell us so, and they prove it from the Scriptures...the Creed likewise declares the same. The Apostles' Creed requires us to believe in two of these Marks: I "believe the HOLY CATHOLIC Church;" and the Nicene Creed requires a belief in all four: "I believe ONE, HOLY, CATHOLIC, and APOSTOLIC Church." [*See the 8th of the 39 Articles; which shows that Protestants believe and teach, that the Church must have these four marks.*]

I. The true Church, then, must be ONE:—Thus, the Scripture says: "One Lord, *one faith*, one baptism;[88] i.e., as there is but one Lord, and one baptism, so there can be but *one faith*." Again: "Every kingdom divided against itself shall be made desolate."[89] Now, the Church is called "a kingdom that shall never be destroyed......but shall stand for ever."[90] "There shall be *one fold*, and *one shepherd*."[91] "We being many, are *one body* in Christ."[92]

Now, *the Catholic Church* ALONE is One:—She is one body; for all her members are united in the same *faith*—in the same *communion*—and under the same

(87) * "Magnum compendium, nulluslabor.
(88) Ep. iv., 5.
(89) Matt. xii., 25.
(90) Dan. ii., 44.
(91) John x.. 16.
(92) Rom. xii., 5.

Head. Though they are spread over all nations, and differ in everything else—in language, laws, customs and political interests: yet they are all united in Religion: so that, as to religion, a Catholic may be said to be at home anywhere. We are thus united, and always shall be, because we have the principle of unity: we have one fixed infallible rule to go by—the unerring decisions of the Church: *unerring*, because secured from error by the promises of Christ. And hence, we are united in faith and communion; we always have been so united; and we always shall be.

But, no sooner do persons leave our Communion, and form themselves into new *Sects*, than they are torn asunder by divisions. Thus the followers of the Reformation are divided, and subdivided without end. They are spotted like a leopard.[93] And how could it be otherwise; since they have within them the very principle of division, viz., Private Judgment?

They have no common centre: they differ therefore; and they differ in essentials: and they have frequently excommunicated each other.

II. The true Church must be HOLY:—It must necessarily be so, because it comes directly from God. St. Paul tells us, that "Christ loved the Church, and delivered himself up for it; that he might *sanctify* it, ...that it should be *holy*, and without blemish."[94] The true Church can teach none but true and holy doctrines—it must supply its members with motives, and efficacious means, to become holy—and it must lead many to holiness. All this is essential to the true Church.

Now, the *Catholic Church* ALONE is HOLY:—There is perfect agreement in all her doctrines; and this is an evidence of their truth—every article of her faith tends to holiness—she affords motives, and efficacious

(93) Apoc. xiii., 1, 2. (94) Eph. v. 25, 26, 27.

means, for becoming holy—and thousands of her children have arrived at holiness—all the Saints were Catholics, whose holiness has been attested by undeniable miracles; and this is the grand proof of the holiness of the Catholic Church.

But *Sects*, instead of having perfect agreement in all their doctrines, fall into inconsistencies; and, therefore, into evident falsehood—they even teach immoral doctrines—and they have had no sanctity attested by miracles.

III. The true Church must be CATHOLIC; i.e., not confined to one nation, nor to one century; but spread over all nations, and existing in all ages:—1. It was instituted *to be diffused* over the whole world: "Going, therefore, teach *all nations*;......and behold I am with you *all days*, even to the end of the world."[95] "Go ye into the *whole world*, and preach the Gospel to *every creature*."[96]——2. The success of its preaching was foretold: "Their sound hath gone forth into all the earth."[97] "All the ends of the earth shall be converted to the Lord (Christ), and he shall have dominion over the nations."[98]——3. All this has been verified: "The truth of the Gospel is come unto you, as also it is in the whole world."[99] "Your faith is spoken of in the whole world."[100]

Now, the *Catholic Church is* ALONE Catholic.—She alone has fulfilled Christ's commission; for she alone has converted infidel nations to the Christian Religion—she has been always extending—when one nation has fallen off, others have been converted—in many nations there is no other Religion known—and she is found in all nations.

But *Sects* seldom extend over one nation; they bear the name of the place to which they are confined, or

(95) Matt. xxviii., 19, 20. (96) Mark xvi., 15, 16. (97) Ps. xviii., 5. (98) Ps. xxi., 28, 29. (99) Col. i. 5, 6. (100) Rom. i., 8.

of the founder, who, long after the Apostles, gave them birth. Their missionary accounts of success are completely false.[1]

IV. The true Church must be APOSTOLICAL:—Evidently, no Religion *can* be the true one except *that* which was founded by the Apostles, and which has received her *faith*, her *orders*, and her *mission* from them, by an uninterrupted succession: "For this cause I left thee in Crete, that thou shouldst *ordain* priests in every city, as I also appointed thee."[2] *Mission*, as well as order, is essential to the true Church: "As the Father hath *sent* me, I also *send* you."[3] "Going, therefore, teach all nations; *baptizing* them, &c."[4] "How can they preach, unless they be *sent?*"

Now, the *Catholic Church* ALONE is Apostolical:—Each generation, from the Apostles, has received and handed down in the Catholic Church, "all truth" taught by God. We have an unbroken succession of Pastors; whose orders and mission have come down, without interruption, from the Apostles: We can name every Pope from the present one, up to St. Peter.

But *Sects* are far from being Apostolical. Protestants acknowledge they have no orders or mission, except what they had received from the Catholic Church; but they have received none from us—and no other religions pretend to have any. *All*, except Catholics, came 1500 years too late to be Apostolical. They cannot show any time, since the Apostles, when *we* began; but we can show *when*, *where*, and *by whom* THEY began.

CONCLUSION:—It is evident from what has been said, that the Catholic Church alone has these four Marks. Therefore, she alone is the true Church of

(1) *See* Wiseman's Lectures on the Principal Doctrines and Practices of the Catholic Church.—*Vol.* 1, *Lect.* vi.

(2) Tit. i., 5.
(3) John xx., 21.
(4) Matt. xxviii., 19, 20.
(5) Rom. x., 15.

Christ, from which we are to receive our Faith. And, being infallible, she cannot lead us into error; we have *Christ's word* for it, that she shall not; but that he will always be with her in her teaching; and that the Holy Ghost will also be with her for ever, guiding her into all truth.

INSTRUCTION XXI.

NINTH ARTICLE CONCLUDED.

The Communion of Saints—and Purgatory.

What is meant by the Communion of Saints?—That, in the Church of God, there is a Communion of all holy persons in all holy things.

And have we any Communion with the Saints in heaven?—Yes; we communicate with them as our fellow members, under the same head Jesus Christ; and are helped by their prayers.

And are the souls in Purgatory helped also by our prayers?—Yes; they are.

What do you mean by Purgatory?—A middle state of souls suffering for a time on account of their sins.

What souls go to Purgatory?—Such souls as depart this life in lesser sins, which we call *venial*.

Do any other souls go to Purgatory?—Yes; such souls as leave this world before they have fully discharged the debt of *temporal* punishment due for their *mortal* sins; the guilt and *eternal* punishment of which have been remitted.

How do you prove there is a Purgatory?—Because the Scripture often teaches, that God will render to every man according to his works, and that nothing defiled can enter heaven; and that some Christians shall be saved, yet, so as by fire.

I. COMMUNION OF SAINTS:—The Christian Church is but "*one body:*"[6] All its true members are styled

(6) Rom. xii., 5.

"*Saints*;" because they either are so in reality; or, having been sanctified by Baptism, are called *to be Saints.* All these members, throughout the whole Church, are united together by a mutual interchange of good offices; which is called "*The Communion of Saints.*"

The Church of Christ consists of three parts, viz., the Church *Triumphant* in heaven—*Militant* on earth—and *Suffering* in purgatory. All these participate in the "Communion of Saints," and are united—

1. By being all under the same head, Jesus Christ, as his members—

2. By the promise of the same good; which some already possess--some are secure of possessing—and the rest, in a state of uncertainty, are labouring to possess.

3. By partaking in the prayers and good works of each other. For prayers, good works, sacraments, and sacrifice, are common goods of the Church; in which all on earth, in heaven, and in Purgatory participate, as far as they are capable.

Do persons who are in mortal sin participate in the "Communion of Saints?" Such continue to be members of the Church; but they are *dead members*, united externally, i.e., by faith, hope, and a right to the sacraments, as means of pardon.

Do excommunicated persons participate? . . . . No, but they are still subjects of the Church: the same is to be said of heretics and schismatics. Unbaptized persons (as Quakers, Jews, Pagans,) have no communion with the Church in any way; they are not even subjects of the Church.

How do we communicate with the Saints in heaven? We honour their memory; we join with them in blessing and praising God; and we ask them to obtain blessings for us, by interceding in our favour. They do intercede for us, and procure us many assistances—many favours both spiritual and temporal.

How do we communicate with the souls in Purgatory? By praying, offering the Holy Sacrifice, and performing good works in their behalf; and so obtaining a remission of their punishment; when they, in return, will pray for us.

II. PURGATORY :—*What do you mean by Purgatory?*—**A middle state of souls, suffering for a time on account of their sins.**

Purgatory is a place of suffering in the next world, prepared by Almighty God for the expiation of venial sins—of the punishment due to them—and of the temporal punishment due to mortal sin, the guilt and eternal punishment of which have been remitted in this life.

What souls go to Purgatory?—

They who leave this world in the state of *perfect innocence*, which they had either always preserved, or else recovered, after having lost it, go straight to heaven—They who die in the *guilt* of mortal sin, go straight to hell, and are lost eternally.

But they, who, being free from the *guilt* of mortal sin, depart this life, 1, In the guilt of venial sins—or, 2, Before they have fully satisfied Divine Justice for the punishment due to them—or, 3, Before they have discharged the whole debt of temporal punishment due to their remitted mortal sins, go to Purgatory. Whoever, therefore, at the time of his departure hence, is in all or any of these three last-mentioned states, will be condemned to a place of punishment for a time; and, when he shall have fully satisfied God's Justice by his sufferings, he will be translated to heaven, to be there happy with God for ever.

How do you prove there is a Purgatory?—Because the Scripture often teaches, that God will render to every man according to his works—that nothing defiled can enter heaven—and that some Christians shall be saved, yet, so as by fire.

Proofs that there is a Purgatory:—

1. Divine Justice demands satisfaction for sin by temporal punishments, AFTER the guilt and eternal punishment have been forgiven, (*Example of Adam*, whose sin, though pardoned, brought severe temporal punishments both upon himself and all his posterity ;[7] *Example of Moses*, who, for his sin in striking the rock twice, was not permitted, even after forgiveness, to enter the promised land[8] —*Example of David*, whose sin in numbering the people, caused, even *after* his repentance, 70,000 persons to die by pestilence ;[9] —and whose sins of adultery and murder were severely punished, *after* the Prophet Nathan had declared them forgiven.[10]

Now this debt of temporal punishment *must* be discharged *somewhere*. But, suppose the sinner die *before* he has discharged it: the debt must still be paid ; but where ? in what place ? Certainly not in heaven, because there are no punishments there ; nor in hell, because the *guilt* of sin is forgiven, and because " out of hell there is no redemption." Where then ? In that prison of which Christ speaks, when he says : " Be at agreement with thy adversary betimes, whilst thou art in the way with him : lest the adversary deliver thee to the Judge, and the judge deliver thee to the officer, and thou be cast into prison. Amen I say to thee, thou shalt not go out from thence, till thou repay the last farthing."[11]

(7) Gen. iii., 17 to 24 ; Rom. v., 12.
(8) Num. xx., 7 to 12 ; Deut. xxxii., 48 to 52.
(9) 1 Par. xxi., 9 to 14.
(10) 2 Kings xii., 14.
(11) Matt. v., 25, 26.

2. Venial sin does not *destroy* the state of grace: for a "*just man* shall fall seven times, and shall rise again;"[12] and "in many things we *all* offend;"[13] and "if we say we have *no sin*, we deceive ourselves, and the truth is not in us."[14] Yet these venial sins *defile* the soul, and increase our debt of punishment. Therefore, if we die in the guilt of venial sin *only*, what must become of us? We cannot go immediately to heaven, because "there shall not enter into it (the heavenly Jerusalem) anything defiled."[15] We must be first purified by punishment. But where? Not in hell, because, not being in mortal sin, we are not to go thither; for "God will render to every man according to his works."[16]——Divine Justice will not punish us *beyond* what we shall deserve: now, we cannot suppose that God would condemn any one to *eternal* flames for a mere "idle word;" and yet Christ assures us, that, at his tribunal, "men shall render an account for every idle word that they shall speak."[17] Where, then, is this purgation to be made, except in a middle place, where souls suffer for a time, on account of their sins?

3. "He that shall speak against the Holy Ghost, it shall not be forgiven him; neither in this world, nor in the world to come."[18] These words show, that there are some sins which can be forgiven in the world to come.

4. "Other foundation no man can lay, but that which is laid; which is Christ Jesus. Now, if any man build upon this foundation gold, silver, precious stones, wood, hay, stubble: every man's work shall be manifest; for *the day of the Lord* shall declare it, because it shall be revealed *in fire*; and the fire shall try every man's work, of what sort it is. If any

(12) Prov. xx[illegible], [illegible].
(13) James iii., 2.
(14) 1 John i., 8.
(15) Apoc. xxi., 27.
(16) Rom. ii., 6.
(17) Matt. xii., 36.
(18) Matt. xii., 31, 32.

man's work abide which he hath built thereupon; he shall receive a reward. If any man's work *burn*, he shall *suffer loss*; but *he himself* shall be saved, yet so AS BY FIRE."[19]

Here we see, that those souls whose works are perfectly good, without any admixture of evil, will, when judged after death, receive an immediate reward. But those, whose good works are found to be mixed with imperfections or venial faults (with wood, hay, and stubble), will be condemned to "suffer loss"—to have those venial faults punished by fire; but not *eternally*; because they "shall be saved," after they shall have suffered the loss. Now, *where* is this loss to be suffered? It can neither be in heaven nor in hell; it must be in some other place.

5. This belief, and the practice of praying for the dead, are older than Christianity. Judas Machabeus "sent 12,000 drachms of silver to Jerusalem for sacrifice, to be offered for the *sins of the dead*..... It is, therefore, a holy and wholesome thought to pray for the dead, that they may be loosed from sins."[20] Hence, before Christ, the people of God believed it to be a holy practice to *pray for the dead*, and believed that such prayer *loosed from sin*.

Severity of the Sufferings of Purgatory.

The poor souls that are condemned to "suffer loss" in that place of punishment, shall indeed be saved; but they shall be saved "*by fire*." They learn, by painful experience, "that it is a fearful thing to fall into the hands of the living God."[21]

They can do nothing for themselves: for "the night" has come upon them, "wherein no man can work."[22] Yet God is pleased to accept our prayers, &c., in their behalf.

(19) 1 Cor. iii., 11 to 15.
(20) 2 Mac. xii., 43 to 46.
(21) Heb. x., 31.
(22) John ix., 4.

It is a very great act of charity to pray for them; it is pleasing to God, and advantageous both to them and to us: Hence, the Scripture calls, it "a *holy* and *wholesome* thought to pray for the dead." As an inducement to pray for them consider *who* they are—what they *suffer*—and how *easily* you can relieve them. Those whom we pray for, will pray for us when they get to heaven.

CONCLUSION:—The existence of Purgatory, and the severity of its sufferings, show how *great* is the *evil* of venial sin; and how advantageous are present sufferings, (whether voluntary, or sent by Divine Providence,) if they be embraced and endured in a spirit of penance.

INSTRUCTION XXII.

TENTH ARTICLE.

The Power of Forgiving Sins—Original Sin—Mortal Sin—Venial Sin.

What is the Tenth Article of the Creed?—The forgiveness of sins.

What is meant by this Article?—That there is in the Church of God forgiveness of sins, for such as properly apply for it.

To whom has Christ given power to forgive sins?—To the apostles and their successors, the bishops and priests of his Church.

By what Sacraments are sins forgiven?—By baptism and penance.

What is sin?—An offence of God, or any thought, word, or deed, against the law of God.

What is original sin?—It is the sin in which we were all born.

How came we to be born in sin?—By Adam's sin when he eat the forbidden fruit.

What is actual sin?—Every sin which we ourselves commit.

How is actual sin divided?—Into mortal and venial sin.

What is mortal sin?—It is a grievous offence against God.

Why is it called mortal sin?—Because it kills the soul and deserves hell.

How does mortal sin kill the soul?—By destroying the grace of God, which is the supernatural life of the soul.

What is venial sin?—That sin which does not kill the soul, yet displeases God.

Why is it called venial sin?—Because it is more easily pardoned than mortal sin.

I. POWER TO FORGIVE SINS.—The Catechism teaches, in accordance with the doctrine of the Church, "that there is in the Church of God forgiveness of sins, for such as properly apply for it," and that the power of communicating this forgiveness to those who do properly apply for it, has been given by Christ "to the apostles and their successors, the bishops and priests of his Church."

Nothing can be more clearly proved from Scripture than this doctrine. I will say only a few words on the subject, in this place; because the proofs of it will be more fully given, in the Explanation of the Sacrament of Penance.

Christ worked a miracle to prove, that, AS MAN, *He* had the power of forgiving sins on earth: "Jesus said to the man sick of the palsy: Be of good heart, son, thy sins are forgiven thee. And behold some of the scribes said within themselves: He blasphemeth. And Jesus seeing their thoughts, said: Why do you think evil in your hearts? whether is it easier to say, Thy sins are forgiven thee, or to say, Arise and walk? But that you may know that the SON OF MAN hath power on earth to forgive sins, (then he said to the man sick of the palsy,) Arise, take up thy bed, and go into thy house. And he arose, and went into his house. And the multitudes seeing it, feared, and glorified God, that *gave such power to men.*"[23]

Now, this same power Christ gave to his Apostles, after his resurrection, when, appearing to them, he said: "Peace be to you: *As* the Father hath sent *me*, I also send *you.* When he had said this, he breathed on them: and he said to them: Receive ye the Holy Ghost: whose sins *you* shall forgive, they are forgiven them; and whose sins *you* shall retain, they are retained."[24] These words, of course, have a meaning; but what *can* they mean, except that Christ gave to his Apostles *the power of forgiving and retaining sins?*

God alone can forgive sins in his own name, and by his own power; but he can commission others to do it as his ministers in his name and by his power: as, in fact, he *has* commissioned the Apostles and their successors. The means by which this power is exercised, and forgiveness applied to our souls, are the Sacraments of Baptism and Penance; by Baptism is remitted original sin, and also actual sins, if any have been committed before the reception of this Sacrament; but by Penance are remitted *all* sins, however grievous, committed *after* baptism: the Sacrament of Penance is of no avail whatever, in blotting out the sins of a person who is not baptized.

Christ, then, has left in his Church the power of forgiving sins. But—

What is sin?—Sin is an offence of God; or any thought, word, or deed, against the law of God.

II. ORIGINAL SIN:— *What is* ORIGINAL *sin?*—It is the sin in which we were all born.

How came we to be born in sin? —By Adam's sin, when he eat the forbidden fruit.

(23) Matt. ix., 2 to 8. (24) John xx., 21, 22, 23.

When Adam sinned, *he* and *his posterity* thereby lost original justice--became children of wrath, subject to concupiscence, to labours, sickness, and death, and were under the threat of eternal death: "In what day soever thou shalt eat of it thou shalt die the death."[25]

In consequence of Adam's fall, we are all born in sin: As by one man sin entered into this world, and by sin death; so death passed unto all men, *in whom all have sinned*."[26]

The sin of Adam, which thus "*passed unto all men*," would have excluded both him and us eternally from heaven, had not the Son of God purchased our Redemption. The merits of this Redemption are applied to us, for the pardon of *original* sin, by Baptism: "Unless a man be born again of water and the Holy Ghost, he cannot enter into the kingdom of God."[27]

III. Mortal Sin.—*What is* mortal *sin?*—It is a grievous offence against God.

Mortal sin is a most dreadful evil! It destroys the state of grace; renders the soul hideous and hateful to God; closes heaven against us; and condemns us to hell: hence, it is the greatest of all evils!

The greatness of this evil proved:—

1. Mortal sin is a grievous injury, an outrageous insult offered to the infinite Majesty of God. By how much greater is the dignity of the person offended, above that of the offender; by so much greater is the insult. Now, by mortal sin, the creature rises up against the Creator—a mere worm against infinite Majesty!

2. God's hatred to sin is infinite and eternal. Being infinitely *holy*, he cannot but hate and abhor

(25) Gen. ii., 17. (26) Rom. v., 12. (27) John iii., 5.

sin. "To God the wicked and his wickedness are hateful alike."[28]

3. Hence, he has *punished* mortal sin most severely, even in this life. Of this the sacred Scriptures furnish many Examples: Being *just*, God has not punished sin more than it deserves; but, being *merciful*, much less. Now, *one sin* stripped Adam of original justice, corrupted all human nature, doomed the whole of mankind to suffer death, and closed the gates of heaven against us. Mortal sin brought down upon the whole earth the waters of the deluge;"[29] called down fire and brimstone upon Sodom and Gomorrha, and the neighbouring cities;"[30] armed the destroying Angel against the first-born of Egypt;[31] caused the earth to open beneath the feet of Core, Dathan, and Abiron, and to swallow them down alive into hell;[32] delivered to destruction 23,000 of the children of Israel on one occasion,[33] and 24,000 on another,[34] to be slain by the command of their offended God; and it has drawn down many other severe chastisements, which are also recorded in the sacred Scriptures.

4. Mortal sin contains the blackest ingratitude to Jesus Christ. Our obligations to him are beyond conception; for without him we must have been for ever miserable.

5. The effects of mortal sin on the soul are most lamentable! It destroys the spiritual life of the soul; and for this reason it is that it is called *mortal*, or *deadly*: "All iniquity is like a two-edged sword; the teeth thereof are the teeth of a lion, killing the souls of men."[35]——A soul *in grace* is beautiful, like an

(28) Wisd. xiv., 9.
(29) Gen. vi., 5, 6, 7;
Gen. vii., 11, 12, 21 to 24.
(30) Gen. xviii., 20;
Gen. xix., 13, 15, 24, 25.
(31) Exod. xii., 29, 30.
(32) Num. xvi., 28 to 35.
(33) Exod. xxxii., 7, 27, 28.
(34) Num. xxv., 1, 2, 9.
(35) Eccl. xxi., 3, 4.

Angel; and is pleasing in the sight of God: but, by sin, she becomes ugly, abominable, hateful: He that doth these things is abominable before God."[36]——He who is the child of God, and the temple of the Holy Ghost, becomes a slave of the devil, and the habitation of unclean spirits.——Sanctifying grace being lost, the merit of all past and present good works is consequently lost: "All his justices, which he *hath* done, shall not be remembered."[37]

6. Mortal sin deprives us of the sovereign good, of infinite happiness, and condemns us to an inconceivable and endless misery!

Such is the enormity, such the malice of this greatest of all evils! and such are the direful consequences which it brings upon them that commit it!——How is it that Christians, who know all this, should dare to sin? The reason is, because they do not think. amused by pleasures, . . by the world, . . they spend their time in dissipation, . . . and give none to reflection: "With desolation is all the land made desolate, because there is none that considereth in the heart."[38] "They take the timbrel, and the harp, and rejoice at the sound of the organ: they spend their days in wealth, and in a moment they go down to hell."[39]

IV. Venial Sin.—*What is* venial *sin?*—That sin which does not kill the soul, yet displeases God.

Venial sin, although immensely less grievous than mortal sin, is, nevertheless, a very great evil; because it offends God, weakens grace, cools the fervour of charity, renders the soul less holy, less pleasing to God, and deserving of severe chastisements. What can show more clearly the greatness of the evil of

(36) Deut. xxii., 5.
(37) Ezech. xviii., 24.
(38) Jer. xii., 11.
(39) Job xxi., 12, 13.

venial sin than the alarming denunciation directed against the Bishop of Laodicea: "I know thy works that thou art neither cold nor hot. I would thou wert either cold or hot; but because thou art lukewarm, and neither cold nor hot, *I will begin* to vomit thee out of my mouth."

Proofs that all sins are not mortal:—"A *just man* shall fall seven times, and shall rise again,"[41] yet, all the time, he is called a "*just man.*"——"In many things *we all* offend;"[42] and "if we say *we* have no sin we deceive ourselves, and the truth is not in us."[43] Yet, who will say that these Apostles were in *mortal* sin? or that they charge *all* others with being in *mortal* sin?——"Every idle word that man shall speak, they shall render an account for it at the day of judgment."[44] Yet, who will say that a mere "idle word" would condemn a soul to the eternal torments of hell?

If sometimes we fall into venial sins, *through frailty* or *inadvertence*, (as "idle words," distractions in prayer, &c.,) we should lament them, and humble ourselves; but not be surprised, or uneasy, because we are not angels, but men; and must expect to experience human frailty. But if we fall into them *deliberately*, or *through habit*, we should look upon them as very *great evils:*—

1. Because they are deliberate offences against an infinite Majesty.

2. Because they lessen our love of God, and increase our love of creatures.

3. Because they render us disagreeable to God, and provoke him to withdraw his graces: "Because thou art lukewarm, I will begin to vomit thee out of my mouth."[45]

(40) Apoc. iii., 16. (41) Prov. xxiv., 16. (42) James iii., 2. (43) 1 John i., 8. (44) Matt. xii., 36. (45) Apoc. iii., 15, 16, 17

4. Because a habit of venial sin disposes and leads to such as are mortal: "He that contemneth small things, shall fall by little and little."[46] "Behold how small a fire what a great wood it kindleth."[47]

It is evident, from all this, with what care we should avoid venial sins, especially such as are deliberate or habitual; seeing the great evil which they contain, and the fearful consequences which they produce. Bear in mind, that, by contemning these smaller sins, you will fall by little and little into greater; till you provoke God "to vomit you out of his mouth." Never, then, commit *any* sin *deliberately*, however small; and employ the proper means for this purpose, viz., Prayer—Meditation—frequent and fervent Reception of the Sacraments — Mortification — constant watchfulness over your senses—and great care to keep away from the occasions of sin.

INSTRUCTION XXIII.

ELEVENTH AND TWELFTH ARTICLES.

Death—Resurrection—Hell—Heaven.

What is the Eleventh Article of the Creed?—The Resurrection of the body.

What means the Resurrection of the Body?—That we shall rise again with the same body at the day of judgment.

What is the Twelfth Article of the Creed?—Life everlasting.

What means life everlasting?—That the good shall live for ever happy in heaven.

What is the happiness of heaven?—To see, love, and enjoy God for evermore.

And shall not the wicked also live for ever?—They shall live and be punished for ever in the flames of hell.

(46) Eccli. xix., 1. (47) James iii., 5.

1. DEATH :—*What is* DEATH ? It is the separation of the soul from the body.—Before the general resurrection, all mankind must die; even Enoch and Elias will return to the earth, and die. Death is the punishment of sin, decreed against the whole human race without exception : " By one man sin entered into this world, and by sin death ; and so death passed unto *all men*."[48]

That you *must die* is *certain ;* therefore *prepare ;*—That you may die *any moment* is also *certain :* therefore prepare *immediately* , and keep yourselves *always prepared ;*—That you can die but *once*, is likewise *certain ;* therefore, to prepare for death is the most *important business* of your life.

II. GENERAL RESURRECTION :—*Will the body ever* RISE AGAIN ? Yes. When ? At the last day.—After the whole world has been destroyed by fire from heaven, and when there will not be a single person *living* on the face of the earth, the *General Resurrection* will take place. God will send his Angel to call the dead to life : " For the trumpet shall sound, and the dead shall rise again incorruptible."[49] Each soul will be reunited to its own body—the same body which it had in this life : " I know that my Redeemer liveth : and in the last day I shall rise again ; and in my flesh I shall see my God : whom I myself shall see, and my eyes shall behold."[50]

We shall rise in the perfect state of man ; but there will be a great difference between the good and the bad : the just shall rise in bodies glorious, brilliant, impassible ; the wicked in bodies deformed, hideous, loathsome, and fitted for sufferings.

The dead being risen again, we shall all be summoned before the tribunal of Jesus Christ, to be judged—to be sentenced by him according to our

(48) Rom. v., 12. (49) 1 Cor. xv., 52. (50) Job. xix., 25, 26.

works.——The explanation of this last judgment was given in the Instruction on the Seventh Article of the Creed, and need not be repeated here: I will proceed, therefore, to explain the state of mankind *after* the general judgment; and this is what we are taught in the Twelfth Article.

III. HEAVEN:—*What is the Twelfth Article of the Creed?*—LIFE EVERLASTING.

What means life everlasting?—That the GOOD shall live for ever HAPPY IN HEAVEN.

We are all created for the enjoyment of eternal happiness; and we are placed in this world, in order that, by loving and serving God, we may arrive at that end of our creation.

In what does the happiness of heaven consist? It consists in the *Beatific Vision*—in seeing, loving, and enjoying God for ever. The unceasing raptures of delight, which the Saints derive from this, are inconceivable: For "eye hath not seen, nor ear heard, neither hath it entered into the heart of man, what things God hath prepared for them that love him."[51] Perpetually beholding and contemplating God's infinite Perfections, the Blessed in heaven are incessantly adoring, praising, and loving him, with all the ardour of their souls; and from this they derive continual and unspeakable happiness. Their society is that of all the best and noblest of God's creatures; all exulting in ecstasies of delight, and rejoicing in each other's happiness, as if it were their own. The time of trials and of labours will then be at an end: For "God shall wipe away all tears from their eyes; and death shall be no more, nor mourning, nor crying, nor sorrow shall be any more; for the former things are passed away."[52] But they will possess and enjoy all that

(51) 1 Cor. ii., 9. (52) Apoc. xxi., 4.

can be desired; and they will possess and enjoy it for ever: they will live for ever, in order to be happy for ever.

IV. HELL:—*And shall not the* WICKED *also* LIVE FOR EVER?—They shall live and be punished for ever IN THE FLAMES OF HELL.

The wicked will live for ever, but only to be eternally miserable: "They shall have their portion in the pool burning with fire and brimstone, which is the second death:"[53] "And the smoke of their torments shall ascend up for ever and ever, neither have they rest day nor night."[54] They are doomed to hell, to suffer there all kinds of torments—perpetual remorse—bitter and fruitless repentance—always dying, yet never to die—agonizing in flames, tortured by merciless devils, and gnashing their teeth unceasingly, in pangs of the deepest despair. They are separated from God, and from all that is good. which will afflict them with inconceivable grief. Their misery is unceasing and eternal; and the thought of this eternity is a severe pang to every torment which they have to endure. Their doom is *fixed* for ever: "Depart from me, ye cursed, into everlasting fire."[55]

CONCLUSION:—Often think on the torments of hell, with the view of escaping them; nothing but sin can condemn you to hell; be careful, therefore, to avoid it. ......Considering, on the other hand, the greatness of the happiness which is promised to the Saints, be diligent in serving God: Strive to "enter in at the narrow gate; for wide is the gate, and broad is the way, that leadeth to destruction; and many there are who go in thereat. But how narrow is the gate, and strait is the way, that leadeth to life; and few there are that find it!"[56] Again, our Blessed Lord says: "Strive

(53) Apoc. xxi, 8.
(54) Aqoc, xiv., 11.
(55) Matt. xxv., 41.
(56) Matt. vii., 13, 14.

to enter by the narrow gate; for many, I say to you, shall seek to enter, and shall not be able."[57] It is, then, not by merely *seeking*, but by *striving*, that you are to enter into heaven; strive, therefore, earnestly: "The kingdom of heaven suffereth violence; and the violent bear it away."[58] It is only the diligent servant that enters into the joys of his Lord; whilst the slothful servant is "cast out into the exterior darkness, where there shall be weeping and gnashing of teeth."[59]

Watch, and pray—frequent the Sacraments—resist temptations—carry your cross with patience, &c.; and encourage yourself in all this with the prospect of future glory. Think on what so many Martyrs have suffered for the gaining of eternal happiness: for it is "through many tribulations we must enter into the kingdom of heaven."[60] Look up to that kingdom, and see that "the sufferings of this present time are not worthy to be compared with the glory to come, that shall be revealed in us."[61] "For that which is at present momentary and light, of our tribulation, worketh for us above measure exceedingly an eternal weight of glory."[62]

EXPLANATION OF GRACE AND PRAYER.

INSTRUCTION XXIV.

The Necessity of Good Works, and of Grace, for Salvation.

Will faith alone save us?—No; it will not without good works.

Can we do any good work towards our salvation of ourselves?—No; we cannot without the help of God's grace.

(57) Luke xiii., 24. (58) Matt. xi., 12. (59) Matt. xxv., 22, 13, 30. (60) Acts xiv. 21. (61) Rom. viii., 18. (62) 2 Cor. iv., 17.

How may we obtain God's grace?—By Prayer and the holy Sacraments.

I. GOOD WORKS:—In the *Creed* we are instructed in what relates to FAITH: we come now to the explanation of what relates to HOPE. Faith is *necessary*, in order to be saved; for, "without faith it is impossible to please God:"[1] yet, it is not alone *sufficient;* for good works are also necessary.

That a man is *justified by faith alone*, is a doctrine started by Martin Luther: "Faith *alone* (he says) is necessary for our justification; all other things are completely optional, being no longer either commanded or forbidden."[2*]

The same doctrine is taught by the Protestant Church; for the 11th of the Thirty-ninth Articles says: "Wherefore, that a man is *justified by faith only*, is a most wholesome doctrine, and very full of comfort." One might think, that they who drew up this Article, could not have read the Epistle of St. James: "What shall it profit, my brethren, if a man say he hath faith, but hath not works? shall faith be able to save him?......Do you see that *by works* a man is justified, and NOT *by faith only?*......For even as the body without the spirit is dead; so also faith without works is dead."[3] We must leave Protestants to reconcile their doctrine with that of St. James, if they can.

Luther Rejected St. James's Epistle, as being unworthy of an Apostle, calling it "an Epistle of Straw." This Reformer has even gone so far as to say: "A person who is baptized, *cannot* (though he *would*) lose his salvation by any sins, however grevious, unless he refuse to believe: *for no sins can damn him, but unbelief alone*."[4] †

(1) Heb. xi., 6.

(2) * "Sola fides necessaria est ut justi simus; *cætera omnia* liberrima, neque præcepta amplius, neque prohibita." *In Cap. 2, ad Gal.*

(3) James ii., 14, 24, 26.

(4) † "Nulla peccata damnare possunt, nisi sola incredulitas."—*De Capt. Babyl., tom. 2, fol. 74, Edit. Wittemb.*

How horrible is the tendency of his doctrine! how it opens the door to every kind of wickedness! At the judgment-seat of Christ, our sentence will be attributed to our having done, or neglected to do, good works: therefore, we must not only *have faith*, but we must *practise it*, by doing good works.

II. GRACE:—But *can* we do good works of ourselves? *Of ourselves* we can do nothing meritorious of eternal life—we cannot "avoid evil and do good," without grace. And there are two kinds of grace. *actual* and *sanctifying*.

1. What is ACTUAL GRACE? It is a supernatural help to "avoid evil and do good;" and it operates in the soul, by enlightening us *to see* what is good, and what is evil—by inclining us *to choose* the good, and *reject* the evil—and by enabling us *to act* accordingly. "It is God who worketh in you, both to will and to accomplish, according to his good will."[5]

We cannot, by our own natural strength, unassisted by grace, do anything *towards our salvation*. This is a most important truth—it is the foundation of Christian humility: "Without me (says our Lord) you can do nothing."[6] Yet grace will not work alone; but God requires us to co-operate with his grace: For, "he who made us without our concurrence, (says St. Augustin,) will not save us without our concurrence."

Works, performed without grace, may be good *natural* actions, but not *meritorious*. For our works can only become meritorious through the merits of Christ; and his merits cannot be applied to us without grace.

Does God give to *all* men *sufficient* grace? Yes; and by corresponding with it, it is rendered *efficacious*. St. Paul says: "To every man is given grace."[7] And this is true even of *blinded* and *hardened* sinners; yet from such God withdraws his special and more

(5) Phil. ii., 13. (6) John xv., 5. (7) Eph. iv., 7.

abundant graces; then they are in danger of every kind of crime—they are in a most alarming state! but God never takes from them the grace of *prayer*, by a good use of which they may obtain such further graces, as will enable them to save their souls. If they are lost, it is through their own fault.

When Providence provides for us admonitions, instructions, opportunities of spiritual reading, and such like occasions of spiritual profit, these are what are called *external* graces, and they are the ordinary occasions on which God gives his *internal* graces. Therefore attend to them, and profit by them; bearing always in mind, that you must account for them hereafter.

2. What is SANCTIFYING GRACE? It is a supernatural gift which cleanses the soul, and makes it pleasing in the sight of God—it is "the charity of God, poured forth in our hearts by the Holy Ghost."[8] St. Peter calls it that which makes us "partakers of the Divine nature."[9] For, as iron when heated, partakes of the nature of fire, so the soul, when raised to the state of sanctifying grace, receives some participation of the Divine nature.

When first we receive this precious gift, we pass from the state of sin to the state of grace; hence it it called *sanctifying* grace.

Its Effects:—1st, It destroys all the *guilt* of mortal sin 2nd, It renders the soul beautiful and pleasing in the eyes of God. 3rd, It makes us become temples of the Holy Ghost, and heirs of heaven. 4th, It gives value and merit to our good works. 5th, It gives us a title to eternal happiness.

From all this it is evident, that we ought to esteem the gift of grace above everything in this world: "I

(8) Rom. v., 5. (9) 2 Peter i., 4.

preferred her before kingdoms and thrones, and esteemed riches as nothing in comparison of her."[10]

Can sanctifying grace be increased, diminished, or lost? Yes.——When we have lost it by sin, what dispositions are necessary for recovering it? Faith, Fear, Hope, and sincere Repentance, joined with *Prayer* and the Holy Sacraments.

In the next Instruction, I will explain the duty of *Prayer*, which is the first means of grace.

INSTRUCTION XXV.

Prayer, Vocal and Mental—the Obligation of Prayer—and the Dispositions with which it should be accompanied.

How may we obtain God's grace?—By prayer and the Holy Sacraments.

What is Prayer?—It is the raising up of our minds and hearts to God.

How do we raise up our minds and hearts to God?—By thinking of God who is above all; and by offering our affections and desires to him.

Do those pray well who at their prayers, do not think of God or of what they say?—If their distractions are wilful, they do not pray well; for such prayers, instead of pleasing God, offend him.

I. Nature of prayer:—Prayer is the "raising up of our minds and hearts to God," to beg his grace and other blessings, or to avert evils: it is a conversation with God; and it may be either *vocal* or *mental.*

1. What is *Vocal Prayer?* It is that in which we use a set form of words; as, for example, when we say the Lord's Prayer, or recite any of the public Prayers of the Church.

2. What is *Mental Prayer?* It is that in which we

(10) Wisd. vii., 8.

exercise, 1st, our *Memory*, in calling to mind some Truth of Religion. 2ndly, our *Understanding*, in reflecting upon it, for the purpose of drawing therefrom practical conclusions, and of exciting corresponding affections. 3rdly, our *Will*, in adopting those practical conclusions, by passing from mere affections to the forming of resolutions, and in pouring forth our soul in fervent supplications for grace, that we may be enabled to accomplish our resolutions.

II. Obligation of Prayer:—Prayer is a most necessary Christian duty, required of us by the institution and command of God. We can do nothing meritorious without grace; now, Prayer is divinely appointed *as the means* of obtaining grace: "Ask, and you shall receive."[11] "You have not, because you ask not."[12]

How great is the Divine goodness, in having appointed so easy a means of grace as that of Prayer! a means which leaves us without the possibility of excuse for neglecting it! Yet, how many *vain excuses* are made, to justify this neglect!

1. Some say *they have no time* to pray:—But what is time given us for? is it not to save our souls? and is not salvation our most important business? and besides, cannot you pray *at all times* even *during your work?*

2. Others imagine they have no convenient or *proper place*:—But is not God present everywhere? Is there any place where you cannot address him? (*Example:* The martyrs prayed amidst their torments—the penitent thief prayed on the cross.)

3. Some pretend they *know not how* to pray:—Know not how! but, if you were in corporal distress and had a promise of relief on condition of asking for it, would you excuse yourself by saying: "I know not

(11) John xvi., 24. (12) James iv., 2.

how to ask?" Cannot you say the "Our Father," and "God be merciful to me a sinner," and other such prayers?

4. Others excuse themselves on the ground of being such *great sinners:*—But this, instead of being an excuse for neglecting prayer, shows that it is the more necessary for them: it is a means by which they are to obtain the grace of repentance, and of perseverance.

There can be no excuse sufficient to justify the neglect of Prayer. Daniel chose to be cast into the lions' den, rather than neglect this important duty.[13]

III. DISPOSITIONS REQUIRED:—Prayer is a *certain* means of grace, if accompanied with *proper dispositions.* What are the proper dispositions? This is a very important point; because it is the want of these dispositions, that renders our prayers ineffectual.

1. We must pray with the disposition, or *desire of renouncing all sinful habits;* because these are obstacles to grace.

2. We must pray *in the name of* JESUS CHRIST:—"If you ask the Father anything *in my name*, he will give it you."[14] To pray in his name, we must ask for such things as are worthy of Christ; and we must ground all the hope of our prayer being heard, on his infinite merits. Hence, most of the prayers of the Church terminate in these or similar words: "*Through our Lord Jesus Christ.*"

3. We must pray *with attention:* For otherwise, our prayer could not be said to be "a raising up of our minds and hearts to God," nor "a conversation with him;" for, if the inattention or distractions be wilful, then the prayer offends God, instead of pleasing him.——Are all distractions, then, sinful? No; for we cannot help having distractions sometimes: They are not sins, when they are not wilful; and, in this

(13) Dan. vi. (14) John xvi., 23.

case, they do not hinder the effect of our prayer: but when they *are* wilful, they will certainly be laid to our charge: "Ye hypocrites, well hath Isaias prophesied of you, saying: This people honoureth me with their lips, but their heart is far from me."[15]

To avoid distractions, (such, at least, as are *wilful*, we should practise what the Scripture directs: "Before prayer, prepare thy soul, and be not as a man that tempteth God;"[16] i.e., cast away all over-solicitude about earthly things—place yourselves in the presence of God—resolve to pray attentively—and reject distractions, as soon as you perceive them.

4. We must pray *with confidence* in the goodness and promises of God: "Let him ask *in faith*, nothing wavering...Let not that man (who wavereth) think that he shall receive anything of the Lord."[17]

To animate your confidence, think on the infinite goodness of God—and on his unlimited promises: "All things whatsoever you shall ask in prayer, *believing*, (i.e., *having confidence*,) you shall receive."[18] "Be it done unto you *according to your* FAITH,"[19] (i.e., *your confidence.)*

5. To our confidence in God, we must join an humble diffidence in ourselves—we must pray *with humility of heart:* i.e., we must cast ourselves entirely on the Divine mercy; acknowledging sincerely, that, on account of our sins and unworthiness, we deserve not the blessings we ask, but severe chastisements.—— This humble disposition is most powerful in inclining God to mercy: "To whom shall I have respect, but to him that is poor and little, and of a contrite heart, and that trembleth at my words?"[20] "The prayer of him that humbleth himself shall pierce the clouds, and it will not depart till the Most High behold."[21]

(15) Matt. xv., 7, 8. (16) Eccli. xviii., 23. (17) James i., 6, 7. (18) Matt. xxi., 22. (19) Matt. ix., 29. (20) Is. lxvi., 2. (21) Eccli. xxxv., 21.

6. We must pray *with perseverance:* We must persevere in our prayer, when God seems not to hear us Christ teaches, that "we ought always to pray, and not to faint."[22] Sometimes God grants our petition insensibly by little and little; sometimes he defers, that he may grant it afterwards more to our advantage, and as a reward of our perseverance: "Know ye that the Lord will hear your prayers, if you continue with perseverance."[23]

CONCLUSION:—As your wants and miseries cease not, but with your life; so let your supplications also cease not. Endeavour to become truly men of prayer; and then, like David, you will soon become also men according to God's own heart;[24] you will be enabled to pass through all the trials and temptations of this life, without sin; because the grace of God will be with you, and his protecting hand will preserve you. Though a thousand should fall by your side, and ten thousand by your right hand, the evil will not be allowed to come near you; because you will "dwell in the aid of the Most High"—you will abide securely "under the protection of the God of heaven."[25]

INSTRUCTION XXVI.

The Lord's Prayer.

What is the best of all prayers?—The Lord's Prayer

Who made the Lord's Prayer?—Christ our Lord.

Say the Lord's Prayer?—Our Father, who art in heaven, hallowed be thy name; thy kingdom come; thy will be done on earth, as it is in heaven. Give us this day our daily bread; and forgive us our trespasses, as we forgive them that trespass against us; and lead us not into temptation; but deliver us from evil. Amen.

(22) Luke xviii., 1.
(23) Judith iv., 1.
(24) Acts xiii., 22.
(25) Ps. xc.

Who is it that is here called Our Father?—God, who made us all, and who, by his grace, is the Father of all good Christians.

Why do you say Our Father, and not My Father?—Because we are not to pray for ourselves only, but for all others.

What do we pray for, when we say, Hallowed be thy name?—We pray that God may be honoured and served by all his creatures.

What do we pray for when we say, Thy kingdom come?—We pray that God may come and be king in all our hearts, by his grace, and may bring us all hereafter to his heavenly kingdom.

What do we pray for, when we say, Thy will be done on earth, as it is in heaven?—We pray that God will enable us by his grace, to do his will in all things, as the blessed do in heaven.

What do we pray for, when we say, Give us this day our daily bread?—We pray that God will continually give us all that is necessary for soul and body.

What do we pray for, when we say, Forgive us our trespasses as we forgive them that trespass against us?—We pray that God would forgive us our sins, as we forgive others the injuries they do to us.

What do we pray for, when we say, Lead us not into temptation?—We pray that God would give us grace not to yield to temptation.

What do we pray for, when we say, Deliver us from evil?—We pray that God would free us from all evil of soul and body, in time and eternity.

This prayer, which our Lord has made, is *short*, that all may learn it; but, though short, it contains all we can want, or need ask for; it contains Acts of the most sublime virtues; and expresses sentiments of the highest perfection.——When Christ had explained the manner and dispositions in which we should pray, his disciples said to him: "Lord, teach us to pray." In compliance with their request, he said: "Thus, therefore, shall you pray: Our Father, who art in heaven, &c."[26]——This Prayer contains *seven petitions*, introduced by the words, "*Our Father, who art in heaven.*"

God is our FATHER both *by creation*, and *by adoption;* and we are hereby admonished, that we should go to him with confidence, as Children to a good and kind Father—that we are all brethren—and that we should pray for one another, as members of the same family: "Pray for one another, that you may be saved."[27]

FIRST PETITION:—What do we pray for, when we say: "*Hallowed be thy name?*" We pray for the greater honour and glory of God; or that we may all praise, love, and serve God, on account of his Divine Perfections. And, in order that we may be enabled to do so, we beg in the next petition, that he would come and establish his kingdom in our hearts.

SECOND PETITION:—What do we pray for, when we say: "*Thy kingdom come?*" We pray that God would come into our hearts, and reign there by his grace—that he would rule our actions, and conduct us in the path of virtue—and would thus make us true members of his spiritual kingdom here on earth, as a sure means of bringing us to his eternal kingdom in heaven. And, in order that we may be worthy of that heavenly kingdom, we next pray that we may, in all things, accomplish his holy will.

THIRD PETITION:—What do we pray for, when we say: "*Thy will be done on earth, as it is in heaven?*" Considering, that, in the kingdom of heaven for which we have prayed, its blessed inhabitants always do God's will, we pray that *we* may do the same.——The Divine will should be the rule of all our actions: "My meat is to do the will of him that sent me."[28] When we repeat this petition, we should, at the same time, *re-*

(26) Matt, vi., 5 to 13; Luke xi., 1 to 4. (27) James v., 16.
(28) John iv., 34.

solve to do what we pray for; and, as a means of being enabled to do God's holy will, we next pray for a continual supply of his graces—for the daily spiritual food of our souls.

FOURTH PETITION.—What do we pray for, when we say: "*Give us this day our daily bread?*" We pray for the daily supply of all our wants, both corporal and spiritual; and thereby we acknowledge our total dependence on God.——As to *corporal* wants, we are admonished to be content with necessaries; and, for these, to rely entirely on Providence: "Be not solicitious for to-morrow."[29] "But having food, and wherewith to be covered, with these we are content."[30]——As to *spiritual* wants, we pray for Divine grace, as being our daily spiritual food, without which the soul languishes and dies in sin: we pray for the Blessed Eucharist—that "bread of life,"[31] in which we receive Christ himself, who is able to strengthen our souls to every good work. But then, conscience tells us we are sinners, and, as such, unworthy of this great blessing, therefore, in the next petition we implore forgiveness.

FIFTH PETITION:—What do we pray for, when we say: "*And forgive us our trespasses as we forgive them that trespass against us?*" Knowing ourselves to be sinners, subject to *daily* weaknesses and transgressions, (for, "in many things we all offend,"[32]) we pray *daily* for pardon.——This petition shows the necessity of our forgiving others, Christ having made this forgiveness a condition of our obtaining pardon from God: "If you will not forgive men, neither will your Father forgive you your offences"[33]——Having asked the pardon of past sins, we pray that we may not fall again.

(29) Matt. vi., 34.
(30) 1 Tim. vi., 8.
(31) John vi., 48, 52.
(32) James iii., 2.
(33) Matt. vi., 15.

SIXTH PETITION :—What do we pray for, when we say : "*And lead us not into temptation?*" We beg of God either to preserve us from temptation, or to support us in time of temptation ; or, in the words of St. Paul, we pray that "God would not suffer us to be tempted, above that which we are able ; but would make with temptation issue, that we may be able to bear it."[34]—God does not himself *tempt us to sin*, but he *permits* us to be tempted for our trial. So long as we are living in this world, we can never be secure from temptations ; for "the life of man upon earth is a warfare."[35] But in this warfare, "the grace of God is sufficient for us."[36]

SEVENTH PETITION :—What do we pray for, when we say : "*But deliver us from evil?*" Having prayed for the pardon of past sins, that we may not fall into them again, we then beg to be delivered from the consequences of sin ; viz., from all evils of soul and body. But, as regards temporal evils—such as sickness, losses, famine, distress, &c., we should pray in the spirit of resignation : "Not my will, but thine be done."[37] Resignation, patient suffering, and a penitential spirit, can convert these evils into real good. But the evils from which we principally pray to be delivered, are the punishments of sin in the next life.

"AMEN :"—Having thus prayed for all we can need, we confirm our prayer by saying : "*Amen.*" This word is called by Jerome, "The seal of the Lord's prayer." It means, *so be it :* i.e., may God grant these our petitions.

CONCLUSION :—Never let a day pass without saying this prayer. The words "*this day,*" and "*daily,*" show that it is intended to be said at least *every day* Say it then often ; but always attentively, devoutly

(34) 1 Cor. x., 13.
(35) Job vii., 1.
(36) 2 Cor. xii., 9.
(37) Luke xxii., 42.

and slowly; so as to enter into the spirit and meaning of it. For if you do so, it will be to you a source of many graces and blessings.

INSTRUCTION XXVII.

The Invocation of Saints and Angels—They can hear us—They pray for us—We may ask them to pray for us.

May we desire the Saints and Angels to pray for us?—Yes; we may.

How do you prove that the Saints and Angels can hear us?—"There shall be joy before the Angels of God over one sinner doing penance."[38]

Having addressed ourselves to God in the "*Our Father*," we are taught next to engage the Saints in our favour, that, through their intercession, we may be heard: we beg of the blessed in heaven to join *their* prayers with *ours*, and to present both to God; because we feel conscious, that God will hear *them* sooner than *us sinners*.

I. But "how do you prove that THE SAINTS AND ANGELS CAN HEAR US?"

1. Christ assures us, that, as the shepherd calls upon his friends and neighbours to rejoice with him, when he has found his lost sheep; "even so there shall be joy in heaven upon one sinner that doth penance, more than upon ninety-nine just who need not penance....... There shall be joy before the Angels of God upon one sinner doing penance."[39] These words evidently show, that the Angels in heaven *know* what goes on here upon earth; that they know when a sinner repents—when he repents *sincerely;* and, consequently, that *they know* what takes place *in a sinner's*

(38) Luke xv., 10. (39) Luke xv., 7, 10.

heart; and, therefore, they must know when he prays. The same words still further show, that the Angels not only know when we pray, but that they take an interest in our welfare. What is here said of the *Angels* is equally applicable to the *Saints* in heaven; because, "the Saints are as the Angels of God in heaven:"[40] "For they are equal to the Angels."[41]

2. Our Lord cautions us against despising or scandalizing those who believe in him, on account of their Guardian Angels: "See that you despise not one of these little ones; for I say to you, that their Angels in heaven always see the face of my Father who is in heaven."[42] Now, how can we offend the Angels, by despising or scandalizing the little ones whom they have to guard, unless the Angels *know it?* If they did not know it, these words would be without meaning.

3. In the Revelations made to St. John, our Blessed Lord says: "He that shall overcome, and keep my works unto the end, I will give him *power over the* NATIONS; and he *shall rule them* with a rod of iron."[43] Evidently this is spoken of *the Saints*—of those who have kept Christ's works "*unto the end;*" and, therefore, it is spoken of the Saints *after they have finished their mortal life.* Now, these must *know* what passes among the *nations;* for otherwise, how could they be said to exercise "power over the nations," and to "rule them?"

All these Texts clearly prove that the Angels and Saints in heaven both *know*, and *take an interest in* what goes on upon earth.

II. But, DO THEY PRAY FOR US? Yes; for,

1. The Archangel Raphael said to Tobias: "When thou didst pray with tears, and didst leave thy dinner,

(40) Matt. xxii., 30.
(41) Luke xx., 36.
(42) Matt. xviii., 10.
(43) Apoc. ii. 26, 27.

and didst bury the dead, *I offered thy prayer to the Lord*......For I am the Angel Raphael, one of the seven, who stand before the Lord."[44]

2. When the prophet Jeremias, long after his death, appeared to Judas Machabeus, the Second Book of Machabees says of him: "This is a lover of his brethren, and of the people of Israel: this is he that *prayeth much for the people*, and for all the holy city, Jeremias the prophet of God."[45]

The various Sects of Protestants do not receive these two Books (Tobias and Machabees) as inspired Scripture; but they *do* and *must* regard them as undeniable evidence of what was the belief of the Jews (i.e., of the people of God), before Christ——But, without these Texts, we have, in what Protestants do receive as the inspired Word of God, all the evidence we can need, to prove that the Angels and Saints *do pray in our behalf*, and that God *receives their prayers* Thus,

3. The Prophet Zacharias relates the prayer of an Angel in heaven for God's people on earth: "And the Angel of the Lord answered, and said: O Lord of Hosts, how long wilt thou not have mercy on Jerusalem, and on the cities of Juda, with which thou hast been angry? this is now the seventieth year. And the Lord answered the Angel, that spoke in me, good words, comfortable words......Therefore thus saith the Lord: I will return to Jerusalem in mercies."[46] Here, then, an Angel *implored mercy* for the people of God, and obtained it.

4. The New Testament, also, contains evidence equally strong. For, in the Book of the Apocalypse, it is said: "And I saw seven Angels standing in the presence of God......And another Angel came, and stood before the altar, having a golden censer; and

(44) Tobias xii., 12, 15. (45) 2 Mac. xv., 14. (46) Zach. i., 12, 13, 15.

there was given to him much incense, that he should offer of the prayers of all saints upon the golden altar, which is before the throne of God. And the smoke of the incense of the prayers of the saints ascended up before God, from the hand of the Angel."[47]—— How evident, then, that Angels present our petitions to God, and join with them the incense of their own! How perfectly does this accord with what was revealed to Tobias: "When thou didst pray with tears... .I offered thy prayer to the Lord......For I am the Angel Raphael, one of the Seven, who stand before the Lord?"[48]

5. And of the SAINTS *in heaven*, the same Book says: "The four-and-twenty ancients fell down before the Lamb, having every one of them harps, and golden vials full of odours, which are the prayers of Saints."[49] These four-and-twenty ancients are *Saints* in heaven; for they say to Christ, in the next verse: "Thou hast redeemed us to God, in thy blood, out of every tribe, and tongue, and people, and nation." Now, in the above passage, these Saints in heaven are spoken of, as falling down before Christ, in our favour; and also as offering our prayers to Him.

Thus, then, we are taught, both in the Old and New Testament, that the Saints and Angels in heaven *pray for us* who are on earth.

III. But MAY WE ASK THEM TO PRAY FOR US? Yes; we may.

Do we not thereby injure the Mediatorship of Christ? No; not in the least degree.

But does not the Scripture say, that there is only one Mediator between God and us? The Scripture says: "There is one Mediator between God and man, the man Christ Jesus, *who gave himself a ransom for all;*"[50] that is to say, there is *only one* who *ransomed*

(47) Apoc. viii., 2, 3, 4. (49) Apoc v. 8, 9. (50) 1 Tim. ii., 5,
(48) Tobias xii., 12, 15.

us—only one who can interpose his *own* merits in our favour; but this is no reason why others may not intercede for us (not indeed by their *own* merits, but) through the infinite merits of Him who ransomed us.——St. Paul teaches us that there may be such intercessors: "I desire that prayers and intercessions be made for all men."[51] It is just the same, as regards any injury done to the Mediatorship of Christ, whether these intercessors be in heaven or on earth at the time of their interceding. We expect nothing from them, except THROUGH CHRIST.

That we *may* pray to the Blessed in heaven, the Scripture plainly shows:—

1. Jacob *prayed to an Angel*, saying: "I will not let thee go, except thou bless me;......and he blessed him in the same place."[52] The Prophet Osee, relating this event, says: "Jacob prevailed over the Angel, and was strengthened; he wept, and *made supplication to him*."[53] Here is supplication made to an Angel, and a blessing obtained.

2. Abraham *prayed to the Angel* who was going to destroy Sodom, begging that he would not "slay the just with the wicked;"[54] and Lot was accordingly spared.

3. Lot, also, *prayed to the Angel* who conducted him out of Sodom, beseeching him to spare the small city of Segor: "And he (the Angel) said to him: Behold also in this, I have heard thy prayers, not to destroy the city for which thou hast spoken."[55]——In both these instances, prayers were made to Angels, and the petitioners obtained their requests: for Lot was not slain with the wicked; and the small city of Segor was spared.

4. Again, when Jacob was on his death-bed, he

(51) 1 Tim. ii., 1 (53) Osee xii., 4. (54) Gen. xviii., 23, 25
(52) Gen. xxxii., 26 29 (55) Gen. xix., 18 to 22.

blessed his two Grandsons; and, in order to obtain a blessing from heaven upon them, he *invoked* not only God, but *his Guardian Angel* also, in their behalf: "God, that feedeth me from my youth until this day; *the Angel* that delivereth me from all evils, bless these boys, and let my name be called upon them."[56] Here Jacob not only prayed to God, but, in the very same sentence, *he implored a blessing from the Angel* who had been his constant protector. That holy Patriarch would not have done so, unless it were lawful; and from the manner in which the Scripture relates it, it is plain, that he did nothing then, but what was good and lawful: But, if it was good and lawful *for him*, is it not so *for us?—for us*, who, (according to St. Paul.) in the New Law, "are come," not only "to the city of the living God" (the Church); "and to Jesus Christ, the Mediator of the New Testament;" but also "to the company of many *thousands of Angels*, and to the Church of *the first-born*, who are written in the heavens, and to *the spirits of the just made perfect*,"[57] i.e., to the Saints.

After all these proofs from Scripture, that the Angels and Saints in heaven *pray for us*, and that we *may ask them* to do so, one must feel surprised that this doctrine has ever been doubted. For, is it not most strange, that Protestants should deny a doctrine for which there is such Scriptural evidence? How their rejection of this doctrine shows the force of prejudice!

INSTRUCTION XXVIII.

Our Guardian Angel—The "Hail Mary."

May we desire the Saints and Angels to pray for us?—Yes; we may.

How do you prove that the Saints and Angels can hear

(56) Gen. xlviii., 15, 16.

(57) Heb. xii., 22 to 24.

us?—"There shall be joy before the Angels of God over one sinner doing penance."

What is the prayer to our Blessed Lady which the Church teaches?—The Hail Mary.

Say the Hail Mary?—Hail Mary, full of grace, the Lord is with thee: blessed art thou amongst women, and blessed is the fruit of thy womb, JESUS. Holy Mary Mother of God, pray for us sinners, now and at the hour of our death. Amen,

How many parts are there in the Hail Mary?—Three parts.

Who made the first two parts?—The Angel Gabriel and St. Elizabeth, inspired by the Holy Ghost.

Who made the third part?—The Church of God, against those who denied the Virgin Mary to be the Mother of God.

Why do you say the Hail Mary so often?—To put us in mind of the Son of God being made man for us.

For what other reason?—To honour the Blessed Virgin, Mother of God, and to beg her prayers for us.

It has been proved from Scripture, that the Angels and Saints in heaven *pray for us*; and that we *may ask them* to do so.—But,

1. GUARDIAN ANGEL:—Is there any one of the *Angels* whom we should invoke *more particularly*? Yes; OUR GUARDIAN ANGEL.

God has given an Angel to each of us, to be our special Guardian: "He hath given his Angels charge over thee, to keep thee in all thy ways. In their hands they shall bear thee up, lest thou dash thy foot against a stone."[58] Christ teaches this same truth, when he says: "See that you despise not one of these little ones; for I say to you, that *their* Angels in heaven always see the face of my Father who is in heaven."[59]

As the wicked spirits tempt us to evil, by their suggestions; and endeavour to deprive us of happiness,

(58) Ps. xc., 10, 11, 12. (59) Matt, xviii., 10.

so our Guardian Angel directs us to good, by inward inspirations; preserving us from dangers, and from many evils: "The Angel of the Lord shall encamp round about them that fear him, and shall deliver them."[60]——Thus, he delivered Judith from being injured by Holofernes: "As the Lord liveth, his Angel hath been my keeper both going hence, and abiding there, and returning from thence hither."[61] Thus, also, he preserved and delivered Daniel in the Lions' den;[62] and he delivered Peter and other Apostles out of prison.[63]

Our Guardian Angel prays particularly for us; and presents our petitions to God. We should frequently invoke him—we should pay great respect and attention to his presence—and we should take care not to do in his presence, what we should be ashamed to do before men: "Behold I will send my Angel, who shall go before thee, and keep thee in thy journey......Take notice of him, and hear his voice, and do not think him one to be contemned: for he will not forgive, when thou hast sinned; and my name is in him."[64] How very little is this admonition of the Almighty attended to?

II. THE HAIL MARY:—Is there any one among the *Saints*, whom we should ask *more particularly* to intercede for us? Yes, THE BLESSED VIRGIN MARY.

The Blessed Virgin, being the Mother of God, is above all the Angels and Saints—she is pronounced "*blessed amongst women*,"[65]—and is to be called "*blessed*" by the faithful throughout all generations;[66] Christ appointed her as OUR MOTHER, and as as HER *children*, in the person of St. John: "Behold thy son:......Behold thy Mother."[67]

(60) Ps. xxxiii., 8. (61) Judith xiii., 20. (62) Dan. vi., 21, 22. (63) Acts v., 19; Acts xii., 7 to 11. (64) Exod. xxiii., 20, 21. (65) Luke i., 28. (66) Luke i., 48. (67) John xix., 26, 17.

We should frequently implore her intercession. Such has been the practice of the Saints—they were remarkable for their tender devotion to her: witness, for example, St. Bernard, St. Bonaventure, St. Dominic, St. Alphonsus Liguori, &c. The Saints have received many and great blessings, through her intercession and so may *we*, if, like them, we will be fervent and devout in imploring her assistance. Have recourse to her, then, frequently and fervently, and on all occasions, especially in your temptations, and spiritual necessities. Ask her to obtain your requests, placing the greatest confidence in her intercession; for, if *she* prays for you, you may rest assured that God will grant what she asks. Hence, St. Bernard says, that "never hath any one been known to have recourse to her protection, implore her aid, or ask her intercession without obtaining relief!"

The manner in which our Lord granted her request, at the marriage feast in Cana of Galilee, shows the power of her intercession: "The wine failing, the Mother of Jesus (requesting him to supply some by his Divine power) saith to him: They have no wine. And Jesus saith to her: Woman, what is it to me and to thee? my hour is not yet come (for working miracles. But, persevering in her request,) his Mother saith to the waiters: Whatsoever he shall say to you, do ye. Jesus (yielding) saith to them: Fill the water-pots with water. And they filled them up to the brim. And Jesus saith to them: Draw out now, and carry to the chief steward of the feast. And they carried it." And it was found to be wine, as the Blessed Virgin had requested.[68]——With reason, then, may we say, that, if *she* intercedes in our favour, God will grant her request.

What is the prayer to her, which the Church

(68) John ii., 1 to 10.

teaches? The "HAIL MARY;" otherwise called "*The Angelic Salutation.*"

"The Angel being come in, said to her: Hail! full of grace, the Lord is with thee: blessed art thou amongst women."[69] She is thus "blessed," because she is gifted with the highest graces and virtues; and because she is chosen for the special privilege of being the Mother of God.

St. Elizabeth, being visited by the Blessed Virgin, said to her: "Blessed art thou amongst women; and blessed is the fruit of thy womb."[70] That is to say, of all women thou art the most blessed, because thou art to bring forth the world's Redeemer.—On account of the Son, we honour the Mother; it is on *His* account, that "all generations" are to call her "blessed."[71]

In the third part of the Hail Mary, which has been added by the Church, we declare the Blessed Virgin Mary to be the "*Mother of God*," against the Nestorians, who assert, that the Son of God, and the Son of Mary, were two distinct persons. This heresy was condemned in the third General Council at Ephesus, in 431. The Blessed Virgin is the Mother of *Him*, who, besides being man, is also God; in Christ there is but *one person*, and she is *his Mother*; "Whence is this to me, that the mother of my Lord should come to me?"[72]

In this third part, we also declare ourselves to be "*sinners*;" and as such, we beg her intercession—"*now*;" i.e., always at the present time, because we always need God's mercy; "*and at the hour of our death*" more especially; because *then* we stand in more need of help; and because all depends on dying well.

(69) Luke i., 28.
(70) Luke i., 42.
(71) Luke i., 48.
(72) Luke i., 43.

EXPLANATION

OF THE

TEN COMMANDMENTS.

INSTRUCTION XXIX.

FIRST COMMANDMENT.

The Commandments in general; What the First Commandment requires—and what it forbids.

How many Commandments are there?—Ten.

Who gave the Ten Commandments?—God himself in the Old Law, and Christ confirmed them in the New.

What is the First Commandment?—"I am the Lord thy God, who brought thee out of the Land of Egypt, and out of the house of bondage. Thou shalt not have strange Gods before me. Thou shalt not make to thyself any graven thing, nor the likeness of anything that is in heaven above, nor in the earth beneath, nor in the waters under the earth; thou shalt not adore them, nor serve them."

What are we commanded to do by the First Commandment?—By the First Commandment, we are commanded to believe in one only true and living God, and no more; to hope in him, to love him, and to serve him all our days.

What is forbidden by the First Commandment?—The First Commandment forbids us to worship false gods or idols, or to give to any creature whatsoever the honour which is due to God.

What else is forbidden by this Commandment?—All false religions, and dealing with the devil; and the inquiring after things to come by fortune-tellers, or superstitious practices.

What else?—All charms, spells, and heathenish observations of omens, dreams, and such like fooleries.

I. The Commandments in General:—The Commandments contain God's Law, directing what is to be done by us, and what is to be avoided: they are an epitome of our duties towards God, towards our neighbour, and towards ourselves.

In the beginning, God impressed upon the heart of man a sense of right and wrong, called *the light of nature*—he gave man a *conscience*. By disregarding the light of nature and the voice of conscience, men soon became wicked—so wicked as to induce Almighty God to say: "I will destroy man whom I have created;... for it repenteth me that I have made them.........The earth is filled with iniquity through them, and I will destroy them with the earth."[1] After the Deluge, men soon became wicked as before; so that the earth was again "filled with iniquity;" habits of crime silenced, in a great measure, the voice of conscience; and, by darkening the light of nature, almost deadened man's sense of right and wrong. As a means of preserving it amidst the general corruption, God wrote his Law or Commandments on two tables of stone. He wrote them in the midst of thunder and lightning, to signify what *they* might expect, who should dare to transgress them.[2] ——In the Gospel these Commandments are confirmed by Christ. For, when "one came and said to him: Good Master, what good shall I do that I may have life everlasting?" Jesus said to him: "If thou wilt enter into life, keep the Commandments."[3]

Men, enslaved to vice, have said it is impossible to keep the Commandments. It is impossible, without the help of God's grace; but perfectly possible, when we have his grace to assist us. Now, his grace will never be wanting to those who will take the *proper means* of having it. The words addressed to St. Paul apply to each of us: "My grace is *sufficient* for thee."[4] And every one of us may say with that Apostle: "I can do all things in him that strengtheneth me."[5] "God

(1) Gen. vi., 7, 13. (3) Matt xix., 16, 17. (5) Philip. iv., 13
(2) Exod. xix.; and xx. (4) 2 Cor. xii., 9

is faithful, who will not suffer you to be tempted above that which you are able; but will make also with temptation issue, that you may be able to bear it."[6] —— God requires us to keep his Commandments, under pain of eternal condemnation; therefore, they are *possible*, and also *obligatory:* for it would be against the Attributes of God, to command impossibilities, and then punish us for not doing the things commanded.

These words, "I am the Lord thy God, who brought thee out of the land of Egypt, and out of the house of bondage,"[7] are an introduction to the Commandments: they show, that God has a right to command us, as being "*the Lord our God;*" and that we ought to obey his commands, out of gratitude also for what he has done for us, as having delivered us *from the bondage of sin and Satan.*

II. The First Commandment *requires us* to worship God by Faith, Hope, Charity, and Religion:—

1. *By Faith*, in paying homage to his Truth: and this we do, when we believe all that he has revealed, and believe it upon the authority of his word; i.e., *because* He has revealed it.

2. *By Hope*, in paying homage to his power, goodness, and infidelity: and this we do, when, acknowledging our own insufficiency, we confidently expect all good from God alone, through the infinite merits of Christ.

3. *By Charity*, in paying homage to his infinite Perfections, which render him infinitely deserving of our love: and this we do, when we love God for his own sake, above all things; when, for his own sake, we would rather be deprived of all things—of our pleasures, possessions, health, and even life itself, than act against his will. This is the most acceptable homage we can give to God; and we have examples

(6) 1 Cor. x., 13. (7) Exod. xx., 2.

of it in all the Martyrs. We show that we worship God by charity, when we keep his Commandments: "If you love me, keep my commandments."[8] "He that keepeth his word (his law), in him in very deed the charity of God is perfected; and by this we know that we are in him."[9]

4. We are required to worship God *by the virtue of Religion*, in paying homage to his infinite Majesty and supreme dominion over us; and this we do, when we adore him as our first beginning and our last end, acknowledging our entire dependence on him; when we offer him the tribute of our praise and thanksgiving, or address our supplications to him; when we give him public and external worship (which is of obligation); and especially, when we celebrate or hear Mass, wherein we offer him a complete acknowledgment of his dominion over us, and of our dependence on him.

III. WHAT THE FIRST COMMANDMENT FORBIDS: I have now explained what the First Commandment *requires us to do;* but WHAT IS FORBIDDEN by the First Commandment?—

1. *Idolatry*, which is giving to a creature the adoration or supreme honour, which is due to God alone. This is a grievous crime, directly opposed to the First Commandment. We need only use our common sense, to see the extreme folly of it.

2. *False Religions;* i.e., such as are different from *that one* which the Apostles established, and which has come down from them by a regular sucession.—— May we go and join with false religions in their worship? No. But, suppose the members of those religions oblige their servants to go with them to their places of worship; may a Catholic servant go and join with them? No; certainly not. When servants engage themselves to Protestants of any denomination,

(8) John xiv., 15. (9) 1 John ii., 5.

they should not neglect to provide against this evil; and parents should be careful to make this provision for their children. A Catholic must give up a situation, rather than be compelled to join in a false worship. We cannot join at all, *in religion*, with the members of an heretical church.

3. *Superstition*, which consists in turning away from God, to seek help from the devil—in withdrawing from God's Providence, and from the means of help which he has ordained; to follow the delusions of the devil, by using means appointed by him, for obtaining something which we wish to have: such means, for example, as consulting fortune-tellers, for the purpose of learning what is to happen; or beginning harvest, or any other important affair, on a particular day of the week, for the purpose of securing good luck. These and such like means are called *superstitious practices*, because they have no natural connexion with the ends to be obtained, and have not been instituted by any proper authority to be supernatural means of obtaining those ends. To put any confidence in omens, charms, dreams, and such like things, is superstitious and sinful.

Omens are what superstitious people take to be *signs of what is to happen;* as, certain days being considered lucky or unlucky—spilling the salt on the table being looked upon as foretelling some misfortune to the person towards whom it falls, &c. What folly it is (as well as sin), to place the least confidence in these things!

Charms and *Spells* are certain words, sentences, or things, which are kept by superstitious persons as *preservatives from some particular evils;* as, charms to prevent or cure the tooth-ache—a horse-shoe placed over a door to prevent any one from going through that door to do any mischief, and similar follies. What gross ignorance! what weakness of mind, and want of common sense!

These follies, and also *witchcrafts* of every kind, are displeasing to Almighty God, and strictly forbidden: "Let there not be found among you any one that consulteth soothsayers, or observeth dreams and omens; neither let there be any wizard, nor charmer, nor any one that consulteth pythonic spirits, or fortune-tellers. ....For the Lord abhorreth all these things."[10] "Wizards thou shalt not suffer to live."[11]

The observance of *dreams*, or taking them to be signs of what is to happen, is foolish, superstitious, and sinful. We do indeed read, in Scripture, of God having sometimes made known future events in dreams or visions. Thus, he showed Joseph his future superiority over his brethren in Egypt;[12] he made known to Pharaoh the seven years of plenty, and the seven of famine;[13] he showed Nabuchodonosor a statue which represented four kingdoms, to be succeeded and broken to pieces by the kingdom of Christ, which should stand for ever;[14] and, by a vision in the night," the king's dream, with its interpretation, was revealed to Daniel.[15] These, and such like dreams, or rather visions, which were either to great Saints or Prophets, or to great public characters, and for the public good, cannot by any means authorize us to observe dreams; since God gives us a general prohibition: "Neither let there be found among you any one that......observeth dreams......For the Lord abhorreth all these things."[16]——How can mere fancies of the brain, arising from constitution, from habit of body, or from previous ideas, be signs of what is to happen? "Dreams have deceived many."[17]

(10) Deut. xviii., 10, 11, 12.
(11) Exod. xxii., 18.
(12) Gen. xxxvii., 5 to 10.
(13) Gen. xli., 1 to 7.
(14) Dan ii.
(15) Dan ii., 19.
(16) Deut. xviii., 10.
(17) Eccli, xxxiv., 7.

4. *Sacrilege* is also forbidden by the First Commandment. Sacrilege is the abuse or profanation of holy persons, holy places, or holy things.

First, by *holy persons* are to be understood *persons consecrated to God;* as, Priests, and the members of Religious Orders. It is a sacrilegious crime to strike them maliciously, to violate them, or to treat them with any other great irreverence: "Touch not my anointed; and do no evil to my Prophets."[18] "With all thy soul fear the Lord, and reverence his Priests."[19]

Secondly, By *holy places* are meant *places consecrated to God;* as, consecrated churches, or burial grounds. When these places are pillaged, or profaned by heretical worship, it is the crime of sacrilege.

Thirdly, *Holy things* are such as either are consecrated to God's service, or relate to him in a special manner; as, a consecrated chalice, the relics of a canonized Saint, the Sacraments, or the Sacrifice of the Mass. It is a sacrilegious crime to steal these things, or to employ them in sinful or profane uses; or to receive Sacraments unworthily: "They (the laity) shall not touch the vessels of the Sanctuary, lest they die."[20] Baltassar, King of Babylon, serves as a striking example of the great evil of sacrilege. In a feast, which he made for his nobles, he used, as drinking cups, the sacred vessels which his father Nabuchodonosor, had taken from the temple of Jerusalem. This crime cost him his life; for scarcely had he committed the sacrilege, when he saw a hand writing his sentence on the wall.[21]

We should cherish in our hearts a great respect for Religion, and for whatever is consecrated to God's service, or relates more particularly to him.

(18) Ps. civ. 15.
(19) Eccli. vi., 31.
(20) Numb. iv., 15.
(21) Dan. v.

INSTRUCTION XXX.

FIRST COMMANDMENT CONCLUDED.

The Lawfulness of making Images—of honouring the Angels and Saints—and of showing Respect to Relics, Crucifixes, and holy Pictures.

Does the First Commandment forbid the making of Images?—The First Commandment does not forbid the making of Images, but the making of idols; that is, it forbids making Images to be adored, or honoured as God.

Does the First Commandment forbid us to give any kind of honour to the Saints and Angels?—No; it only forbids us to give them that supreme or Divine honour, which belongs to God alone; but it does not forbid us to give them that inferior honour, which is due to them, as the faithful servants and special friends of God.

And is it allowable to honour Relics, Ccruifixes, and holy Pictures?—Yes; with an inferior and relative honour, as they relate to Christ and his Saints, and are memorials of them.

May we pray to Relics or Images?—No, by no means; for they have no life nor sense to help us.

I. Making Images:—When the First Commandment says: "Thou shalt not make to thyself any graven thing, nor the likeness of any thing that is in heaven above, or in the earth beneath, or in the waters under the earth;" these words, were we to reason upon them as Protestants do, would render it equally unlawful to make any image or picture at all, sacred or profane. But, that their mode of reasoning is false, is evident from the fact, that, after giving this Commandment, God said to Moses: "Thou shalt make two Cherubims of beaten gold on the two sides of the oracle."[22] "And the Lord said to Moses: Make a brazen serpent, and set it up for a sign."[23] Accord-

(22) Exod. xxv., 18. (23) Numb. xxi., 8.

ing to God's direction, Solomon ornamented the temple with religious images or pictures: "He graved Cherubims on the walls......He made also in the house of the holy of holies two Cherubims of image work; and he overlaid them with gold."[24]

These Texts evidently show, that it is lawful to make images or pictures, and to fix them in places of worship. The First Commandment, then, does not forbid us to make them *as pictures and images*; it only forbids us to make them *as idols.* God himself explains the Commandment in this sense, by saying: "Thou shalt not *adore* them, nor *serve* them."[25] And again: "You shall not make *gods* of silver, nor shall you make to yourselves *gods* of gold."[26] Now, when we make images and place them in our Churches, it is not to make *gods* of them; but it is for the same purpose, as Moses made the Cherubims and placed them on each side of the oracle; and as Solomon put Cherubims of image-work in the Temple. Protestants will not dare to charge *them* with the crime of breaking the First Commandment by so doing; then, why do they charge *us* with it?

II. Honouring Saints:—But do we not break the First Commandment, when we *honour the Saints and Angels?* for does not this Commandment forbid us to give any kind of honour to the Saints and Angels? No; for it is lawful and proper to give them that inferior and relative honour, which is due to them as the faithful servants and special friends of God; and which we would show towards a good and virtuous person on earth—we would honour such a person *for God's sake.*

The words "*honour*" and "*worship*" on account of the strong prejudices of Protestants, require some explanation. If we use these words with reference to

(24) 2 Par. iii., 7, 10. (25) Exod. xx., 5. (26) Exod. xx., 23.

the Saints, we are charged with giving them *supreme homage;* but the words have only this meaning, when they are referred to God. For, when referred to creatures, they merely mean respect, veneration, great reverence. This used to be the common meaning of the word "*worship.*" How strange, then, and how unjust it is in Protestants, to charge us with giving Divine honour to the Saints, merely because this word has been retained to express our veneration? especially as they have retained the *same word* in the *same sense?* For, in their Marriage-Service, they direct the husband to say to his wife: "With my body *I thee worship.*" This only means, that he will show her great respect. Again, they say to the Magistrates: "*Your worship,*" and they call them "*Worshipful.*" Now, we do not charge *them* with making *gods* of wives and magistrates on account of using towards them the word "*worship;*" then, why do they charge *us* with making *gods* of the Saints, because we use towards them the same word?

In order, then, to know what kind of honour is expressed by any word, we must consider the *intention* of him who uses it: this *may* and *does* give quite a different character to the same outward expression. For example, bowing the head, or bending the knee, may be used in *adoration* of God, or *as respect* to an earthly superior. A child, for instance, may kneel and bow to ask pardon of God, or of his offended parent: in the first case, it is an act of *supreme adoration;* and in the second, an act of filial *submission.*

The same external actions or words, then, may express (according to the intention) different kinds of honour—either that *inferior honour* due to creatures, or that *supreme honour* due to God alone.

That this inferior and relative honour may be lawfully given to creatures, is clear from many passages of Scripture, several of which I will quote.

"And David commanded all the assembly: Bless ye the Lord our God. And all the assembly blessed the Lord, the God of their fathers: and they bowed themselves and WORSHIPPED God, and then *the king*."[27] [*The Protestant Version says: They "bowed down their heads, and worshipped the Lord and the king*."] Here, civil (relative) honour, and also Divine honour, are expressed by the very same word "*worship*," and by the self-same act of *bowing*.——When three Angels appeared to Abraham, "as soon as he saw them he ran to meet them from the door of his tent, and adored down to the ground."[28] [*The Protestant Version says: "He ran to meet them...and bowed himself towards the ground*."]——Lot gave this same mark of honour to two Angels;[29] and so did Josue to another.[30]

In objection to all this, it is said, that, when St. John fell at an Angel's feet to worship him, the Angel said: "See thou do it not; I am thy fellow-servant, and of thy brethren, who have the testimony of Jesus. Adore God."[31] [*According to the Protestant Version, it is: "Worship God*."] But this Text, instead of opposing, confirms our doctrine; for, the *proffered worship* was either *Divine* or *not*: if *Divine*, then the Apostle must have taken the Angel to be Christ, for surely we must not charge *him* with offering *Divine* worship *knowingly* to a *mere Angel*. In this case, the passage is not against our doctrine, which condemns *as idolatry* the offering of *Divine* worship to Angels But if not *Divine worship*, then it could not have been refused as being unlawful. For, *that* honour and worship which it was lawful for Abraham, Lot, and Josue to give to angels, and for those Angels to receive, could not be unlawful for St. John to give, nor

(27) 1 Par. xxix., 20. (28) Gen. xviii., 2. (29) Gen. xix., 1. (30) Josue v., 13, 14 (31) Apoc. xix., 10

for this Angel to receive from him. Why, then, did the Angel refuse it? It was out of humility, and of respect for St. John, which he shows by styling himself as being merely his "*fellow-servant.*"——And, besides, we find St. John offering it a second time, after having been thus admonished; which we cannot suppose he *would* have done, unless he knew it was right.[32]

And, indeed, let each one (whatever be his religion) only appeal to his own heart on this subject: Suppose, for example, that this Angel who appeared to St. John, or St. John himself, or St. Peter, or St. Paul, were to appear to you; *ought* you not, and *would* you not, show to him, for God's sake, all the honour, and respect you could (except *Divine*)? Now, this is all that the Catholic Church teaches on this subject.

We may, then, honour the Angels and Saints.

III. HONOURING CRUCIFIXES:—*Is it allowable to honour Relics, Crucifixes, and Holy Pictures?*—Yes; with an inferior and relative honour, as they relate to Christ and his Saints, and are memorials of them.

With regard to *Relics*, the Council of Trent teaches, "That the sacred bodies of the Martyrs, and of the other Saints......are to be held in veneration by the faithful." And, with regard to Crucifixes and holy Pictures, the Council also teaches, "That the Images of Christ, of the Virgin Mother of God, and of the other Saints, are to be had, and retained, especially in Churches; and that due honour and veneration are to be given to them; but that this honour is referred to the Prototypes whom they represent."[33]

Now, if we *may* and *do* respect the *Temple*, because it is dedicated to God's worship; if we may and do respect the *Bible*, because it represents to our minds,

(32) Apoc. xxii., 8, 9. (33) Conc. Trid., Sess. 25, De Invocatione

when we read it, the very words spoken by God; why may we not respect the *Crucifix*, for the very same reason—because *it* represents also to our minds, when we look upon it, the very sufferings endured by Christ for our salvation? In all these and such like cases, it is not the mere materials that we respect or venerate; but the Temple, the sacred Volume, the Crucifix, &c., are merely the vehicles, through which our respect is conveyed to God.

Do not Protestants do the very same thing towards the pictures and keep-sakes of their deceased parents and friends? and is not this the natural feeling of the heart? Why, then, do they condemn us for what they themselves do?

For, let Protestants, in this also, only appeal to their own heart: Suppose any of them possessed the body of St. Peter, or Paul, or the mantle of Elias, &c., would they not preserve it with very great respect, and consider it as a most precious Relic? If so, then why condemn us for what they themselves would do? and for what they actually *do* do towards the keep-sakes of their departed friends?

It has been now shown, that our doctrines, on this subject, are both reasonable and Scriptural. Protestants, then, should take care how they charge *us* with breaking the First Commandment, by honouring the Saints, or what relates to them; lest, instead of proving the charge against us, they bring upon themselves the heavy guilt of transgressing that *other* Commandment which saith: "Thou shalt not bear false witness against thy neighbour."[34]

(34) Exod. xx., 16.

INSTRUCTION XXXI.

SECOND COMMANDMENT.

How we are to speak of God—Vows and Oaths—Cursing, Blaspheming, and Profane Words.

What is the Second Commandment?—Thou shalt not take the name of the Lord thy God in vain.

What are we commanded by the Second Commandment?—By the Second Commandment we are commanded to speak with reverence of God and all holy things, and to keep our lawful oaths and vows.

What is forbidden by the Second Commandment?—The Second Commandment forbids all false, rash, unjust, and unnecessary oaths; as also cursing, blaspheming, and profane words.

The Second Commandment is: "Thou shalt not take the name of the Lord thy God in vain: for the Lord will not hold him guiltless that shall take the name of the Lord his God in vain."[35]

I. Object of this Commandment:—By this Commandment we are commanded to *speak with reverence of God*, and to *avoid speaking of him with irreverence.* Its object, therefore, is to direct us how we are to *worship God in our words:* and it is a natural consequence of the First Commandment; for, if we love God, and adore and serve him, as that Commandment requires, then we shall speak of him with love and respect.

This Second Commandment enjoins the *duty of praising God*, i.e., of extolling his Greatness, his Goodness, his Bounty towards us, and his other Divine Perfections. This is man's noblest employment: it is that which is to be continued eternally in heaven.

(35) Exod. xx., 7

II. Oaths and Vows:—This Commandment still further requires us to respect God's name, *by keeping our lawful Oaths and Vows.*

1. What is a *Vow?* It is *a free and deliberate promise, made to God, of doing something good, with the intention of binding one's-self to do it.* A Vow, in the making of it, is a free act; but, when made, it is binding under the strictest obligation: "When thou hast made a vow to the Lord thy God, thou shalt not delay to pay it; because the Lord thy God will require it: and if thou delay, it shall be reputed to thee for a sin."[36] It is much better not to vow, than, after a vow, not to perform the things promised."[37]——It is more meritorious to perform good works by vow, than without a vow; because, by a vow, we sacrifice our liberty to God—we give him, not only *the fruit*, but the *tree itself*.

Never make vows of such things as are trivial; much less of such as are sinful. A vow to do anything sinful, is itself a sin; and such a vow must not be kept. But all other vows must be fulfilled; unless for some reasonable cause, a dispensation or commutation be obtained from a proper authority.

2. What is an *Oath?* It is *calling on God to witness the truth of what we say: and to punish us, if what we say is false.* Is it lawful to swear or take an oath? Yes, when God's honour, or when our own or neighbour's just defence, requires it: "Thou shalt fear the Lord thy God, and thou shalt swear by his name."[38] An oath is the greatest pledge we can give of the truth of our words. [*Explain the words,* "So help me, God;" *i.e., may God send me blessings or punishments, according as my words are true or false.*]

Three *Conditions* are necessary for taking an Oath; and they are expressed in the words of Jeremias:

(36) Deut. xxiii., 21. (37) Eccles. v., 4. (38) Deut. vi., 13.

"Thou shalt swear as the Lord liveth, in *truth*, and in *judgment*, and in *justice*."[39] That is to say, the oath must be true—it must be taken with mature deliberation—and for a good and reasonable cause. We sin against the first of these conditions, by perjury or *false* swearing; against the second, by *rash* swearing; and against the third, by *unjust* or *unnecessary* swearing. "Swear not at all;"[40] i.e., do not swear at all in your common conversation. It is a sin to take an oath of doing anything unlawful; it is a sin also to observe such an oath. (*Example:* Herod sinned by the oath, which he took to the daughter of Herodias, that he would give whatsoever she should ask: This oath was both rash and unjust, because he knew not what unreasonable or unjust thing she might ask. He sinned again, and more grievously, by keeping the oath—by commanding the head of St. John the Baptist to be given to her.[41])

Perjury, or false swearing, is a transgression against the *most essential* condition of an oath, viz., against its truth. We become guilty of this,

First, If we know the oath to be false, when we take it—

Secondly, If we think it to be false, although it should happen to be true—

Thirdly, If we are uncertain whether it be true or false—

Fourthly, If, without a just cause, we refuse to fulfil what we have promised upon oath.

Perjury is a very grievous crime—it is a contempt of God, and an injury to society; and yet, how common it is in this country!

But, as to *rash*, *unjust*, and *unnecessary* oaths, how still more common are they! How many people have a habit of uttering oaths, without any just reason, on

(39) Jer. iv., 2. (40) Matt. v., 34. (41) Mark vi., 21 to 28.

every occasion? These oaths are, for the most part, *rash*, and therefore sinful; many of them are *unujst* which is worse; and all of them are *unnecessary*. This habit of swearing on every occasion, is a disedifying, detestable, and irreligious practice.

III. CURSING AND BLASPHEMING:—But the habit of *cursing* and *blaspheming* is even more common still!

1. What is *Cursing?* It is *calling down judgments or some evil upon one's-self, one's neighbour, or some other creature of God.* It is a horrible, impious, and diabolical practice; for it is imitating the devil, who is always wishing and seeking to bring evils upon us. Persons, who are addicted to cursing, should reflect, that their curses fall not, upon those against whom they are directed, but upon themselves only; and that most heavily. (*Example:* The Jews pronounced a curse upon themselves, when they said: " His blood be upon us, and upon our children."[42] And how literally has their curse been executed! for his blood *has* been upon them!

2. What is *Blaspheming?* It is *speaking evil of God, or of his Saints; or speaking of them with contempt; or speaking contemptuously of the truths revealed by God, or of his Church; or of the means of grace which Christ has established in his Church, such as the Sacraments, and the Sacrifice of the Mass.* The mere description of blasphemy cannot but raise in our minds very serious reflections. For what is more common in this country, than to hear those of other religions railing against the Saints—casting slights upon the Blessed Virgin Mary—speaking against, and turning into ridicule, those truths which have been taught by the Son of God himself, and those sacred means of grace which he has instituted in his Church!

For, what horrible blasphemies are uttered against

(24) Matt. xxvii., 25.

the holy Sacrifice of the Mass, and the Sacrament of the Blessed Eucharist! Christ, the Eternal Truth, declares: "The bread that I will give *is my flesh*;"[43] "Take ye, and eat: this *is my body*....Drink ye all of this: for this *is my blood*."[44] But, instead of believing, they deny his word: for, whilst *He* declares it *is* his body and blood; *they*, setting their own private judgment above every other rule, declare it *is not*.

But, not content with merely denying this truth, they make it the subject of ridicule, sarcasm, and abuse. Other truths are blasphemed in a similar manner. Indeed, there is scarcely one doctrine of the true Church of Christ, which is not misrepresented, abused, reviled, and scoffed at! How literally do they fulfil the prophecy of St. Peter: "There shall be among you lying teachers, who shall bring in sects of perdition......And many shall follow their riotousness, *through whom the way of truth shall be evil spoken of*. .....They fear not to bring in sects, *blaspheming*...... But these men,......*blaspheming those things which they know not*, shall perish (he says) in their corruption."[45]

3. What are *profane words?* They are such words as "*the devil*"—"*devilish*"—"*hell*"—"*hellish*," &c., introduced into common conversation. This is an irreligious way of speaking—it is unbecoming a Christian, and gives disedification to others: "Let no evil speech proceed from your mouth; but that which is good to the edification of faith, that it may administer grace to the hearers."[46]

(43) John vi., 52.
(44) Matt. xxvi., 26, 27, 28.
(45) 2 Pet. ii. 1, 2, 10, 12.
(46) Eph. iv., 29.

INSTRUCTION XXXII.

THIRD COMMANDMENT.

Its Obligation transferred from Saturday to Sunday—its Design—its Importance—the Duties it requires from us.

What is the Third Commandment?—"Remember that thou keep holy the Sabbath Day."

What are we commanded by the Third Commandment?—By the Third Commandment we are commanded to spend the Sunday in prayer and other religious duties.

What do you mean by religious duties?—Hearing Mass, going to the Sacraments, and reading good books.

What is forbidden by this Commandment?—The Third Commandment forbids all unnecessary servile work and sinful profanation of the Lord's day.

The Third Commandment is: "Remember that thou keep holy the Sabbath-day. Six days shalt thou labour and do all thy work; but on the Seventh day is the Sabbath of the Lord thy God: thou shalt do no work on it; thou, nor thy son, nor thy daughter, nor thy man-servant, nor thy maid-servant, nor thy beast, nor the stranger that is within thy gates. For in six days the Lord made heaven and earth, and the sea, and all things that are in them; and rested on the Seventh day; therefore the Lord blessed the Seventh day, and sanctified it."[47]

I. The Sabbath Day:—What day of the week is the *Seventh* or *Sabbath*-day? It is *Saturday*. Then why do we not keep Saturday holy? Because the Church, in the Apostles' time, transferred the obligation from the Seventh to the *First* day of the week. ——Why was this done? In honour of Jesus Christ: and therefore the first day of the week is called "*The Lord's day.*"[48]

(47) Exod. xx., 8 to 11. (48) Apoc. i., 10.

It was on the First day of the week (or Sunday), that Christ rose from the dead—that he commissioned his Apostles to teach all nations—that he empowered them to forgive sins—that he sent down upon them the Holy Ghost—it was on this day that the Apostles began to preach the doctrines of Christ, and to establish the Christian Religion.——Protestants profess to learn the whole of their religion from the Bible; but where does the Bible tell them that the *obligation* of the Sabbath is transferred from the Seventh to the First day of the week?

II. DESIGN OF THIS COMMANDMENT:—What is the object or *Design* of the Third Commandment? It is this: To determine, by a positive precept, what particular portion of our time shall be dedicated *specially and immmediately* to God; instead of leaving it to the mere natural law, which, without such precept, requires that we should set apart *some* portion of our time for his immediate service.

To understand this more clearly, it should be observed, that man's actions are of two kinds: 1*st*, Those which immediately and specially regard the service of God, and the care of our soul—and, 2*ndly*, Those which regard worldly affairs and the care of the body. Now, as the *soul and eternity* are of far more importance, than the body and the mere temporal pursuits; so is the service of God of much greater consequence, than the seeking of earthly possessions. ——*All* our time belongs to God; yet he is satisfied, if a portion of it only be devoted *immediately*, and *in a special manner*, to his service. But, if it were left to ourselves to choose this particular portion of time, we should be too apt to neglect it, by giving to earthly cares *that time* which ought to be given specially to God. Therefore, in order to prevent such neglect, God has specified and fixed, by a positive command, the time which he requires to be thus given to him,

Such is the object and design of the Third Commandment.

III. IMPORTANCE OF THIS COMMANDMENT:—The *importance* of this precept, and the *strictness* of its obligations, are indicated by the word "*Remember*;" by the *great blesssings* promised to those that keep the Sabbath—and by the *severe punishments* denounced against them that shall dare to trangress it: "Thus saith the Lord: Blessed is the man that respecteth the Sabbath from profaning it......They that keep my Sabbaths, I will give them an everlasting name that shall never perish:......I will make them joyful in my house of prayer;......and their victims shall please me upon my altars."[49]——"Keep my Sabbath.......He that shall profane it, shall be put to death."[50]

IV. THE DUTIES IT REQUIRES:—The observance of this Commandment requires of us two things: 1*st*, That we should rest from unnecessary servile work; and 2*ndly*, That we should spend the time in such exercises, as may be said to sanctify the day.

1. As to *resting:* All such works are forbidden, as are *servile;* i.e., such kinds of bodily works, as are commonly done by servants, mechanics, tradesmen, &c., for gaining a livelihood.——Is it never lawful to do such works as these? Yes; when they are really necessary: as *to provide food for the day:* "Doth not every one of you, on the Sabbath-day, loose his Ox or his Ass from the manger, and lead them to water?"[51] *To attend the sick:* "Love is the fulfilment of the law."[52]——But nothing should be done on the Sunday which can be done beforehand, or deferred till another day.

2. But, when we are commanded to *rest* from servile works on the Sunday, we are not to imagine

(49) Is. lvi., 1 to 7.
(50) Exod. xxxi., 14.
(51) Luke xiii., 15.
(52) Rom. xiii., 10.

that we may spend the day *in idleness;* nor should we consider it sufficient, merely to hear Mass. We are commanded to keep holy *the day;* "Remember that thou keep holy the Sabbath-*day.*"

To *hear Mass* is what the Church, by a positive precept, *obliges* us all to do. If we absent ourselves from Mass on Sundays, without any necessity, we become guilty of mortal sin; and if we are *wilfully* absent, or *wilfully* distracted, during *any part* of it, we render ourselves guilty of sin more or less. If any person be hindered by necessity, or some sufficient cause, from attending, he does not sin by not hearing Mass; but he should not neglect to pray at home.—It is with good reason, that the Church obliges all her children to be present at this holy Sacrifice; because hearing Mass is the best means we have of sanctifying the Sunday.

THE VESPERS, or *Afternoon-Service*, should also be attended; unless persons be excused, by great distance, or by some other great inconvenience; and, in these cases, they should say prayers at home. But such persons as live near, and yet are in the habit of neglecting on the Sunday-afternoons, what can be thought of them, except that they are slothful,.....or indifferent....? Are they not of the number of those of whom God says: "I know thy works, that thou art neither cold nor hot; I would that thou wert either cold or hot; but, because thou art lukewarm, and neither cold nor hot, I will begin to vomit thee out of my mouth"[53] It is by serving God diligently and devoutly on Sundays, that you draw down a store of graces for the rest of the week.

Salvation is your most important affair—the *only* affair of *real* importance: unless you succeed in it, you must be miserable for ever. But can you expect to succeed in it, without taking the necessary pains?

(53) Apoc. iii., 15, 16.

If you only hear Mass on the Sunday morning, can you say you have consecrated *the day* to God's service? St. Gregory says: "We rest from worldly employments in order to pray." St. Peter Damian also says: "He only celebrates the Sabbath *properly*, who so rests from worldly occupations as to *spend the time in* SPIRITUAL OCCUPATIONS." The Council of Tours, and of Aix-la-Chapelle teach, that, besides hearing Mass, we are to spend *the day* in serving God: this, at least, is the *spirit* of the Commandment.

For, though the Afternoon-Service is not expressly and explicitly commanded, does not *the spirit* of the law require it? Is not this the proper means of sanctifying the *second part* of the day, as hearing Mass is the means of sanctifying the *first part?* The Church does not indeed *command*, but she strenuously *exhorts* all her children to attend at her public Services. The Catechism of the Council of Trent, enumerating what religious duties are to be done on Sundays and Holidays, gives these heads: 1, "*To assist at Mass*"—2, "*To frequent the Sacraments*"—3, "*To confess one's sins*"—4, "*To receive the Holy Eucharist*"—5, "*To hear Sermons*"—6, (Besides the works of piety already mentioned,) "*To supplicate and praise God;*" (or, as the same Catechism explains it: "*The Faithful ought also to be diligent in attending to other prayers and Divine praises;*")—and, 7, "*To be present at the Catechetical Instructions.*"[54*]——They who are negligent in this point must answer for the effects of their example on others. Such persons should consider the example of the first Christians, who not only spent the first day of the week in God's service, but attended the

(54) * "*Agenda diebus Festis:* Missæ interesse; —Sacramenta frequentare; Peccata confiteri; Eucharistiam percipere; Conciones audire; Orare Deum et laudare (Exercitatio item, atque studium Fidelium in precibus divinisque laudibus frequens esse debet); Catechismis interesse." *Cat. Conc. Trid*, *part.* 3, *cap.* 4, *De Tertio PræceptoDecal. n.* 35.

public Prayers *every day*, spending therein a great part of the day; for the services of the Church were much longer in those days. Absence was looked upon *by them* as great negligence.

Remember, that *public* prayers, offered *in the name of the Church*, and by *the Ministers* of the Church, are more effectual, than mere private devotions. Go, then, and unite *your* voice with the rest of the Faithful, and with the whole Church. Let not trifling inconveniencies hinder you from doing so.

You should also spend *some* time in *reading and reflecting* on the great truths of Religion; such as Death, Eternity, &c., &c.

An exercise of piety very proper for sanctifying the Sundays, is to prepare for and receive the Holy Sacraments. Almighty God says: "You shall afflict your souls on that day;"[55] i.e., you shall examine your consciences—lament your sins—and take the means of obtaining pardon, and of persevering afterwards in grace.

[*What is here said with reference to Sundays, applies equally to Days of Obligation.*]

INSTRUCTION XXXIII.

FOURTH COMMANDMENT.

The Obligation of Children to be dutiful to their Parents—the Duties which this Obligation requires from them.

What is the Fourth Commandment?—"Honour thy Father and thy Mother."

What are we commanded by the Fourth Commandment?—By the Fourth Commandment we are commanded to love, honour, and obey our parents in all that is not sin.

Are we commanded to obey only our father and mother?—

(55) Levit. xxiii., 28.

We are commanded to obey not only our father and mother, but also our bishops, pastors, magistrates, and masters.

What is forbidden by the Fourth Commandment?—The Fourth Commandment forbids all contempt, stubbornness, and disobedience to our lawful superiors.

The Fourth Commandment is: "Honour thy father and thy mother, that thou mayest be long-lived upon the land which the Lord thy God will give thee."[56]

This Commandment teaches the mutual duties of Children towards their Parents, and of Parents towards their Children; and also the duties of all inferiors towards their superiors, and of superiors towards their inferiors.

1. The Obligation of Children to be dutiful to their Parents:—Are Children *obliged* to honour and obey their Parents? Yes, they are. Whence arises this obligation? It arises,

First, From the positive Law of God—from his express command; and, therefore, obedience to Parents is obedience to God.

Secondly, From the natural law, which is also very clear on this point.

Thirdly, From gratitude towards Parents; for what labours, inconveniences, anxieties, and sufferings do not Parents undergo for their Children.

Fourthly, From necessity; for dutifulness to parents is a necessary means not only of obtaining the blessings promised by God to dutiful Children, but also of escaping the judgments denounced against those who are undutiful. Almighty God promises, saying: "He that honoureth his mother is as one that layeth up a treasure: he that honoureth his father shall have joy in his own children, and in the day of his prayer he shall be heard."[57] But, on the other hand, he says

(56) Exod. xx. 12 (57) Eccli. iii., 5, 6

"Cursed be he that honoureth not his father and mother."[58] "Children, (says St. Paul) obey your parents in the Lord, for this is just. *Honour thy Father and thy Mother;* which is the first commandment with a promise: *that it may be well with thee, and that thou mayest be long-lived upon earth.*"[59]

II. THE DUTIES WHICH CHILDREN OWE TO THEIR PARENTS:—Children, then, are under, a strict obligation of being dutiful to their parents; but, what are the *particular duties* which this obligation requires from them? They are these: *To love their Parents —to honour them and to obey them.*

1. We must LOVE our Parents:—We are commanded to love *all* persons; how much more, then, our Parents? We are bound to love God, as our Creator, from whom we have received our being—as our constant Protector by whom we are preserved from evils, and as our bountiful provider from whom we derive all that we have. Now, in all these characters, our parents represent God in our regard; and consequently, we should love them most after God. We are bound to love our parents *sincerely*—with real affection, wishing them well from our hearts.——If our love be of this character, it will show itself outwardly in our words and actions, and in our whole conduct towards them; it will lead us to pray for them, and it will make us ready, on all accasions, to assist them in their necessities, both corporal and spiritual.

To act contrary to this love is grievously sinful. Of this sin we become guilty.

First, If we entertain feelings of hatred or dislike towards our Parents. It is a sin to hate *any one;* how much more, then, to hate our Parents?

Secondly, If we show this dislike by curses, or any

(58) Deut. xxvii., 16. (59) Eph. vi., 1, 2, 2.

other injurious language; which increases the guilt. Against such as treat their Parents in this manner, God pronounces the severest judgments: "He that curseth his Father and Mother, his lamp shall be put out in the midst of darkness; i.e., he shall die in his sins."[60]

Thirdly, If we strike them; which makes the matter still worse. He is a most unnatural child, who lifts up his hand against them who gave him birth.

Fourthly, If we refuse or neglect to relieve them in their necessities, it is a proof that there is a want, not only of love but also of gratitude.

2. We must HONOUR and respect our Parents:—We should have, and should cherish, a heartfelt esteem for them; and we must not allow their condition in life to interfere with this duty: for, whatever may be their poverty or infirmities, they are still our Parents; and, therefore, demand our honour and respect. And, as our *love* should show itself in our outward conduct, so likewise should the *respect* which we owe them: for we should honour them in our words, and in our behaviour towards them; and we should take every opportunity of showing our respect.

III. WE SIN AGAINST THIS DUTY OF HONOURING OUR PARENTS:—

First, If we reproach or mock them, or give them any kind of ill language.

Secondly, If we speak to them in a hasty, harsh, or passionate manner; or if we give them short and sharp answers, or contradict them in an abrupt manner; vexing and irritating them by such undutiful behaviour, especially in the presence of others.

Thirdly, If we make known their weaknesses and defects, instead of concealing them; or if, in any way, we expose them to contempt or ridicule.

(60) Prov. xx., 20.

Fourthly, If we refuse to consult them in affairs of great importance.

3. We must obey our parents:—This is a duty which God *strictly* commands; and the observance of it is very pleasing to him: "Children, obey your parents in all things, for this is well pleasing to the Lord."[61]

In order to comply with this duty of obedience to Parents,

First, We must do what they command; and avoid what they forbid.

Secondly, We must do this readily and in a pleasant manner, without seeking needless excuses or delays; without murmuring or disputing the point; without showing opposition or stubbornness: for all such resistance is opposed to that dutiful obedience which Children owe to their Parents.

Thirdly, We must also receive correction from them *patiently*, and with filial submission; acknowledging our fault, asking pardon, and promising amendment.

Fourthly, When Children are sent to school, they should consider their Teachers as holding the place of Parents in their regard; and, consequently, they should treat their Teachers with respect; obeying them as they would their Parents. They should strive to learn: and avoid giving unnecessary trouble. They should receive correction at school, with the same submission as they should receive it from their Parents.

If Children would duly comply with all these duties towards Parents, as the Fourth Commandment requires, what a happiness it would be for both! how pleasing it would be to God! and how meritorious in his sight!

(61) Coloss. iii., 20.

INSTRUCTION XXXIV.

FOURTH COMMANDMENT CONTINUED.

Duties of Parents towards their Children.

What is the Fourth Commandment?—"Honour thy father and thy mother."

What are we commanded by the Fourth Commandment?—By the Fourth Commandment we are commanded to love, honour, and obey our parents in all that is not sin.

And what is the duty of Parents and other Superiors?—To take proper care of all under their charge, and to bring their children up in the fear of God.

The Fourth Commandment not only requires children to be dutiful to their Parents (as was explained in the last Instruction), but it also requires *Parents* to discharge the duties which *they owe* towards their children.

Of these duties, some regard the *body* and the *temporal welfare* of their children. About these, Parents are generally too solicitous: so that it is unnecessary to enforce them. But there are others which regard their children's *soul*, and their *eternal welfare* These are of the strictest obligation, and of the utmost consequence: the happiness of Parents and of their children, both here and hereafter, depends very much upon them; and therefore Parents should be careful both to learn what those duties are, and also to discharge them faithfully.

I. LOVE:—The first thing which Parents should attend to, is, *to regulate aright their* LOVE for their children: very much depends upon this. Their natural love for their children too often degenerates into a passionate fondness, which is ruinous both to Parent and child.

How many Parents know whether they are *too fond* of their children? They may know it by these signs:—

1. If they are blind to their children's faults, and displeased when told of them: this is a pretty sure sign that they are too fond of their children;—

2. If they cannot bear to hear them cry; and so cannot use proper correction, nor refuse what they ask, lest they should cry:—

3. If, in consequence of thus neglecting correction, they have allowed them to become headstrong; so that, instead of having proper authority over their children, the children have authority over them: not bearing to be denied anything which they want, they *must* have their own will; and they manage to have it, by *forcing* their fond Parent to yield;—

4. If they allow their children to be guilty of great rudeness in their presence; and overlook in their own, what they condemn in other children.

These are signs that Parents are *too fond* of their children.

THE CONSEQUENCES of this over-fondness are most ruinous:—For, 1*st*, It makes children obstinate and stubborn—they soon get to such a state that they must and will have their own way; 2*ndly*, It renders it difficult to send them to school; and, when they are there, they will not receive correction; for, when correction is attempted, they become obstinate, refuse to learn, and, when asked a question, will not speak; 3*rdly*, But, the most lamentable consequence of all is, that their vices and passions become ungovernable; so that they grow up in habits of sin.

Therefore, Parents MUST *regulate* their natural love of their children. But how are they to do it: by what rule? They are to regulate it by a supernatural love—by the love of charity—by that love which Religion teaches.——Now.

Religion teaches parents to love their children's *souls* more than their *bodies*—to be more solicitous for their *eternal*, than for their *temporal*, welfare. Consequently, knowing that their children are *commanded*, under pain of sin, *to obey;* they will, if actuated by a true Christian love for them, MAKE *them obey:* it is the duty of parents to do so, and a very important duty.

II. RULES TO BE OBSERVED BY PARENTS:—In order to act in accordance with that love which Religion teaches, what rules should Parents follow, in the treatment of their children?—

1. They must have every order obeyed, cry or not cry: and in this they must be *firm* and *persevering*. Thus they will teach their children proper obedience.

2. When they see a child impatient to have any particular thing, they should mortify that impatience. Thus they will teach their children to be submissive, instead of self-willed.

3. When they give a child anything, they should require to be thanked for it, as for a favour. Thus they will teach their children filial love and gratitude.

4. When any one of their children does what is evil, Parents should never laugh at it, but always show displeasure. Thus they will teach them a general horror of sin, and a love of virtue.

5. They must correct their children, whenever circumstances require it. But, in doing this, they should try the easiest and mildest means first; for instance, they should show their displeasure, advise, threaten, and, if all this be not sufficient, then they should inflict some kind of chastisement. But they should first take the child aside, and show *the evil* that has been done, and *why* the punishment is inflicted. When children do evil, Parents should never allow it to pass, without some kind of correction: "Bow down his neck, while he is young; and beat his sides

while he is a child: lest he grow stubborn, and regard thee not; and so be a sorrow of heart to thee."[62]——Correction ought never to be given in a passion; nor harshly, which breaks a child's spirit.——When one Parent is correcting a child, the other should never interfere, by excusing the child, or blaming the correction.

III. Other Duties of Parents:—Besides the duties already explained, there are also others which are of a most important character, and of serious obligation; and for the neglecting of which, Parents will have much to answer for. And they are these: To instruct their children—to give them good example—to watch over them—to pray for them.

1. Parents must INSTRUCT their children: "Hast thou children? Instruct them, and bow down their neck from their childhood."[63] They should teach them their Prayers and Catechism—how to hear Mass, and how to prepare for Confession and Communion—to love God, and, for his sake, to love virtue, and hate sin. The Mother of St. Louis the Ninth used to say to him: "Though I love you most tenderly; yet, my son, I would rather see you dead before me, than guilty of a mortal sin!"——Parents are obliged to prepare their children for the instructions of their Pastor; and to *send them* to him, at the appointed times.

2. Parents must set their children GOOD EXAMPLE: The best instructions are but of little use, if they who give them set bad examples. Children have a natural tendency to follow example, especially that of their Parents. (*Example:* the descendants of Cain were wicked like himself; whilst those of Seth were good.)——The experience of all past ages shows the importance and necessity of good example in Parents.

(62) Eccl. xxx., 12. (63) Eccl. vii., 5

3. Parents must watch over their children, as the shepherd does over a young flock: They must see that they perform their Christian duties—they must keep them from evil—from bad company—and from all other occasions of sin—they must not allow them to run out at nights where they please, but keep them in.

4. Parents may PRAY FOR THEIR CHILDREN, in order to draw down upon them the Divine blessing: For, "unless the Lord build the house, they labour in vain that build it: unless the Lord keep the city, he watcheth in vain that keepeth it."[64] As Job offered sacrifices daily for his children;[65] so should all Parents let them share in their daily prayers; and whenever they assist at Mass, they should then especially commend them to God, imploring for them his grace and protection.

If parents would but faithfully discharge all these duties towards their children, the world would soon become very different from what it is at present. Instead of being overrun with vice, as it is, it would soon become a world of saints!

INSTRUCTION XXXV.

FOURTH COMMANDMENT CONCLUDED.

The Duties of Servants and Masters towards each other—of Subjects towards the Civil Power—and of the People towards their Pastors.

What is the Fourth Commandment?—"Honour thy father and thy mother."

What are we commanded by the Fourth Commandment?—By the Fourth Commandment we are commanded to love, honour, and obey our Parents in all that is not sin.

(64) Ps. cxxvi, 1. (65) Job i. v.

Are we commanded to obey only our Father and Mother?—We are commanded to obey not only our Father and Mother, but also our Bishops, Pastors, Magistrates, and Masters.

What is forbidden by the Fourth Commandment?—The Fourth Commandment forbids all contempt, stubbornness, and disobedience to our lawful superiors.

And what is the duty of Parents and other Superiors?—To take proper care of all under their charge, and to bring their children up in the fear of God.

Is it the duty of the Faithful to contribute according to each one's ability, towards the support of their Pastors?—Yes; for it is just, and agreeable to the spirit of the Old and New Testament, and to the practice of the Christian Church, that the Faithful should contribute to the temporal support of those, from whose ministry they receive spiritual blessings.—*See* 1 Cor. ix.

The Fourth Commandment obliges children to be dutiful to their Parents; and it requires Parents to take proper care of their children, by a due discharge of those important duties which they owe towards them: so far this Commandment has been explained.

I will now proceed to explain the duties of Servants and Masters towards each other—of Subjects towards the Civil Power—and of the Faithful towards their Pastors.

1. What, then, are THE DUTIES OF SERVANTS TOWARDS THEIR MASTERS?—

1. They must be *just* and *faithful* to them:—The Master entrusts his goods and works to the care of his Servants; now, they are unfaithful to his trust, and become guilty before God, 1*st*, If they wrong their Master in his goods, by taking them for their own use, or by giving them to others, or by carelessly injuring, waisting, or destroying them—2*ndly*, If they suffer others to do so, without taking such means, as are in their power, to prevent them. For, the duty of *fide*

lity obliges them to protect their Master from these injustices, when they can; either by telling him, or by admonishing the delinquent, or in such other way as prudence shall suggest—*3rdly*, If they neglect their work; or do it in a bad or insufficient manner; or if they idle away the time for which they are paid; or if they encourage others to do these things.

2. They must be *obedient* to their Masters:—"Servants, be obedient to them that are your Masters,...... not serving to the eye, as it were pleasing men; but doing the will of God from the heart;"[66] and "not gainsaying."[67]

3. They must show *respect* to their Masters:—"Whosoever are servants under the yoke, let them count their Masters worthy of all honour; lest the name of the Lord, and his doctrine, be blasphemed."[68] They should show this respect in their conduct, with reference to their Master, whether he be present or absent. They should not expose his faults, as many do; nor betray family secrets, as they so often do, when they get into a new situation.

As regards *fellow-servants*, besides these duties which they owe towards their Masters, there are certain mutual duties which they owe towards each other. For, they should strive to live together in peace and good-will; and therefore they should never say or do anything that would breed discord or misunderstanding between each other, or between them and their Master: "The tale-bearer shall defile his own soul, and shall be hated by all."[69] "Refrain from strife, and thou shalt diminish thy sins."[70] It would contribute much to this peace and good-will, if fellow-servants would be always ready to assist one another in what they have to do: for how frequently does the want

(66) Eph. vi., 5, 6. (67) Tit. ii., 9. (68) 1 Tim. vi., 1. (69) Eccli. xxi., 31. (70) Eccli. xxviii. 10.

of this cause quarrels and disputes amongst them? "Bear ye one another's burdens; and so you shall fulfil the law of Christ."[71]

II. What are THE DUTIES OF MASTERS TOWARDS THEIR SERVANTS?

1. Masters should consider that their authority *comes from God*. "For there is no power but from God."[72]—They should take care, therefore, how they use their authority; because they will have to render a strict account of it, immediately after death.

2. They should consider, that, like their servants, *they* are also *servants of God*:—"Both you and they have a Master in heaven; and there is no respect of persons with Him."[73] Hence, considering themselves as *fellow-servants* of God, they should act towards their servants with humility and brotherly love: "The princes of the Gentiles lord it over them;......it shall not be so among you."[74]

3. They should act towards them with *mildness and fellow-feeling*:—"Be not as a lion in thy house, *terrifying* them of thy household, and *oppressing* them that are under thee."[75] How generally is this divine admonition disregarded!

4. They should treat their servants *with justice*:—"Masters, do to your servants that which is just and equal, knowing that *you also* have a Master in heaven."[76]

5. They should behave towards them *with gratitude*:—"If thou hast a faithful servant, let him be to thee as thy own soul; treat him as a brother."[77]

6. They should *allow them time*, on Sundays and Holidays, for the service of God—for assisting at Mass, for receiving the Sacraments, and for getting instructed. Masters should bear in mind, that God has a prior

(71) Gal. vi., 2.
(72) Rom. xiii., 1.
(73) Eph. vi., 9.
(74) Matt. xx., 25, 26.
(75) Eccli. iv., 35.
(76) Col. iv., 1.
(77) Eccli. xxxiii., 31.

right to man's service, on the days dedicated to him; and, consequently, that to deprive their servants of time for the Divine Service on those days, is to deprive God of his right.

7. They should *look to the conduct* of their servants; taking care not to expose them to occasions of sin; and endeavouring to make them do their duty; and for this purpose, they should *set them good example:* "If any man have not care of his own, and especially those of his house, he hath denied the faith, and is become worse than an infidel."[78]

III. What are THE DUTIES OF SUBJECTS TOWARDS THE LAWS AND NATIONAL RULERS?

They are *Respect* and *Obedience.* We must show respect and submission toward those, whom the country has placed in authority over us; and we must respect and obey the laws of the land, unless we are commanded what is sinful: "Let every soul be subject to the higher powers: for there is no power but from God; and those that are, are ordained by God. Therefore, he that resisteth the power, resisteth the ordinance of God. And they that resist, purchase to themselves damnation."[79]

IV. What are THE DUTIES OF THE FAITHFUL TOWARDS THEIR PASTORS?

1. To honour and respect their Pastors as "the Ministers of Christ, and the dispensers of the mysteries of God:"[80] "With all thy soul fear God, and reverence his priests."[81] "He that despiseth you, despiseth me."[82]

2. To obey them in spiritual matters: "He that heareth you, heareth me."[83] "Obey your Prelates, and be subject to them. For they watch as being to

(78) 1 Tim. v., 8. (80) 1 Cor. iv., 1. (82) Luke x., 16.
(79) Rom. xiii., 1, 2. (81) Eccli. vii., 31. (83) Luke x., 16.

render an account of your souls: that they may do this with joy and not with grief."[84]

3. To *contribute to their temporal support*: "For (as the Catechism teaches), it is just, and agreeable to the spirit of the Old and New Testament, and to the practice of the Christian Church, that the Faithful should contribute to the temporal support of those, from whose ministry they receive spiritual blessings.

First, That it is JUST, is evident, when we consider what a Pastor is. He is one chosen by Divine Providence to attend to the immediate service of God, and to the care of souls committed to him. His duties are *many* and *weighty*, and *of great* RESPONSIBILITY: He has to offer prayers for them daily, and Sacrifice frequently, to administer the Sacraments to his people, and to instruct them diligently, to console the afflicted, to attend the sick (frequently at the hazard of his life), to be ready at all times, night or day, to answer the calls of his flock: and, that he may have no earthly cares to draw him off from these duties, he is forbidden to marry, or to engage in worldly business.

Now, when a person thus dedicates himself to the special service of the people, *how is he to live? to whom* must he look for support? Is it not "just, that the Faithful should contribute to the temporal support of those, from whose ministry they receive spiritual blessings," and who dedicate their whole lives to their spiritual good? "Let him that is instructed in the Word, communicate to him that instructeth him, in all good things."[85] For Christ says on this subject: "The labourer is worthy of his hire."[86]

Secondly, That it is, "*agreeable to the spirit of the* OLD *Testament*," is evident from the fact of God having chosen the tribe of Levi for the work of the ministry, and expressly commanded the other tribes to

(84) Heb. xiii., 17. (85) Gal. vi., 6. (86) Luke x., 7.

maintain them. And on this account, in the division of the promised land, *no share* was given to the tribe of Levi.

Thirdly, That it is "*agreeable to the spirit of the* NEW *Testament*" also, as well as of the *Old*, is evident from the 9th Chapter of the 1st Epistle of St. Paul to the Corinthians, wherein that Apostle strongly enforces this duty on the Faithful.

As a great part of that Chapter is on this subject, I will quote it to you:—

1 CORINTHIANS, CHAPTER IX.

"1. Am not I an Apostle? Are not you my work in the Lord?...

4. Have we not power to eat and drink?...

7. Who serveth as a soldier at any time, at his own charges? Who planteth a vineyard, and eateth not of the fruit thereof? Who feedeth the flock, and eateth not of the milk of the flock?

8. Speak I these things according to man? Or doth not the law also say these things?

9. For it is written in the law of Moses: *Thou shalt not muzzle the mouth of the ox that treadeth out the corn.* Doth God take care for oxen?

10. Or doth he say this indeed for our sakes? For these things are written for our sakes: that he that plougheth, should plough in hope; and he that thrasheth, in hope to receive fruit.

11. If we have sown unto you spiritual things, it is a great matter if we reap you carnal things?

12. If others be partakers of this power over you, why not we rather? Nevertheless we have not used this power: but we bear all things, lest we should give any hinderance to the Gospel of Christ.

13. Know you not, that they who work in the holy place, eat the things that are of the holy place; and they that serve the altar, partake with the altar?

14. So also the Lord ordained, that they that preach the Gospel, should live by the Gospel.

15. But I have used none of these things. Neither have I written these things, that they should be so done unto me: for it is good for me to die, rather than that any man should make my glory void.

16. For if I preach the Gospel, it is no glory to me; for a necessity lieth upon me: for woe is unto me if I preach not the Gospel."

This is a very unpleasant subject for a Pastor to give instructions upon to his own flock. But his office, as a Pastor, requires him to teach them *all* their Christian duties, so as not to leave them ignorant of any of them, through his own fault. Whether they practise them or not, after having been taught them, is a matter for self-examination which rests between their consciences and God.

INSTRUCTION XXXVI.

FIFTH COMMANDMENT.

Murder—Quarrelling—Anger, Revenge, Envy, and Hatred—giving Scandal, and bad Example.

What is the Fifth Commandment?—"Thou shall not kill."

What is forbidden by the Fifth Commandment?—The Fifth Commandment forbids all wilful murder, hatred, and revenge.

Does it forbid striking?—Yes; as also anger, quarrelling, and injurious words.

What else?—Giving scandal, and bad example.

The fifth Commandment is: "Thou shalt not kill;" and its general *design* is this: to direct us in what regards the preservation and protection of our own and neighbour's life and person, both as to soul and body.

It forbids all actions that may have any (even remote) tendency to *destroy* life unjustly; and even the affections of the soul that have such a tendency: "You have heard that it was said to them of old: Thou shalt not kill; and whosoever shall kill shall be in danger of the judgment: But *I* say to you, that whosoever is ANGRY with his brother, shall be in danger of the judgment."[87] *Anger*, therefore, and *murder*, and all the *intermediate degrees* between them, are forbidden.

I. MURDER is a most grievous crime!! it is one of the four sins that cry to heaven for vengeance: "Cain rose up against his brother Abel and slew him. And the Lord said to Cain: what hast thou done? *The voice of thy brother's blood crieth to me from the earth.*"[88] The crime of the murderer haunts him day and night—his conscience cannot rest—at all times he seems to hear God saying to him: "What hast thou done? I will require of thee blood for blood, life for life, and soul for soul."[89]——Some murders are more heinous than others; as, for instance, killing those who are consecrated to God, or who are the near relatives of the murderer. When persons wilfully cause a miscarriage, they are guilty of a real murder, and one of the worst kind, because it is the murder of their own child, as to its *soul* as well as its body!——We may lawfully defend ourselves, if unjustly attacked; and we are not obliged to suffer ourselves to be killed in order to spare the life of an unjust aggressor.——Suicide, or self-murder, is also forbidden by this Commandment; for it says simply: "Thou shalt not *kill.*" God only has the power of life and death. How awful it is, to go before the judgment-seat of God uncalled for, as the suicide does!

II. *Uncharitable disputes — contentions—strifes—*

(87) Matt. v., 21, 22. (89) *See* Exod. xxi., 23; *and* Ezech. xxxiii., 6, 8.
(88) Gen. iv., 8, 9, 10.

quarrelling—fighting, and the like, are forbidden by the Fifth Commandment.

Why are these forbidden? 1*st*, Because they *tend* towards murder: "Injurious words go before blood."[90] "A hasty contention kindleth a fire; and a hasty quarrel sheddeth blood."[91]—2*ndly*, Because they are injurious to the *person* of his neighbour, by afflicting either his mind or his body.—3*rdly*, Because they are opposed to fraternal charity: "The works of the flesh are manifest, which are...enmities, contentions, wraths, quarrels, dissensions;...of which I foretell you, that they who do such things shall not obtain the kingdom of God."[92]

III. *Anger—Revenge—Envy—and Hatred* are also strictly forbidden.

1. What is *Anger?* It is a feeling of displeasure on account of some real or supposed injury, with some desire of punishing the offender. This is not always sinful: for, there is *just* as well as *unjust* anger. Anger is *just* when the cause of it is just; when the feeling is moderate, and subjected to reason; and when the desire of punishment is proportioned to the offence, and not from a spirit of revenge. This is rather a *zeal* than anger; as in a Parent, correcting his child for having done evil; "Be angry and sin not."[93] Anger is *unjust*, when any one of the above-mentioned conditions is wanting. Then it very soon degenerates into revenge.

2. What is *Revenge?* It is rendering evil for evil, or desiring to do so. This is a sin against Charity, which, as St. Paul says, "is not provoked to anger;" but "is patient, and beareth all things, endureth all things."[94] Revenge is quite contrary to the virtue of Christian patience, and to the precept of returning good for evil.[95]

(90) Eccl. xxii., 30.
(91) Eccli. xxviii., 13.
(92) Gal. v., 19, 20, 21.
(93) Ps. iv., 5.
(94) 1 Cor. xiii., 4, 5.
(95) Rom. xii., 19, 20, 21; 1 Pet. iii., 9.

3. What is *Envy?* It is a repining or uneasiness at another's good, as lessening one's own. This is likewise opposed to Charity, which "is kind and envieth not."[96] St. Paul says: "Rejoice with them that rejoice, and weep with them that weep."[97] But envy leads a man to do quite the contrary; and it even renders his disposition conformable to that of the devil, who, through envy, grieves at our happiness, and rejoices at our misery.

4. What is *Hatred?* It is a feeling of mind which is the very opposite to love; and, therefore, it is a direct breach of that great Commandment which requires us to love every neighbour as ourselves. Hatred is a state of mind most displeasing to God; and most gloomy and miserable to the sinner.

IV. *Giving scandal, or bad example*, is also forbidden by the Fifth Commandment; being destructive, not indeed of the body, but of the soul of our neighbour. Scandal is any word or action, which, being in itself evil, or having the appearance of evil, is the occasion of sin to others.—There are three kinds of scandal:—

1. There is what is called *malicious* scandal; or, doing what is in itself evil, either with the *intention* of causing sin, or when the person *knows* or *ought to know*, that it will cause it, or that it is calculated to cause it; as, giving bad example to inferiors—enticing others to sin—ridiculing virtue—advising or encouraging what is sinful—flattering others for doing evil—or uttering immodest words. "Woe to the world, because of scandals. For it must needs be that scandals come; but nevertheless, woe to that man by whom the scandal cometh."[98] "He that shall scandalize one of these little ones that believe in me, it were better for him that a mill-stone should be hanged about his neck, and that he should be drowned in the

(96) 1 Cor. xiii., 4. (97) Rom. xii. 15. (98) Matt. xviii., 6, 7.

depth of the sea."[98]——The company of scandalizing sinners should be shunned as much as possible; for "evil communications corrupt good manners."[99]

2. There is likewise what is called the scandal of *weak brethren*; or, doing what has *only the appearance* of evil, from which ignorant or weak persons take occasion of sin: as, for instance, when a person, who is lawfully dispensed with from the law of abstinence, eats meat on a forbidden day in the presence of others, forseeing, or having reason to believe, that they will take scandal at it. The doing of this and of such like things, which are not evil, but merely have an appearance of evil, is not a sin, except when we forsee, or have reason to believe, that scandal will be taken at it; and when circumstances are such as to require us to remove the cause of scandal.

3. There is also a *pharisaical* scandal, or scandal *taken* but not *given*; i.e., when a person, from an evil and malicious disposition, takes scandal, without any reason, at our actions, and even at good actions; putting the worst construction upon them, and attributing them to some bad intention. This is called *pharisaical* scandal, because it is such as the Pharisees took at the words and actions of our Blessed Redeemer. Evidently, this is no sin, except in the persons who *take* the scandal. We are not to avoid doing good, because malicious people choose to take scandal at it.

But, as to real scandal, avoid everything that would *really* give cause to others for being scandalized, and avoid it with the greatest care; because scandal is a very grievous crime, being a spiritual murder: "Woe to that man by whom the scandal cometh." Strive rather to set good example—to lead others to virtue: "Let your light so shine before men, that they, seeing your good works, may glorify your Father who is in heaven."[100]

(99) 1 Cor. xv., 33. (100) Matt. v., 16.

INSTRUCTION XXXVII.

SIXTH AND NINTH COMMANDMENTS.

Chastity commanded—Impurity forbidden—In what this Vice consists—its Remedies.

What is the Sixth Commandment?—"Thou shalt not commit adultery."

What is forbidden by the Sixth Commandment?—The Sixth Commandment forbids all kinds of sins of uncleanness with another's wife or husband

What else?—All other kinds of immodesties, by kisses, touches, looks, words, or actions.

And what ought we to think of immodest plays and comedies?—That they are also forbidden by this Commandment; and it is sinful to be present at them.

What is the Ninth Commandment?—"Thou shalt not covet thy neighbour's wife."

What is forbidden by the Ninth Commandment?—The Ninth Commandment forbids all lustful thoughts and desires, and all wilful pleasures in the irregular motions of the flesh.

The Sixth and Ninth Commandments relate, both of them, to the same object; and they have both the like design: for they both relate to carnal pleasures; and for the purpose of directing us with regard to them. By these two Commandments, impurity is strictly forbidden; and chastity is commanded.

I. *Chastity* is a most amiable virtue: the practice of it makes us rather like Angels, than the fallen children of Adam: it renders us most pleasing in the eyes of God. It was for this virtue, that the Blessed Virgin Mary was chosen to be the Mother of God; and that St. John was beloved by Christ above the rest of the Apostles. Those who have preserved their chastity, are represented, in the Apocalypse, as being most honoured in heaven, by being chosen to be the immediate attendants of our Blessed Saviour: "These are they who are not defiled with women, for they are Virgins; these follow the Lamb whithersoever he goeth."[1]

II. IMPURITY: The amiable virtue of Chastity is sullied, and innocence lost, by every defilement of *impurity*, or of unlawful carnal pleasure. With the exception of what marriage allows, the natural law strictly forbids us to seek or indulge carnal pleasure, in any degree whatever, by immodest thoughts, or desires, or words, or looks, or actions; and whenever we do so *with full deliberation and consent*, it is a mortal sin; as is evident from the declarations of Scripture—from the punishment of this vice—and from its effects on the sinner.

1. *From the declarations of Scripture:*—Our Blessed Redeemer tells us, that "evil thoughts, adulteries, fornications......are the things that *defile* a man."[2] Sins of impurity defile both soul and body. Now, St. Paul says: "Know you not that your members are the temple of the Holy Ghost, who is in you?......... Know you not that you are the temple of God? But if any man *violate* the temple of God, *him shall God destroy.*"[3] "Fornication, and all uncleanness, let it be not so much as named among you, as becometh Saints."[4] Frequently, in Scripture, the Almighty expresses his hatred of these sins, by calling them *detestable things*"—"*abominations:*" "Every soul that shall commit any of these abominations, shall perish from the midst of his people."[5]

2. *From the punishments of this vice:*—The terrible judgments which have been executed upon mankind on account of the vice of impurity, show that it must be very displeasing to God. For, being infinitely *just*, God never inflicts upon any sins more punishment than they deserve; but, being infinitely *merciful*, he may

(1) Apoc. xiv., 4. (3) 1 Cor. vi., 18, 19; & iii. 17. (5) Levit. xviii. 29.
(2) Matt. xv., 19. (4) Eph. v., 3.

inflict much less. Now, he *has* executed the most *severe vengeance* upon this vice. For,

First, When "all flesh had corrupted its way upon the earth," (by yielding to this vice,) "God said: I will destroy man, whom I have created, from the face of the earth; from man even to beasts; for it repenteth me that I have made them."[6] And, in accordance with this terrible threat, he covered the earth with a universal deluge, which destroyed the whole human race, except Noe and his family.[7]

Secondly, When the Inhabitants of Sodom, and of the neighbouring cities, gave themselves up to sins of the flesh, their crimes were so grievous, that the Scripture says *they cried to heaven for vengeance.* And, in his anger, God showered down fire and brimstone from heaven, and destroyed them all, except Lot and his family.[9]

Thirdly, Onan, for defiling the marriage-bed, was struck dead, "because (says the Scripture) he did a detestable thing."[10]

Fourthly, Four-and-twenty thousand of the Israelites were, on one occasion, put to death by God's command, for crimes which they had committed against the Sixth Commandment; i.e., for adultery and fornication.[11]

Fifthly, Sins against this Commandment exclude those who die guilty of them, from the kingdom of heaven; and condemn them to everlasting torments; "The works of the flesh are manifest, which are, fornication, uncleanness, immodesty, luxury;......of the which I foretell you, that they who do such things shall not obtain the kingdom of God."[12] "But (Almighty God declares) the *abominable*...shall have their portion in the pool burning with fire and brimstone, which is the second death."[13]

(6) Gen. vi., 1 to 13. (9) Gen. xix., 24, 25. (12) Gal. v., 19,21.
(7) Gen. vii., 21, 22, 23. (10) Gen. xxxviii., 10. (13) Apoc. xxi., 8
(8) Gen. xviii., 20, 21. (11) Num. xxv., 1 to 9

3. *From the fatal effects which this vice produces on those who are addicted to it*:—For,

First, Sins of this kind darken and blind the understanding—they produce great hardness of heart, and spiritual insensibility—and they lead to many other sins.

Secondly, When habitual, they render conversion very difficult; for they corrupt the heart to such a degree, as seems to deprive the sinner almost of the power of resistance. It is of these sins chiefly, that it is said. "If the Ethiopian can change his skin, or the leopard his spots; you also may do well, when you have learned evil."[14] And again: "His bones shall be filled with the vices of his youth, and they shall sleep with him in the dust."[15] By a habit of sensual indulgences, the sinner becomes so hardened, that the most awful threats can make no impression upon him.

Thirdly, The vice of impurity destroys all happiness, and makes life a complete burden; it disgraces the sinner; ruins his health; and oftentimes brings on a most loathsome disease, which reduces the body, even whilst living, to a state of putrefaction.

III. WHAT THE GUILT CONSISTS IN:—In what does *the sin* of Impurity consist?—As was said just now, all kinds and degrees of this vice are strictly forbidden; so that every *voluntary and deliberate* consent to the carnal pleasure of impurity, whether it be *in thought*, *word*, or *action*, is a mortal sin.

Is it a sin to be *tempted?* No; the sin consists in either *wilfully and unnecessarily causing* the temptation, or *entertaining* it, or *taking pleasure* in it, or *yielding consent* to it.

Plays and promiscuous meetings for dancing, are very often *causes* of temptations, and of sins: they are

(14) Jer. xiii., 23. (15) Job xx., 11.

dangerous, and should, therefore, be avoided. For, "he that loveth the danger shall perish in it."[16] By these dangers thousands have lost their innocence. Hence, the Pastors of the Church have always declaimed against them. St. John Chrysostom says: "Can any one touch boiling pitch, and not be defiled with it?" And the Book of Proverbs also says: "Can a man hide fire in his bosom, and his garments not burn? or can he walk upon hot coals, and his feet not be burnt?"[17] In like manner it may be asked: Can you wilfully run into temptations of impurity, and not fall a prey to sin?

IV. REMEDIES:—You cannot avoid these sins, without taking the *necessary precautions*, and using the *proper means:* which are these:—

1. Fly with horror all *occasions* that are calculated to lead to sin; such as mixed dances, dangerous interviews with persons of the other sex, bad company; indeed, all that *tends* to excite improper thoughts, or to inflame the passions.

2. Keep a strict *watch over yourselves;* guarding especially your *eyes*, and your *ears*: "Turn away thy face from a woman dressed up; and gaze not upon another's beauty, for many have perished by another's beauty; and hereby lust is enkindled as a fire."[18]

3. Resist *with vigour* and *resolution*, and IMMEDIATELY, the first attacks: "Resist the devil, and he will fly from you."[19]

4. Have recourse frequently to *fervent prayer*, and join with it the practice of *mortification:* "And as I knew that I could not otherwise be continent, except God gave it, (and this also was a point of wisdom, to know whose *gift* it was;) I went to the Lord, and *besought him with my whole heart.*"[20] "This kind of devil (the *unclean* spirit,) is not cast out but by prayer

(16) Eccli. iii., 27. (17) Prov. vi., 27, 28 (18) Eccli. ix., 8. (19) James iv., 7. (20) Wisd. viii., 21.

and fasting."[21] "I chastise my body, and bring it into *subjection*; lest, perhaps, when I have preached to others, I myself should *become a cast-away*."[22] "If you *live according to the flesh*, you shall die; but if, by the spirit, you *mortify* the deed of the flesh, you shall live."[23]

5. Practise *humility*, and place great *confidence in God*.

6. Be devout to the *Blessed Virgin Mary*

INSTRUCTION XXXVIII.

SEVENTH AND TENTH COMMANDMENTS.

Acts of Injustice—Restitution to be made—Covetousness to be avoided.

What is the Seventh Commandment?—"Thou shalt not steal."

What is forbidden by the Seventh Commandment?—The Seventh Commandment forbids all unjust taking away, or keeping what belongs to another.

What else?—All manner of cheating in buying and selling; or in any other way of wronging our neighbour.

Must we restore ill-gotten goods?—Yes, if we are able; or else the sin will not be forgiven; we must also pay our debts.

What is the Tenth Commandment?—"Thou shalt not covet thy neighbour's goods."

What is forbidden by the Tenth Commandment?—The Tenth Commandment forbids all covetous thoughts and unjust desires of our neighbour's goods and profits.

The *Design* of these two Commandments is, to direct us in our duties towards our neighbour with regard to his *property* and temporal goods; requiring us to act honestly towards him, by forbidding all kinds of

(21) Matt. xvii., 20. (22) 1 Cor. ix., 27. (23) Rom. viii., 13.

injustice, whether it be in stealing from him—in cheating or defrauding him—in deceiving, or over-reaching him in business—in imposing upon him—in wilfully damaging his possessions, or in coveting them.

1. Acts of Injustice :—The Seventh Commandment forbids all unjust taking away or retaining what belongs to another person against his will. If this be done by secret fraud, it is called *theft;* if by open violence, it is called *robbery.* This is always a sin; which is greater or less, according to the amount of the injury done, and to the disposition of him who does it. For it is a greater sin to steal twenty shillings than to steal one. But if, in stealing the one shilling, a person had the actual disposition and intention of stealing twenty, then his *guilt* is the same as if the twenty had been stolen. Although the trifling amount of an injustice committed and the absence of all disposition to commit a greater, may render this sin venial, yet injustice is, in its own nature, *a mortal sin.* Thus, St. Paul says: "You do wrong and defraud; and that to your brethren, Know you not that the unjust shall not possess the kingdom of God? Do not err. Neither idolaters, nor thieves, nor covetous persons, nor extortioners, shall possess the kingdom of God."[24] Again, he says: "This is the will of God......that no man overreach, nor circumvent his brother in business: because the Lord is the avenger of all these things."[25] By these tranagressions against the Seventh Commandment, we violate two very important virtues, viz., Charity and Justice: and we act in direct opposition to the precept of Christ: "As you would that men should do to you, do you also to them in like manner."[26]

(24) 1 Cor. vi., 8, 9, 10.
(25) 1 Thess. iv., 3, 6.
(26) Luke vi. 31.

Almighty God frequently punishes sins of injustice by executing vengeance even in this life: "He that hath gathered riches, and not by right, in the midst of his days he shall leave them."[27] Honesty, therefore, is the best policy; for ill-gotten goods *seldom prosper:* "Some distribute their own goods, and grow richer; some take what is not their own, and are always in want."[28]

There are *many ways* by which persons become guilty of injustices:—

1. By unjustly taking away or keeping what belongs to another, against the owner's will;

2. By destroying or damaging another's property, wilfully and maliciously, or mischievously;—

3. By passing bad money knowingly;—

4. By selling things for what they are not, or concealing their defects;—

5. By taking undue advantage of a person's ignorance, or of his necessities;—

6. By servants wasting their master's goods; or giving meat and drink to others, without his knowledge, and against his will;—

7. By workmen doing their work insufficiently, or idling away the time for which they are hired;—

8. By persons in trust taking bribes to overlook injuries done to their employer;—

9. By contracting debts, without any prospect of paying them; or by refusing to pay just debts. Debts should be paid when due, if required then: for a refusal to pay them is an unjust retaining of what belongs to another; it causes loss to the creditor, and frequently occasions his failure in business;—

10. By defrauding labourers of their wages: "The cry of them hath entered into the ears of the Lord:"[29]—

(27) Jer. xvii., 11. (28) Prov. xi., 24. (29) James v., 4.

11. By oppressing the poor and helpless: "*Defraud* not the poor of alms, bow down thy ear to the poor, and pay what thou *owest*;[30] —

12. By usury; i.e., by requiring and taking for the loan of money more than is allowed by public authority, without any just grounds. This is an oppression—it is taking advantage of a neighbour's necessity. "Do good and lend, hoping for nothing thereby."[31]

II. RESTITUTION:—When these or other injustices have been committed, what is required to be done? Restitution *must* be made, by giving back what has been taken away, or its value; or by repairing the damage which has been done. This is of strict obligation, if we are able to do it; but if we are not able, then we must be in a disposition to do it, when we shall become able, otherwise the sin will not be forgiven. And this obligation of making restitution, and compensation, rests not only on the person who has *performed* the unjust act, but also on every one who has been a real and guilty *cause* of it.

III. COVETOUSNESS:—As a means of avoiding injustices, we should banish (according to the Tenth Commandment) all dispositions to *covetousness;* and we should rely on Divine Providence.

What is *covetousness?* It is having too great a desire and concern for money or possessions, so as to set one's heart upon them. There are two kinds of covetous persons: 1*st*, Those who love money so much as to take *unjust means* of getting it: "There is not a more wicked thing than to love money; for such a one setteth even his own soul to sale......Nothing is more wicked than the covetous man."[32] 2*ndly*, Those who do not indeed take unjust ways of getting money, but pursue it *too ardently*, and possess it *too closely or fondly:* "If riches abound, set not the heart upon

(30) Eccli., 4, 8.
(31) Luke vi., 35.
(32) Eccli x., 9, 10.

them."[33] "Thou fool! this night do they require thy soul of thee; and whose shall those things be which thou hast provided?"[34]

How may persons know when they are covetous? They may know it by their conduct in *acquiring*, *possessing*, or *losing*.

1. *In acquiring:* If they let their mind be habitually occupied about their interests; or neglect their spiritual duties, for the sake of earthly gains; they may then conclude that they are not free from covetousness.

2. *In possessing:*—If their possessions make them proud and haughty—if they trust in them—if they are too sparing to themselves, or hard-hearted to the poor—if they cannot pay their debts, without feeling great difficulty in parting with the money; then also they are to believe that they are covetous.

3. *In losing:*—If they are very fretful, uneasy, and allow their peace of mind to be habitually disturbed, at every loss that happens to them; they may then likewise conclude that they are covetous. Riches, to a good man may be compared to his clothes, which are put off without pain; but, to a covetous man, they may be compared to his skin, which is not put off without great torment. The good man receives losses with resignation: when they befall him, he can say with holy Job: "The Lord gave, and the Lord hath taken away: as it hath pleased the Lord, so is it done: blessed be the name of the Lord."[35]

The good man relies, not on earthly possessions, but on *Providence;* according to the injunction of Christ, who says: "Be not solicitous, saying: What shall we eat, or what shall we drink, or wherewith shall we be be clothed? for your Father knoweth that you have need of all these things. Seek ye therefore *first* the

(33) Ps. lxi., 11. (34) Luke xii., 20. (35) Job i., 21.

kingdom of God, and his justice; and all these things shall be added unto you."[36]

INSTRUCTION XXXIX.

EIGHTH COMMANDMENT.

Lies—Rash Judgment, Calumny, and Detraction.

What is the Eighth Commandment?—"Thou shalt not bear false witness against thy neighbour."

What is forbidden by the Eighth Commandment?—The Eighth Commandment forbids all false testimonies, rash judgments, and lies.

What else?—All backbiting and detraction, or any words or speeches by which our neighbour's honour or reputation is any ways hurt.

What is he bound to do who has injured his neighbour by speaking ill of him?—He must make him satisfaction and restore his good name as far as he is able.

The Eighth Commandment is: "Thou shalt not bear false witness against thy neighbour;"[37] and its design is, to direct us in what we owe to *truth*; and also in the duties which we owe to our neighbour with regard to his *reputation*. It forbids lies of every kind; and all unjust injuring of our neighbour's character, either by rash judgments, or by calumny or detraction.

I. LIES:—*What is a* LIE? It is any word or action whereby (for the purpose of deceiving) we give others to understand what we believe at the time to be false; or, in the words of St. Augustin, it is "having one thing in the mouth, and another in the mind."

Are all lies *sins?* Yes, if deliberately wilful: "A lie is a foul blot in a man."[38] But every lie is not a mortal sin; for there are some kinds which are *venial;* as lies of mere jesting, or excuse, when they do no in-

(63) Matt vi., 31, 32, 33. (37) Exod. xx., 16. (38) Eccli. xx., 26

jury to any one.—It is never lawful to tell a lie, even though great advantage may arise from it? No; we must not do evil that there may come good from it.[39]

Are not some lies *mortal sins?* Yes, as is evident from the declarations of Scripture: "The mouth that belieth killeth the soul."[40] "Lying lips are an abomination to the Lord."[41] "All liars shall have their portion in the pool burning with fire and brimstone."[42]

When are they mortal sins?

1. When told to oppose the great truths of Religion—

2. When to praise vice, or condemn virtue: "Woe to you who call good evil, and evil good"[43]—

3. When to protect or forward wickedness—

4. When to injure one's neighbour in anything of consequence—or when a person foresees, or has reason to believe, that his lie will cause such an injury—

5. When a person *forsees* or *ought to forsee*, that it will be the cause of great scandal to others—

6. When lies, though otherwise venial, are confirmed by oath—

7. When persons break their promises in matters of consequence. For promises (made and accepted) give a full right to the thing promised: they are of strict obligation. The breach of them is a double sin, being a violation of *justice* as well as of *truth.*——Equivocations and mental reservations, (*properly such*) are lies, and therefore forbidden by the Eighth Commandment.

II. Injuring our Neighbour's Character:—This Commandment forbids all unjust injuring of our neighbour's character; whether it be in one's own mind only, by rash judgments; or in the minds of others, by calumny, and detraction.

(39) Rom. iii., 8. (40) Wisd. i., 11. (41) Prov. xii., 22, (42) Apoc. xxi., 8. (43) Is. v., 20.

1. *What is* RASH-JUDGMENT? It is judging evil without reasonable grounds, as,

First, When, at first sight, from a person's looks, we form a bad opinion of him—

Secondly, When we attribute good or indifferent actions to bad intentions—

Thirdly, When from the past, we judge of the present state of a person: or, from the present, we judge of his past or future state—

Fourthly, When we condemn any one without hearing him, or without hearing both sides of the case.

These rash judgments are uncharitable and sinful: "Charity thinketh no evil,"........but "hopeth all things."[44] "Judge not, that you may not be judged."[45] "Condemn not, and you shall not be condemned."[46] They betray, moreover, a corrupted heart; for "out of the abundance of the heart, the mouth speaketh."[47] "Why seest thou the mote in thy brother's eye, but *the beam that is in thine own eye*, thou considereth not."[48] "Wherein thou judgest another, thou condemnest thyself: for thou dost the same things which thou judgest."[49]

But suppose there are strong proofs, is it *then* sinful? No, if there be these two conditions: 1*st*, if the proofs be well founded; and, 2*ndly*, if the person be heard in his own defence, or if both sides of the case be duly considered. *Appearances*, however strong, are not not to be relied upon, for they often deceive us. (*Examples:* How strong and suspicious were the appearances against Benjamin, when he was accused of having stolen Joseph's silever cup; and when, upon search being made, it was found concealed in his sack? and yet he was innocent of the crime.[50] How strong also were the appearances, and how satisfactory did

(44) 1 Cor. xiii., 5, 7.
(45) Matt. vii., 1.
(46) Luke vi., 37.
(47) Matt. xii., 34.
(48) Luke vi., 41.
(49) Rom. ii., 1.
(50) Gen. xliv., 1, &c

they seem to be in the eyes of the people, against Susanna, in Babylon, when two judges accused her of adultery, and appeared as eye-witnesses against her? Upon their testimony she was condemned; but still she was innocent, as Daniel afterwards proved, by examining the two judges separately, and convicting them out of their own mouth, of having borne false testimony against her.[51]

2. *What is* CALUMNY OR SLANDER? It is speaking evil of our neighbour, when we know it to be *false*. ——*What is* DETRACTION? It is speaking ill of our neighbour, when we know it to be *true*, but *secret* or only known to a few.

Calumny and Detraction are grievous sins, being against both Charity and Justice. They are frequently the cause of anger, hatreds, animosities, quarrels, &c.; and they spring from a depraved and malicious heart: "They have whetted their tongues like a sword."[52] "His words are smoother than oil; and the same are darts."[53] Again: "They have sharpened their tongues like a serpent, and the venom of asps is under their lips."[54]

Some persons are so given to these sins, that, as soon as they have heard anything against their neighbour, off they go, and: "Have you heard what such a one has done?! I could not have believed it! But I fear it is too true; and if you will promise me not to speak of it again, I will tell you." Then out it comes, and involves both of them in sin.

When they know no evil of their neighbour, or hear him praised for some good which they cannot deny: "Ah! well! (they will say,) he is not the man the world takes him to be. For my part......; but I will say nothing; for least said is soonest mended." Or

(51) Dan. xiii., 1, &c.
(52) Ps. lxiii., 4
(53) Ps. liv., 20.
(54) Ps. cxxxix., 4.

they will shake their head, and put on a significant smile, with: "I *could* say something, if I chose." This is most uncharitable, unjust, and malicious: "They have whetted their tongues like a sword."[55]

Sometimes they will even pretend esteem; but only to give greater effect to their detraction. Thus, they will say: "He is a person I have great esteem for: for he has some good qualities: BUT I am sorry to find he is given to such and such things." "I always looked upon him as a good man; BUT it is a pity he is not more on his guard against such a practice." These *buts*, at the end, are like the sting in a serpent's tail—they carry *venom* with them: "Their words are smoother than oil, and the same are darts."[56]......... "The venom of asps is under their lips."[57]

May we *never* speak of our neighbour's faults, or make them known to others? Sometimes we *may*, and even *ought*: for, we may speak of them (with the view of getting the evils corrected) to those whose business or duty it is to correct them. We may speak of them, also, when it is necessary to guard others against injury. We *may* likewise speak of them, when the evil is *quite public*, and we speak of it merely as a public event, without taking pleasure in speaking of it as an evil in our neighbour.

Is it, then, a sin to speak *with pleasure* of the *known* faults of our neighbour? Yes; it is what is called *backbiting:* it is not doing as we would be done by.

Carrying tales backwards and forwards, so as to make mischief among neighbours, is uncharitable, and sinful: "The tale-bearer shall defile his own soul, and shall be hated by all."[58]

Is it also a sin to LISTEN to calumny, detraction, and backbiting? Yes, when we consent to it, or take

(55) Ps. lxiii., 4.
(56) Ps. liv., 20.
(57) Ps. cxxxix., 4.
(58) Eccli. xxi., 31.

pleasure in hearing it; or when, by our attention, questioning, &c., we encourage the detractor to go on.

Instead of listening to detractors we should *shun* their company: "My son......have nothing to do with detractors."[59] "Hedge in thy ears with thorns, and hear not a wicked tongue."[60] If *obliged* to hear, then take the part of the person against whom the detraction is directed; or reprove the detractor; show displeasure; or turn aside; or introduce some other subject of conversation, which, if done abruptly, will serve as an admonition to the detractor.

Calumniators and detractors, who, by their evil-speaking have lessened the reputation of others, or have caused them to suffer any other loss, are *obliged* to make satisfaction, by retracting what they have said, if it were false; and by repairing the whole injury in whatever way they can.

This obligation, together with the injustice and uncharitableness of these sins, should lead you to avoid them with the greatest care: and should make you ready (as the Wise Man exhorts) even to "melt down your gold and silver, in order to make a balance for your words, and a just bridle for your mouth."[61]

INSTRUCTION XL.

NINTH AND TENTH COMMANDMENTS.

The Government of the Heart—Evil Thoughts, and Desires—Temptations arising therefrom—the Means to be employed against them.

What is the Ninth Commandment?—"Thou shalt not covet thy neighbour's wife."

What is forbidden by the Ninth Commandment?—The

(59) Prov. xxiv., 21. (60) Eccli. xxviii., 28. (61) Eccli. xxviii., 29.

Ninth Commandment forbids all lustful thoughts and desires, and all wilful pleasures in the irregular motions of the flesh.

What is the Tenth Commandment?—"Thou shalt not covet thy neighbour's goods."

What is forbidden by the Tenth Commandment?—The Tenth Commandment forbids all covetous thoughts and unjust desires of our neighbour's goods and profits.

The Ninth and Tenth Commandments have, in great measure, been explained in the Instructions on the Sixth and Seventh.

The Sixth and Seventh Commandments forbid all *actions* contrary to chastity and justice. The Ninth and Tenth forbid all *wilful thoughts and desires* contrary to those two virtues. Their *design*, therefore, is to teach us the proper regulation of our thoughts and desires: that is to say, the government of the heart.

I. Government of the Heart:—Nothing is of greater importance than this *government of the heart*; for the neglect of it is the cause of all the other sins we commit. For, "from the heart (when not properly governed) come forth evil thoughts, murders, adulteries, fornications, thefts, false testimonies, blasphemies;" indeed, all kinds of wickedness.[62] "For out of the abundance of the heart the mouth speaketh. A good man, out of a good treasure, bringeth forth good things; and an evil man, out of an evil treasure, bringeth forth evil things."[63] Therefore, according as the desires and dispositions of the heart are, so will our outward conduct be—good or evil. How important, then, it must be, that we should properly *govern and regulate the heart*.

II. Evil Thoughts and Desires:—Whatever it is a sin to *say* or to *do*, it is a sin also to *consent to* in thought or desire. "Evil thoughts are an abomina-

(62) Matt. [illegible], 19 (63) Matt. xii., 34 35

tion to the Lord."[64] Indeed, the *malice* of sin properly consists in the *disposition* of the heart—in the *consent of the will:* "Whosoever shall look on a woman to *lust after her*, hath already committed adultery with her *in his heart.*"[65] (*Examples:* When a person breaks his fast *knowingly* and wilfully, on a day when he is obliged to fast; the OUTWARD ACT is exactly the same, as when he breaks his fast *unknowingly* and innocently, yet, in the former case, it is a sin; but in the latter, it is no sin at all. Now, that which makes all the difference, is the *intention and disposition* of the heart. Again, the same must be said of taking and spending another man's money, *believing* it to be *his*; and doing the same outward act, *believing* the money, by mistake, to be *one's own*. In the one case, it is a formal injustice, and a sin; in the other there is a material injustice, but no *guilt* of sin at all.) ——-Thus, the performance of the *very same outward action* is sinful or not sinful in him who performs it, according to the *intention and dispositions* of his heart. Hence, it may be said, that if these two Commandments be duly observed, (that is to say, if the heart be properly governed,) the whole law will be fulfilled.

III. TEMPTATIONS by evil thoughts and evil inclinations:—Is every evil thought *a sin?* No; it may be only *a temptation*. For, if we give no wilful occasion to such thoughts; as, by reading bad books—looking at improper objects—keeping bad company, &c.; and if we do not consent to them, but oppose them; then they are not, properly speaking, *our own;* and they will not be imputed to us as *sins*. Indeed, instead of injuring us, they are *then* an advantage, because they serve to prove our fidelity to God—to obtain for us greater graces—to increase our merits, and, conse-

(64) Prov. xv., 26. (65) Matt. v., 28.

quently, to procure for us a greater degree of glory hereafter.

We make the evil thoughts *our own*, and render them sinful—

1. If we bring them into our mind *wilfully*, being aware, in some degree, at least, of the evil we are doing :—

2. If we love the evil, and *wilfully* allow our thoughts to *dwell* upon it ;

3. If we *consent* with our *will* to any evil proposed to us by the thoughts:

4. If we *desire* or *intend* to commit it ; for this is what is directly forbidden by the Ninth and Tenth Commandments.

We can *never be secure* against these temptations; evil thoughts, bad desires, and the corrupt inclinations of the heart, are what we shall have to fight against all the days of our life. For the human heart is corrupted by the fall of Adam—it is *naturally* bent upon evil. This is what makes "the life of man upon earth a warfare;"[66] and puts us continually in danger of sin, unless we use proper means for curbing and correcting our natural inclinations.

IV. THE MEANS *proper for curbing and correcting our inclinations or passions :—*

1. Acquire *a habit of attention*, i.e., direct your mind habitually to some useful subject; and never allow it to run wilfully or wildly on *any* subject that presents itself. Thus, you will be enabled to keep a constant vigilance over the motions of your heart: "Watch and pray, that you enter not into temptation."[67]

2. Acquire *a habit of industry;* i.e., be always employed for some useful purpose—let the devil *never* find

(66) Job. vii., 1. (67) Matt. xxvi., 41.

you idle. For indulging in sloth, and in the love of ease, is the cause of many temptations.

3. *Avoid the occasions* of temptation: such as reading dangerous books—looking at dangerous objects—keeping bad company—intemperance, &c.

4. *Banish the first thought* IMMEDIATELY *and* RESOLUTELY; as you would cast off a spark from your clothes.

5. *Turn immediately to God:*—Think of his being present—think on Christ's passion—implore the Divine assistance—have recourse to the Blessed Virgin Mary.

6. If the temptation continues to trouble you, *treat it with contempt*; engaging your mind on your employment, or on any other subject which will most easily take up your attention.

7. *Put great confidence in the Divine grace and protection:* "My grace is sufficient for thee."[68] "God is faithful, who will not suffer you to be tempted above that which you are able; but will make with temptation issue, that you may be able to bear it."[69] "Though I should walk in the midst of the shadow of death, I will fear no evils; for *thou*, O Lord, art with me."[70]

(68) 2 Cor. xii., 9. (69) 1 Cor. x., 13. (70) Ps. xxii., 4.

EXPLANATION

OF THE

COMMANDMENTS OF THE CHURCH.

INSTRUCTION XLI.

FIRST AND SECOND COMMANDMENTS OF THE CHURCH.

The Obligation of obeying the Church—of observing the Holidays—and of hearing Mass on all Sundays and Holidays.

Are we bound to obey the Commandments of the Church?—Yes; because Christ has said to the Pastors of the Church: "He that heareth you, heareth me; and he that despiseth you, despiseth me."

How many are the Commandments of the Church?—Chiefly six.

What is the First Commandment of the Church?—To keep certain appointed days holy, with the obligation of resting from servile works.

What are these days called?—They are called holy days of obligation.

What is the Second Commandment of the Church?—To hear Mass on all Sundays and holy days of obligation.

By the "*Commandments of the Church*" we mean those *general* laws and regulations, which the Pastors of the Church have made and rendered binding on the Faithful, by an authority received from Christ. That such a power is given to the Pastors of the Church, is evident from our Saviour's own words: "To thee I will give the keys of the kingdom of heaven: And whatsoever *thou shalt bind upon earth*, it shall be *bound also in heaven;* and whatsoever thou shall loose upon earth, it shall be loosed also in heaven."[1] And again: "What-

(1) Matt. xvi., 19.

soever *you* shall *bind upon earth*, shall be *bound* also in heaven; and whatsoever you shall loose upon the earth, shall be loosed also in heaven."[2] "Take heed to yourselves, and to the whole flock, wherein the Holy Ghost hath placed *you Bishops to* RULE *the Church of God.*"[3]

I. WE MUST OBEY THE CHURCH:—Are the laws or Commandments of the Church *binding in conscience?* Yes; they are of strict obligation. For,

1. Christ considers disobedience to the Pastors of his Church, the same as disobedience to himself: "He that heareth YOU, heareth ME; and he that despiseth YOU, *despiseth* ME."

2. Christ shows that they who disobey are guilty of a grievous sin; for he ranks them with heathens and publicans: "If he will not hear the Church, let him be to thee as the heathen and publican."[5]

3. St. Paul directly commands, and strongly enforces, this obedience and subjection: "Obey your prelates, and be subject to them."[6] And again: "Let every soul be subject to the higher powers, for there is no power but from God: and those that are, are ordained of God. Therefore, he that resisteth the power, resisteth the ordinance of God: and they that resist, purchase to themselves damnation."[7]

4. Indeed, the Church gives her commands by the guidance and authority of the Holy Ghost: "It hath seemed good *to the Holy Ghost* and to us."[8]

How many are the Commandments of the Church?— Chiefly six.

These six Commandments of the Church are regarding duties, which God himself commands: the Church

(2) Matt. xviii., 18.
(3) Acts xx., 28.
(4) Luke x., 16.
(5) Matt. xviii., 17.
(6) Heb. xiii., 17.
(7) Rom. xiii., 1, 2.
(8) Acts xv., 28.

has only determined what God left undefined, viz., the *times* and *manner* of fulfilling them; for she fears, and with reason, that, if we were left to ourselves with regard so these duties, the greater part of us would neglect them.

II. WE MUST KEEP THE DAYS OF OBLIGATION:—*What is the First Commandment of the Church?*—To keep certain appointed days holy, with the obligation of resting from servile works.

This Commandment directs us in the *times* we are to set apart for the more immediate service of God; it *obliges* us to devote to him certain festival days, which have been instituted by the Church, for the purpose of commemorating and gratefully acknowledging God's special benefits. Those festival days are, 1st, The Nativity of our Lord, or Christmas-day: 2nd, Th Circumcision, or New-year's-day: 3rd, The Epiphany: 4th, The Ascension: 5th, Corpus Christi: 6th, SS. Peter and Paul: 7th, The Assumption of the Blessed Virgin Mary: 8th, All Saints.——These are the eight *Days of Obligation*, which we are required to devote to God's service.

In what manner should these days be kept? The same as Sundays; i.e., they should be *kept holy* by resting from all unnecessary servile works—by hearing Mass—by Prayer—by reading good books—and by other religious duties. *To rest* from servile works, and *to hear Mass*, are of STRICT OBLIGATION, because they are *commanded* by an authority received from Christ.

Would it, then, be a *mortal sin* to work on Days of Obligation? Without either *necessity* or a *dispensation*, it most certainly *would* be a mortal sin, the same as on a Sunday, because *the resting* on these days is commanded by the very self-same authority as the resting on Sundays; and also because to disobey or disregard the Commandments of the Church, is the same thing as disregarding the Commandments of God himself: For, "He that *despiseth* YOU, despiseth ME:" and, if he will not hear the Church, let him be to thee as the heathen and publican."[9] The Commandments of the Church are from God's authority, just as much as the Ten Commandments given on Mount Sinai.

But, is it not a great disadvantage in business, and loss of time, to devote so many days to religious duties? In answer to this it may be asked,

1. Is it not a much greater loss, to *lose one's soul* by neglecting to serve God? "What doth it profit a man, if he gain the whole world, and suffer the loss of his own soul?"[10]: "Thou fool! this night do they require thy soul of thee; and whose shall those things be which thou hast provided?"[11]

2. How many days are given to idleness, dissipation, and sin, without complaint or regret? Is it not a pity and a shame, too, to grudge every moment dedicated to God's service; whilst *whole days* can be given to vanity or sin without a murmur? When persons are thus so afraid of giving a little time to God's service, and look upon such time as lost, does it not show a greater concern for this world, than for the next; and a lamentable indifference for salvation? and does it not prove, that they have not a sufficient confidence in Divine Providence?——For,

3. Has not God a thousand ways of recompensing you, for the time you give to him, by giving a blessing to the time which he allows you to employ for yourselves? and has he not promised to do so? "Behold the birds of the air: for they neither sow, nor do they reap, nor gather into barns; and your Heavenly Father feedeth them......How much more *you*, O ye of little faith? Be not solicitous, therefore, saying: What shall we eat, or what shall we drink, or wherewith shall

(9) Matt. xviii., 17. (10) Matt. xvi., 26. (11) Luke xii., 20.

we be clothed?...For your Father knoweth that you have need of all these things. *Seek ye therefore* FIRST *the kingdom of God, and his justice; and* ALL THESE THINGS SHALL BE ADDED UNTO YOU."[12] Depend upon it, you will not be losers by giving these days to God.——But,

4. What blessing can you expect, if you love and prefer your temporal interests before God? If you *offend him*, by refusing him the service which he requires from you, and by rebelling against the Church which he commands you to obey, you then take the means of drawing down upon yourselves judgments, instead of blessings.

III. WE MUST HEAR MASS :—*What is the Second Commandment of the Church?*—To hear Mass on all Sundays and holy days of obligation.

This Commandment directs us as to the *manner* of employing the days set apart for God's service—it obliges us to hear Mass on all such days.

Why are we commanded, in particular, to *hear Mass?* Because the Sacrifice of the Mass is the most solemn and essential act of religious worship, and the most perfect homage which man can pay to God; it is an act of homage the most pleasing to him, and the most effectual in drawing down his blessings. And therefore, to hear (or celebrate) Mass *attentively* and *devoutly*, is the best means we have of keeping the day holy. Hence, what a pity it is that so many persons either neglect this holy Sacrifice, when the Church requires them to assist at it; or are present at it without attention or devotion; and thereby, not only run their souls into sin by violating this Second Commandment of the Church; but lose, moreover, the many and great

(12) Matt. vi., 26 to 33.

spiritual blessings, which a devout assistance at Mass would draw down upon them!

To *fulfil* this Commandment of hearing Mass on all Sundays and Days of Obligation, you must be present during the *whole Mass*, from beginning to end. To be absent *wilfully*, without a necessary or sufficient cause, during all or *any part* of it, is a sin; and the longer the absence the greater the sin; if it be during two or three minutes only, the sin is venial; but if during a considerable or an essential part, then it is mortal.——The same is to be said of *wilful* distractions during Mass.

What is meant by *Days of Devotion?* They are festival days on which it is proper and *advisable* that you should hear Mass, and perform more exercises of piety, than on common days; although there is no *command* or strict *obligation* to do so. They were formerly Days of Obligation; but on account of the tepidity and negligence of Christians, the obligation has been removed.

INSTRUCTION XLII.

THIRD COMMANDMENT OF THE CHURCH.

Abstinence and Fasting shown to be Scriptural—the Times and Manner of Fasting—its Advantages—Objections answered.

What is the Third Commandment of the Church?—To keep the days of fasting and abstinence appointed by the Church.

What is meant by fasting days?—Days on which we are allowed to take but one meal, and are forbidden to eat flesh meat.

Which are the fasting days?—The forty days of Lent; certain Vigils; the Ember days; and in England, the Wednesdays and Fridays in Advent.

Why does the Church command us to fast?—That by fasting we may satisfy God for our sins.

What is meant by days of abstinence?—Days on which we are forbidden to eat flesh meat, but are allowed the usual number of meals.

Which are the days of abstinence?—All Fridays, except the Friday on which Christmas-day may fall; and the Sundays in Lent, unless leave be given to eat meat on them.

This Third Commandment of the Church directs us as to *the times* and *manner* of complying with the duty of Fasting, which duty God himself requires of us—it obliges us to refrain, on certain appointed days, from taking our usual food; either as to *quality* only, and then we call it Abstinence; or as to both *quality and quantity*, and then we call it Fasting.

I. ABSTINENCE AND FASTING:—Are Abstinence and Fasting *in accordance with Scripture?* Yes, nothing cane be more so.

I. *As to Abstinence*, the Scriptures contain many passages which strictly enjoined it. Thus, for instance, the very *first* and *only* command given to Adam and Eve in Paradise, was one of *Abstinence:* "Of the tree of knowledge of good and evil, thou shalt not eat. For, in what day soever thou shalt eat of it, thou shalt die the death."[13]——Noe likewise received a precept of *Abstinence:* "Flesh with blood you shall not eat."[14]——The Israelites also were commanded to *abstain* from several kinds of flesh: "The flesh of these (*viz. the hare, the swine, &c.*) you shall not eat; and their carcasses you shall avoid......Do not *defile your souls*, nor touch aught thereof."[15] (*Examples of the strict observance of this precept among the Jews:*—Eleazer preferred death, and suffered death, rather than transgress this law of God, by eating forbidden

(13) Gen. ii., 17. (14) Gen. ix., 4. (15) Levit. xi., 8, 11, 43,

meats. So likewise did the Seven Machabees, with their mother."[16] Daniel also, in the Babylonish captivity, "proposed in his heart that he would not be *defiled* with the king's (Nebuchodonosor's) table;" and to the officer appointed over him, he said: "Try, I beseech thee, thy servants for ten days, and let pulse be given us to eat."[17])——The Apostles commanded the converts to *abstain* from blood, and things strangled· and they gave this command in the name and by the authority of the Holy Ghost: "It hath seemed goo to the Holy Ghost and to us, to lay no further burden upon you than these necessary things: that you *abstain* from these things sacrificed to idols, and from blood, and from things strangled."[18]

What practice, then, can be more Scriptural, than that of Abstinence? How strange, therefore, it is, and how inconsistent, that *they* who pretend to take the Bible as their sole rule of faith, should not only reject, but even ridicule a practice which is taught in almost every page of Scripture!

2. *As to Fasting*, the evidences for it in Scripture are numerous and decisive. Thus, in the Old Testament, God commanded, saying: "Blow the trumpet in Sion: *sanctify a fast*; call a solemn assembly......Be converted to me with all your heart *in fasting*, and weeping, and mourning; and rend your hearts, and and not your garments."[19]——In the New Testament, Christ also commands fasting: "Then came to him the disciples of John, saying: Why do *we* fast often, but thy disciples do not fast? And Jesus said to them: Can the children of the Bridegroom mourn, as long as the Bridegroom is with them? But the days shall come when the Bridegroom shall be taken away from them, and *then* THEY SHALL FAST."[20]——And, accordingly,

(16) 2 Mac. vi., and vii. (18) Acts xv., 28, 29. (20) Matt. ix., 14, 15.
(17) Dan. i., 8, 12. (19) Joel ii., 1, 12, 13.

he gave rules for fasting to be then observed: "When you fast, be not as the hypocrites, sad. For they disfigure their faces, that they may appear unto men to fast. Amen I say to you, they have received their reward. But thou, when thou fastest, anoint thy head, and washthy face; that thou appear not to men to fast, but to thy Father who is in secret: and thy Father who seeth in secret, will repay thee."[21]—— Both the Old and New Testament testify, that Fasting has, at all times, been practised by the greatest servants of God Moses fasted forty days, without eating anything[22]— Elias also fasted forty days, in the same manner[23]— David likewise fasted much: "My knees (he said) are weakened through fasting;"[24] The Apostles fasted: "When they had ordained to them priests in every Church, and had prayed *with fasting;* they commended them to the Lord;"[25] Christ himself fasted: "And when he had fasted forty days, and forty nights, he was afterwards hungry."[26]——Notwithstanding all these Scriptural evidences for fasting, how frequently do we hear the doctrine of it rejected, and its practice called superstitious!

III. TIME AND MANNER OF FASTING:—Almighty God, then, requires us to fast; the Church (as I have already said) determines *the times* and *manner* of fulfilling what God thus requires.

1. *With regard to the* TIMES *of fasting*, the Church obliges us to keep, as fast-days, 1st, *The forty days of Lent;* for from Ash-Wednesday to Easter, every day, except the Sundays, is a fasting day; 2ndly, *Certain Vigils*, viz., the Vigils of Christmas-day, of Whit-Sunday, of SS. Peter and Paul, of the Assumption of the Blessed Virgin Mary, and of All Saints; 3rdly, *The Ember-days*, i.e., the Wednesdays, Fridays, and

(21) Matt. vi., 16, 17, 18. (23) 3 Kings xix., 8. (25) Acts xiv., 22.
(22) Exod. xxxiv., 28. (24) Ps. cviii., 24. (26) Matt iv., 2.

Saturdays in the first Week of Lent, in Whitsun-week, in the third week of September, and in the third week of Advent; 4thly, in England, all the *Wednesdays and Fridays of Advent.*

2. *With regard to the* MANNER *of fasting*, the Church restricts all her subjects, who have not a lawful cause of exemption, to only *one full meal* in the day, with *a collation* at night; but, in this country, custom has authorized us to take also something in the morning. What is thus taken in the morning must be *but a little* (one ounce, or, *at most*, two ounces); and the evening collation, according to the common teaching of Divines, must not exceed eight ounces of food.[27*] As to the *quality* of what may be taken morning and evening, according to the present discipline in England, it must not be flesh-meat, nor anything produced from animals, as milk, butter, cheese, eggs, &c.; but

(27) * Bishop Hays says; "As for the *quantity* to be used at Collation, this must depend a great deal upon circumstances, though *the general voice of Divines* agree that it ought not to exceed about eight ounces."—*Sincere Christian*, *Vol.* 1, *Chap* 15, *Ques.* 39.

St. Alphonsus Liguori, quoting the opinion of some Divines, who permit a quarter of the usual full meal to be taken at the evening collation, says: "But of this rule I do not approve, because either it might possibly be too indulgent (at least with respect to some persons), or is at best very obscure, and liable to cause scruples. It is better therefore to follow that opinion, given by other Divines, which is commonly received at the present day, and which allows eight ounces to all persons indiscriminately (even to those who require but little food)." "Circa *quantitatem* alii Permittunt quartam partem cœnæ consuetæ; sed hæc regula mihi non probatur, quia aut potest esse nimis indulgens (saltem respectu aliquorum), aut saltem est nimis obscura et scrupulosa. Melius igitur est sententiam sequi aliorum communiter hobi accep tam, quæ omnibus indiscriminatim (etiam illis qui parvo cibo indigent) permittit quantitatem octo unciarum."—*Hom. Apostol.*, *tract.* 12. *n.* 16.

"The quantity of eight ounces (he says again) is so adopted in practice at the present day, that it is indiscriminately allowed even to those whose appetite is fully satisfied with it."—"Cæterum quantitas octo unciarum ita hodie usu recepta est, ut indistincte permittatur, etiam iis qui cum illa ad satietatem reficiuntur." — *Theol. Moral.*, *lib.* 3, *tract*, 6. *n.* 1025.

It must consist of such things as are produced by the earth, as bread, fruit, olive-oil, &c, [*These regulations are liable to be varied by the Lental Pastorals.*]

Every fasting day is also a day of abstinence; but it has long been customary, in England, to be allowed to eat flesh-meat at the full-meal, on the Tuesdays and Thursdays in Lent; except the Thursday after Ash-Wednesday, and the Tuesdays and Thursdays in Holy-Week. [*But this dispensation is liable to be altered by the Bishop.*]

In the earlier ages of the Church, fasting was much more rigorous than it is at the present time.

Does the Church oblige all her members to fast? No; none are commanded to *fast*, until they have completed their twenty-first year of age. And, even then, many are exempted—some by the weakness of their constitution, or by sickness; some by their laborious employments; some on account of their being in the family-way, or their having a child at their breast; some by a dispensation lawfully obtained from their Pastor. But all are obliged to *abstain* from flesh-meat on days of fasting and abstinence, after they have completed their seventh year of age; unless, for some just cause, they are dispensed with.

Would it be a mortal sin to transgress the laws of fasting and abstinence? Yes; unless it be done from some necessity, or by a lawful dispensation. In order to obtain a lawful dispensation, a *just cause* is necessary.

III. ADVATANGES OF FASTING.—WHY *does the Church command us to fast?*—That by fasting we may satisfy God for our sins.

It is with good reason that we are commanded to fast; because fasting is attended with *many* and *very great* ADVANTAGES. For,

1. It is very *powerful* in appeasing the anger of

God, and in averting his judgments. (*Example of the Ninivites.*[28])

2. It satisfies the Divine Justice, by discharging, or considerably lessening, the debt of temporal punishment due to our past sins.

3. It acts as a preservative against future transgressions; because it tames the violence of our passions, and weakens temptations.

4. It renders the soul more spiritual—more fit for Prayer, Meditation, and other religious Exercises.

IV. Objections Answered:—The advantages of fasting being so great, and the Scriptures so clear, so explicit, and so strong in its favour, *why do other religions object so much against the practice of it?* They do not like fasting, and therefore they are glad to catch at every trifling objection against it.

1. They say: "*It is not that which goeth into the mouth, that defileth a man;*"[29] and they apply this as an objection against fasting and abstinence: but it is evident that they misapply the text. For, what was it that defiled Adam and Eve? was it not the apple going into their mouth contrary to God's command? Would not the eating of Nebuchodonosor's meats have defiled Daniel? and swine's flesh the Jews? and was it not to avoid this defilement that Eleazer, and the seven Machabees, with their Mother, suffered death?

2. They say: "*Flesh is as good on Friday as on other days.*" Certainly, *it* is as good; but the ACT *of eating it* is not so good, because forbiden by lawful authority. The *forbidden* apple was as good as the others; but, &c......Leven bread was forbidden to the Jews, during the week of the passover; so that they would have sinned by eating it;[30] yet it was as good during that week, as at other times when allowed.

(28) Jonas iii., 8, 9, 10. (29) Matt. xv., 11.
(30) Exod xiii., 3, 7; Deut. xvi., 3, 4.

3. They object against us these words of St. Paul "*Whatsoever is sold in the shambles, eat; asking no question for conscience sake.*"[31] But this text, instead of opposing, rather confirms our doctrine. The first Christians were forbidden to eat things, which had been offered to idols; and, in the very Chapter, from which the above passage is taken, St. Paul confirm that prohibition; and then teaches that the Christians were not to be *scrupulous* in its observance; for, that, so long as *they did not know* that the meat had been offered to idols, they might eat it, without first asking the question, whether it had been offered to idols. "But (*he adds*) if any man say: This has been sacrificed to idols; *do not eat of it*, for his sake that told it, and FOR CONSCIENCE SAKE."[32]

But, how can Protestants object to the doctrine and practice of either fasting or abstinence, since their "Book of Common Prayer" enjoins both? and since, by Protestant laws, it is the duty of Churchwardens to see that the Parishioners have no flesh on their table on fish-days, i.e., on days of Fasting and abstinence? Existing laws require them to levy penalties for eating flesh on those days;[33] and also to present the transgressors to the Protestant Bishop at the Visitation. The Protestant clergy are required by the Canons, under pain of censure, to declare to the people every Sunday, at the time appointed in the Communion-book, whether there be any *Fasting-days* the week following.[34]

(31) 1 Cor. x., 25. (32) 1 Cor. x., 28.
(33) 5 Eliz., cap. 5 — *See* Burn's Justice, Art. Churchwardens Sect. vi., Duties of Churchwardens in general.
(34) Canon 64.

INSTRUCTION XLIII.

FOURTH, FIFTH, AND SIXTH COMMANDMENTS OF THE CHURCH.

Annual Confession—Easter-Communion—Prohibitions regarding Marriage.

What is the Fourth Commandment of the Church?—To confess our sins to our Pastor, at least once a year.

At what time should children go to confession?—When they come to the use of reason, so as to be capable of mortal sin, which is generally supposed to be about the age of seven years.

What is the Fifth Commandment of the Church?—To receive the Blessed Sacrament once a year, and that at Easter or thereabouts.

At what age are Christians bound to receive the Blessed Sacrament?—When they are sufficiently capable of being instructed in that sacred mystery.

What is the Sixth Commandment of the Church?—Not to solemnize marriage at certain times, nor within certain degrees of kindred; nor privately without witnesses.

I. Annual Confession:—The Fourth Commandment of the Church requires us to go to Confession, in obedience to the general command of God: it fixes a period, beyond which we are not allowed to defer the confession of our sins to our Pastor.

The *general command of God* is implied in the very *institution* of Confession: for, as this institution renders Confession a necessary condition of reconciliation, it follows that God requires it of every sinner. When Christ gave to his Apostles and their successors the power of forgiving and retaining sins, he thereby constituted his ministers the judges of consciences. Now, they cannot exercise this office, without confessions being made to them.

The Church *commands us* to comply with this general precept of God, at the VERY LEAST *once a year*. When does this obligation begin to bind us? When we come to the use of reason, so as to be capable of mortal sin—when we are able to distinguish good from evil, so far as to be accountable to God for the morality of our actions. They who have not made their first confession, are (obliged, if ignorant) to get instructed, in order to learn how to make it; and they are obliged to prepare themselves for it; and they must never afterwards neglect beyond a year.

But, is once a year often enough to go to confession? It is all that the Church expressly *commands;* but not all that *she wishes.*[35]*——After we have fallen into mortal sin, God requires us to return to him, without delay, by sincere repentance: "*Delay not* to be converted to the Lord, and defer it not from day to day: for his wrath shall come on a sudden, and in the time of vengeance he will destroy thee."[36] When a person, who has committed a mortal sin, neglects for a long time to have recourse to the appointed means

(35) * The Catechism of the Council of Trent says: "There is nothing which ought to be an object of so much care to the Faithful, as to study to purify their souls by the *frequent* confession of their sins. For when any one is oppressed with any deadly sin, nothing can be to him more salutary, than to confess his sins *immediately;* on account of the many dangers which hang over our lives."—*Cat. Conc. Trid., part 2, cap. 5, de sacr. pœnit., n.* 70.

The same Catechism, teaching what works of piety ought to be done on Sundays and Holidays, says: "They are such as these: *Often* to make use of the Sacraments of the Church; which were instituted for our salvation, and for curing the wounds of our souls. Nor is there anything which can be more seasonable or better for Christians [*on those days*], than *often* to confess their sins to the Priests...But the Pastor shall not only excite the people to that Sacrament [Penance]; but he shall with diligence exhort them to it again and again. In order that they may *frequently* receive the holy Sacrament of the Eucharist"—*Cat. Conc. Trid., part 3, cap 4, de tertio præcepto Decalogi, n.* 25.

(36) Eccli. v., 8, 9.

of reconciliation, can we suppose that God is not offended by such neglect? Can we suppose that such a person is not violating the precept of loving the Lord his God with his whole heart, and soul, and mind, and strength?——Whenever we have been so unhappy as to become guilty of mortal sin we should repent *immediately*, and prepare ourselves for approaching *soon* to the Sacrament of reconciliation...... If this were done, how many sins would be thereby prevented?

For, Confession is not only a *remedy* for sins already committed, but is also a *preservative* against committing them in future. When a person is *enslaved* to any vice; when his heart is corrupted, and the powers of his soul are weakened, by a habit of falling; when he *desires and endeavours* to reform his conduct, but *has not the strength* to do so; frequent Confession is to such a sinner a most powerful help—it is sometimes the only means, *that will be effectual*, of overcoming temptations.——They whose repeated falls give them occasion to lament their weaknesses, but who cannot be induced to go to Confession oftener than once a year; must have great reason to apprehend, that they are far from being really in earnest about their salvation—that they are very indifferent —that they are worse than mere lukewarm. How seldom it is that this neglect of Confession is effectually corrected, when once the habit of it has been contracted? This is a negligence which generally grows upon those who are guilty of it, and too often accompanies them to their death-bed. With expressions of bitter regret, they then resolve and promise to do better in future, if God will only spare them. But no sooner do they find that they have been spared, than, forgetting their resoultions, they become as negligent as before

II. Easter Communion :—*What is the Fifth Commandment of the Church?*—To receive the Blessed Sacrament once a year, and that at Easter or thereabouts.

The Fifth Commandment of the Church requires us to receive the Holy Communion, in obedience to the general command of God: and it specifies a time beyond which we are not allowed to defer the reception of this Sacrament.

That *general command of God* is evident from these words of Christ: " Amen, amen, I say unto you: Except you eat the flesh of the Son of Man, and drink his blood, you shall not have life in you."[37]

At what age are Christians bound to receive the Blessed Sacrament?—When they are sufficiently capable of being instructed in that sacred mystery.

Observe, the Catechism does not say: " When they are *sufficiently instructed;* but: " When they are *sufficiently* CAPABLE *of being instructed.*" For they are then bound to get instructed, and to make all necessary preparations for receiving the Holy Communion:—Parents will have much to answer for, if they suffer their children to neglect......(and how many Parents do?) The negligence of children is almost always traceable to neglect in Parents. What a terrible account must await those Parents, who are guilty of such neglect!

Would it be a grievous sin to omit one's *Easter Communion*, without necessity or some just cause? Yes; and the longer people neglect, the more guilty they become. St. Alphonsus Liguori says, that, if any one has been prevented from communicating at Easter, he is bound to communicate *as soon afterwards as he can —or at the earliest opportunity;* because both the di-

(37) John vi., 54.

vine and the ecclesiastical precept require him to do so."[38]*

But, if persons communicate at Easter, is that *sufficient?* It is as often as the Church positively *commands;* but not as often as she desires and advises,[39]* nor as often as our necessities require. The Holy Eucharist is called: "Our daily bread;"[40] it is "the bread of life," given for the food and nourishment of our souls: "The bread that I will give, is my flesh for the life of the world......For my flesh is meat indeed, and my blood is drink indeed."[41] Now, as the body languishes and dies, unless frequently nourished with corporal food; so does the soul languish and lose its spiritual life, if deprived of this *bread of life.* For so Christ declares: "Amen, amen, I say unto you: Except you eat the flesh of the Son of Man, and drink his blood, you *shall not have life in you.*"[42]

(38) * "Sicut diximus de confessione [*vide supra, n,* 36], ita dicimus de communione, quod si quis tempore Paschali non potuit communicare, tenetur ad quamprimum communicandum, quia urget præceptum tam divinum (ab Ecclesia determinatum ut observetur quolibet Pascha), quam ecclesiasticum quod assignat tempus Paschale non ad finiendam, sed ad solicitandam satisfactionem."—*Hom. Apost., tract.* 12, *n.* 40.

(39) * "The Holy Synod [the Council of Trent], with paternal affection, admonishes, exhorts, implores, and entreats all Christians, through the bowels of the mercy of our God,...to believe and venerate the sacred mysteries of our Lord's body and blood with such constancy and firmness of faith, and with such devotion, piety, and reverence of mind, that they may be able to receive *frequently* this supersubstantial bread, and that it may truly be to them the life of their soul, and the perpetual health of their mind."—*Conc. Trid., Sess.* 13, *de Euch. cap.* 8.

The Catechism of the Council of Trent says: "Let not the Faithful think it enough, if, in obedience to the authority of this decree, they receive the Lord's body *once a year* ONLY; but let them know, that the Communion of the Eucharist should be received *oftener.* But whether it be more expedient to receive it every month or every week, or every day, no fixed rule can be prescribed for all persons. Yet this rule of St. Augustin is most certain: 'So live, that thou mayest receive every day.'" —*Cat. Conc. Trid. part.* 2, *cap.* 4, *n.* 6.

(40) Luke xi., 3.

(41) John vi., 48, 52, 56.

(42) John vi., 54.

How many are there among the faithful, who seem to make it a point to approach the Holy Communion once a year *only?* But what can be thought of them, except that they are in a deplorable state of soul? for, to whom are these terrifying words of the Apocalypse more strictly applicable: "I know thy works, that thou art neither cold nor hot. I would that thou wert cold, or hot; but because thou art luke-warm, and neither cold nor hot, I will begin to vomit thee out of my mouth."[43]

If such persons will only look well into their own hearts, and observe what passes there, it is to be feared that they will find this threat already executed upon them—that they will find themselves deprived of the protecting and supporting graces of God—left a prey to frequent and violent temptations—and repeatedly falling, so as to be continual slaves to their passions.

III. Prohibitions regarding Marriage:—*What is the Sixth Commandment of the Church?*—Not to solemnize marriage at certain times, nor within certain degrees of kindred; nor privately without witnesses.

1. Those *forbidden times* are, from the first Sunday in Advent to the Epiphany, and from Ash-Wednesday to Low-Sunday *inclusively.* These are times set apart for public penance, or for particular devotion. Marriages *solemnized* at these forbidden times are unlawful, but not invalid. It is not right to take any part in the solemnization of a marriage, to which this prohibition of the Church applies.

2. The Sixth Commandment of the Church forbids marriage between relations to the fourth degree of kindred. Brothers and sisters are the first degree from the common stock; their children, or first cousins, are the second degree; and so on to the third cousins, who

(43) Apoc. iii., 15, 16.

are the fourth degree, and included in the prohibition. When the parties are not equally distant from the common stock, from which both of them proceed, they are related to each other in the degree of the one who is farthest removed.

It also forbids marriages between those who are within the fourth degree of affinity, arising from lawful marriage. Speaking of man and wife our Blessed Lord says: "They are not two, but one flesh;"[44] so that the relations of one of the parties by consanguinity, are related to the other party by *affinity*.——An unlawful cohabitation creates the same kind of affinity, which prevents marriage with the relatives of each other to the second degree.—Godfathers and Godmothers contract a spiritual relationship or affinity with *the person* for whom they are Sponsors, and also with the *Parents* of that person; which prevents them from marrying any one of the three; and this applies also to those who are Sponsors in Confirmation.

In all these cases the marriage would be null and void, if celebrated without a dispensation.

3. In places where the decree of the Council of Trent, concerning clandestine marriages, is in force, any marriage which is not contracted before the proper Pastor of one of the parties, and in presence of at least two witnesses, is null and void.

(44) Matt. xxix., 6.

EXPLANATION

OF

THE SACRAMENTS.

INSTRUCTION XLIV.

On the Sacraments in general.

What is a Sacrament?—A Sacrament is an outward sign of inward grace, or a sacred and mysterious sign and ceremony, ordained by Christ, by which grace is conveyed to our souls.

Do all the Sacraments give grace?—Yes; to those who receive them with due dispositions.

Whence have the Sacraments the power of giving grace?—From Christ's precious blood.

Is it a great happiness to receive the Sacraments worthily?—Yes; it is the greatest happiness in the world.

How many Sacraments are there?—These Seven: Baptism, Confirmation, Holy Eucharist, Penance, Extreme Unction, Holy Orders, and Matrimony.

Our eternal salvation depends very much on the use we make of the Sacraments; because they are *the means of grace* instituted by Christ our Lord for the sanctification of mankind. It is very important, therefore, that the Sacraments should be well *understood* by all Christians, in order that they may be able to receive them with greater advantage to their souls.

1. The Essentials of a Sacrament:—*What is a Sacrament?*—A Sacrament is *an outward sign of inward grace*, or a sacred and mysterious sign and ceremony *ordained by Christ*, by which grace is conveyed to our souls.

Three things are necessary to constitute a Sacrament: 1st, Some external sensible thing; which is to be applied by the Minister of the Sacrament, whilst he pronounces a set form of words: All this is the *Sign*, or the *outward part* of the Sacrament.—2ndly, This external thing, with the application of it to the Receiver, (that is to say, the entire sign or outward part of the Sacrament), must both *signify* inward grace, and have the power of *producing* it in the soul.—3rdly, This sign, or outward part of the Sacrament, must have been permanently *instituted by Christ* in his Church, to be a means of producing grace.

1. *The outward Sign*:—An external sensible *Sign* is something which we can see or hear, &c.; it is something which can be perceived by our *senses*; pointing out something else which we do not see, or hear, or perceive with any of our senses; for example, when we see smoke rising out of the top of a chimney, we know by that *outward sign*, that there is fire inside the house; although the fire itself is not perceived by any of our senses. The external sensible *thing*, with the application of it, is called the *matter* of the Sacrament; the *words* which are pronounced at the same time, by the Minister applying the matter, are called the *form* of the Sacrament. Thus, the *matter* of the Sacrament of Baptism is the water, with the application of it to the person who is being baptized, [the water itself is the *remote* matter, and its application [or the ablution) is the *proximate* matter]:[1]* and the *form* of this Sacrament is the sentence, "I baptize thee, &c.," pronounced while the the water is being poured. "Withhold the word, (says St. Augustin,) and what is the

(1) * "*Materia* est res corporea et sensibilis, quæ suscipienti applicatur, v g, aqua chrisma, oleum sanctum, &c. Et hæc est materia *remota*; nam *proxima* est ipsa applicatio materiæ, ut ablutio, unctio," &c.—*S. Alph Lig.*, *Hom. Apostol.*, *append.* 3, *n.* 5.

water, but mere water? The word is joined to the element, and it becomes a Sacrament."[2] *

The union between the application of the matter, and the pronouncing of the form, ought to be such, that, according to the moral estimation of men, the words may be considered as affecting the matter, and as constituting with it *one whole Sign.*[3] †

Every Sacrament has a *matter* and *form;* which are its *outward part*, applied by the person who administers the Sacrament.

2. *The inward Grace:*—There is also, in *every* Sacrament, an *inward part*, or *grace*, given by Almighty God to the soul, at the very same instant in which the outward part is performed. This inward grace is *certain;* it is infallibly produced in the soul of the person receiving the Sacrament, unless he prevent it by putting some obstacle in the way: "If any one shall assert, (says the Council of Trent,) that the Sacraments of the New Law contain not the grace which they signify, or that they do not confer that grace upon those who put no obstacle in the way; let him be Anathema."[4] ‡

Why is this inward effect *certain?* Because God has *promised* it, and is *faithful* to his promises. Of Baptism, for instance, Christ has declared, saying: "Unless a man be *born again* of water and the *Holy Ghost*, he

(2) * "Detrahe verbum, quid est aqua, nisi aqua? Accedit verbum ad elementum, et fit Sacramentum."—*Tract,* 80 *in Joannem.*

(3) † "Ut Sacramentum sit validum, debet inter materiam et formam (v.g., inter effusionem aquæ et pronuntiationem verborum) tanta esse conjunctio, ut secundum moralem hominum æstimationem, spectata natura cujusque Sacramenti, una alteram afficiat; hoc est, ut *verba* censeantur cadere in talem rem, et cum ea UNUM TOTALE SIGNUM constituere." - *S. Alph. Lig., Theol. Mor., lib.* 6, *tract.* 1, *n.* 9

(4) ‡ "Si quis dixerit, Sacramenta novæ legis non continere gratiam, quam significant, aut gratiam ipsam non ponentibus obicem non conferre; anathema sit."—*Conc. Trid., Sess.* 7 *de Sacr. in genere, can.* 6.

cannot enter into the kingdom of God;"[5] but "he that believeth and is baptized, shall be saved;"[6] Of the Holy Eucharist he has also promised: "He that eateth my flesh and drinketh my blood, abideth in me, and I in him:...he hath everlasting life; and I will raise him up at the last day;"[7] Of Penance likewise he has promised, saying to his ministers: "Whose sins you shall forgive, they *are forgiven them*;"[8] Of Extreme Unction: "And if he (the sick person) be in sins, they *shall be* forgiven him."[9] Now, Christ says of his promises: "Heaven and earth shall pass away, but my word shall not pass away."[10] For, as the rain and the snow come down from heaven, and return no more thither; but water the earth, and make it to spring and give seed to the sower, and bread to the eater: *so shall my word be*, which shall go forth from my mouth; it shall not return to me *void*; but it shall do whatsoever I please, and *shall prosper in the things for which I sent it*."[11]

The outward part which is performed by the Minister of the Sacrament, is called a SIGN *of the inward grace*, because it *signifies and represents outwardly* what is *done inwardly and invisibly* in the soul. These *sacramental* signs (very different from others) actually effect or *give* what they represent: for example, in Baptism, the application of the water, and the pronouncing of the accompanying words, are A SIGN which not only *represents* the cleansing of the soul from sin, but actually *effects* that cleansing.

3. *The Institution of Christ*:—A Sacrament must be an *Institution of Christ*: He is the Author of all the Sacraments. For no one, but God, can give to material things, or to outward signs, the power of producing grace in the soul.

(5) John iii., 5.
(6) Mark xvi., 16.
(7) John vi., 54, 55.
(8) John xx., 23.
(9) James v., 16.
(10) Mark xiii., 31.
(11) Is. lv., 10, 11

II. THE NUMBER OF THE SACRAMENTS:—How many Sacraments *has* Christ instituted? Seven. This is an Article of Faith: "If any one shall assert, (says the Council of Trent,) that the Sacraments of the New Law were not all of them instituted by Jesus Christ our Lord; or that there are more or fewer than seven; viz., Baptism, Confirmation, Eucharist, Penance, Extreme Unction, Order, and Matrimony; or even that any one of these seven is not truly and properly a Sacrament; let him be Anathema."[12]

These seven Sacraments supply the various *wants* of the *spiritual life*, corresponding to those of the temporal life.

1. In order to live a temporal life we must be born. But we are born in a state of sin; and, therefore, before we can live the life of grace, we must be purified from our guilt—we must receive a spiritual birth; and this we receive by means of the Sacrament of Baptism.

2. After being temporally born, we are, for some time, weak and helpless infants; we have to grow up and acquire strength, in order to be equal to the labours and duties which we shall have to perform. So likewise, after being spiritually born, our life of grace is but weak and feeble—we are in a state of spiritual infancy: we are indeed *Christians* and *Servants* of Christ; but we have to become *strong and perfect* Christians and *Soldiers* of Jesus Christ; and this we become by receiving the Sacrament of Confirmation.

3. As, in the temporal life, we must be frequently supplied with nourishing food, in order to preserve life, and to maintain and increase our strength; for otherwise we should soon languish and die: so, in order to maintain and perfect that spiritual life, which we received in Baptism, and which was strengthened

(12) Conc. Trid., Sess. 7, de Sacr. in genere, can. 1.

in Confirmation, we stand in need of a spiritual nourishment—of a continual supply of graces: our souls must be frequently fed with "*the bread of life*;" and this is given to us in the Sacrament of the Holy Eucharist.

4. But, however strong and healthy we may have become, we are liable to be seriously or mortally wounded, or to lose our health and strength under the enfeebling influence of some disorder; we are liable to fall into such a state, that even the very food which should administer health and strength, would become pernicious and fatal to us: we stand in need, therefore, of some healing remedy—of one that possesses the property of curing our wounds, and of restoring to us the health which we have lost. Now, (applying all this to the spiritual life,) that necessary remedy, capable of healing the wounds of mortal sin, of restoring us to the state of grace, and of enabling us again to partake of "the bread of life" with advantage to our souls—that necessary and healing remedy is provided for us in the Sacrament of Penance.

5. But, after all, we must die: the sentence of death is passed upon all mankind; and, sooner or later, enfeebled nature must yield to the execution of that sentence: it is then difficult to avoid sinking under the pains, infirmities, languor, &c., of our last sickness and we need special consolation and special assistances. *Spiritually* also, we are then in the greatest need; for the devil exerts himself then to the utmost of his power in tempting us, especially to impatience and despair: and we, being weakened by disease, are less able to stand his attacks: but the special consolation and support—the special assistances which we then need, are communicated to us in the sacrament of Extreme Unction.

6. Society requires a Government and Administrators of the laws. So, in Religion, we stand in need

of *spiritual* Rulers, Teachers and Guides: and these are supplied, together with the powers and graces necessary for them, by the Sacrament of Holy Orders.

7. Marriage is necessary, in order to supply children for succeeding generations; and as the general happiness of mankind, and the temporal good of society, (being composed chiefly of married persons,) depend very much on the proper discharge of the duties of the married state, and especially on the manner in which parents bring up their children; so, the Sacrament of Matrimony has been instituted, to give to married persons the graces which are required for the due fulfilment of their duties, and for training up their children *religiously*, so that they may thus people the Church with *good Christians*, and heaven with *Saints*.

You see how these seven Sacraments serve to *sanctify every stage and condition of life*—how you ought, therefore, to thank God for having instituted them—and also how inexcusable you are, if you live and die in sin.

III. The Minister of the Sacraments:—Christ, having instituted the Sacraments, left the administration of them to Priests, who are ordained "for the work of the ministry."[13] And whether the Minister of a Sacrament be virtuous or wicked, it produces the same *effects* in the receiver. All that is necessary in the Minister for conferring the Sacraments *validly*, is, 1st, That he have *the power* of administering them; 2ndly, That he have *jurisdiction*, with regard to those Sacraments which require it; 3rdly, That he perform all the *essential* rites; and 4thly, That he have "*an intention* of at least doing what the Church does."[14]

(13) Eph. iv., 12. (14) Conc. Trid., Sess. 7, de Sacr. in genere, can. 11 et 12.

IV. THE EFFECTS OF THE SACRAMENTS:—All the Sacraments give grace to those who receive them with due dispositions.

It is of the nature of two of them, viz., Baptism and Penance, to give the *first grace*; i.e., to produce sanctifying grace in those who are *destitute of it*—they put *sinners* in a state of grace—they raise souls that are dead in sin, to the life of grace: (Hence, they are called *Sacraments of the dead.)*——It is of the nature of the other five to *increase* sanctifying grace in those who *already possess it*: for the worthy reception of these five requires a *previous* state of grace: (Hence, they are called *Sacraments of the living.)* Nevertheless, there may be circumstances in which even these five confer the *first* grace; that is, they may restore us, like the Sacrament of Penance, to the *the state of grace*[15]*

(15) * "Gousset, Archbishop of Reims, says: "They are called Sacraments *of the living*, because they cannot *ordinarily* be received with fruit, except by those who are *living* the life of grace. We say, *ordinarily*; for, by an *extraordinary* effect, they sometimes confer the *first* grace. Thus: if a person, who is under the guilt of some mortal sin, believes himself to be in a state of grace; and, in preparing himself to receive a Sacrament *of the living*, is moved (we do not say to perfect contrition, but) to a feeling of *attrition*, such as is necessary for receiving sacramental absolution: then the Sacrament will have all its effects — by communicating grace to him who receives it, it will itself obtain for him pardon and remission of all his sins..This is not an opinion held by a *few* Theologians *only*, but it is the most common doctrine of Divines—it is that which is the most generally received (*Communior Theologorum sententia*)...It is not *the state* of sin, but the *affection* to mortal sin, which is the obstacle (or *obex*) to the entrance of grace into the soul."—*Gousset Theologie Morale. tome* 2, *n.* 22.

St. Alphonsus Liguori says: "Of these (seven Sacraments) some are called Sacraments *of the dead*, as Baptism and Penance, which produce the *first* grace, and can therefore be received even by a sinner. Others are called Sacraments *of the living*, as the Eucharist and the rest. But, notwithstanding this, even the Sacraments of the living may sometimes confer the *first* grace! as, for instance, when any one, not thinking himself to be in a state of mortal sin, or considering himself

Besides thus producing or increasing *sanctifying* grace, each Sacrament gives a grace proper to itself, called *sacramental* grace. Thus, Baptism gives a spiritual birth, or the life of grace, making us Christians, and heirs of heaven; Confirmation gives us the Holy Ghost, with his seven-fold gifts; the Holy Eucharist gives us Christ himself, the Author of all grace, for the food and nourishment of our souls; Penance cancels the sins committed after Baptism, and reconciles us again to God; Extreme Unction gives us the grace of patience and resignation in our last sickness; the grace of resisting temptations to despair, and of

to be contrite, approaches to the Sacrament *with attrition*; as St. Thomas teaches, *p.* 3, *q.* 79, *art.* 3, where he says: '*This Sacrament* (the Holy Eucharist) *may, however, operate the remission of sins;.. even when received by him, who, without being conscious of it, is in mortal sin. For, perhaps, he was not at first sufficiently contrite; but, approaching devoutly and reverently, he will obtain by this Sacrament the grace of Charity, which will perfect his contrition, and complete the remission of sin*' St. Thomas confirms this doctrine in another place, *q.* 72, *art.* 7, *ad* 2; and Divines, with common voice, teach the same concerning the other Sacraments (of the living). *Reason:* because, in the Council of Trent, *Sess.* 7, *Can.* 6, it is said: "*If any one shall assert that the Sacraments of the New Law ..do not confer grace upon those who put no obstacle in the way; let him be anathema.*' He, therefore, who approaches to a Sacrament of the living *with attrition*, which excludes both actual and habitual affection to sin, ceases to put an obstacle in the way; and therefore he receives grace, provided he have a desire of the Sacrament of Penance." *S, Alph. Lig., Theol., Mor., lib.* 6, *tract.* 1, *n.* 6,——It is said: "*Provided he have a desire of the Sacrament of Penance,*" i.e., provided he be so disposed, that he *would* approach the Sacrament of Penance, if he *knew* that he needed it, and were able to have recourse to it; so far, indeed, as regards the receiving of the Holy Eucharist, there is a command of the Church to, that effect.—*Vide Conc. Trid. Sess.* 13, *de Euchar., cap.* 7.

Indeed, if *the slate* of sin were *itself* an obstacle to grace, it is evident that *every* Sacrament would then *necessarily* require to be received in the state of sanctifying grace; and. consequently, *no* Sacrament would be able to produce the *first* grace, since *the very want* of the first grace would be an obstacle against its reception.

making due preparation for death; Holy Orders give the power of the Priesthood, and grace to discharge properly the functions of it; Matrimony confers such grace as is required for the fulfilment of the duties of the married state.

The Sacraments produce grace *through the merits of Jesus Christ;* through his merits, they produce it *of themselves—by virtue of their very institution;* and not by virtue of the merits either of him who administers them, or of him who receives them. In order to *receive* the grace of a Sacrament, it is, indeed, necessary to be in good dispositions; but those dispositions do not *produce* the grace—they only *remove the obstacles* which would otherwise prevent its reception. For example, a room, in order to receive light, must have a window, or some aperture in the wall, through which the light may pass; yet the window does not *make* the light, but only removes the obstacles to its entering.

When a sacrament is knowingly received without the *necessary* good dispositions, i.e., when it is received *unworthily*, it then stamps upon the soul the *guilt of Sacrilege.*

V. The Reiteration of the Sacraments:—Can each Sacrament be received more than once? Three of them, viz., Baptism, Confirmation, and Holy Orders, can be received *only once* during life: and the reason is, because they imprint a *character*, or spiritual mark on the soul, which can never be cancelled.[16]. This spiritual mark, or character, consecrates the soul to God in a special manner: for his *servants*—for his *soldiers*—for his *ministers.* It will add to our glory and happiness in heaven; or to our disgrace and misery in hell. How careful, therefore, each one should be to fulfil the obligations which these Sacra-

(16) Conc. Trid., Sess, 7, de Sacr. in genere, can. 9.

ments impose! Extreme-Unction can be received as often as we are in *danger of death by sickness;* but not twice in the *same* danger.——The Sacrament of Matrimony cannot be repeated whilst *both* the parties live; but, if one die, it can be received again by the surviving party.

The Sacraments of Penance and Holy Eucharist can be received very often, and even daily. We should prepare ourselves for that of Penance whenever we have had the unhappiness of falling into *mortal sin;* and we should *frequently* partake of "the bread of life" in the Holy Communion.

EXHORTATION :—The Sacraments were instituted for the *sanctification of our souls:* they are the *means* appointed by God for this purpose. In vain, therefore, do you hope for sanctification or salvation, if you will not make use of the Sacraments—if you neglect the *means* of obtaining that which you hope for. And yet, how general is such neglect! How many are there whom no exhortations, no entreaties of their Pastor can induce to have recourse to the Sacraments, those life-giving institutions of God's mercy and goodness; and who thus live in the most imminent danger of dying without sanctifying grace, and of losing their souls!

Most earnestly, therefore, do I exhort you to make a proper use of these efficacious means of grace; and, in particular, to approach *very frequently* to the Sacraments of Penance and Holy Communion, and to be diligent and devout in preparing yourselves for them. Then will you obtain, from these Divine institutions, such graces as will enable you to "avoid evil and do good"[17]—such graces as will enable you to say with St. Paul: "I live; now not *I*, but *Christ liveth in me.*"[18]

(17) Ps. xxxiii., 15. (18) Gal. ii., 20.

INSTRUCTION XLV.

BAPTISM.

Baptism is a true Sacrament—its Effects—its Minister—its Necessity—the Preparation required in Adults—Sponsors—Ceremonies.

What is Baptism?—Baptism is a Sacrament; by which we are made Christians, children of God, and heirs of heaven; and are cleansed from original sin, and also from actual sin, if we be guilty of any.

How is Baptism given?—By pouring water on the child, whilst we pronounce the words ordained by Christ.

What are those words?—"I baptize thee in name of the Father, and of the Son, and of the Holy Ghost;" which words must be said at the same time the water is poured.

What do we promise in Baptism?—To renounce the devil, with all his works and pomps.

The design of this Sacrament is to cleanse the soul from original sin; and also from actual sins, if any have been committed previous to its reception; to make us Christians, and members of the Church; and to give us a right to the other Sacraments. It confers upon us a *new or spiritual birth*, whereby we become children of God, and heirs of his kingdom.

I. Baptism is a true Sacrament:—It has all that is necessary to constitute a Sacrament. For,

1. There is the "*outward Sign*" (or the outward part which the Minister performs), viz., the pouring of the water, and the pronouncing of the words.——The water used in Baptism must be natural water, such as rain water, or that which is taken from a well, or a river, or the sea. It must be poured on the head, if possible; and in sufficient quantity to run, or so as that it may truly verify the words, "I *baptize* thee," i. e., I *wash* thee.——The word must be said at the

same time the water is being poured—*all* of them must be said—and by *that person* who pours the water.—— There is, then, in this Sacrament, the *matter* and the *form;* which are its outward Sign.

2. There is the "*inward Grace*" (or that inward invisible part which God gives), viz., that sacramental grace whereby the soul is cleansed from *all* stain of original and actual sin, and restored to spotless innocence: "Do penance, and be baptized every one of you, . . . for the remission of your sins."[19] "Rise up, and be baptized, and wash away thy sins."[20] "Christ loved the Church, and delivered himself up for it; that he might sanctify it, cleansing it by the laver of water in the word of life."[21]——This grace, or inward cleansing of the soul is *signified* by the outward sign of Baptism, which is called a *sign* for this very reason.

3. There is the "*Institution of Christ:*" For he instituted it when he commissioned his Apostles to administer it, saying to them: "Going, therefore, teach all nations, baptizing them in the name of the Father, and of the Son, and of the Holy Ghost."[22]

II. Effects of baptism:—Besides that inward *sacramental* grace, which has just been mentioned, whereby the soul is cleansed from all *stain* of sin, and put in a state of *sanctifying* grace, there are also other inward graces or effects: For,

1. By Baptism, we are freed, not only from *guilt*, but also from the *temporal punishment* due to sin.

2. We are adorned with the Theological virtues of Faith, Hope, and Charity; which are infused into the soul.

3. A Character, or spiritual mark, is imprinted on the soul, which consecrates us to God as Christians,

(19) Acts ii., 38. (20) Acts xxii., 16.
(22) Matt. xxviii., 19. (21) Eph. v., 25, 26.

and servants of Christ; and which, being indelible, prevents this Sacrament from being received more than once.

4. A *right* is given us to the other Sacraments—and a *title* to the kingdom of heaven.

But, though Baptism destroys all guilt of sin, and the temporal punishment due to it; yet the soul remains subject to concupiscence and human infirmity. And why so? To keep us humble: To detach our hearts from the love of this life: To make us sigh after heaven: To try our fidelity to God in resisting temptations, &c. . . .

III. Minister of Baptism:—The proper Minister of this Sacrament is a Bishop or Priest; or Deacon if he be duly commissioned for the purpose. No other person can baptize *solemnly* or with the ceremonies; nor can any others *lawfully* baptize, except in cases of necessity. But, in cases of necessity, when a Priest cannot be had, *any* person (man or woman) may baptize; and not only *may* but *must*, rather than let any one die without Baptism. Consequently, all persons should know how to baptize.

IV. Necessity of Baptism:—Is Baptism necessary for salvation? Yes; it is the most necessary of all the Sacraments. We are not members of the Church without it, nor even Christians; nor can we receive any of the other Sacraments, until we have received this. Its necessity is plainly declared in the Scriptures. For,

1. Our Blessed Lord assures us, that we cannot be saved without Baptism: "Amen, amen, I say to thee, unless a man be born again of water and the Holy Ghost, he cannot enter into the kingdom of God."[23]

2. When giving commission to his Apostles to "preach the Gospel to every creature," our Lord

(23) John III., 5.

added: "He that believeth and *is baptized*, shall be saved."[24] This shows that Baptism is a necessary condition of salvation.

3. After St. Peter's first sermon, the people who were converted by it said to the Apostles: "What shall we do, men and brethren? But Peter said to them: Do penance, and *be baptized every one of you* in the name of Jesus Christ, for the remission of your sins."[25]

4. When St. Paul, on his way to Damascus, cried out: "Lord, what wilt thou have me to-do?" the Lord said to him: "Arise, and go to Damascus; and there it shall be told thee of all things that thou *must* do." And when he came to Damascus, Ananias said to him: "Rise up, and *be baptized, and wash away thy sins*."[26]

Is it *impossible*, then, in any case to be saved without being *actually* baptized? No; for when a person *cannot* be actually baptized, then martyrdom, or an ardent desire of Baptism, accompanied with faith and true repentance, may supply its place. In these cases, the person is said to be baptized *in his own blood*, or in *desire*.

What becomes of children who die unbaptized? It has not been revealed where they *go to*; but they are certainly excluded from heaven—from the beatific vision. Hence, how careful Parents should be to have their children baptized......!

V. Preparation for Baptism:—Children, of course, can make no preparation, nor is any required from them; but they who have come to the use of reason before they are baptized, must get instructed in the doctrines of the Church, and must believe them: "He that *believeth* and is baptized, shall be saved; but he that *believeth not*, shall be condemned."[27]

(24) Mark xvi., 15, 16. (26) Acts xxii., 10 to 16. (27) Mark xvi., 16
(25) Acts ii., 37, 38.

"Going, therefore, *teach* all nations, baptizing them in the name of the Father, and of the Son, and of the Holy Ghost."[28] They must also have true repentance, and resolve to lead a Christian life: "*Do penance*, and be baptized every one of you,......for the remission of your sins."[29]

VI. SPONSORS:—A Godfather and Godmother are provided for those who are baptized. Why so? To answer and promise in the child's name: To be sureties for the fulfilment of the baptismal promises: To be the instructors of their godchild, in case the parents should neglect their duty in this respect, or be prevented by death, or otherwise, from performing it. Hence, Sponsors must be themselves sufficiently instructed; they must lead a Christian life; and must be, at least, Easter-Communicants: otherwise they cannot be admitted as Sponsors. They contract a spiritual relationship with their godchild, and also with its parents, which prevents them from marrying either one or the other.

VII. CEREMONIES:—*How is Baptism given*.--By pouring water on the child, whilst we pronounce the words ordained by Christ.

Having explained the *Sacrament* of Baptism, it remains now to say a few words on the *Ceremonies* used in its administration.

All the Sacraments are accompanied with Ceremonies, instituted by Christ or his Church for good reasons. For what reasons? To give greater solemnity to their administration: To serve as outward expressions of those inward dispositions which are required: To present the mysteries of Religion in a sensible manner to the eyes of the people.——All the Ceremonie of the Church are full of useful meaning.

(28) Matt. xxviii., 19. (29) Acts ii., 38

The Ceremonies *used in Baptism* are all taken, either from the Scriptures, or from some important truth of Religion. Some of them serve to represent the *dispositions* for receiving Baptism; some its beneficial *effects;* and some its *obligations.* Therefore all Christians should know them.

Of these Ceremonies, some *precede* the essential act of Baptism, some *accompany* it, and some *follow* it.

1. *The Ceremonies immediately preceding Baptism:—*

First, The Child, or person to be baptized, stops at the porch or door of the Church; and there the Priest declares the advantages and obligations of the faith which is asked of the Church of God.

Secondly, The Priest breathes on the face of the child, saying: "Depart from him, unclean spirit; and give place to the Holy Spirit." For, as Almighty God, when he created Adam, "breathed into his face the breath of life; and man become a living soul:"[30] so Baptism (as this ceremony represents), causes the soul, that is dead in sin, to become "a living soul," by conferring sanctifying grace.

Thirdly, The Priest makes a cross upon the forehead, to teach us that we are not to be ashamed of the Cross of Christ; and also upon the breast, to signify that we are to cherish an affection for it in our hearts.

Fourthly, He puts into the mouth a few grains of blessed salt, saying: "Receive the salt of wisdom." For salt is an emblem of wisdom; hence, Christ says to his Apostles: "You are the salt of the earth."[31]

Fifthly, He exorcises the child, commanding the devil to depart from him; and then introduces him into the Church, going to the Font (if there be one); and the Sponsors recite with the Priest the "Apostles' Creed," and the "Our Father."

Sixthly, He touches the ears and nostrils with spittle,

(30) Gen. ii., 7. (31) Matt. v., 13.

saying: "Ephphetha, which is, Be opened." This is taken from the example of Christ, who did the same, when he cured the deaf and dumb man.[32]

Seventhly, He interrogates the child, saying: "Dost thou renounce Satan?—and all his works and all his pomps?" The Sponsors answer in its name: "I do renounce him—I do renounce them." This is a public, solemn, and binding engagement.

Eightly, The Priest annoints the child on the breast, and between the shoulders, saying: "I annoint thee with the oil of salvation, in Christ Jesus, our Lord:" This is in accordance with what God directed Mosses to do. "Thou shalt consecrate all (the things dedicated to the Divine service), with the oil of unction, that they may be most holy."[33]

Ninthly, The Priest inquires concerning faith in the Blessed Trinity, and in the incarnation, saying: "Dost thou believe, &c.?" The Sponsors answer: "I do believe." For an explicit belief of these mysteries is necessary for the child, when he shall come to the use of reason.

Tenthly, He asks: "Wilt thou be baptized?" To which the Sponsors answer: "I will."

2. *The Ceremonies accompanying the act of Baptism:—*

Then the Priest baptizes the child; in doing which, he pours the water three times on the head of the child, each time in the form of a cross; and while he is pouring the water, he says: "N., I baptize thee in the name of the Father, and of the Son, and of the Holy Ghost." The water he uses is blessed, according to the form prescribed in the Ritual.

When a lay person baptizes, he does not use this blessed water. All that such a person has to do is this: Take *common* water, and pour it upon the head of the

(32) Mark vii., 32 to 35. (33) Exod. xl., 11.

child', and, *at the same time* say these words: "I baptize thee in the name of Father, and of the Son, and of the Holy Ghost."

3. *The Ceremonies immediately following the Baptism:—*

First, The Priest anoints the child with the Chrism on the crown of the head; and thus are the members of the Church consecrated to God; so that it may be said of them, in the words of St. Peter: "You are a chosen generation, a holy nation."[34]

Secondly, The child is clothed with a white garment—the emblem of spotless innocence. In delivering it, the Priest says: "Receive this white garment, and see thou carry it without stain before the Judgment-seat of our Lord Jesus Christ, that thou mayst have eternal life."

Thirdly, Then the Priest gives a lighted taper, saying: "Receive this burning light, and keep thy Baptism, so as to be without blame; keep the commandments of God; that when the Lord shall come to the Nuptials, thou mayst meet him in the company of all the Saints in the heavenly Court, and have eternal life, and live for ever and ever." This lighted taper is an emblem of the *light of Faith;* and also of *good Example.* Thus, Christ says: "So let your light shine before men, that they may see your good works, and glorify your Father who is in heaven."[35]

Fourthly, The Priest concludes by saying: "N., Go in peace; and the Lord be with thee."

EXHORTATION:—As you have had the happiness of receiving Baptism, you should frequently thank God for this great blessing. You should think on the promises you then made; and resolve to fulfil them; but, if you have broken them, lament the loss of your baptismal innocence; lose no time in recovering it,

(34) 1 Pet. ii. 9. (35) Matt. v., 16.

by sincere repentance; and approach to the Sacrament of Penance for this purpose: *Delay not* to be converted to the Lord, and defer it not from day to day, for his wrath shall come on a sudden, and in the time of vengeance he will destroy thee."[36]

INSTRUCTION XLVI.

CONFIRMATION.

Confirmation is a true Sacrament—its Effects—its Minister—its Necessity—the Preparation required—its Ceremonies.

What is Confirmation?—Confirmation is a Sacrament, by which we receive the Holy Ghost, in order to make us strong and perfect Christians and soldiers of Jesus Christ.

Who is the ordinary Minister of this Sacrament?—A Bishop only.

How does the Bishop administer this Sacrament?—He prays that the Holy Ghost may come down upon us; He imposes his hands over us; and makes the sign of the cross with Chrism on our foreheads, at the same time pronouncing a set form of words.

What are these words?—"I sign thee with the sign of the cross, I confirm thee with the chrism of salvation, in the name of the Father, and of the Son, and of the Holy Ghost."

The great *object* of the Sacrament of Confirmation is to complete the life of grace received in baptism; by giving the Holy Ghost with his sevenfold gifts to dwell in our souls—to strengthen our faith—and to enable us to withstand whatever oppositions we may meet with in the practice of our Religion.

The Catechism of the Council of Trent says: "If

(36) Eccli. v., 8, 9.

the diligence of Pastors in explaining the Sacrament of Confirmation were ever required, certainly there is need, in these times, to put it in as clear a light as possible; seeing that this Sacrament is wholly neglected by many in God's holy Church, and that there are very few who endeavour to draw from it that fruit of grace which they ought. Wherefore the Faithful are to be in such a manner instructed concerning the nature, the efficacy, and the dignity of this Sacrament, that they may not only know that it must not be neglected, but that it is to be received with the greatest piety and devotion; lest, through their own fault, and to their extreme spiritual injury, this Divine benefit be conferred upon them in vain."[37]

I. CONFIRMATION IS A TRUE SACRAMENT:—It has those three things which are essential to the nature of a Sacrament. For,

1. There is the "*outward Sign*" (or that part which is outwardly performed by the Bishop), viz., the Bishop imposes his hands over all that are to be confirmed, praying the Holy Ghost to come down upon them with his sevenfold gifts. Then, as the essential matter and form, he lays his right hand upon the head of each one; and with the thumb of the same hand, he anoints the forehead with the holy Chrism, saying at the same time: I sign thee with the sign of the cross, and I confirm thee with the Chrism of salvation, in the name of the Father, and of the Son, and of the Holy Ghost." All this is the outward *sign* or visible part of this Sacrament of Confirmation.

2. There is also the "*inward grace*" (or that part which is invisibly performed by God), viz., the Holy Ghost, with his gifts and strengthening graces, is, in a special manner, given to the soul. For, the Scripture says of this Sacrament: "The Apostles (Peter

(37) Cat Conc. Trid., de Sacr. Confirm., n. 1.

and John) *prayed* for them (the Samaritans), that they might receive the Holy Ghost; then they *laid their hands upon them*, and they *received the Holy Ghost.*[38]

These inward graces are *signified and represented* by the outward *sign.* For, the imposing of the hand over the person who is being confirmed represents the imparting of the Holy Ghost; and the anointing with Chrism, saying: "I sign thee with the sign of the cross, and I confirm thee with the Chrism of salvation, in the name of the Father, and of the Son, and of the Holy Ghost," signifies both the *fulness* and the *nature* of the grace received.——*Chrism* is oil of olives mixed with Balm of Gilead, solemnly consecrated by the Bishop on Maunday Thursday. *The oil*, of which it is composed, represents *fulness* of grace; because it is of such a nature, that it easily flows, and *spreads*, and *penetrates;* and, being a smooth and mild substance, it represents also the spirit of patience in bearing contradictions and oppositions. And the *Balm of Gilead*, of which the Chrism is also composed, represents, by reason of its fragrance, the practice of a virtuous life, which is called in Scripture, an odour of sweetness in the sight of the Most High;"[39] and, as it possesses, moreover, the property of preserving bodies from putrefaction, it represents thereby, that the grace of Confirmation has the effect of preserving the soul from the corruption of sin. Thus, then, the outward part of this Sacrament is a SIGN of the inward grace it confers.

3. There is the *Institution of Christ:* That this Sacrament was instituted by Christ, is proved from the *fact*, that the Apostles administered it *as a means of grace.* In the Acts of the Apostles it is related, that, after the Samaritans had been baptized by Philip the Deacon, the Apostles sent to them Peter and

(38) Acts viii., 15, 17. (39) Eccli. xxxv., 8; 2 Cor. ii., 15.

John; who, when they were come, prayed for them that they might receive the Holy Ghost; then they laid their hands upon them, and they received the Holy Ghost."[40]

II. EFFECTS OF CONFIRMATION:—Like all the other Sacraments, Confirmation produces sanctifying grace; but (as *peculiar* to confirmation or as sacramental) it is the grace of *spiritual growth* and *strength*; that is to say, it is a grace which *augments* and *perfects* that of Baptism, and *strengthens* us against the enemies of our salvation—it renders us perfect Christians, and makes us soldiers of Jesus Christ.

This Sacrament gives us the *plenitude* of the Holy Spirit, who adorns and enriches our souls with those interior graces, with which he sanctified and strengthened the Apostles on the day of Pentecost. For, in this Sacrament we receive the sevenfold gifts of the Holy Ghost; viz., "*the spirit of wisdom, and of understanding, the spirit of counsel, and of fortitude, the spirit of knowledge, and of godliness, and the spirit of the fear of the Lord.*"[41] These gifts are certain supernatural dispositions or habits of soul, imparted to us by the Holy Ghost; and they lead us to act according to the inspirations and motions of his grace; which inspirations and motions of grace are given to us in those particular times and circumstances when we stand in need of them, or when they will be of service to us. [*See* INSTRUCTION LXXI. *where these seven Gifts of the Holy Ghost, and the twelve Fruits which they produce in the soul, are explained.*]

Although Confirmation is a Sacrament *of the living*, it may, nevertheless, produce even the *first* grace; that is, it may restore us, like the Sacrament of Penance, to the state of grace. [*See Note* 15, *page* 253.]

There is another effect of Confirmation, similar to

(40) Acts viii., 15, 17. (41) Is. xi., 2, 3.

what is produced in Baptism and Holy Orders; which is, that it imprints a character or spiritual mark on the soul, which can *never* be effaced. This spiritual character distinguishes us as the Soldiers of Christ; and, abiding in the soul for ever, it will either add to our glory and happiness in heaven, or to our disgrace and misery in hell.

III. Minister of Confirmation:—It is an Article of Faith, that the *ordinary* Minister of Confimation is a *Bishop only*.[42] He is called the *ordinary* minister, because the administration of this Sacrament belongs to the proper office of a Bishop; so that he can confirm his own subjects, without needing to be *specially* delegated for the purpose. But it belongs not to the proper office of a Priest; so that, if he should be empowered to confirm, he would act as the *extraordinary* minister of this Sacrament. In cases of necessity, the *Pope* can delegate or commission a Priest to administer Confirmation. But a Priest cannot administer it, without this special papal delegation.

IV. Necessity of Confirmation:—Is it necessary for every one to receive the Sacrament of Confirmation? The reception of this Sacrament is not so necessary, as to be an *essential* means of salvation, (hoc Sacramentum non est necessarium *necessitate medii*); but when persons have an opportunity of receiving it, by the Bishop's coming to administer it, they cannot then wilfully neglect to receive it without a sin, unless they be prevented by some reasonable cause.[43] There is more necessity of receiving it in a

(42) Conc. Trid. Sess. 7, de Confirm. can. 3.

(43) * "In hoc ergo casu aliquam esse negligentiam salutis et perfectionis, ideoque culpam venialem, non diffiteor." —*Billuart. Tract. de Confir.*, *Art.* 6.

But St. Alphonsus Liguori says;—"Opinio supra relata nimirum non teneri Fidelis sub gravi ad Confirmationem suscipiendam, hodie non videtur satis probabilis."—*Lib.* 6, *Tract.* 2, *cap.* 2, *n.* 182, *Parag.* "*Verumtamen.*"

persecuting country; or in a country like this, where Catholic faith and practice are so much opposed and ridiculed by those amongst whom we live.

In the Apostles we have a striking example of the necessity, or extreme utility of receiving the special graces of the Holy Ghost, such as are conferred upon us in Confirmation. The Apostles had been three years with Christ,—had seen his miracles,—heard his instructions,—witnessed his example, &c.; yet they had not courage to profess and practise what he required from them: they even forsook him,—denied him,—durst not show themselves in public, or appear to be his Disciples. But no sooner did they receive the Holy Ghost, with his gifts and graces, than their minds were enlightened......and their hearts inflamed......; they were filled with zeal and courage ......; and being thus endued with power from on high,"[44] they boldly professed......, publicly preached ......, and courageously, and even joyfully suffered for the Religion which they professed and preached. The Sacrament of Confirmation works the like beneficial effects in the souls of those who receive it worthily.

V. Preparation for Confirmation:—To receive Confirmation *worthily*, it is necessary to make a *good preparation*. In what does this preparation consist? It consists chiefly in these three things:—

1. In getting sufficiently instructed in the nature, effects, &c., of this Sacrament; and in our Religion generally. Hence they who are about to be confirmed should attend the preparatory instructions.

2. In putting one's self in a state of grace: For, "the Holy Spirit will not enter into a malicious soul, nor dwell in a body subject to sin."[45] Therefore, every one who is conscious of sin, should receive worthily the Sacrament of Penance.

(44) Luke xxiv., 49. (45) Wisd. i., 4, 5.

3. In spending some time in prayer, previous to the reception of Confirmation; after the example of the Apostles, who from Ascension-day to Pentecost, "were persevering with one mind in prayer, with Mary the Mother of Jesus."[46] Therefore, they who are about to be confirmed, should be more recollected and retired;—should frequently invite the Holy Ghost to come into their souls by the communication of his graces, and for this purpose it would be well to say occasionally the "*Hymns to the Holy Ghost;*"—they should desire ardently, and implore earnestly, the plenitude of those strengthening graces which Confirmation is intended to confer: For "your Heavenly Father will give the good Spirit to them that ask him."[47]

VI. Ceremonies of Confirmation:—I have now to say a few words on the Ceremonies of Confirmation.

How does the Bishop administer this Sacrament?—He prays that the Holy Ghost may come down upon us; he imposes his hands over us; and makes the sign of the cross with Chrism on our foreheads, at the same time pronouncing a set form of words.

1. The Bishop, turning towards the people, imposes his hands over those who are to be confirmed, and prays that God would send down upon them the Holy Ghost, the Paraclete, with his sevenfold gifts. The people, uniting their intention with that of the Bishop, should make the same supplication for themselves.

2. Then they go and kneel one by one before the Bishop, who dips the thumb of his right hand in the holy Chrism, and laying that hand upon the head of the person kneeling before him, he anoints his forehead with the Chrism in form of a cross, saying at

(46) Acts i, 14. (47) Luke, xi. 13.

the same time: "N., I sign thee with the sign of the cross, and I confirm thee with the Chrism of salvation, in the name of the Father, and of the Son, and of the Holy Ghost."—By this we are admonished that we must not be ashamed of the Cross of Christ, but boldly profess our faith, and fight manfully under the standard of the cross against all the enemies of our salvation.

3. This being done, the Bishop gives a slight blow on the cheek of him whom he has just confirmed, to remind him, that, being now a perfect Christian and a Soldier of Jesus Christ, he ought to be prepared to suffer any kind of contempt, of insult, and of humiliation, for the name of Christ. The Bishop says, at the same time: "Peace be with thee," to give him to understand, that it is only by his patience that he can preserve his peace of soul: "In your patience (says our Lord) you shall possess your souls."

4. The Bishop then begs of God to confirm the blessing which has been conferred, saying: "Confirm, O God, what thou hast wrought in us."[48] And he prays that the Holy Ghost, having come down upon them, would vouchsafe to dwell in their hearts, as in his holy temple. And he concludes by giving his Episcopal benediction. The persons confirmed should make the like petitions for themselves; and, moreover, they should spend some time after Confirmation in thanksgiving and prayer, in the same manner as after the Sacraments of Penance and Holy Communion.

If a person, after having been confirmed, unhappily fall into mortal sin, and thereby lose the grace of this Sacrament, he can recover it by sincere repentance and penance; because it revives in the soul, when she is clothed again with the robe of sanctifying grace.

(48) Ps. lxvii., 29.

INSTRUCTION XLVII.

HOLY EUCHARIST.

The Outward Sign of the Holy Eucharist—its Inward Grace—its Institution, the Scriptural Account of which proves the Real Presence—Objections answered.

What is the Holy Eucharist?—It is the true body and blood of Christ, under the appearances of bread and wine.

Why has Christ given himself to us in this Sacrament?—To feed and nourish our souls, and to enable us to perform all our Christian duties.

The Holy Eucharist is the greatest of all the Sacraments, because we receive therein, not only *grace*, but Jesus Christ himself, *the Author of all grace.*

Its *object* is "to feed and nourish our souls," in order that the life of grace, which we received in Baptism, and which was strengthened and perfected in Confirmation, may be preserved and increased: "I am the living bread, which came down from heaven; if any man eat of this bread, he shall live for ever: and the bread that I will give, is my flesh for the life of the the world."[49] The Holy Eucharist is intended to do for the soul, what corporal food does for the body.

The Blessed Eucharist is a *true Sacrament;* that is to say, it is *an outward sign—of inward grace—instituted by Christ.*

I. There is the "OUTWARD SIGN" (or the visible sensible part), viz., the *bread and wine*,— the *words of consecration* which are pronounced over them—and the *species* or *outward appearances* of bread and wine, which appearances remain after consecration.

II. There is the "INWARD GRACE" (or the inward invisible part), viz., the body and blood of Christ,

(49) John vi., 51, 52.

together with his soul and Divinity; that is to say, Jesus Christ himself, the Author of *all grace*, who gives himself to us in this Sacrament, to feed and nourish our souls.

This inward grace (or spiritual nourishment) is *signified* by the outward *sign*. For, as bread and wine are the food and nourishment of the body; so their outward appearances, which remain after consecration, *represent* the spiritual food and inward nourishment of the soul—they represent that "bread of life, of which whosoever eateth shall live for ever."[50]

III. There is the INSTITUTION OF CHRIST. And as the Scriptural account of its Institution, besides proving that it *was* instituted by Christ, proves also the doctrine of the REAL PRESENCE, i.e., that this Sacrament does really contain the body and blood of Christ, under the outward appearances of bread and wine; I will relate that account, from the first promise of this Divine Institution, to its final accomplishment.

1. *The Words of Promise:*—Though our Lord did not institute this Sacrament, till the night before his Passion; he had long promised it. He took occasion from the miraculous multiplication of the five loaves, to make this promise. For, after having prepared the minds of the people for this mystery, by feeding 5,000 persons with five loaves, he said to them: "Labour not for the meat which perisheth, but for *that* which endureth unto life everlasting, which the Son of Man will give you....... I am the *living bread* which came down from heaven, if any man eat of this bread he shall live for ever: *and the bread that I will give*, IS MY FLESH *for the life of the world.*"[51]

The Jews understood him to speak of giving them *his real flesh:* this is evident from the objection which

(50) John vi., 48, 51, 52 (51) John vi., 27, 51, 52.

they instantly made, saying: "How can this man give us HIS FLESH *to eat?*"[52]

In answer to this objection, far from explaining away his words, he confirmed them by the most positive declarations:

"Then Jesus said to them: Amen, amen, I say unto you: Except you eat *the flesh* of the Son of Man, and drink *his blood*, you shall not have life in you.

"He that eateth *my flesh*, and drinketh *my blood*, hath everlasting life; and I will raise him up at the last day.

"For *my flesh* is meat INDEED; and *my blood* is drink INDEED.

"He that eateth *my flesh*, and drinketh *my blood*, abideth in me and I in him.

"As the living Father hath sent me, and I live by the Father: so he that *eateth me*, the same also shall live by me.

"*This* is the bread that came down from heaven Not as your fathers did eat manna, and are dead: he that eateth *this* bread shall live for ever."[53]

After these *plain*, and *positive*, and *repeated* declarations, the Jews clearly saw that he *meant* to give them his *real* flesh and blood: yet they would not believe, but *still objected:* "Many therefore of his disciples, hearing it, said: This saying is *hard*, and who can hear it?"[54]

In answer to this second objection, he still did not tell them that they mistook his meaning; but, on the contrary, he reproached them for their unbelief; "Doth this scandalize you? If then you shall see the Son of Man ascend up where he was before?"[55] i.e., if you cannot believe that I can give you my flesh to eat and my blood to drink, now that I am here with

(52) John vi., 53.
(53) John vi., 54 to 59.
(54) John vi., 61.
(55) John vi., 62, 63.

you *on earth*; how will you believe it, when you shall have seen me ascend up into heaven? And thus, he anticipated the objection of later *Protesters* against his doctrine, who say: "The natural body and blood of our Saviour Christ are *in heaven*, and *not here*; it being against the truth of Christ's natural body, to be at one time in more places than one."[56]

Then he proceeded to show *the reason* why they could not believe his doctrine: it was because they followed their own corrupt *fleshy* reasoning, instead of listening to *the Spirit* of God; and therefore he said to them: "It is *the* Spirit that quickeneth; *the* flesh profiteth nothing: the words that I have spoken to you, are spirit and life."[57] Then, reproaching them for their unbelief, he added: "But there are some of you that believe not. For Jesus knew from the beginning who they were who did not believe. And he said: Therefore did I say to you, that no man can come to me, unless it be given him by my Father;"[58] i.e. unless he be *quickened by the Spirit of God* to believe.

"After this, many of his disciples," (seeing that he *really meant* to give them his *very flesh and blood*,) "went back; and walked no more with them."[59] He then let them go, without intimating to them that such was not his meaning. "Then Jesus said to the twelve: Will you also go away? And Simon Peter (in the name of himself and of the other Apostles) answered him: Lord, to whom shall we go; thou hast the words of eternal life."[60]

How many are there, in these days, who follow the unbelieving Jews, by going away from the Church of Christ; saying, like them, in the spirit of unbelief:

(56) Book of Common-Prayer, Declaration at the end of the Communion Service.

(57) John vi., 64.

(58) John vi., 65, 66; 44.

(59) John vi., 67.

(60) John vi., 68, 69.

"How *can* it be the real flesh of Christ, that is given to us in the Eucharist:—This saying is *hard*, and who *can* hear it?"——Catholics alone imitate the faith of the Apostles.

2. *The Words of Institution:*—Although the Apostles *believed* the words of Christ, wherein he promised to give them his flesh to eat and his blood to drink; yet they could not *understand* now those words were to be accomplished, until they saw our Lord actually fulfil them, by *giving* what he had thus *promised.*

"And when the hour was come (the night before his death), Jesus sat down and the twelve Apostles with him. And he said to them: With desire I have desired to eat this pasch with you before I suffer."[61] "And whilst they were at supper, Jesus took bread, and blessed, and broke; and gave to his disciples, and said: Take ye, and eat: This is my body. And taking the chalice, he gave thanks; and gave to them, saying: Drink ye all of this: For *this is my blood* of the New Testament which shall be shed for many unto remission of sins."[62]

Here we see the complete *fulfilment* of what had been long before promised. Christ declared what he gave to his Apostles to be HIS BODY and HIS BLOOD—the very body which should be delivered for them[63]—the very blood which should be shed for many unto remission of sins.[64] Now, when he says: "This *is* my body—This *is* my blood:" are we to contradict him, and say: "It is not so"? On the contrary, ought we not to say with St. Peter: "Lord, to whom shall we go?" in whom shall we find truth, if not in thee? for "thou hast the words of eternal life."[65]

IV. OBJECTIONS ANSWERED:—It remains now to answer some of the chief objections, which the un-

(61) Luke xxii., 14, 15. (63) 1 Cor. xi., 24. (65) John vi., 68, 69
(62) Matt. xxvi. 26, 27, 28. (64) Matt. xxvi., 28.

believers of our days raise against this doctrine, to justify their unbelief.

1. They say: "*Christ spoke figuratively at the last Supper.* For, if his words were figurative, when he said: "*I am the door*[66] —*I am the vine*;"[67] why not also, when he said: "*This is my body—This is my blood?*" This objection is as much as to say: "Christ spoke figuratively *sometimes*; therefore, why not *always?*"

"*I am the door*:"—The Evangelist *expressly shows* that these words were spoken in explanation of a *parable*: "*This proverb* Jesus spoke to them, but they understood not what he spoke to them."[68]——But when he said: "This is my body—This is my blood," there is no expression used to show, that his words were a proverb, or the explanation of a parable.

"*I am the vine*:"—The Evangelist plainly shows that these words are the application of a *comparison*. "As *the branch* cannot bear fruit of itself, except it *abide in the vine*; NO MORE *can you*, except ye abide *in me*." This is the comparison. Then comes the application: "*I* am *the* vine; *ye* are *the* branches, ...if any one abide not in me, he is cast forth as *a branch*."[69]——Evidently, therefore, this is no *real* or *valid* objection.

2. But does not Christ say: "Do this *for a commemoration* of me?"[70]——Yes; but, *do what?* Why, what *he* had just done, i.e., consecrate bread and wine (as I have done) into my body and blood, and eat and drink the same "for a commemoration of me,"—when you eat my body, and drink my blood, bear in mind that *that* SAME BODY, which you eat, was "delivered for you" on the Cross; and *that* SAME BLOOD, which you drink, was there "shed for the remission of your sins."

(66) John x., 7.
(67) John xv., 5.
(68) John x., 6.
(69) John xv., 5, 6
(70) Luke xxii., 19. 1 Cor. xi. 24, 2

Thus it is that St. Paul explains these words, by immediately adding: "For as often as you shall eat this bread, and drink the chalice, you shall SHOW THE DEATH OF THE LORD, until he come."[71] For, eating *the body and drinking the blood* of a person necessarily SHOWS *his death:* but receiving mere bread and wine does not.

3. But (they say), does not St. Paul still call the Eucharist "*bread,*" after consecration?——Yes; and the reason is, 1st, Because it has still the appearances of bread; as Angels are sometimes called "*men,*"[72] and the Holy Ghost "*parted tongues,*"[73] because they had the appearances by being such;—2ndly, Because it *had* been bread; as, for this same reason, the serpent was still called a *rod:* "But Aaron's *rod* devoured their *rods.*"[74]——This, therefore, is a groundless objection.

And, indeed, in the very same Chapter from which this objection is taken, St. Paul argues on the Blessed Eucharist in such a way, as to give the strongest proofs that HE *believed* it to be (not bread and wine, but) *the real body and blood of Christ.* For, after relating the words of consecration, he reasons thus: "*Therefore,* whosoever shall eat this bread, or drink the chalice of the Lord *unworthily*, shall *be guilty of the* BODY AND BLOOD *of the Lord*......For he that eateth and drinketh *unworthily*, eateth and drinketh *judgment* to himself, NOT DISCERNING *the body of the Lord.*"[75]

Here St. Paul evidently speaks of Christ's REAL *body and blood.* For HOW could any one be guilty of our Lord's body and blood, by eating *mere bread?* How could any one commit an outrage against the body of Christ, if it were not there to be outraged?

(71) 1 Cor. xi., 26.
(72) Gen. xix., 1, 10.
(73) Acts ii., 3.
(74) Exod. vii., 12.
(75) 1 Cor. xi., 27, 29.

How could an unworthy Communicant bring judgment upon himself for "not discerning the body of the Lord," if it were not there to be discerned?—Evidently, then, St. Paul *believed* the Blessed Eucharist to be Christ's real body and blood; and *taught the Corinthians* to believe it also. Therefore, the Catholic Church believes and teaches the same: whilst they who have left her Communion, follow the example of the unbelieving Jews, who went away from Christ, "and walked no more with him."

I have now explained the *outward Sign*, and the *inward grace*, of this Sacrament; and have shown that it was *instituted by Christ*, to be the spiritual food of our souls; and also that its institution, as related in the sacred Scriptures, affords abundant proofs of the doctrine of the Real Presence.

INSTRUCTION XLVIII.

HOLY EUCHARIST CONTIUNED.

Power given to consecrate—Transubstantiation—Communion in one Kind—the Effects of Communion.

What is the Holy Eucharist?—It is the true body and blood of Christ, under the appearances of bread and wine.

Why has Christ given himself to us in this Sacrament?—To feed and nourish our souls, and to enable us to perform all our Christian duties.

How are the bread and wine changed into the body and blood of Christ?—By the power of God, to whom nothing is impossible or difficult.

When is this change made?—When the words of consecration ordained by Jesus Christ, are pronounced by the priest in the Mass.

It has been shown in the last Instruction, how the

Blessed Eucharist is a true Sacrament—how it has an *outward Sign* and an *inward Grace*; and how the Scriptural Account of its Institution, besides proving that it *was instituted by Christ*, proves also the Catholic doctrine of the *Real Presence*.——I will now enter into a further explanation of this Sacrament.

I. POWER OF CONSECRATING, *given by Christ to his Apostles and their Successors*:—When our Lord instituted the Blessed Eucharist, he said: "*Do this* for a commemoration of me:"[76] and by these words, he gave POWER AND COMMISSION to his Apostles and their Successors *to do what he had done*; namely, to change bread and wine into his body and blood, and to administer the same to others.——It is in the Mass, that this change is made: it is made in the name, and by the power of Christ. In *His* name, the Priest says: "THIS IS MY BODY—THIS IS MY BLOOD;" and in the very same instant in which these words are pronounced, the bread and wine become, by virtue of a Divine power, the body and blood of Christ. The *appearances* indeed, remain the same as before; but the *substance* is changed.

II. TRANSUBSTANTIATION:—This change is called *Transubstantiation*. In all bodily and material objects, there are these two things; viz., the outward sensible *appearances*, and the inward *substance* which exists under those appearances or qualities. Now, faith teaches us, that, by the words of Consecration, this inward substance of the bread and of the wine is changed into the substance of the body and blood of Christ; the outward appearances all remaining the same as before.

Objections answered:—"But (exclaim the unbelieving followers of the Reformation), how is this possible?"

(76) Luke xxii., 19.

The Catholic answers: "By the power of God, to whom *nothing is impossible or difficult.*" Such an objection ill becomes us: it is not for us to limit our Creator's power, by setting bounds to his Omnipotence! Since Christ *has said it*, we know it must necessarily be true: what he has said, we *must* believe; and not say with the unbelieving Jews: "How *can* this man give us *his flesh* to eat? This saying is *hard*, and who can hear it." But rather should we say with St. Peter: "Lord, to whom shall we go? thou hast the words of eternal life."[77]——Did not Christ change water into wine in Cana of Galilee?[78] Was not water changed into blood in Egypt? and the dead rod of Aaron into the *body and blood* of a living serpent?[79]

"But (adds the Objector) *there* I could *see* a change; but *here* I can see none—it appears to be bread and wine as before—am I not to believe my senses?" Yes, we *do* believe our senses; for they tell us there are all the appearances of bread and wine; and we believe this testimony of our senses, for there *are* those appearances. But faith tells us, that under those appearances are the body and blood of Christ. Thus, then, our senses are not deceived. (*Example:* Had we been present, when "the Holy Ghost descended in bodily shape as a dove;"[80] and when he again descended under the outward appearances of "parted tongues, as it were of fire;"[81] our senses would have told us, that there were there *all the appearances* of a dove, and of parted tongues; but faith tells us that there was no dove, no tongue there, but the Holy Ghost under those appearances. Just so in the Holy Eucharist......)

Under the appearances, then, of bread and wine,

(77) John vi., 53, 61, 69. (78) John ii., 1 to 11. (79) Exod. vii., 20, 10. (80) Luke iii., 22. (81) Acts ii., 3.

are really contained the *body* and *blood* of Christ. Anything else? Yes; his *soul* and *Divinity:* "If any one shall deny, (says the Council of Trent,) that the body and blood, together with the soul and Divinity of our Lord Jesus Christ, and therefore the whole Christ, are truly, really, and substantially contained in the Sacrament of the most holy Eucharist; let him be Anathema."[82]

III. COMMUNION UNDER ONE KIND:—The body blood, soul and Divinity of Christ are present under one kind only, just as much as under both. For, Christ is present in the Holy Eucharist in a LIVING state, having risen from the dead to die no more;[83] and therefore, where his body is, there *must* also be his blood, his soul, and his Divinity: for these are inseparable in Christ's *living* body.

For the same reason, Christ is present whole and entire, not only under each kind, but also under every particle. Hence, St. Paul says: "Whosoever shall eat this bread, OR drink the chalice of the Lord unworthily shall be guilty of the *body* AND *blood* of the Lord."[84]

From this it evidently follows, that they who communicate *under one kind only*, receive Christ just as much as if they communicated under both; for, in either case, they receive Christ entire; there being no difference, except in the appearances.—(*Example*: If the Apostles had received the Holy Ghost under the appearances both of a dove, and of tongues, at the same time, they would have received no more than they did, but exactly the same; all the difference would have been in the outward appearances. Just so in the Holy Eucharist......)

The Priest, however, *must* consecrate and receive *both*, whenever he celebrates Mass. And the reason is,

(82) Conc. Trid., Sess. 13, de Euchar., can. 1. (83) Rom. vi., 9. (84) 1 Cor. xi., 27.

because the Mass is a *Sacrifice*, the object of which is to "*show Christ's* DEATH"[85]—to represent and continue the Sacrifice of the Cross: and this is shown by the separate consecration of the bread and wine.

In receiving, then, the Blessed Sacrament, (whether under one or under both kinds,) we receive Jesus Christ—his body and blood, soul and Divinity: and therefore, when we receive this Sacrament *worthily*, it must produce the most happy effects in the soul.

IV. EFFECTS OF COMMUNION:—The effects which the Blessed Eucharist produces in the soul of the worthy Receiver, are these:—

1. It *unites us to Jesus Christ:* "He that eateth my flesh, and drinketh my blood, abideth in me, and I in him."[86] Thus we become one with him; for, by means of the Holy Communion, "we are made partakers of the Divine nature."[87] The effect of the happy union will be, to make our lives resemble his; so that we may be enabled to say with St. Paul: "I live, now not *I;* but *Christ* liveth in me."[88] What bounty! what excess of love and condescension, on the part of our Blessed Redeemer!

2. It *supports and strengthens the soul*, by giving an INCREASE OF GRACE:—It is not, indeed, intended to *put* the soul *in a state of grace*, (although there are cases wherein it may have this effect;[89*]) but its ob-

(85) 1 Cor. xi., 26. (87) 2 Pet. i., 4. (88) Gal. ii., 20.

(86) John vi., 57.

(89) * St. Alphonsus Liguori, speaking on the effects of this Sacrament, says: "Its first and chief effect is, to confer an increase of grace: and sometimes to confer, accidentally, the *first* grace; as, for instance, if any one, not knowing himself to be in mortal sin, or believing that he has *contrition*, approaches to Communion *with attrition only;* then, from being *attrite*, he is rendered *contrite*. (St. Thomas and other Divines, almost with common voice, teach the same.) Because it belongs, generically to the nature of Sacraments, to confer grace upon those who are disposed for it by supernatural repentance, and who put no obstacle in the way."—*S. Alph. Lig., Theol. Mor., lib.* 6, *tract.* 3, *n.* 269.

See Note 15, page 236.

ject is to preserve us in that state: "He that eateth me, the same also shall live by me: He that eateth this bread shall live for ever;"[90] i.e., he shall have strength to persevere in the life of grace. For the Holy Communion inflames our soul with divine love; and imparts such an increase of grace, as will enable us to avoid sin, by assisting us to overcome all our temptations: "Thou hast prepared a table before me, against them that afflict me."[91]

3. Not only does it support us in our spiritual warfare, by strengthening our souls, but also by *weakening our passions.* The passions are those natural inclinations, which are the unhappy causes of sin: Now, in the Holy Communion, we receive our spiritual Physician, who, as the Psalmist says, "healeth all our diseases;"[92] i.e., cures our disorderly inclinations, by lessening their violence, and bringing them into perfect subjection to reason. If, then, temptation attack and trouble you, hasten to Jesus Christ in the Holy Communion, with an entire confidence that he will give you a complete victory over them. For, as "he commanded the winds and the sea, and there came a great calm;"[93] so will he command your passions, and the violence of your temptations, that they may not lead you into sin.

4. This Sacrament, moreover, is a *pledge of a glorious resurrection.* Everlasting life consists in possessing God eternally in heaven: now, Christ gives himself to us in this sacrament, during life, as a pledge of a glorious immortality; according to his express promise. "He that eateth my flesh and drinketh my blood, hath everlasting life; and I will raise him up at the last day;" (i.e., to eternal glory.)

Such are the happy effects which this Sacrament

(90) John vi., 5. (92) Ps. cii., 3.
(91) Ps. xxii., 5. (93) Matt. viii., 26.

produces in those who receive it with proper dispositions. Every worthy Communion makes us partakers of these inestimable advantages! Have recourse, then, frequently to this Divine Institution—to this efficacious means of grace. But take care to be always duly prepared; for otherwise, instead of receiving these *happy* fruits of Communion, you would bring judgment upon yourselves, by becoming "guilty of the body and blood of the Lord:" You would commit, therefore, a most grievous sacrilege!——The *manner of preparing* for Communion shall be the subject of the next Instruction.

INSTRUCTION XLIX.

HOLY EUCHARIST CONTINUED.

How to prepare for Communion.

How must we prepare ourselves to receive the Blessed Sacrament?—We must be in a state of grace, and be fasting from midnight.

Is it a great sin to receive it unworthily?—Yes, it is: "For he that eats and drinks unworthily, eats and drinks judgment to himself."—1 Cor. xi., 29.

What is it to receive unworthily?—To receive in mortal sin.

Communion is the receiving of the body and blood of Christ, for the food and nourishment of our souls.

In the last Instruction, I explained the *happy Effects* of a worthy Communion; showing how it unites us with Jesus Christ—how it supports us in our spiritual warfare, by strengthening us with an increase of grace, and by weakening our enemies—and how it gives us a pledge of a glorious immortality. But, to receive these happy Effects, we must be *properly pre-*

pared: and, according to the degree of our preparation, we receive these Effects more or less abundantly. It is for want of due preparation, that so many derive little or no profit from their Communions.

How, then *must we prepare ourselves to receive the Blessed Sacrament?*—We must be in a state of grace, and be fasting from midnight.

In order, then, to receive this Sacrament properly, two things are required; *first*, preparation of the body; and, *secondly*, preparation of the soul.

I. As regards the body, we are required, by a positive precept of the Church, to be fasting from midnight; i.e., from twelve o'clock, at the midnight immediately preceding Communion; we must avoid taking even the least thing by way of eating or drinking; otherwise, we could not lawfully communicate that day. It is out of respect and reverence to the Blessed Sacrament, that this command of the Church is given; in order that, on the day of our Communion, this spiritual food of the soul may be the first food we receive.

But this command of being fasting does not include those, who, being in danger of death by sickness, receive the Holy Communion by way of *Viaticum*, i.e., as an immediate preparation for their passage into eternity; for, in this case, the Blessed Sacrament may be received any day or hour, and whether the sick person be fasting or not.

II. As regards the soul, we are required to be in proper dispositions.

1. *We must be in a state of grace;* i.e., free from all guilt of mortal sin. For, as food is of no advantage whatever to a *dead body;* so the Holy Communion can do no good to a *soul*, when *dead in sin.*

To receive this Sacrament in the known guilt of mortal sin, is to commit the greatest of crimes. To those who are guilty of this sacrilegious crime, may be applied these words of our Blessed Lord: "Friend, how camest thou in hither, not having on a wedding garment (i.e., sanctifying grace)? Then the king said to the waiters: Bind his hands and his feet, and cast him into the exterior darkness; there shall be weeping and gnashing of teeth."[94] St. Paul declares, that they who receive unworthily, or in mortal sin, are "guilty of the body and blood of the Lord;" and that they "eat and drink judgment to themselves;" Therefore he says: "Let a man prove himself; and so let him eat of that bread, and drink of the chalice:"[95] i.e., before Communion you must examine the state of your soul; and if you find yourselves defiled with mortal sin, you must seek forgiveness by sincere repentance; and for this purpose, in compliance with a positive precept of the Church, you must have recourse to the Sacrament of Penance."[96]

Not only must you be free from the guilt of mortal sin; but moreover, you should adorn your soul with virtue, endeavouring to enter into such sentiments of piety, devotion, and love, as so great and holy a Sacrament demands.——And therefore,

2. *On the Eve of your Communion*, you should be more than usually retired and recollected; in order to think on the great work which you are about to perform, and to dispose your soul for a more immediate preparation. Let your *intention* be, to please God, and to advance in virtue.

3. *On the morning of Communion*, employ yourselves in fervent acts of *Faith*, *Adoration*, *Humility*, *Contrition*, *Divine Love*, *Desires* of being united to Jesus Christ, and *Supplications* for his grace.

(94) Matt. xxii., 12, 13.
(95) 1 Cor. xi., 27, 28, 29.
(96) Conc. Trid., Sess. 13, de Euchar., cap. 7.

First, FAITH :—Make *acts* of a firm and lively *Faith* in the real presence—remember what Christ said to Thomas: "Blessed are they that have not seen, and have believed."[97] Faith assures us, that, in receiving the Holy Communion, you receive Jesus Christ—"your Lord and your God." This Faith, if it be lively, will naturally lead you to pay him supreme homage.

Secondly, ADORATION :—Bow down your soul, therefore, in *acts of Adoration.* If Jesus Christ were to appear visible before you, what would you do? Would you not adore him in the most perfect manner you could? Now, we have his positive declaration, that he is really present: and therefore, we are as sure of his presence as if we actually saw him. Adore him, therefore, in this Sacrament, with all the fervour of your soul.

Thirdly, HUMILITY :—Then make *acts of Humility*, considering *His* greatness and *your* nothingness: the God of infinite Majesty comes to a mere worm! to a sinner! Oh! if your faith were lively, you would humble yourselves to the very dust; exclaiming with the Centurion: "Lord, I am not worthy that thou shouldst enter under my roof; but only say the word, and my soul shall be healed."[98]

Fourthly, CONTRITION :—This thought of your unworthiness should lead you to make fervent *acts of Contrition.* You may, indeed, hope to have received pardon in the Sacrament of Penance; but the true penitent has his sins "always before him"—he continues to lament them, and to crave mercy and forgiveness: with the penitent David he cries out: "Have mercy on me, O God, according to thy great mercy...Wash me *yet more* from mine iniquity; and cleanse me from my sin."

(97) John xx. 28, 29. (98) Matt. viii., 8.

Fifthly, HOPE :—After this make *acts of Hope* and confidence in the Divine goodness. *He*, whom you are about to receive, is, indeed, Lord of heaven and earth; and *you* a miserable sinner: but he is *infinitely good* and *merciful*, and invites you to have recourse to him: "Come to me, *all you that labour* and are *burdened*, and I will refresh you."[99] Go to him, therefore, with great confidence in his goodness.

Sixthly, CHARITY :—But, above all, go with a heart inflamed with an ardent *Charity*—love him with your whole heart and soul, in return for the great love which he manifests to you in giving you himself: this is the return which he expects from you. Make, then, fervent *acts of love*.......

Seventhly, DESIRES :—As the time of Communion draws near, rouse all your devotion—redouble your fervour; make *acts of ardent Desires* to receive Jesus Christ—to be united to the beloved of your soul: "As the hart panteth after the fountains of water, so my soul panteth after thee, O God."[100]

Eighthly, SUPPLICATIONS :—Conclude your preparation, by begging of your Blessed Lord to infuse these virtues plentifully into your soul—to perfect them—and to supply, by his grace, whatever is wanting in your preparation. And ask the Blessed Virgin Mary, and other Saints, to join their prayers with yours, and to obtain the grant of your petitions

(All this you will find expressed in the "*Prayers before Communion*," which are provided for you in your Prayer-Books.)

4. *At the moment of Communion*, after acknowledging again your unworthiness, ("Lord, I am not worthy," &c.,) receive your Redeemer with the greatest reverence and humility.——Having received, employ

(99) Matt. xii., (100) Ps. xli., 2.

all the powers of your soul in silent adoration of Jesus Christ, whom you inwardly possess.

5. *Immediately after Communion*, you should spend some time in acts of *thanksgiving and love;* you should make an *offering of your entire selves* to God; and pray for such graces and blessings, as you stand in need of.

First, Having, then, returned to your place, and adored your Lord who is present with you; *thank* him for all his blessings; and especially for having thus given himself to you: and *invoke* all creatures to join with you in blessing, and praising, and thanking him. Gratitude for favours received is the way to insure a continuance of them.

Secondly, Testify, therefore, your gratitude by *offering your whole self* to his love and service. Resolve that all your thoughts, words, and actions shall be directed to his glory, &c......

Thirdly, The time after Communion is *most precious;* because then you possess the Author of all grace. Employ it therefore in presenting fervent petitions to him: beg of him to adorn your soul with his gifts and graces—to strengthen you against temptations—to give you the grace of perseverance, &c.

(These sentiments and petitions you will find expressed in your Prayer-Books.)

6. *During the day of Communion*, keep yourselves retired and recollected; frequently call to mind the great blessing you have received; be particularly watchful against all occasions of sin; resolve to persevere in God's service, and frequently renew this holy resolution.

INSTRUCTION L

THE MASS.

Sacrifice in general—the Four Ends of Sacrifice—the Sacrifice of the Mass—Proofs—the Mass answers all the Ends of Sacrifice.

What is the Mass?—It is the unbloody sacrifice of the body and blood of Christ,

What are the ends for which we are to offer up this Sacrifice?—1st, For God's honour and glory. 2ndly, In thanksgiving for all his benefits, and as a memorial of the passion and death of his Son. 3rdly, for obtaining pardon for our sins. And, 4thly, For obtaining all graces and blessings through Jesus Christ.

The Mass is *the Sacrifice of the body and blood of Christ, offered on our altars under the appearances of bread and wine, to commemorate and continue the Sacrifice of the Cross.*

The Holy Eucharist is not only a *Sacrament*, but a SACRIFICE also: and this double mystery is accomplished in the Mass. Hence, the Mass is the most sacred, solemn, and sublime act of Religious Worship that we can perform. Of all the treasures which Christ has left to his Church, this Institution is the richest and most precious—it is the greatest display of his bounty and love towards us. Yet, alas! how unknown: how little understood! how many know not its value, nor how to apply its advantages to their souls! Pay attention, therefore; because it is very necessary to be well instructed on this important subject.

WHAT IS SACRIFICE IN GENERAL? It is *an offering* of some external *sensible thing*, made to *God* by a *lawful Minister*, to acknowledge by *its destruction or change* God's absolute Dominion over us, and our entire dependence on him, and thereby to pay him *the supreme homage of adoration.* Hence, sacrifice can be offered *only* to God.

To offer sacrifice, then, is to offer *to God* some *external thing* in testimony of his absolute Dominion, and our entire dependence. Thus, Cain offered his first-fruits; and Abel the first born of his flock: thus, also, Noe, Abraham, Melchisedech, &c., offered Sacrifice. In the Mosaic Law, God appointed Aaron and his descendants to be the only lawful Ministers of Sacrifice.[1] Core, Dathan, and Abiron, for usurping this office, were punished most severely by Almighty God. For he was so offended at their conduct, that he caused the earth to open beneath their feet, and to swallow them down alive into hell, together with those who joined in their schismatical worship.[2]

In offering Sacrifice, the victim undergoes a real or mystical destruction, to testify thereby that *we* deserve destruction at the hands of God. In the Old Law, this was signified by the person, for whom the victim was offered, putting his hand upon its head.

II. THERE ARE FOUR GREAT ENDS, which the servants of God have always had in view, in offering sacrifice; viz., 1*st*, to adore God, by giving him supreme homage; 2*ndly*, to thank him for his blessings; 3*rdly*, to appease his anger, and satisfy his justice; 4*thly*, To obtain his graces, and all the blessings we stand in need of.

But all the sacrifices of sheep and oxen could never (of themselves) answer these ends—they could never "take away sin,"[3] nor render to God the homage worthy of his Majesty.

In order that Sacrifice may be worthy of God's acceptance, and capable of atoning for sin, the victim must be of infinite value; because God, against whom

(1) Exod. xxviii., 1, 4; and xxix; Num. i., 48 to 51.
(2) Num. xvi., 1, &c. (3) Heb. x., 4.

sin had been committed, is infinite. Man had no such victim to offer; but God, in his mercy, supplied us with one—the Son of God himself became our great high priest and victim: by offering himself in sacrifice on the cross, he made full atonement for sin, and purchased redemption for *all* mankind IN GENERAL.

And to apply the merits of that *general* redemption to our souls *individually*, he has left in the Church an Institution for this purpose, viz., the Mass.

III. WHAT IS THE MASS? It is the unbloody Sacrifice of the body and blood of Christ;" offered on our altars under the appearances of bread and wine, to represent and continue the sacrifice of the Cross.

How does the Mass *represent*, or perpetually "*show* (as St. Paul says) the death of Christ?"[4] By the very act whereby he is rendered present; i.e., by the separate consecration of the bread and wine. Christ died by *really* shedding his blood; and thereby the Sacrifice of the Cross was accomplished: now, this shedding of his blood—this separation of the blood from the body, is represented in the Mass by the act of separate consecration. The Priest says in the name of Christ: "This is my body;" and, by these words, the bread is changed into the body of Christ: again, he says, "This is the chalice of my blood;" and thereby the wine is changed into the blood of Christ. The body and blood are *represented*, therefore, as separated from each other; and thus, our Lord offers himself to his eternal Father under *the appearance* of death, or, "*as it were* slain."[5]

But, the Mass is not a mere representation of the Sacrifice of the Cross; it is a *continuation* of the same Sacrifice: for the Priest and the victim are the same; the only difference being in the manner of offering:

(4) 1 Cor. xi., 26. (5) Apoc. v., 6.

on the Cross, Christ *really* shed his blood, and *really* died; but in the Mass, he sheds his blood *mystically* and is, "*as it were* slain."

IV. Proofs of the Mass, from the Scriptures:—

1. The Mass is *that perpetual Sacrifice*, of which God (after having declared that he would *reject the Jewish* Sacrifices) says: "From the rising of the sun, even to the going down, my name is great *among the Gentiles; and* in *every place* there is *sacrifice;* and there is offered to my name a *clean oblation.*"[6]

2. It is *that Sacrifice*, which Christ offered at the last supper: "This is my body which *is* given for you;"[7] "This is my blood of the New Testament which shall be shed for many unto remission of sins."[8]

3. It is *that Sacrifice*, which he commanded and empowered his Apostles and their successors to offer, till the end of the world, when he said: "*Do this* for a commemoration of me......For, as often as you shall eat this bread, and drink the chalice; you shall *show the death* of the Lord *until he come.*"[9]

4. It is *that great Sacrifice*, for the perpetual offering of which Christ is called "a Priest *for ever*, according to the order of *Melchisedec.*"[10]

V. The four Ends for which the Mass is offered:—The Mass, by reason of its infinite value, fully answers the four great Ends of Sacrifice.——For,

What are the Ends for which we are to offer up this Sacrifice?—

1*st*, *For "God's honour and glory:"*—We owe to God supreme homage of adoration, whereby we are to testify that he has absolute Dominion over us—that he is "the Lord our God." But if (independently of

(6) Mal. i., 11. (7) Luke xxii., 19, 20. (8) Matt. xxvi., 28. (9) 1 Cor. xi., 24, 25, 26. (10) Heb. v, 6.

Christ) we are to offer to him our whole selves, and all that belongs to us; it would not be a sacrifice worthy of his acceptance.——Now, in the Mass, we have a victim which is in every way worthy of God namely, Jesus Christ, who offers himself in our behalf, as *a Sacrifice of Adoration:* and, by uniting our intention with his, when we assist thereat, we are enabled to offer to God a homage which is *supreme* and perfectly pleasing to him.

"*2ndly, In thanksgiving for all his benefits:*"—We owe infinite thanks to God, for the blessings we have received from him: but, *of ourselves*, we have no return that we can make, worthy of God's acceptance.—Now, in the Mass, Jesus Christ offers himself for us, as *a Sacrifice of Thanksgiving:* and thereby he enables us to return adequate thanks for all the blessings which God has bestowed upon us.

"*3rdly, For obtaining pardon of our sins:*"—We have frequently sinned against God; we owe him, therefore, a Sacrifice of Propitiation: but al the repentance and penance which *we* could offer, would not be sufficient or available, without the merits of Christ.——Now, in the Mass, Christ offers himself for us, as a *Sacrifice of Propitiation:* and, by offering the same in union with him, we are enabled to repent effectually, to appease the anger of God, and to satisfy his justice; for the Mass applies to our souls the merits of Christ for this purpose.

"*4thly, For obtaining all graces and blessings, through Jesus Christ:*"—We need a constant supply of God's graces, and of his other blessings: but we cannot obtain them, except through the merits of Christ.——Now, in the Mass, Jesus Christ offers himself for us, as *a Sacrifice of Impetration*, to obtain for us all the graces and blessings of which we stand in need.

CONCLUSION:—You see, from what has been said,

how perfectly the Mass answers the four Ends of Sacrifice—how it is the most sacred, solemn, and sublime act of Religious Worship that we can perform—the most pleasing to God—and the most advantageous to our souls. You see, therefore, what esteem and veneration you should have for this sacred Institution of God's mercy—and with what reverence, attention, and devotion, you ought to assist at it. Remember, this Sacrifice is the *means of applying* the merits of the Cross to your souls; but that this application is more or less abundant, according to your devotion; therefore, with what earnestness you should assist at it! for otherwise, what immense spiritual losses you will sustain! how many and precious are the graces of which you will be deprived!

INSTRUCTION LI.

THE MASS CONTINUED.

Manner of assisting at Mass: By using a Prayer-Book—By reflecting on the Passion—By attending to the four Ends of Sacrifice.

What is the Mass?—It is the unbloody Sacrifice of the body and blood of Christ.

What are the Ends for which we are to offer up this Sacrifice?—1st, For God's honour and glory. 2ndly, In thanksgiving for all his benefits, and as a perpetual memorial of the Passion and Death of his Son. 3rdly, For obtaining pardon for our sins. And 4thly, For obtaining all graces and blessings, through Jesus Christ.

How must we hear Mass?—With very great attention and devotion.

In the last Instruction, I explained the Nature, the Necessity, and the Ends of Sacrifice—and particularly of the great Christian Sacrifice--I showed how the Mass is the most sacred, solemn, and sublime act of Religious Worship, that we can perform; the most pleasing to God, and most advantageous to us: it is a most inestimable treasure, provided for us by the Divine goodness; for, one Mass, *heard well*, is sufficient to enrich our souls with special graces, and to make us Saints.

Why, then, do so many persons who hear Mass, derive therefrom so little benefit? That proceeds from their *defective manner* of assisting at it.

MANNER OF ASSISTING AT MASS:—As three kinds of persons were present at the Sacrifice of the Cross on Mount Calvary; some crucifying and insulting their Redeemer—others satisfying their curiosity, or merely passing away their time—and some few, (as the Blessed Virgin Mary, St. John, &c.,) with feelings of devotion, love, and compassion: so, how many, in like manner, are there, who, going to Mass in a state of mortal sin, are so far from repenting, or seeking forgiveness, that they persevere in their sinful dispositions; and who, by their presence, do not honour, but rather "crucify again the Son of God?"[11]—How many also are there, who only go to see and be seen; who are, indeed, present at the Holy Sacrifice, but with indifference—without attention or devotion?—How few there are, who, by their conduct and dispositions during Mass, imitate the devotion of the Blessed Virgin or of St. John?——I will now explain the manner of hearing Mass.

In order to assist at Mass properly and with spiritual advantage, 1st, you should show great devotion and respect in your outward behaviour; and, 2ndly, you should also strive to enter into such sentiments and feelings as this great Sacrifice ought to inspire.

(11) Heb. vi., 6.

I. By using a Prayer-book :—For this purpose, read attentively the *Prayers for Mass*, either in your Missal or in some other Prayer-book. If you have a Missal, you have then the very same prayers which the Priest says; but, after the "*Agnus Dei*," take another book, or pray mentally. If you use a "Garden of the Soul," or any similar Prayer-book, you have prayers which are expressive of the sentiments proper for each part of the Mass. Accompany the Priest, by reading the prayer corresponding to what he is saying; and strive to enter into the spirit of each prayer.——While you are hearing Mass, never lose sight of this truth, namely, that you are then assisting at the same Sacrifice, as that which Christ offered on the Cross; and, consequently, that you should have the same sentiments as you would have had, if you had been present on Mount Calvary; viz., a lively representation of the Sufferings of Christ—devotion—love—gratitude—contrition—and hatred of sin, with a firm resolution to avoid it in future. You will find all these sentiments expressed in your Prayer-books; and you should strive to excite them in your soul.

II. By reflecting on the Passion of Christ :—Those who *cannot read*; or, who can read, but prefer to *pray mentally*, may employ themselves in reflecting on the Passion and Death of Christ, and in exciting the sentiments and feelings just mentioned, accompanying their reflections with frequent aspirations, pious affections, and frequent acts of love and contrition, &c.——To assist you in following this method, I will now show you how the different Ceremonies of the Mass may serve to remind you of the different stages of our Lord's Passion. While hearing Mass according to this method, you should bear in mind, that it is *Jesus Christ* who is then offering himself in Sacrifice to his eternal Father, by the ministry of the

Friest; and that he is thus offering himself, in order to apply the merits of Redemption to your soul.

1. The Priest goes to the Altar, with the Clerks, *to begin Mass.*——This may remind you of Christ going to the Garden of Gethsemani, with three of his Apostles, *to commence his Passion.* [*Enter into sentiments of resignation to God's will; casting yourselves entirely on his mercy, in the spirit of Penance.*]

2. The Priest *prays* at the foot of the Altar, *bowing down* at the "Confiteor."——Christ *prays* in the Garden, *prostrating* himself on the ground, his soul being "sorrowful even unto death;"[12] so much so, that "his sweat became as drops of blood trickling down upon the ground."[13] [*Think of your sins; excite contrition; implore forgiveness.*]

4. The Priest *ascends* up to the Altar; and, having kissed it, *goes* to the Epistle-side to read the "Introit," then he *returns* to the middle to say the "Kyrie,"—he *goes again* to the Epistle-side to read the "Collects" and the "Epistle"—he *returns again* to the middle and *prays*—then he *goes* to the other side to read the "Gospel.——"Christ having *risen* from his prayer, is led by the Jews to Annas and Caiphas—then to Pilate—from him to Herod—and back again to Pilate; and in these stages of his Passion, he is ill-treated by his enemies, mocked, spit upon, struck on the face, condemned, and delivered up to be crucified. [*Make Acts of meekness, patience, humiliation, &c.*]——The reading of the Gospel represents our Lord's preaching. [*During the "Gospel" and the "Creed," make lively Acts of Faith; and resolve to practise what Faith teaches, begging God's grace for this purpose.*]

4. The Priest *uncovers* the Chalice, and *offers* the Host.—Christ is *stripped* of his clothes; and, after having been scourged and crowned with thorns, he is ex-

(12) Matt. xxvi., 38 (13) Luke xxii., 44.

hibited to the people: "Behold the man"[14] Our Blessed Lord *offered* all these sufferings, to atone for our sins of sensuality, pride, and vanity. [*Make acts of contrition for these sins; and of love and gratitude towards Christ, from the consideration of what he has done to expiate them.*]

5. The Priest *washes* his hands, to show the purity of heart with which we ought to assist at the Holy Sacrifice.——This may remind us of Pilate "washing his hands before the people, saying, I am innocent of the blood of this just man."[15] But Pilate was not innocent, for "he delivered up Jesus to be crucified."[16] [*Think how often* YOU *also have been guilty of similar self-delusions; deplore these unhappy delusions—and beg of God to preserve you from them in future.*]

6. The Priest, going to the middle of the Altar, *bows down* in silent prayer; then, *turning towards the people*, he says: "Brethren, pray that my Sacrifice and yours may be acceptable to God the Father Almighty."——Christ, going to Calvary, *falls down;* and then *turning round to the pious women*, says: "Daughters of Jerusalem, weep not over me; but weep for yourselves and for your children."[17] [*Mere compassion for his sufferings is not sufficient; but we must hate and lament* THE CAUSE *of them, viz., our own sins: and we should beg of God to accept this Sacrifice, in satisfaction for what we owe to his Justice; that both we and our offering may be pleasing in his sight.*]

7. The Priest, having *come to the* "*Canon,*" commences that part of the Mass wherein the *Sacrifice* or *mystical Immolation* properly takes place.——This may represent Christ *arrived at Calvary*, when the Jews begin to *nail him to the Cross.* [*Endeavour to*

(14) John xix., 5.
(15) Matt. xxvii., 24.
(16) Matt. xxvii., 26.
(17) Luke xxiii., 28.

die to sin, to your passions, to the world; and resolve by daily mortification and self-denials, to offer yourself a continual sacrifice or oblation to God.]

(During this portion of the Mass, the bread and wine are consecrated; and are then no longer bread and wine, but the body and blood of Christ, who is then truly present on the altar, under the appearance of bread).

8. After pronouncing the words of Consecration, the Priest *elevates* and adores. The Elevation may remind us of Christ's being *raised up* on the Cross; and the separate consecration represents the shedding of his blood for us. [*At this solemn part, bow down in silent adoration—offer your whole heart and soul to your Blessed Redeemer, dedicating yourself irrevocably to his service, and pouring forth fervent Acts of love, gratitude, and contrition. These are most precious moments; take care, therefore, to employ them well.*]

9. After the Elevation, the Priest, *extending* his hands, says a number of prayers *in silence.*——Christ, with his hands extended on the Cross, *silently* offers his Sufferings and Sacrifice to his Father; and gives up his soul, with perfect resignation, into his hands.[18] [*Join with your Redeemer in offering the same; and pray most earnestly, that the merits of this Sacrifice may be applied to you for the pardon of your sins, and for the enriching of your soul with all the graces and blessings you stand in need of.*]

10. At the "Agnus Dei," the Priest *strikes his breast*, saying: "Lamb of God, who takest away the sins of the world, have mercy on us."——Say the same yourself with heartfelt sorrow; like the Jews, who "returned home striking their breasts," and saying: "Indeed, this was the Son of God,"[19] whom

(18) Luke xxiii., 46. (19) Matt. xxvii., 54; Luke xxiii., 48.

we have crucified! [*Think with sorrow how often* YOU *have crucified him again by your sins;*[20] *and strike your breast, to testify your sorrow; and implore his mercy.*]

11. The Priest *breaks* the Host, dividing it into three parts.——The soldiers *pierce* the side of Christ, as if to open to us a way to his Divine heart—that treasury of all graces. [*Beg of your Lord to inflame your heart with an ardent love of him; and conceive longing desires of being united to him, that he may enrich your soul with the treasure of his graces.*]

12. The Communion may remind you of Christ's *Burial*, and of his *descent* into Limbo. [*If you have not the happiness to receive your Blessed Lord sacramentally, make here a* SPIRITUAL COMMUNION; that is, make an Act of lively Faith in what the Church teaches concerning the Holy Communion—an Act of Hope or Confidence in the goodness and bounty of Christ—a fervent Act of Charity, uniting therewith sentiments of sincere repentance for your sins—then conceive in your heart an ardent desire of being united with Christ in the Holy Communion; and, in these dispositions, entreat him to come into your soul by a *spiritual Communion*, and to confer upon you those precious gifts and special graces, which he communicates so abundantly to those happy souls, who, being duly prepared, receive him *sacramentally.*]

13. After the Communion, the Priest turns towards the people, and says: "*The Lord be with you.*"——After his Resurrection, Christ says to his Apostles: "*Peace be with you.*"[21] [*Implore the grace of perseverance; that, avoiding sin in future, you may enjoy the* PEACE *of a good conscience; and that, advancing continually in virtue, you may arrive at that perfection to which God calls you.*]

14. Before leaving the Altar, the Priest *blesses* the

(20) Heb. vi., 6. (21) John xx., 19, 21.

people.——Christ *blesses* his Apostles, before he leaves them, by ascending into heaven. [*Receive this blessing with great devotion, humility, and confidence in the Divine goodness.*]

Thus, you see, how every part of the Mass may serve to remind you of some circumstances of our Lord's Passion; and to excite within you corresponding sentiments of piety, such as are proper for the time of Mass.

III. BY ATTENDING TO THE ENDS OF SACRIFICE: Another method of assisting at Mass with great advantage, is to confine yourself chiefly to the *four great ends of Sacrifice;* viz., 1st, to adore God; 2ndly, To supplicate him for mercy and pardon; 3rdly, To implore his graces and blessings; and, 4thly, To thank him for all his benefits.

1. In the *First Part* of the Mass (which is from the beginning, to the end of the Gospel or Creed), employ yourself in making *Acts* of profound adoration and humility; acknowledging God's supreme dominion over you, and your entire dependence on him......

2. In the *Second Part* (which is from the Offertory to the Canon), call to mind your sins—lament them in bitterness of soul—send forth to God repeated and fervent supplications for mercy, imploring the gift of true repentance, that you may obtain the Divine forgiveness. To these acts of contrition, join firm purposes of amendment—resolve to avoid sin in future, and make your resolutions *decisive* and *practical*, praying for grace, that you may be enabled to reduce them to practice....

3. The *Third Part* of the Mass is from the "Canon" to the "Pater Noster." At the Elevation, bow down in silent adoration of Jesus Christ, who is then present on the Altar; and offer him your whole heart and soul. Employ the rest of this Part in begging, through the merits of this Divine Sacrifice, all the

gifts and graces you stand in need of, and the virtues which ought to be your daily practice, viz., Faith, Hope, and Charity. Humility, and Chastity, Patience, Resignation, and Conformity to God's will—the spirit of Mortification and Penance, &c. Make similar petitions for your friends, and for *all* mankind....

4. The *Fourth Part* is from the "Pater Noster" to the end of the Mass. In this part make a *spiritual Communion*, by conceiving an ardent desire to receive your Blessed Lord; and by inviting him to come and take up his abode in your soul; that henceforth you may abide in him, and he in you. Then, considering the great and special favours you have received from God, thank him for them from your heart, and beg a continuance of them—deplore your past ingratitude—and resolve to be more grateful in future, and to testify your gratitude by a good life......

The Mass being finished, thank God for the favour of having been allowed to assist at it; and leave the Church with the same feelings of compunction, gratitude, and love, with which you would have left the crucifixion on Mount Calvary.

CONCLUSION:—If you had always assisted at Mass in this devout manner, how many graces and blessings would you have thereby obtained! Be resolved now at least to correct all past negligences, by hearing Mass in future "with very great *attention* and *devotion*;" and then you will not fail to advance rapidly in virtue......

[When persons are prevented, by an unavoidable impediment, from being present at Mass, they may, in some measure, supply for their absence, by attending *in spirit* during the time that the Holy Sacrifice is being offered; and they may thus obtain very great spiritual advantages.]

For this purpose, let them (while Mass is being said) represent themselves as being actually present before the Altar of God, joining with the Priest, and with the assembled Faithful, in offering up the adorable Sacrifice; and then let them go through the same devotions, and endeavour to excite the same sentiments and feelings, and make the same petitions as they would do if they were assisting at Mass really. Let them not forget to commemorate the Passion of Christ—to attend to the four great Ends of Sacrifice—and to make a Siritual Communion—and also to beg of God, with all the fervour of their soul, to bestow upon them those special graces and blessings, which he gives to the Faithful who hear Mass attentively and devoutly.]

INSTRUCTION LII.

PENANCE. I.

Penance is a true Sacrament, i.e., an Outward Sign—of Inward Grace—instituted by Christ—its Minister—its Necessity—its Effects.

What is the Sacrament of Penance?—Penance is a Sacrament in which, by the Priest's absolution, joined with contrition, confession, and satisfaction, the sins are forgiven which we have committed after Baptism.

How do you prove that the Priest has power to absolve sinners if they be truly penitent?—From the words of Christ: "Whose sins you shall forgive, they are forgiven"—John xx., 23.

How wonderfully God has manifested towards us his goodness, bounty, and love, in the Institution of the three Sacraments already explained; for, in Baptism, he gives us a new and spiritual birth; whereby we receive the life of grace, are made members of the Church of Christ, and heirs of his heavenly Kingdom; in Confirmation, he imparts to us the Holy Ghost; with his seven-fold gifts; whereby we are strengthened against our spiritual enemies; in the Holy Eucharist, Jesus

Christ communicates to us his own body and blood, for the food and nourishment of our souls; whereby we receive grace to enable us to perform all our Christian duties. But, notwithstanding all this bounty and goodness on the part of God, what would still become of us, if, after having lost his grace by mortal sin, we had no means of recovering it? We should have to live and die in sin, and be lost eternally! God *might*, in his justice, have left us without such a means of pardon as he left the fallen Angels!

How consoling, then, for us is the reflection, that God, in his tender mercy, has provided for sinners an efficacious means of reconciliation with him! This means is the *Sacrament of Penance*. How very important, therefore, it must be, that you should be well instructed in the nature of this Institution of Mercy, and in the manner of making a good and profitable use of it; for, it is for the want of such instruction, that many sinners neglect the Sacrament of Penance—that many others derive but little benefit from it—and that many even make it a means of increasing their guilt, by sacrilegiously profaning it. I will endeavour, therefore to give *full* Instructions on each part of this Sacrament.

I. PENANCE AS A SACRAMENT.—*What*, then, *is the Sacrament of Penance?*—Penance is a Sacrament in which, by the Priest's absolution, joined with contrition, confession, and satisfaction, the sins are forgiven which we have committed after Baptism.

There is a difference between penance as a *Virtue* and penance as a *Sacrament*. [*Show the difference.*] I have to speak of it now as a *Sacrament*, *i.e.*, as an outward Sign—of inward Grace—instituted by Christ.

1. *There is the* "OUTWARD SIGN" (or that part which is performed externally by the penitent and the Priest),

viz., the three acts of the penitent—*contrition*, *confession*, and *satisfaction*, which are *as the matter* of this Sacrament;[22]* and the *words of absolution*, pronounced by the Priest, which are its *form*.——The three acts of the penitent, being outwardly expressed or externally manifested, are properly and naturally taken to *signify* an inward change of heart—they have been divinely appointed to be signs of inward remission; and the words of absolution determine those acts more clearly to this signification; for the absolution, pronounced over the self-accused penitent outwardly *expresses*, and therefore *signifies*, the inward remission which it operates.

2. *There is the* "INWARD GRACE" (or inward part of this Sacrament), namely, the remission of the *guilt* of sin. For thus Christ says to the Pastors of his Church: "Whose sins you shall forgive, they are forgiven them; and whose sins you shall retain, they are retained."[23] Therefore, when the Priest pronounces absolution over a penitent sinner, God ratifies the sentence, and *gives sanctifying grace* to the soul.

3. *There is the* "INSTITUTION OF CHRIST." For

(22) * Gosset, Archbishop of Reims, says: "Scholastic divines make the distinction of *remote* and *proximate* matter of the Sacrament of Penance: the sins of the penitent are the remote matter; and his acts are the proximate matter: but it would be more correct to say, that the sins are the matter of the *Confession*, and not of the *Sacrament*. At all events, the opinion now generally received is, that the Sacramental matter of Penance consists in the external acts of the penitent, which are contrition, confession, and satisfaction."—*Theologie Morale*, tome 2, n. 388.

St. Thomas says: "The proximate matter of the Sacrament of Penance are the acts of the penitent." *(Materia proxima Sacramenti Pœnitentiæ sunt actus pœnitentis.)—Sum.*, p. 3, q. 84, a. 2.

The Council of Trent says: "The acts of the penitent himself, to wit, contrition, confession, and satisfaction, are, *as it were, the matter of* this Sacrament." *Sunt autem* quasi materia *hujus Sacramenti ipsis pœnitentis actus, nempe contritio, confessio et satisfactio.)*—Sess. 14, de Pœnit, cap. 3.

(23) John xx., 23

Christ instituted this Sacrament, and gave the power of administering it, when he said to the Apostles: "Receive ye the Holy Ghost: whose sins you shall forgive, they are forgiven them; and whose sins you shall retain, they are retained."[24] He had previously promised this power, saying: "Whatsoever you shall bind upon earth, shall be bound also in heaven; and whatsoever you shall loose upon earth, shall be loosed also in heaven."[25]

Proofs that the Church has this Power:—

1. When Christ cured the Paralytic, he worked that miracle for the express purpose of proving, that he, *as man*, had "power on earth to forgive sins."[26] ——Now,

2. Christ sent the Apostles (and through them their successors) with the same power. For, on the day of his resurrection, he appeared to the Apostles, and said: "Peace be to you. *As* the Father hath sent me, *I also* SEND YOU. And when he had said this, he breathed on them, and he said to them: Receive ye the Holy Ghost: whose sins *you* shall forgive, they ARE FORGIVEN them, and whose sins *you* shall retain, they are retained."[27] "Whatsoever *you* shall bind upon earth, shall be bound also in heaven; and whatsoever *you* shall *loose* upon earth, SHALL BE LOOSED ALSO IN HEAVEN."[28]

3. St. Paul declares, that God has given this power to the Church: "God hath reconciled us to himself by Christ: and hath *given to us* the ministry of (this) reconciliation. For God indeed was in Christ, reconciling the world to himself; and he hath *placed in us* the word of reconciliation (i.e., the power of pro-

(24) John xx., 22, 23.
(25) Matt. xviii., 18.
(26) Matt. ix., 6.
(27) John xx., 21, 22, 23.
(28) Matt. xviii., 18.

nouncing the words of Absolution): For Christ, therefore, we are ambassadors."[29]

4. The Church has *constantly taught* this doctrine, and has *always exercised* this power.

5. All the ancient heresies have likewise held the same: and it is even taught by the Protestant Church of England, in the "Order of the Visitation of the Sick."

II. MINISTER:—None but Priests can administer the Sacrament of Penance: and not all Priests: for, besides valid ordination, jurisdiction is also necessary, that is to say, the Priest must have received faculties from the Bishop for the administration of this Sacrament. But the Church supplies all necessary jurisdiction to any Priest, with regard to those who are in imminent or immediate danger of death (*in articulo mortis*).

III. NECESSITY OF PENANCE.—Since its institution, this Sacrament is as necessary for the remission of mortal sin committed *after* Baptism, as Baptism is for the remission of original sin. Hence, whatever good works we might do—however much we might pray, fast, and give alms; even though we should spend our whole lives in repenting and doing penance; we could not obtain pardon of a mortal sin, unless we would comply with this necessary condition of reconciliation—unless we would have recourse to those to whom alone "God hath given the ministry of reconciliation."

When does this obligation of the Sacrament of Penance *urge*, or require the Faithful to have recourse to it? The *Ecclesiastical precept*, *once a year;* but the *natural* and *divine* precept, *after mortal sin*, when we have to receive another Sacrament; and when in

(29) 2 Cor. v., 18, 19, 20.

danger of death[30]* When they who are in mortal sin, neglect or defer the appointed means of pardon, how fearful the danger wherein they live! how awful, how fatal the consequences to which they expose themselves!

IV. EFFECTS:—The *Effects* of this Sacrament are these:—

1. It remits *the guilt* of sins committed *after Baptism:* Whose sins you shall forgive they *are forgiven* them." Therefore, when the Priest absolves a *penitent* sinner on earth, God absolves him at the very same instant in heaven.——This Sacrament remits *all* sins, however grievous or numorous they may be.

2. It remits also the *eternal punishment* due to our sins; but the *temporal* punishment may remain.

3. It restores, (or, if the penitent be already in grace, it increases) *sanctifying grace;* it restores to us also our right and title to the kingdom of heaven, which we had lost.

4. It *revives* in us *the merits*, which we had gained by doing good works in a state of grace, but which we afterwards lost by consenting to mortal sin.

5. It confers *actual* grace, and strength to resist temptations.

In order to obtain these happy effects, four things are required; viz., Contrition, Confession, Satisfaction, and Absolution; that is to say, 1*st*, You must detest and renounce your sins; 2*ndly*, You must confess them; 3*rdly*, You must be resolved to expiate

(30) * The Catechism of the Council of Trent says: "But at what time *especially* we ought to go to Confession, the Holy Church has defined by the Canon of the Council of Lateran; for she commands all the Faithful to confess once a year *at least*. But if we consider what the nature of our salvation demands: *certainly* as often either as the danger of death threatens us: or as we have to do anything which ought not to be done in a state of sin, as when we administer, or receive the Sacraments; so often Confession is not to be omitted."—*Cat. Conc. Trid., part.* 2, *cap.* 5, *n.* 59.

them; *4thly*, You must receive absolution from a Priest.——In the subsequent Instructions, I will endeavour to give a full explanation of each of these necessary conditions of pardon.

CONCLUSION:—Thank the infinite mercy and goodness of God, for having instituted this efficacious means of rescuing us from sin and hell; and of restoring to us his sanctifying grace, and our title to the kingdom of heaven. Whenever you shall have had the misfortune of falling into the dreadful evil of mortal sin, have immediate recourse to this Sacrament of reconciliation; and do not imitate the example of so many unhappy sinners, who refuse or neglect to make use of this effectual means of pardon. For, how many are there, who are so negligent, so indifferent, with regard to this Sacrament, that all the exhortations and entreaties of their Pastors are not sufficient to induce them to have recourse to it. What a dreadful state of spiritual insensibility they must be in! what regret, what bitter remorse they are preparing for the hour of their death! and perhaps for eternity! Never let this be the case with *you;* but, if you have any reason to fear that you are in a state of sin, make your peace with God without delay. [*Exhort to frequent Confession.*]

INSTRUCTION LIII.

PENANCE II.

Contrition: Its Nature—its Necessity—its Qualities.

What are the parts of Penance?—Contrition, Confession, and Satisfaction.

What is Contrition?—Contrition is a hearty sorrow for our sins, by which we have offended so good a God, with a firm purpose of amendment.

What is a firm purpose of Amendment?—It is a resolution, by the grace of God, not only to avoid sin, but also the occasion of it.

Why are we to be sorry for our sins?—The chiefest and best motive to be sorry for our sins, is for the love of God, who is infinitely good in himself, and infinitely good to us; and, therefore, we ought to be exceedingly grieved for having offended him.

What other motives have we to be sorry for our sins?—Because by them we lose heaven, and deserve hell.

The first and most essential part of Penance is Contrition, the *nature*, *necessity*, and *qualities* of which I will now explain; and after that I will show *the means of obtaining it*, and also *the marks* whereby you may judge whether you have it or not.

I. Its Nature: *What*, then, *is Contrition?*—Contrition is a hearty sorrow for our sins, by which we have offended so good a God; with a firm purpose of amendment.

The word "Contrition," means *a breaking to pieces*; and consequently, by a "*contrite* heart," is meant a heart *broken with grief* for sin.

Contrition, therefore, is an inward sorrow—a repentance which grieves and afflicts the soul; arising from the consideration of *the evil* committed against God: "When thou shalt seek there the Lord thy God, thou shalt find him; yet so, if thou seek him with all thy heart, and *with all the affliction of thy soul*."[31] "Rend your hearts and not your garments."[32] This sorrow or repentance necessarily contains two things, viz., *a hatred of one's past life*, and a *resolution of a new life*; so as to be able to say with the penitent David: "I have hated all wicked ways:....I have

(31) Deut. iv., 29. (32) Joel ii., 13.

hated and abhorred iniquity; but I have loved thy law....I have sworn and am determined to keep the judgments of thy justice:......I have inclined my heart to do thy justifications for ever."[33]

II. Its Necessity:—This inward sorrow, or repentance for sin, *is*, and *always was* necessary (necessitate medii et præcepti), being both an essential means of pardon, and also a positive precept of the Divine law: "Be converted to me with all thy heart, in fasting, and in weeping, and in mourning;"[34] "And make to yourselves a *new heart* and *a new spirit*."[35]

Consequently, absolution does not and cannot reconcile a sinner to God, unless he be a truly *penitent* sinner; for, without true repentance, absolution is *null and void*." Therefore, a Priest cannot (and must not) absolve any sinner, when he has reason to believe there is no *true repentance;* and one sign of the repentance not being true is, when the penitent will not adopt *the means* of amendment *prescribed and required* by his Confessor.

You see, then, the nature and necessity of Contrition. And the explanation which I will now give of its essential *qulities*, will show this still more clearly.

III. Its Qualities:—The essential qualities of Contrition are these: it must be *internal*, in its nature, *supernatural* in its motive, *universal* in its extent, and *predominant* in its degree. Both *con*trition and *at*trition (that is to say, both *perfect* and *imperfect* Contrition) must necessarily have these four Qualities.

1. *Internal:* Our Contrition (whether *perfect* or *imperfect*) must spring from, and reside in, the heart; it must be the real inward disposition of the soul. Mere external appearances, therefore, or outward expressions are not sufficient: "Rend your hearts, and

(33) Ps. cxviii., 123, 163, 106, 112. (34) Joel ii., 31. (35) Ez. xviii., 31.

not your garments."[36] "When thou shalt seek there the Lord thy God, thou shalt find him; yet so, if thou seek him with all *thy heart*, and with all the *affliction of thy soul*."[37] It is not enough, then, to *recite* Acts of Contrition, unless *the heart* accord with the words of the mouth; for, it is to the *heart* that God looks. As the malice of sin proceeds from the heart;[38] so likewise must repentance for sin.

2. *Supernatural:* Our Contrition (whether *perfect* or *imperfect*) must spring from supernatural *motives;* i.e., from motives which are taught by Faith, and excited in us by the Holy Ghost. The Council of Trent declares, that *Attrition* is "*the gift of God.*"[39] With what reason, then, must *Contrition* also be said to be *his gift?* Therefore, to God we must apply for it: "Convert us, O Lord, to thee, and we shall be converted: renew our days from as the beginning."[40]

A sorrow for sin may arise from two kinds of motives—*natural* and *supernatural.*——It springs from *natural* motives, when it is excited by considering the evil consequences of sin in the order of *nature;* viz., disgrace and degradation in the eyes of men; the loss of reputation, of health, or of property; civil punishments, &c.: These are mere natural motives of sorrow. (*Examples* of Esau[41]—of Saul[42]—and of Antiochus.[43]) ——Sorrow for sin springs from *supernatural* motives, when it is excited by the consideration of the *supernatural* evils of sin—those evils which we learn from Faith or Religion; viz., the Divine displeasure—ingratitude towards God, and towards Jesus Christ—the loss of grace of God, and of heaven—the Divine vengeance, &c.: These are all *supernatural* motives of

(36) Joel ii., 13.
(37) Deut. iv., 29.
(38) Matt. xv., 8, 18, 19.
(39) Conc. Trid., Sess. 14, de Pœnit., cap. 4.
(40) Lam. v. 21.
(41) Gen. xxvii., 21.
(42) 1 Kings xv., 23, 26, 30.
(43) 1 Mac. vi., 8 to 16; 2 Mac. ix., 4, &c.

sorrow; and from such kind of motives repentance for *sin* must necessarily spring.

But, in these supernatural motives, there is a very great difference, some being far more perfect than others. And it is this difference of the motive, that makes the difference between *Contrition* and *Attrition:* both, indeed, must proceed from *supernatural* motives; but CONTRITION is a sorrow for sin arising *from the pure love of God* or *charity;* as, when we repent of sin, *because* it offends a God who is *infinitely good in himself:* and ATTRITION is a sorrow for sin arising from the fear of punishments in the next life, or from some other supernatural motive, accompanied with *some beginning* of the love of God: "Blessed is the man to whom it is given to have the *fear of God:*" for, "the fear of God is the *beginning of his love.*"[44] ——This difference of the motive is the only difference between Contrition and Attrition, as regards their *qualities;* but as regards their *effects*, there is another difference, which is, that Contrition (which includes a desire of receiving the Sacrament of Penance) remits the guilt of *sin immediately*, before the Sacrament be actually received; whereas Attrition disposes and prepares the penitent for receiving that remission *in the Sacrament;* when the words of absolution are pronounced over him, and not before."[45]

3. *Universal:* Our Contrition (whether *perfect* or *imperfect*) must be universal in its extent; i.e., it must extend to *all* our *mortal* sins, without excepting *any one:* "Be converted, and do penance for ALL your iniquities; and iniquity shall not be your ruin."[46]

Every mortal sin offends God grievously—deprives us of heaven, and renders us deserving of hell. We have the same urgent motives, therefore, for repenting

(44) Eccli. xxv., 14, 15.
(45) *See* Conc. Trid., Sess. 14, de Pœnit., cap. 4. (46) Ezech. xviii., 30.

of *any one* of them, as for repenting of the others. *One* mortal sin cannot be forgiven, without *all* the rest being pardoned with it; because we cannot be in the state of grace and of mortal sin, at the same time.

If a penitent confess both *mortal* and *venial* sins in the same confession, and has Attrition for *all* his *mortal* sins only; then these, and these *only*, will be remitted by absolution. If (not being under the guilt of mortal sin) he confess only venial sins, and has Attrition for *some* of them, but not for the others; then he receives pardon of *those only*, for which he has Attrition: but, if he has Attrition for *none* of them, and knowingly receives the Sacrament in this state of soul; then his confession is *sacrilegious:* and it is for fear of this, that Confessors sometimes tell the penitent to mention some sin of his *past life* for which he is truly sorry.

4. *Predominant:* Our Contrition, (whether *perfect* or *imperfect*) must be predominant in its degree; i.e., our sorrow for sin must predominate in the soul; it must be *greater* than our sorrow for any other evil; we must prefer to suffer any other evil, rather than be under the guilt of mortal sin. The degree of our sorrow *ought*, indeed, to be proportioned to the degree of *evil* for which we grieve: now, sin is the *greatest* of all evils; and therefore, our sorrow for it should be predominant in the soul. We need not, however, FEEL the sorrow so much, or be so SENSIBLY afflicted, as for temporal losses; but sin must *displease us more*, or be more hateful to us, than any other evil; however *sensibly* we may *feel* that evil. Tears and lamentations, (which may be delusive) prove not the greatness of our *sorrow* for sin, but only of our *natural sensibility*. The best and surest sign whereby we may know the greatness of our contrition, and its predominance in the soul, is, when we have a *will* to suffer *anything*. rather than offend God by sin—when we are able with

truth to say, in the words of St. Paul: "Who shall separate us from the love of Christ? Shall tribulation? or distress? or famine? or danger? or persecution? or the sword?......I am sure that neither life nor death; nor things present, nor things to come; nor any other creature, shall be able to separate us from the love of God, which is in Christ Jesus our Lord."[47] This shows the predominance of our sorrow for sin, or that we hate sin above all other evils.

Such are the essential qualities of Contrition, (both perfect and imperfect,) as regards *the past:* but there is another quality, equally essential, as regards *the future;* viz., a firm purpose of amendment. And this will be explained in the next Instruction, together with *the signs* of true sorrow, and *the means* of exciting it in the soul.

INSTRUCTION LIV.

PENANCE III.

What are the parts of Penance?—Contrition, Confession, and Satisfaction.

What is Contrition?—Contrition is a hearty sorrow for our sins, by which we have offended so good a God, with a firm purpose of amendment.

What is a firm purpose of Amendment?—It is a resolution, by the grace of God, not only to avoid sin, but also the occasions of it.

Why are we to be sorry for our sins?—The chiefest and best motive to be sorry for our sins, is for the love of God, who is infinitely good in himself, and infinitely good to us; and therefore we ought to be exceedingly grieved for having offended him.

(47) Rom. viii., 35, 38, 39. *Vide* S. Thomæ, 3 part Sum. Suppl. q. 3, a. 1.

What other motives have we to be sorry for our sins?—Because by them we lose heaven and deserve hell.

How may we obtain this hearty contrition and sorrow for our sins?—We must earnestly beg it of God; and make use of such considerations and meditations as may move us to it.

Having shown the *Nature* and *Necessity of* Contrition, and also its *essential qualities* as regards *the past;* I have now to explain another Quality, equally necessary, which has reference to *the future*, viz., a *firm purpose of Amendment;* after which, I will show *the Marks* of true sorrow, and *the means* of obtaining it.

I. A Firm purpose of Amendment:—You must resolve to amend your life, and to employ the proper means for this purpose; for, without this there can be no true Contrition; and many Confessions are bad for want of it. When persons relapse, after Confession, so soon, so easily, and so frequently, it is *some* SIGN that their Resolution of Amendment was not sincere—that there was not that real *change of heart* which Contrition necessarily includes: "Make to yourselves a new heart, and a new spirit."[48]

As our sorrow for sin must have certain *Qualities*, so likewise must our Resolution of Amendment: it must be sincere—firm and efficacious—universal—and supernatural.

1. *Sincere:* Our Resolution of a new life must come from the heart; and not consist in mere words only: it must be something more than a mere *promise* or outward profession; for it must be a *real determination* of the will—a disposition of the soul, to avoid both sin and the occasions that lead to it. To say we hate sin and will avoid it; and yet frequent and love the occasions of it; is to resolve *in words* only, and not *in*

48) Ezech. xviii., 31.

heart. Such a Resolution is not sufficient—it is not sincere.

2. *Firm and Efficacious:* Our Resolution of Amendment must be (not a vague wish, but) something *decided*—a complete *determination* of the will, not only to avoid sin and the occasions of it, but to take all necessary *means* for this purpose; and to persevere in this, whatever it may cost to our natural inclinations. For otherwise, our Resolution is not firm and efficacious; but only a mere self-delusion.

3. *Universal:* We must have a Resolution to avoid ALL sins, such at least as are *mortal:* "I have restrained my feet from EVERY evil way, that I may keep thy words."[49] There must be *no reserve.*

4. *Supernatural:* Our Resolution must spring, not from mere *human or natural*, but from *supernatural* motives; as, from the love of God, the fear of God, &c.

These Qualities show that our Resolution of Amendment must be *practical;* i.e., we are not to resolve in a mere *general* manner, to avoid sin, and to take the means of avoiding it; but we must descend to *particulars*—we must enter into *details;* we must see *what* means are to be employed in this particular case; and *what* in that; and we must resolve to begin *from the present moment*, to employ them accordingly.

I have now explained the Nature and Qualities of Contrition, both as it regards *sorrow for the past*, and a *Resolution of Amendment for the future;* and I entreat you to examine whether *your* sorrow and Resolution have been such as are required—such as have been described in this and the preceding Instruction.

II. MARKS OF TRUE SORROW FOR SIN:—Although you can never be absolutely *certain*, that your Contrition has been really such as it ought necessarily to

(49) Ps. cxviii., 101.

be; nevertheless, you may have a well-grounded confidence, that it has had at least the *necessary* qualities. And the signs which may give such confidence, are these:—

1. If you *do* really amend your life.

2. If you mortify yourself in expiation of your past sins, and as a preservative against future transgressions.

3. If you are careful and resolute in avoiding the occasions of sin.

4. If, for these purposes, you frequent the Sacraments—pray and meditate—attend to spiritual Reading—and are regular and diligent in your religious duties.

Unless there be such signs as these, you have reason to fear that there has been *some deficiency* either in your Sorrow, or in your Resolution of Amendment.

III. MEANS OF OBTAINING CONTRITION:—I will now explain the *Means* which should be employed in order to excite Contrition in the soul.

1. Consider how sin *provokes the anger of God!*.... For he not only excludes impenitent sinners from his heavenly kingdom, but casts them, body and soul, into hell—"into everlasting fire,"—"where they have no rest either day or night, but the smoke of their torments shall ascend up for ever and ever."[50] Oh! "it is a fearful thing to fall into the hands of the living God."[51]

2. Consider the great evil of sin *in its own nature*: that it is an outrage, offered by a mere worm of the earth, against God's infinite Majesty—against his infinite Goodness and Perfections. Reflect, then, who *you* are,...and who *God* is;...and how great therefore must be the evil of sin!

3. Consider the evil of sin, moreover, *in its conse-*

(50) Apoc. xiv., 11 (51) Heb. x., 31.

quences or effects in the soul, during life: that it deprives you of sanctifying grace, or spiritual life—makes you the enemy of God, and slave of the devil—destroys all your happiness, and peace of mind; renders you always restless and uneasy: "The wicked are like a raging sea, which can never rest; and the waves thereof cast up dirt and mire: There is no peace for the wicked, saith the Lord God."[52]

4. Consider, in sin, *its ingratitude against the goodness and bounty of God*, which are infinite. [*Paraphrase the following words:*] "Judge between me and my vineyard. What is there that I ought to do more to my vineyard, that I have not done to it? Was it that I looked that I should bring forth grapes; and it hath brought forth *wild* grapes? And now I will show you what I will do to my vineyard: I will take away the hedge thereof, and it shall be wasted:...I will make it desolate:...it shall not be pruned, and it shall not be digged; but briers and thorns shall spring up: and I will command the clouds to rain no rain upon it."[53]

5. Consider also, *its ingratitude towards Jesus Christ*, from the view of what he has suffered to expiate his guilt. See him agonizing in the Garden; ...scourged at the pillar;....crowned with thorns;.... nailed to the Cross;.. and expiring upon it in most excruciating tortures! And *why* did he suffer all this? For your salvation. Now, when you commit mortal sin, you make void, in your regard, all that he endured for you: "you crucify again the Son of God."[54]

[*Paraphrase the following Text:*] "O my people, what have I done to thee, or in what have I molested thee? Answer thou me. For I brought thee up out of the land of Egypt; and I delivered thee out of th

(52) Is. lvii., 20, 21. (53) Is. v., 3 to 6. (54) Heb. vi., 6.

house of slaves: and I sent before thy face Moses and Aaron."[55]

Such considerations as these cannot fail to excite within your soul a sorrow for sin; and to make you cry out in deep compunction: "Oh! what an evil I have committed, in committing sin! 'Who will give water to my head, and a fountain of tears to my eyes; and I will weep day and night?'[56] 'O God, be merciful to me a sinner.'"[57]

6. But the *first*—the most *necessary*—and most *efficacious* means of obtaining Contrition, is PRAYER: "Your heavenly Father will give the good Spirit to them that ask him."[58] "Ask, and you *shall* receive."[59] All these Considerations, therefore, and every other Means of Contrition, must be *commenced*, *accompanied*, and *terminated*, by fervent supplications to God; because Contrition is *His gift*.

INSTRUCTION LV.

PENANCE IV.

Perfect and Imperfect Contrition further explained—Advantages of having the fear of God.

What is Contrition?—Contrition is a hearty sorrow for our sins, by which we have offended so good a God, with a firm purpose of amendment.

What is a firm purpose of amendment?—It is a resolution, by the grace of God, not only to avoid sin, but also the occasions of it.

Why are we to be sorry for our sins?—The chiefest and best motive to be sorry for our sins, is for the love of God, who is infinitely good in himself, and infinitely

(55) Mich. vi., 3, 4.
(56) Jer. ix., 1.
(57) Luke xviii., 13.
(58) Luke xi., 13.
(59) John xvi., 24.

good to us; and, therefore, we ought to be exceedingly grieved for having offended him.

What other motives have we to be sorry for our sins?—Because by them we lose heaven, and deserve hell.

I. Perfect and Imperfect Contrition:—In the last two Instructions, it has been shown how a sorrow for sin may spring from *different* supernatural motives.——All the motives that are *good*, are not *equally* good—they are not *equally perfect*; and consequently, the *sorrow* arising from those motives, will not be equally perfect. Hence you see, how there are *two kinds* of Contrition, PERFECT and IMPERFECT. The sorrow which arises from *perfect motives*, is *perfect Contrition*; whilst that which arises from imperfect motives, (if they be good and supernatural,) is *imperfect Contrition*. You will understand th more clearly by an example:—

Example:—We will suppose, then, that there are three brothers, who, by an act of wilful disobedience, have offended a good Father; which is the case with every sinner, whenever he transgresses the laws of God. All three know they have provoked their Father's anger, and they expect punishment; they all *repent*, and *crave pardon*; but from different *motives*:—

The first son really loves his Father—the thought of having displeased him fills his heart with sorrow—he thinks more of this, than of the punishment—he would willingly suffer the punishment to obtain pardon, and would gladly repair the evil he has done. (This is an example of perfect Contrition.)

The second son, as far as regards the love of his Father, cannot (strictly speaking) be said to have any more than "a beginning of love;" for his love is not strong enough *of itself* to induce him to be sorry for the offence; but it requires the assistance of some other motive, such as the baseness of his conduct, the fear of punishment, &c.; he has only (as I said) *some beginning* of love, but he sincrely desires, and firmly resolves, to love his Father in future; and to perfect his love. (This is an example of imperfect Contrition.)

The third son is influenced by *mere* fear—love has no part in his sorrow—he cares not for the displeasure of his Father, but *only* for his chastisements, or vengeance: he resolves, indeed, to obey in future; but *solely* from this *motive of fear.* Evidently, this son, would not deserve to receive pardon, nor to escape punishment. (This is an example of such repentance as falls short of Attrition.)

APPLICATION:—*Perfect Contrition* is a sorrow for sin, arising from the pure love of God—from the pure motive of *Charity*—from the consideration of the infinite perfections of Him whom we have offended; or from the thought of that infinite Goodness, both in himself and to us, which renders him infinitely deserving of our love: it is a sorrow, therefore, which proceeds, not from the fear of chastisements, but from the thought of having offended a God so good. [*Such was the sorrow of the first son.*] As soon as any penitent has this kind of sorrow, he receives *immediate* pardon; yet not without an efficacious desire of receiving the Sacrament of reconciliation, and of doing penance; which are two dispositions necessarily included in perfect Contrition. Of this kind of Contrition Almighty God says: "Charity covereth all sins."[60] "I love them that love me."[61] "He that loveth me shall be loved of my Father; and I will love him."[62]. "He that abideth in charity, abideth in God, and God in him."[63]——This Contrition, perfected by Charity, is exemplified in Magdalen:

(60) Prov. x., 12.
(61) Prov. viii., 17.
(62) John xiv., 21
(63) 1 John iv., 16. *Vide* S. Thomæ, 3 part. Sum. suppl. q 5, a. 3.

When she came into the presence of her Redeemer "she began to wash his feet with tears;" but they were tears flowing from a sorrow which love had excited; and hence our blessed Lord said: "Many sins are forgiven her, *because* she hath loved much."[64]

Although we should always strive to have perfect Contrition, yet it is not *necessary* for absolution.

Imperfect Contrition or *Attrition* is a sorrow for having *offended God*, arising commonly from the consideration of the baseness of sin, or from the fear of hell and of punishments. [*This sorrow was represented by that of the second son.*] A sinner, who has this kind of Contrition, repents partly because, in sinning, he has done something which faith teaches him to be unjust, base, and unworthy of man; or because he dreads hell: and partly because sin displeases God. ——This last motive shows that he has some *beginning* of love: but his love is weak; it requires aid from other motives to give his sorrow and resolution, the necessary qualities. Hence, he considers the evils of sin, in its *own nature*, and in its *present* and *future consequences*.[65]

This imperfect Contrition is not sufficient to obtain pardon for us, without the Sacrament of Penance: indeed, to be sufficient *with* the Sacrament, it must, according to the Council of Trent, have these three qualities or conditions, which I will now mention:—

1. It must contain a sincere, firm, and efficacious *resolution of Amendment*, (such as I have explained it.) The sorrow must be sufficiently strong to produce a firm determination of the will to avoid sin in future: "I have sworn, and am determined to keep the judgments of thy justice."[66]

2. It must contain a *Hope of pardon*, i.e., a con-

(64) Luke vii., 37 to 50.
(65) *Vide* S. Thomæ Sum. 2-2, q. 19, a. 2; *et* 3 part. Sum. suppl. q. 1, a. 3. (66) Ps. cxviii., 106.

fidence that God, in his goodness, will forgive us. This hope rests on, and springs from, the consideration of God's infinite goodness and mercy, of the merits of Christ, and of the Divine promises; and it naturally excites some *beginning* of love.

3. It must contain this *beginning of the love of God—we must begin to love him as the fountain of all justice; i.e.*, as the only one from whom sinners can hope for justification; and from whom we *do* hope for it, as a free gift of his pure mercy and goodness. Without this beginning of love, our sorrow would only be the effect of *mere servile fear* [like that of the third son]—the fear of a *slave*, and not of a *son;* and it would not obtain pardon.

But when, with this fear, there are joined a hatred of sin, and a resolution of avoiding it—a hope of pardon—and some beginning of the love of God; then the sinner has imperfect contrition; and the Sacrament of Penance has the effect of strengthening, and, in some degree, perfecting this love in the soul; because it puts the soul in a state of sanctifying grace, which cannot be without *Charity;* for "Charity and sanctifying grace (says Liebermann) are one and the same thing."67* And therefore, from being *attrite*, when receiving the Sacrament, a penitent is enabled by the power of the keys, to be *contrite* (ex attrito fit contritus); because, together with the remission of his sins, he receives the gift or grace of *Charity*, which perfects Contrition. And hence St. Thomas says, "Some, not being perfectly contrite, (*i.e., being only attrite,*) obtain by virtue of the keys, the grace of contrition."68†

(67) * "Est ergo Charitas quid unum, cum gratia sanctificante."—*Lieb., Institu. Theol., lib.* 5 *de Gratia, part* 1, cap. 1, § 2, *quæs.* 8.

(68) † "Aliqui non perfecte contriti virtute clavium gratiam contritionis consequuntur." — *Div. Thom. in Quodl.* 4, *art.* 1.

When a Penitent, after having committed mortal sin, goes to Confession with only *Attrition*, he goes stained with the

What I have been saying on *Attrition*, as a preparation or disposition for receiving sanctifying grace in the Sacrament of Penance, is in accordance with what the Council of Trent says, when describing the manner in which Adults, who have not been baptized, are prepared for receiving the grace of justification in Baptism :—

"They are disposed unto the said justice, *when*, excited and assisted by Divine grace,......they are freely moved towards God, *believing* those things to be true which God has revealed and promised; and this especially, that God justifies the impious *by his grace*, through the redemption that is in Christ Jesus; and *when*, understanding themselves to be *sinners*," [they are struck with a fear of God, and,] "by turning themselves from the *fear of Divine justice* whereby they are profitably agitated, to consider the *mercy* of God, they are raised unto hope, confiding that God will be propitious to them *for Christ's sake;* and they *begin to love him* as the fountain of all justice; and are therefore moved against sins by a certain *hatred and detestation*, to wit, by that penitence which must be performed before Baptism" [or before Absolution, with regard to sins committed *after* Baptism]; "lastly, *when* they purpose to receive Baptism" [or Penance, if

guilt of sin; but by receiving absolution, his guilt is remitted, and he is gifted and adorned with sanctifying grace, or *Charity*, which then abides in his soul: he ceases, therefore, to have a *mere beginning* of love; because, by means of absolution, his *beginning* of love is *perfected* by the Charity, or sanctifying grace. which he has received. The Penitent, therefore, who, before absolution, could only arrive (but *did* arrive) at Attrition, is enabled, by the effects of Absolution, to make an Act of *Contrition;* because he has sanctifying grace, or *Charity*, abiding in his soul; and thus, from being *attrite*, he is enabled by the Sacrament to be *contrite*. "Et sic intelligitur, (ait S. Alphonsus Liguori,) quomodo peccator *ex attritio fit contritus*, nempe quia virtute clavium æquivalenter contritus redditur."—*Theol. Mor., lib.* 6, *tract.* 4, *n*, 442 *paragr.* Objiciunt autem 1.

the sinner be already baptized], to begin a new life, and to keep the Commandments of God."[69]

From this doctrine of the Council, it is evident, that they who prepare for Confession *sincerely* and *in earnest*, may console themselves with a well-grounded confidence, that they will have the dispositions which are necessary and sufficient for receiving grace in the Sacrament. For those necessary and sufficient dispositions arise from the very EXERCISE of *faith*, *fear of God, and hope of pardon*--SOME BEGINNING OF THE LOVE OF GOD arises from the exercise of these: and you *do* exercise them, in the very act of going through the ordinary preparation, when you go through it *sincerely and earnestly*.

On this point, St. Alphonsus Liguori says: "Whenever a Penitent has an act of sorrow, he has also, even explicitly, acts of Faith and Hope, (not indeed by direct *reflection* upon them, but by actually *exercising* them]; because, without doubt, he does *then* ACTUALLY *believe and hope*, that, in virtue of the merits of Christ, his sins are forgiven him by the Sacrament of Penance......And we say, that *a beginning of love* is found in any *Attrition*—both *in the fear of punishments* to be inflicted by God, according to that of Ecclesiasticus xxv., 16: 'The fear of God is the *beginning of his love*;' and also *in the hope of pardon and of eternal happiness*, according to these words of St. Thomas (1. 2, *q.* 40, *a.* 7): 'From this, that we hope to obtain good things from any one, we *begin to love him*.'"[70*]

(69) *Vide* Conc. Trid., Sess. 6, cap. 6.

(70) * "Pœnitens, semper ac habet actum doloris, etiam explicite (non jam reflexe, sed *exercite)* actus fidei et spei habet: quia tunc sine dubio *exercite* credit et sperat sibi per sacramentum pœnitentiæ, in virtuto meritorum Christi, pecatta remitti.——Et dicimus initium amoris in qualibet attritione reperiri, tum metu pœnarum a Deo infligendarum, juxta illud. *Eccli.* xxv., 16: '*Timor Dei initium dilectionis ejus:*' tum, spe remissionis et beautidinis, juxta illud quod dicit: *S. Thom.: 'Ex hoc, quod per aliquem speramus bona incipimus ipsum diligere.*'"—S. Alph. Lig., Hom. Apostol, tract. 16, n. 13 et 16.

II. ADVANTAGES OF HAVING THE FEAR OF GOD "Ye that fear the Lord, *hope in him;* and *mercy shall come to you* for your delight:"[71] for "the fear of the Lord *driveth out sin.*"[72]

"Ye that fear the Lord, *love him;* and your heart shall be enlightened:"[73] for "the fear of the Lord is *the beginning of wisdom.*[74] "The Fear of God is *the beginning of* HIS LOVE."[75]

Consequently, "They that fear the Lord *will* PREPARE *their hearts;* and in his sight they *will* SANCTIFY *their souls.*"[76] With reason, therefore, it is said: "BLESSED is the man, to whom it is *given* to have THE FEAR OF GOD."[77]

INSTRUCTION LVI.

PENANCE V.

Necessity of Confession proved—and its great Advantages.

What are the parts of Penance?—Contrition, Confession, and Satisfaction.

What is CONFESSION?—It is to accuse ourselves of all our sins to a Priest.

Having explained the first part of Penance, viz., Contrition; we come now to the second, which is *Confession.* I will prove its Necessity, and show its great Advantages: after which, I will describe its necessary qualities—the manner of preparing for Confession, and how the Confession is to be made.

I. NECESSITY OF CONFESSION:—Are we *obliged*

(71) Eccli. ii., 9. (72) Eccli. i., 27. (73) Eccli. ii., 10. (74) Eccli. i., 16. (75) Eccli. xxv., 16. (76) Eccli. ii., 20. (77) Eccli. xxv., 15.

to confess our sins? Yes. Why? In obedience to Christ—to comply with his Institution. For, he has instituted Confession as a necessary condition for obtaining the application of his merits for the pardon of our sins.

Proofs that Confession is a necessary Condition of pardon:—

1. In the Old Law, God *prefigured* this Institution. He ordained that every one infected with leprosy, (a figure of sin,) should be obliged to show himself to the Priest, whom he appointed to be the only authorized judge of leprosy.[78] And he prefigured it still more clearly by directly commanding Confession among the Jews, as a legal observance: "Say to the children of Israel: When a man or woman shall have committed *any* of *all* the sins that men are wont to commit, and by negligence shall have transgressed the commandment of the Lord, and offended; they shall confess their sin."[79]

The *practice* of Confession, here enjoined, is commanded and enforced by the later Scriptures of the Old Testament: "He that hideth his sins, shall not prosper; but he that shall *confess and forsake them*, shall obtain mercy."[80] Again: "For thy soul be not *ashamed* to say the truth. For there is a shame that *bringeth sin*, and there is a shame that *bringeth glory and grace*......Be not *ashamed* to confess thy sins; but submit not thyself to every man for sin."[81] These last words show, that they were, indeed, to submit themselves "*to man*;" yet, not "to *every* man," but only to those who were duly appointed to receive the Confession; and the words "*hideth*" and "*ashamed*" also show, that the Scripture speaks of Confession *to man*.

Thus, then, by a Divine command, Confession was

(78) Levit. xiii., 1, 2, 3.
(79) Num. v., 6, 7.
(80) Prov. xxviii., 13.
(81) Eccli. iv., 24, 25, 31.

practised by the Jews, as an act of Penance: and it continued to be practised by them, till Christ came. For, when St. John the Baptist was preaching penance, and baptizing, "there went out to him Jerusalem and all Judea; ....and were baptized by him in the Jordan, *confessing their sins*."[82] Therefore, Confession is no *novelty*, but much older than Christianity: it is as old as the Scriptures, and God is its author.

2. The practice of Confession, (thus instituted and commanded by God, in the Old Law, as a legal observance conducive to penance,) was raised by Jesus Christ *in the New Law*, to the dignity of being SACRAMENTAL: it was made an *essential* part of penance—a *necessary condition* of pardon.——In fulfilment of what had been prefigured, Christ appointed the Priests of the New Law to be judges of the *spiritual leprosy* of sin, with power of pronouncing pardon in his name: "As the Father hath sent me, I also send you. And when he had said this, he breathed on them, and he said to them: "Receive ye the Holy Ghost: whose sins you shall forgive, they are forgiven them; and whose sins you shall retain, they are retained."[83] "Whatsoever you shall bind upon earth, shall be bound also in heaven; and whatsoever you shall loose upon earth shall be loosed also in heaven."[84] It is evident from these words, that Christ appointed the ministers of his Church *to act as judges of consciences:* now, this judgment is not, of course, to be exercised at random; but with justice and discretion—after a full knowledge of the whole case to be decided. But a full knowledge of the case cannot be obtained, except by the sinner's own Confession: therefore, Confession is necessary for the exercise of that power of forgiving

(82) Matt. iii., 1, 2, 5, 6; Mark i., 4, 5.
(83) John xx., 21, 22, 25. (84) Matt. xviii., 18.

and retaining sins which Christ has given to his Church.

3. Confession having been thus made a necessary part of the Sacrament of reconciliation, *the first converts to Christianity practised* it accordingly: for we read in the Acts of the Apostles, that, when St. Paul had been preaching for two years at Ephesus, "many of them that believed, came CONFESSING *and declaring their deeds*."[85] Now, this must have been done in compliance with St. Paul's teaching.

4. For *the Apostles taught Confession*, as a means of pardon. Thus, St. John says: "If we say we have no sin, we deceive ourselves," (i.e., it is a self-delusion if we expect pardon without complying with the necessary condition of confession;) but, "if we *confess* our sins, God is *faithful* and *just* to forgive us our sins, and to cleanse us from all iniquity."[86]

St. James likewise says: "Confess, therefore, your sins one to another, and pray one for another, that you may be saved."[87] He had just directed that the Priest should be called in to the sick, and had said that their sins should be forgiven through his ministry: "Confess, *therefore*, your sins" to him, "that you may be saved;" because this is a *means* and *necessary condition* of reconciliation.

St. Paul also, speaking of the reconciliation of sinners to God, clearly shows that we must receive it through the ministry of the Priests. For the Apostle says: "God hath reconciled us to himself by Christ; and *hath given* TO US *the ministry of (this) reconciliation*. For God indeed was in Christ, reconciling the world to himself;......and he *hath placed* IN US *the* WORD OF RECONCILIATION, (i.e., the words of absolution.) For Christ therefore we are Ambassadors."[88]

(85) Acts xix., 10, 18. (87) James v., 16. (88) 2 Cor. v., 18, 19, 20.
(86) 1 John i., 8, 9.

——If, then, we would have part in this reconciliation, we must apply to those whom alone God has given the ministry of it.

Thus, then, even from Scripture alone, it is quite evident that Confession is a Divine institution—a necessary part of the Sacrament of Penance—a necessary condition of reconciliation.

5. All this has been declared, moreover, by the infallible decision of the Church.[89]

6. The Arguments, which have been already given, are greatly confirmed by others, drawn from the *constant practice* of the Church—from the very *nature of confession*—and even from the acknowledgments of the first Reformers, after they had abolished it, and had seen the sad consequences of its abolition.——For,

First, As to the CONSTANT PRACTICE OF THE CHURCH, the necessity of Confession is, at the *present time*, the doctrine and practice of the Catholic Church *universally*—in the preceding age it was the same—and so it has been in every age up to the Apostles.

Secondly, Even the VERY NATURE of this duty proves, that it could not have been instituted otherwise, than by *Divine authority*. Confession is a duty so painful to our natural feelings—so humiliating to the sinner, that no *human* power could ever have succeeded in establishing the practice of it. For instance, suppose it to have been introduced at any time since the Apostles: what opposition, what clamours, what outcries, would have been raised against it? Now, we have no accounts of any such opposition; and why? Because it was instituted by God himself. But, when attempts were made to abolish it, we *have* accounts of *that*.

Thirdly, We have even THE ACKNOWLEDGMENTS *of the Reformers themselves* of the evil consequences of

(89) Conc. Trid., Sess, 14, de Pœnit., cap. 5; et can. 6.

having abolished Confession. For, after its abolition, we hear them exclaiming, that all restraints of vice seemed to be removed; that the passions of men were let loose, &c.: "The world grows worse and worse, (says Luther,) and becomes more wicked every day. Men are now more given to revenge, more avaricious, more devoid of mercy, less modest, and more incorrigible; in fine, more wicked, than in the Papacy."[90] "Of the thousands who renounced popery, (says Calvin,) how few have amended their lives? Indeed, what else did the greater part pretend to, than by shaking off the yoke of superstition, to give themselves more liberty, and to plunge into every kind of lasciviousness."[91] "The greater part of the people, (says Bucer,) seem to have embraced the Gospel (by which he means the Reformation), only to live at their pleasure, and to enjoy their lusts and lawless appetites without control."[92] Indeed, such were the sad consequences of having abolished Confession, that the Protestants of Nurremburg sent an embassy to the Emperor, Charles the Fifth, begging him to re-establish Confession by a public edict;[93] but, it was all in vain; for, no other than a Divine authority could establish the practice of Confession.

II. Advantages of Confession:—No wonder there should be cause for such complaints, when we consider the great Advantages of Confession; and in these we see the wisdom of God in giving us this salutary Institution:—

1. Confession *humbles the pride* of the sinner. Pride leads from God; it is the first principle of revolt in

(90) Luth. in Postilla sup. 1 Dom. Advent.; *apud* Amicable Discuss., Vol. 1, letter 2, append. 2 p. 85.

(91) Calv. lib. 6, de Scand.; *apud* Lingard's Tracts, p. 285, edit. 1813.

(92) Buc. de Regn. Christ, lib. 1, cap. 4; *apud* Lingard's Tracts, ibid.

(93) Bergier, Dictionaire de Theol., art. *Confession auriculaire*, paragr. *Plus d'une fois*.

man: The beginning of the pride of man, is to *fall off* from God;......for pride is the beginning of all sin."[94]

Therefore, by appointing Confession as a necessary means of reconciliation, God strikes at the very root of the evil: we forsake God by pride; we must return to him by humiliation.

2. Confession is a means of furnishing us with *suitable remedies* for our spiritual disorders. As, when we would obtain the remedies proper for the cure of bodily diseases, we must *make known* to the Physician the symptoms of our complaint; so, if we would have our spiritual evils cured, we must make known the disorders of our soul.

3. By means of Confession, we obtain *direction* as to when we *may* or *ought* to receive the Holy Communion.

4. Confession is a great *check to vice:* the very thought of having to confess prevents many sins.

5. It is a powerful *support to virtue;* the snares of the enemy, and the delusions of self-love, are thereby detected—suitable advice is obtained—encouragement is given to those who are in spiritual difficulties—and many other spiritual advantages are obtained.

6. Confession promotes *the good of society*. How many enmities are thereby cured—injustices repaired, and frequently prevented—occasions of sin quitted, scandals avoided, and other evils remedied.

But (you will perhaps say) are there no enmities, injustices, scandals, and other such evils among Catholics? Unhappily, there are too many! but among *what kind* of Catholics? Are they found amongst those who frequent, or those who neglect Confession. Their example, then, proves the *advantages* of Confession. It is no wonder, therefore, that the Reformers complained of human passions being let loose—of men becoming every day worse and worse when the prac-

(94) Eccli. x., 14, 15.

tice of Confession had ceased to be in use amongst them.

CONCLUSION:—I have now shown that Confession is a Divine Institution, and an essential part of the Sacrament of Penance; and have described, moreover, some of its great advantages (acknowledged even by its very adversaries). I have yet to explain what kind of Confession is required of us—how to prepare for it—and how to make it.

INSTRUCTION LVII.

PENANCE VI.

The Qualities of Confession; General Confessions.

What is Confession?—It is to accuse ourselves of all our sins to a Priest.

What if one wilfully conceal a mortal sin in Confession?—He commits a great sin by telling a lie to the Holy Ghost, and makes his Confession nothing worth.

What must we do that we may leave out no sin in Confession?—We must carefully examine our conscience upon the ten Commandments and the seven deadly sins.

Having shown the *Obligation* and *Advantages of* Confession, I have now to explain its necessary *Qualities.* I will show, likewise, when a General Confession is required; and how it is to be made.

I. As to the necessary Qualities of Confession, it must be,

1. HUMBLE: Your Confession should be accompanied with a sense of your misery—you should confess as a criminal who is conscious of his guilt: you are not to throw the fault on others, nor to seek excuses, as Adam and Eve did in Paradise: "Adam said: The

(95) Gen. iii. 12, 13.

woman gave me of the tree, and I did eat And she answered: The serpent deceived me, and I did eat."[95] You should receive, in an humble and obedient spirit, the advice and direction given by your Confessor: "He that heareth *you*, heareth *me*."

2. ENTIRE:—Your Confession must contain *all* your sins, at least all that are *mortal;* and the number of each kind; together with all such circumstances as change the nature of any sin; and you should make it your practice, moreover, to mention those circumstances which considerably aggravate the guilt of your sins.——Therefore, you must examine your conscience diligently, and confess all that you recollect; but, if after a diligent examination, you cannot recollect all your sins, you need not be uneasy about that, because the absolution will extend to those sins which you cannot call to mind.——If, with regard to any sin, you have a real doubt, as to whether you committed it or not, or whether it was mortal;[96*] and still more, if, *being certain of the sin*, both as to the *fact* of its commission and the *mortal* degree of its guilt, you have a reasonable doubt of having omitted to confess it; you should (and in the last case you *must*) confess the sin, about which you have any such doubts; not indeed *absolutely*, as if it were certain, but *specifying your doubt*. (But if, on account of being scrupulous, you receive a different rule from your Director, you should fearlessly follow it, by confessing only such sins as are *certain*—*certain* that you have committed them—*certain* that they are mortal—and *certain* that they have not been already confessed.)

(95) Gen. iii., 12, 13.

(96) * "Cæterum in praxi (*ordinaire* loquendo) *omnino* suadenda est Pœnitentibus confessio mortalium tam negative quam positive dubiorum, cum id ordinaire prosit ad conscientiæ tranquillitatem. Dixi *ordinarie*, nam scrupulosi omnino eximi debent ab obligatione confitendi peccata dubia."—*S. Alph. Lig.*, *Theol.*, *Mor. lib.* 6. *tract.* 4. *n.* 476; et. vide *n.* 477.

To omit any mortal sin, through want of due examination of conscience, or wilfully and knowingly *to conceal* any, would render the absolution invalid and sacrilegious. It is to be feared that many, through a false shame, yield to the temptation of concealing their sins; they are ashamed to confess with repentance, what they are not ashamed to take pleasure in committing.

Such false Penitents should remember that they add very considerably to their guilt; for they add the crime of hypocrisy—of telling a deliberate lie to the Holy Ghost—and of a sacrilegious Confession, followed generally by a sacrilegious Communion. They should remember the terrible consequences of sacrilege, as exemplified in Baltassar,[97] in Antiochus,[98] in Judas,[99] in Ananias and Saphira.[100] False Penitents may deceive the Priest, but they cannot deceive God.

To conceal sins in Confession, is the greatest act of folly; because you *must* confess them sooner or later, or else die in the guilt of them: and, in the mean time, your life will be miserable, because your conscience will be troubled.

By concealing your sins *now* from only *one person*, the consequence will be, that, at the last day, they must be exposed to the whole world.

[*Explain the inviolable nature of the seal of Confession.*]

3. SINCERE:—What has just been said of wilfully *concealing* sins, is to be said also of *wilfully disguising or excusing* them. They should be declared *just as they are*, without increasing or diminishing them: what is *certain*, should be confessed as being certain; that is to say, it should be declared *absolutely;* and what is *doubtful*, should be represented as being such. You

(97) Dan. v. (99) Matt, xxvii., 3, 4, 5; (100) Acts v., 1 to 12.
(98) 2 Mac, ix. Acts i., 16, 18.

should endeavour to lay open the state of your conscience, as correctly as *you* know it yourself.

4. Simple :—Confession should be confined to your *sins;* and not be mixed up with the recital of such circumstances, as have nothing to do with the state of your conscience. You should avoid making known *any other person* who may be concerned in the sins you confess.

II. General Confession :—There are *two kinds* of Confession, viz., *Particular*, i.e., of the sins committed since the last Confession; and *General*, i.e., either of one's whole life, or including several particular Confessions.

When is a General Confession *necessary?* when is it *useful?*—and when is it *hurtful?*

First, It is necessary for those who have made *bad Confessions:* i.e., who have been wanting in the necessary *integrity*, *sorrow*, or *resolution.*

If your conscience testifies that you have *always* examined *carefully*, confessed *sincerely*, employed *diligently* the *proper means* of exciting sorrow for your sins, and a resolution of avoiding them in future; and above all, if actual amendment gives reason to believe, that you really had such sorrow and resolution; then thank God—a General Confession is not necessary for you. But if, on the contrary, you find that you have been really wanting in any of these points, you have then sufficient reason to be alarmed.

There are Eight Classes of persons who are under a necessity of making a General Confession:—

1. All those who have wilfully concealed any mortal sin, through fear, shame, or indifference:

2. Those who, instead of having used sufficeint diligence, have been grossly negligent, in the examination of their conscience:

3. Those who have lived in gross and *culpable ignorance* of the necessary points of Faith and Practice:

4. Those who have confessed *without sincere repentance* for the past, or a *firm resolution* to avoid sin, and the occasions of it, in future:

5. Those who have continued both to go to Confession; and to live also in *immediate occasions* of sin, which they *could* but *would not* avoid:

6. Those who have neglected restitution, when they had the power and opportunity of making it:

7. Those who have *continued in vicious habits*, without employing the *ordinary* and *prescribed* means of correcting them:

8. Those who have continued, *after* their Confessions (the same as before) to live on in enmity, hatred, malice, &c.

The Confessions of all such persons have been *bad*, for want of proper dispositions; and *must* be repaired by a *General Confession*. (Examine what your Confessions have been.)

Secondly, A General Confession is USEFUL to those who have been leading a *tepid life*. It is frequently (for such persons) the beginning of a new life: the reason is, because it humbles them in their own eyes; moves them to greater sorrow for their sins, and to a more determined resolution of avoiding them; and it gives an impulse to general fervour in taking proper means both of rooting out all vicious habits, and of advancing in virtue. But its greatest utility and consolation are experienced on the death-bed: for, who would not *then* rejoice at having put his house in order, while in health? What a comfort to have done so! because it is the time *then* (not to *begin* to prepare, but) to *be prepared*.——Before you sleep to-night, imagine yourself on your death-bed; and think what you would wish *then* to have done, and do that now.

Thirdly, Though *necessary* for many, and *useful* to others, there are *some* to whom a General Confession would be *very* INJURIOUS, viz., *scrupulous* and over-timid persons, who frequently wish to make a General Confession, vainly and presumptuously imagining that they will *then* be SATISFIED. Such persons should be satisfied with the *decision* of their Director; to do otherwise, is *not piety*, but obstinacy, and *pride*, and *delusion:* it is not obeying God, but the inspirations of the devil. They can have nothing to fear in obeying an order established by God, and which he requires to be obeyed as himself: they must not proudly set up their own fancies against the decisions of their Director.

III. *How is a General Confession to be made?* The devil will represent it as impossible; and will, perhaps, lead you to exclaim: "How can I make a sufficient examination? How can I recall to my mind all the sins of ten, or twenty, or thirty years?" But the difficulty is *not so great* as it appears to be.

For, in a General Confession, it is not necessary to examine *venial* sins in particular; it is sufficient to accuse one's self of them in general. You need only examine *mortal sins:* and

Your *mortal* sins have either been *habitual* or *not. If habitual*, you cannot know the number of times; but you can say, about how long you had the habit—about how often you fell in the day, week, month, or year—and whether the habit was interrupted by periods of amendment, and about how long those periods were.

If, instead of being habitual, the sins were but *seldom* committed; then it is not very difficult to make out the number of times, or somewhere about it. St. Thomas says: "In Confession, no more is required from man than he is able [i.e., *morally* able] to do."——You will receive great assistance from your Confessor; and much more from God, to whom you should apply for it by frequent and fervent prayer.

INSTRUCTION LVIII.

PENANCE VII.

Preparation for Confession.

What is Confession?—It is to accuse ourselves of all our sins to a Priest.

What if one wilfully conceal a mortal sin in Confession?—He commits a great sin by telling a lie to the Holy Ghost, and makes his Confession nothing worth.

What must we do that we may leave out no sin in Confession?—We must carefully examine our conscience upon the ten Commandments and the seven deadly sins.

How many things, then, have we to do, by way of preparation for Confession?—Four things: 1*st*, We must heartily pray to God for his grace to help us; 2*ndly*, We must carefully examine our conscience; 3*rdly*, We must beg pardon of God, and be very sorry from our hearts for offending him; and 4*thly*, We must resolve to renounce our sins, and to begin a new life for the future.

To obtain a reconciliation with God, we must *confess* our sins *truly*—we must *repent* of them *sincerely*, and we must *resolve firmly* to amend our life. But we cannot do so, unless we know what we have to confess, to lament, and to amend. Therefore, we must *examine* all our thoughts, desires, words, actions, and omissions, whereby we may have violated God's law.

I. *How is this* EXAMINATION *to be made?*

1. We should begin by *imploring light* from above to know our sins. For we are too apt to be blind to our own faults: self-love and our passions naturally prejudice our reason; and the false maxims of the world assist in deluding us. Hence, we should pray with St. Augustin: "Lord, give me grace to know thee; and give me grace to *know myself*." Our na-

tural forgetfulness—the fallibility of our memory, is another reason which should make us earnest, like holy Job, in our petitions for the Divine light, to enable us to know the true state of our consciences, "How many (he says) are mine iniquities and sins? make me know my crimes and offences."[1]

2. You should not only implore the Divine light, to know your sins; but also a sincere detestation and sorrow for them, as offences of God; and a firm resolution of avoiding them, during the remainder of your lives. For these dispositions are necessary for making a good Confession, and they should properly accompany the examination of your conscience; and as they are *gifts* of God, to Him you must apply for them.

3. Having thus prayed to God for his light and grace to help you, the next thing is, to examine the state of your conscience, by considering attentively and diligently what you have committed against God in thought, word, and deed; examining yourselves on the Commandments of God and his Church—on the seven deadly sins—and on the duties of your state of life.[2]*——But,

II. *How much* TIME *and* DILIGENCE *must be given to this examination?*

1. *As to diligence*, you should employ as much attention and diligence in the examination of your conscience, as prudence would require you to give to any other affair of great importance. (*Example:* If some one had unjustly deprived you of your property, and

(1) Job xiii., 23.

(2) * Every person is bound to *know* the duties of his state of life; whoever, therefore, is grossly ignorant of them, must make that ignorance a matter of Confession; and he must resolve, moreover, under pain of sin, to take effectual means of acquiring a sufficient knowledge of his duties. Ignorance of duties cannot excuse a person for transgressing them, when the ignorance proceeds from his own wilful neglect.

taken possession of it himself: what care and diligence you would employ in procuring witnesses, and in proving your right to the property, in order to recover your possession? Now, apply this to your preparation for Confession: Sin has robbed you of sanctifying grace, and of your title to the kingdom of heaven: and absolution, preceded by a good Confession, is the judicial act, by which you are to recover both. What care and diligence, therefore, you ought to employ in your preparation for Confession, which is an affair of so great importance!)

2. *As to time*, no universal rule can be given. The length of time which should be devoted to your examination of conscience, depends very much on the period which has elapsed since your last Confession; and on the kind of life which you have led.

Very little time is sufficient for persons of a timorous conscience, who go *frequently* to Confession. Such persons should be satisfied with the time pointed out for them by their Director.

A much longer time is necessary for those who have lived in habits of sin, and who confess but *seldom*. Such persons should enter seriously into themselves; and be diligent in striving to recollect the *places* where they have been—the *persons* with whom they have had intercourse—and the employments or *pursuits* in which they have been engaged, since their last Confession; for such recollections will assist very much in bringing to mind their transgressions: They should give themselves a reasonable time to discover all the different *kinds* of sin, which they have committed; the *number* of each kind; and all those *circumstances* which ought to be confessed. For, it is not sufficient to say, as some do "I have cursed, I have stolen, I have told lies, I have been vexed, &c.;" but you must endeavour, by examination, to enable yourselves to specify both the number of your sins, and the extent of their guilt. It is to be feared, that many Penitents, through sloth or self-love, make very careless and superficial examinations.

III. When you have finished your examination, seeing *then* your sins *in one view*, endeavour to EXCITE YOURSELVES TO CONTRITION—earnestly craving pardon of God for the sins which you find you have committed, and resolving firmly that you will never commit them any more. [See the *Means of obtaining Contrition*, INSTRUC. LIV., Sect. III., pages 304, 305, 306.]

Remember, that, to form a firm and efficacious resolution of amendment, is a very important point, and a necessary part of *true sorrow;* many Confessions are bad for want of this; many, very many, Penitents may attribute their relapses after Confession to their defective resolutions of amendment.——With regard to your resolution, therefore, sound your heart—ask yourselves the question: "Am I resolved *sincerely, firmly*, and *efficaciously*, to forsake my sins? to avoid *the occasions* of them? and to employ *the proper means* for these purposes?"

Beg of God to give you these necessary dispositions: implore this mercy by many supplications, and with all the ardour of your soul: "Your heavenly Father will give the good spirit to them that ask him:......Ask, and you shall receive."[3] "Call upon me in the day of trouble, and I will deliver thee."[4]

INSTRUCTION LIX.

PENANCE VIII.

Manner of making Confession—Absolution.

What is the Sacrament of Penance?—Penance is a Sacrament in which, *by the Priest's absolution*, joined with Contrition, Confession, and Satisfaction, the sins are forgiven which we have committed after Baptism.

(3) Luke xi, 13. 9. (4) Ps, xlix., 15,

What is Confession?—It is to accuse ourselves of all our sins to a Priest.

After having made all necessary preparation, (as described in the last Instruction,) you may *then* go to Confession: but go with the sentiments and dispositions of the humble Publican—with a deep sense of your guilt and unworthiness.

I. MANNER OF MAKING CONFESSION:—Having arrived at the Confessional, kneel down—make the Sign of the Cross—and ask the Priest's blessing, by saying: "Pray, Father, give me your blessing, for I have sinned." Having received the Blessing, say the first part of the "*Confiteor*," as far as "through my most grevious fault." Then say how long it is since your last Confession—and whether you were then absolved or not—after this, confess all the sins you can recollect, (beginning with the *omissions* of your past Confession and of the obligations then pointed out, if there have been any such omissions.)

Confess with great humility, with truth, candour, and simplicity. Answer sincerely the questions which your Confessor may find it necessary to ask: let your disposition and endeavour be, to lay open the real state of your soul.

When you have declared all that you had to confess, you conclude by saying: "For these, and all other my sins which I cannot at present call to my remembrance, I am heartily sorry, purpose amendment for the future; and most humbly ask pardon of God, and penance and absolution of you, my Ghostly Father Therefore I beseech the Blessed Mary, ever a Virgin &c."

Receive the Penance, enjoined by your Confessor, in the same penitential disposition as holy Job received the afflictions that befel him: "I have sinned, and indeed I have offended; and I have not received what I have deserved."[5]

Whilst your Confessor is giving you direction, do not employ yourselves in examining whether you have forgotten anything; but listen attentively to what he is saying—strive to remember it—and resolve to practise what he advises.

Whilst receiving absolution, renew, with great fervour, your Contrition and Resolution of amendment. But, if it be judged expedient to defer absolution, submit *humbly* to the decision.

II. Absolution:—Absolution is an essential part of the Sacrament of Penance: it is the sentence of pardon, which the Priest pronounces in the name, and by the commission of Christ. For Christ has appointed his Priests to be judges of consciences, with power to *absolve* or *not*, as the case may require: "Whose sins *you shall forgive*, they are forgiven them; and whose sins *you shall retain*, they are retained."[6] Wherefore, the Priest says: "*I*, by *His* authority, absolve thee from thy sins, in the name of the Father, and of the Son, and of the Holy Ghost." When a Priest absolves a Penitent, he does so as *really* and as *effectually*, as if Christ himself pronounced the absolution: because he acts in *His* name, and by *His* authority and commission; (that is to say, he absolves effectually, if the Penitent be *duly disposed*.)

Can a Priest give or refuse absolution, just as he pleases? No; Priests are not the *masters*, but "the *Dispensers* of the mysteries of God."[7] They must follow the rules prescribed by the Church; and must act, to the best of their judgment, as Christ himself would act; otherwise they will have a very severe account to give! (*Example:* A Judge must pronounce sentence *according to the laws*......) Christ has given power to

(5) Job xxxiii., 27. (6) John xx., 23. (7) 1 Cor. iv., 1.

absolve, but on certain conditions, viz., that the sinner *confess,......repent,......resolve,......*and *be in a disposition to satisfy......*When the Priest has *reason* to believe, that *any one* of these is wanting, then he must defer absolution ; otherwise he would ruin both his own soul and the penitent's also. You see, then, how unreasonable it is for any one to take it ill, when absolution is obliged to be deferred : he who does take it ill, shows thereby great ignorance, and proves also his want of proper dispositions ; and he shows, therefore, that the Priest was *right* in refusing absolution. In such dispositions, the absolution would be of no service to the Penitent ; but, on the contrary, it would add to his sins the guilt of *sacrilege.*

What kinds of persons must be *refused* absolution ?

1. They who will not correct, or take means to correct their bad habits, cannot be absolved. For every sinner *must* resolve to employ the necessary means of amendment.

2. They who will not quit and avoid the immediate occasions of sin, cannot be absolved. [*Explain what is meant by occasions of sin ; taking for example, the society of drunkards—the impure acquaintance—vicious companions in general—bad books—&c.*]——No one *can* be a true Penitent, unless he resolve to avoid the immediate occasions of sin ; for how can any one be said to be really disposed to forsake sin, if he will continue to frequent the occasions that lead to it ? " He that loveth the danger shall perish in it."[8] " If thy right eye scandalize thee, (i.e., cause thee to offend God,) pluck it out, and cast it from thee;......and if thy right hand scandalize thee, cut it off, and cast it from thee : for it is expedient that one of thy members should perish, rather than that thy whole body go into hell."[9] By these

(8) Eccli. iii., 27 (9) Matt. v., 29, 30.

words we are given to understand, that the occasions of sin, however near or dear they may be to us, *must* be renounced, if we would escape eternal condemnation. And hence, the Ritual positively says: "*Let not the Priest absolve those who will not quit the immediate occasions of sin.*"

3. They who will not be reconciled to their enemies, are likewise incapable of receiving absolution: For, "if you will not forgive men, neither will your Father forgive you your offences."[10]

4. Neither can they be absolved, who will not (when able) make restitution or reparation for the injustices which they have committed against their neighbour; or who will not pay their just debts.

When a penitent has already promised, in several Confessions, that he would avoid occasions—would be reconciled—or would make restitution; but has neglected, after each Confession, to execute those promises, when it was in his power to do so; he cannot expect that such promises will be again relied on; for he himself, as well as his Confessor, must have sufficient reason to suspect (and more than suspect) their sincerity. Such a penitent, therefore, must expect to be required to *fulfil* his promises, *before* he can be considered as being sufficiently disposed for receiving absolution.

INSTRUCTION LX.

PENANCE IX.

On Satisfaction.

What are the parts of Penance?—Contrition, Confession, and Satisfaction.

What is SATISFACTION?—It is doing the Penance given us by the Priest.

(10) Matt. vi., 15.

The third part of Penance is *Satisfaction*, which consists in repairing the injury done to God by sin. The *true* Penitent must necessarily be *disposed* to make satisfaction to the Divine justice, even when the guilt of sin is remitted.

Satisfaction may be distinguished into *voluntary* and *sacramental*. That satisfaction is called *voluntary*, which we impose upon ourselves, by our own free will: although it be strictly due from us: *sacramental* is that which is enjoined by the Confessor, and which forms a part of the Sacrament of Penance. This, *as to its principle*, or the disposition required in the Penitent, is an *essential* part of the Sacrament; and inseparable from true Contrition (whether perfect or imperfect), whereof it is a necessary consequence. But, *as to its acts*, or the actual imposing of it by the Confessor, and its actual performance by the Penitent, it is only an *integral* part of the Sacrament; and is necessary by a Divine precept; we *cannot* receive absolution, without being *disposed* to satisfy God's justice; but we *can* receive it, validly and worthily, before we have actually *performed* the satisfaction. *As to its effects*, sacramental Penance is more efficacious, than that which is voluntary in expiating the temporal punishment of sin.

I. Application of Christ's merits:—Can we offer to the Divine justice an *adequate* satisfaction? No, not of ourselves: for sin is an outrage against infinite Majesty; and man cannot offer any atonement of his own, which will be equal to such an offence.

But have we *any* means of offering an adequate Satisfaction? Yes; we have the expiatory merits of Christ, which God is pleased to accept in our favour: but then, with his satisfaction, we must join our *own* penitential works. By this means, we can supply, and more than supply, our own insufficiency; because the merits of Christ are infinite.

It is principally in the Sacraments, and the Sacrifice of the Mass, that his merits are applied to our souls and made over to us, as if they were our own. This application is a *pure grace*—a pure bounty, on the part of God. But one condition for obtaining this application in the Sacrament of Penance, is, that we be in a real disposition to do penance ourselves.

II. TEMPORAL PUNISHMENT REMAINING DUE :—Does Divine justice require us to make satisfaction for sin, by temporal punishments, even *after* its guilt and eternal punishment have been remitted? Yes; and this may be proved by a number of examples, recorded in the Scriptures, of such satisfaction having been exacted by the justice of God. Thus—1*st*, In punishment of Adam's sin, although pardoned *as to its guilt*, God inflicted upon Adam himself severe temporal chastisements, and continues still to inflict them upon all his posterity :[11]—2*ndly*, Moses, for his sin of diffidence, which he committed when he struck the rock twice, was punished, after his forgiveness, by not being allowed to enter into the promised land;[12]—3*dly*, David's sin of vanity in numbering the people, was punished, after his repentance, by the destruction of 70,000 of his subjects by pestilence ;[13]—4*thly*, And his sins of adultery and murder were likewise severely punished, *after* the Prophet Nathan had declared that their guilt was remitted.[14] If this temporal punishment be not discharged here, during life, it will be exacted much more rigorously hereafter, in Purgatory.

III. ADVANTAGES OF DOING PENANCE :—Besides satisfying for the temporal punishment of sin, are there any other *advantages* in doing penance? Yes; there are many very great advantages :

(11) Gen. iii, 17 to 24; Rom. v., 12.
(12) Num. xx., 7 to 12; Deut. xxxii., 48 to 52.
(13) 1 Par. xxi., 9 to 14. (14) 2 Kings xii., 13, 14.

1. It is a preservative against sin: for, doing penance makes us careful in avoiding sin—

2. It keeps us humble, by constantly reminding us of our guilt—

3. It cures the infirmities which sins leave in the soul, viz., the spiritual weakness, languor of soul, and repugnance to spiritual exercises, which sins produce; and it renders the soul more active and strong, more fervent and spiritual—

4. It weakens the force of our evil inclinations or passions; and destroys bad habits by contrary practices—

5. It disarms the anger of God, provoked by our sins.[15] (*Example of Achab:* "And when Achab had heard these words, he put hair-cloth upon his flesh, and fasted, and slept in sack-cloth. And the word of the Lord came to Elias, saying: Hast thou not seen Achab humbled before me? Therefore, because he hath humbled himself for my sake, I will not bring the evil in his days."[16] *Example of the Ninevites:* By fasting in sack-cloth and ashes, they saved themselves and their city from the threatened destruction.[17])

6. It makes our life more conformable to that of Christ.[18]

7. It increases our merit, and will add to our future glory.

8. It brings spiritual consolations, and confidence; especially at the approaches of death: for what a comfort it will then be, to have led a penitential life!

IV. EXTENT OF THE PUNISHMENT REMAINING DUE:—What is the *extent of the temporal punishments* which may remain due to sin, after its guilt and eternal punishment have been forgiven? Their extent is much greater than many Penitents imagine.——The

(15) Jer. xviii., 8.
(16) 3 Kings xxxi., 27, 28, 29.
(17) Jonas iii.
(18) *See* Rom. viii., 29

Council of Trent teaches, that the satisfactions, enjoined by Confessors, should bear some proportion to the crimes and ability of the Penitents: "Therefore, the Priests of the Lord ought, as far as the spirit and prudence shall suggest, to enjoin salutary and suitable satisfactions, according to the quality of the crimes and ability of the Penitents; lest, if haply, they.... deal too indulgently with Penitents, by enjoining certain very light works for very grievous crimes, they be made partakers of other men's sins. But let them have in view, that the satisfaction, which they impose, be not only for the preservation of a new life,......but also for the avenging and punishing of past sins."[19] And the practice of the primitive Church, as recorded in the Penitential Canons, may serve to give us some idea of the satisfactions, which, in those days, the Church required as bearing some proportion "to the quality of the crimes and ability of the Penitents." No more was required of Penitents in those first ages, than was justly and strictly due; nor indeed so much; and what was due *then*, is due *now;* because the Divine justice is essentially the same at all times.

That you may see what the ancient penances were, I will quote some few of the Penitential Canons:—

1. They who had denied the Faith, even though it were to save their life, were required to do penance *ten years.*

2. They who had joined in Pagan worship, *two years.*

3. They who had taken a false oath, *forty days on bread and water.*

4. They who had broken a fast, *twenty days on bread and water.*

5. They who had cursed their parents, *forty days*

6. They who had struck their parents, *seven years.*

(19) Conc. Trid., Sess. 14, de Pœnit., cap. 8.

7. They who had done an injury to their parents, *three years.*

Similar penances were inflicted for other mortal sins; and, in some cases, the penance was *for life.*

It may be asked: "Why are less penances enjoined *now;* seeing that sin requires, *at all times*, the same atonement?" Because the spirit of fervour is relaxed; the faith of Christians is less lively; and the Church has accommodated herself to the weakness of her children, lest, if a severer penance were now enjoined, they should become guilty of mortal sin by neglecting to perform it, and so change the temporal punishment into one that is eternal.——The penance, enjoined now, is not considered as being sufficient to expiate the whole temporal punishment; hence, the Priest says: "And *the rest* I leave to the merits of Christ, and to your own pious endeavours."——But, even, at the present time, the Church admonishes her Pastors to impose penances, "as far as the spirit and prudence shall suggest, according to the quality of the crimes and ability of the Penitents, lest they be made partakers of other men's sins."[20]

V. PENANCE TO BE ACCEPTED AND PERFORMED: Must the Penitent *accept* a just penance? Yes, unless it be incompatible with his state or circumstances. Must he *perform* it? Yes; because it is an integral part of the Sacrament of Penance, and required by Divine precept: it would be a sin to neglect it wilfully.

The penance, enjoined in Confession, should be performed *at the time*, and *in the manner*, prescribed; it should be performed with devotion, in a spirit of penance, and also in a state of grace or repentance, because, otherwise it would lose its efficacy as a means of expiation.

(20 Conc. Trid., Sess. 14, de Pœn[illegible], cap. 8.

VI. WORKS OF PENANCE :—Is there an *obligation* to do *more penance*, than that which is enjoined in Confession? St. Thomas says: "If the Priest impose a less penance than the sins deserve, the Penitent *is obliged to do more*; and if he neglect to do it in this life, he must suffer it in Purgatory."[21] The same (as has been already observed) is intimated by the Confessor, when, after, enjoining the penance, he immediately adds: "And *the rest* I leave to the merits of Christ, and to *your own pious endeavours.*"

What are the "*pious endeavours*," whereby that deficiency may be supplied? It may be supplied by Prayer, Alms-deeds, and Fasting.

1. *By Prayer*: by many and fervent supplications, offered up in the spirit of penance; by hearing Mass in the same spirit, by frequenting the Sacraments, being regular and diligent in meditation, and in the general and particular examinations of conscience.

2. *By Alms-deeds:* by performing the works of mercy, corporal and spiritual, in a spirit of penance.

3. *By Fasting:* by observing the fasts and abstinences commanded by the Church, and by voluntary mortifications and self-denials, 1*st*, *of the body* by privations in eating, drinking, sleeping, amusements, and other lawful pleasures; and by bearing pains, sickness, &c., in the spirit of penance; and 2*ndly*, *of the passions*, by denying our own will; and by patiently receiving reprimands, reproaches, contradictions, con tempt, humiliations, injuries, persecutions, &c.; and all this in a spirit of penance—as deserving it.

You see, from all this, with what reason the Archangel Raphael said to Tobias: "Prayer is good with fasting and alms, more than to lay up treasures of gold."[22]

(21) Quodlib. 3, art. 1. (22) Tobias xii., 8.

To animate yourselves to fervour in these penitential works,

First, Consider *the Divine command* to do penance: "Bring forth therefore fruits worthy of penance:"[23] for, "except you do penance, you shall all likewise perish."[24] "The kingdom of heaven suffereth violence; and the violent bear it away."[25] "They that are Christ's, have crucified the flesh with its vices and its concupiscences."[26] "If you live according to the flesh, you shall die; but if, by the spirit, you mortify the deeds of the flesh, you shall live."[27] "Be converted, and do penance for all your iniquities; and iniquity shall not be your ruin."[28]

Secondly, Consider what your sins have deserved; and what penance the souls in hell or in purgatory would do, if they could have the opportunity.

Thirdly, Consider also what penance the first Christians did, as required by the Penitential Canons.

Fourthly, Consider, moreover, what Christ has suffered for the expiation of sin.

Such considerations can hardly fail to animate you to fervour in doing penance.

By these works of penance, joined with an amendment of life, you have the surest proof of the sincerity of your repentance—of your Confessions having been good:—and oh! what joy and confidence will this *practice of penance* give you, at the hour of your death!!!

Always bear in mind these words of St. Augustin: "We must either do penance or burn." For, "all sin must necessarily be punished, either by the *man* PENITENT, or by an *avenging God:* would you that *He* should not punish you? then punish yourselves."

(23) Luke iii., 8. (25) Matt. xi., 12. (27) Rom. viii., 13.
(24) Luke xiii. 3, 5. (26) Gal v., 24. (28) Ezech. xviii., 30.

INSTRUCTION LXI.

PENANCE X.

Indulgences: Partial and Plenary—the Church can grant them—her Intention in granting them—the Dispositions and Conditions for gaining them—Whence they derive their Efficacy

What is Satisfaction?—It is doing the Penance given us by the Priest.

What is an Indulgence?—An Indulgence is a releasing of the temporal punishment which often remains due to sin, after its guilt has been remitted.

In explaining the Catholic doctrine on Satisfaction, in the last Instruction, I showed, that besides the *guilt* and *eternal punishment* of sin, there is a *temporal* punishment due to it—that this temporal punishment (as many Scriptural examples prove) may and often does remain to be expiated, *after* the guilt of the sin has been remitted—that, as to its extent, the debt of punishment thus justly due is according to the quality of the crimes committed, or has some proportion to their number and enormity—that the penance enjoined in Confession, is much less than what is due—and that, if the deficiency be not discharged here, during life, it will be exacted much more rigorously hereafter, in Purgatory. For "we must either do penance or burn."

Is there any means of obtaining *a remission* of this debt of temporal punishment? Yes; by the application of the atoning merits of Christ. How can his merits be applied for this purpose? It was shown, in the last Instruction, that they are applied in the Sacrament of Penance; but that, even then, much may still remain for the Penitent to expiate by his own voluntary works of penance: but there is another means, viz., the gaining of *Indulgences*, whereby the atoning merits of Christ may be efficaciously applied for the discharge even of the *whole debt* of temporal punishment due to our sins.——An Indulgence does not regard the *guilt* of sin at all; but only the temporal punishment due to it.

I. INDULGENCES MAY BE EITHER PARTIAL OR PLENARY:—A *Partial* Indulgence is one which remits *a part* only of the temporal punishment due to sin—it remits so much of it as is specified in the grant of the Indulgence; as forty days, seven years, &c. A *Plenary* Indulgence is an entire remission of the *whole* debt.

The ancient Penitential Canons subjected sinners to long and severe penances: for some sins, the penances enjoined were of many years' duration. An indulgence, when granted in those days, meant, if *Partial*, a remission of so much of the Canonical Penance, and of the temporal punishment corresponding to it, as was specified in the Indulgence; and, if *Plenary*, a remission of the whole of the Canonical Penance, and of all the corresponding temporal punishment.

Although the Church does not now impose those severe penances, yet the justice of God requires as much atonement now as it did then. How few penitents are there, who, since they first came to the use of reason, have not committed sins, which, if put together, would require many years of penance (according to the ancient canons) to expiate them? Perhaps they would require hundreds, perhaps even many thousands of years. How much, therefore, would remain to be atoned for after death, unless remitted by Indulgences? Now, an Indulgence of 40 days, of 100 days, of 7 years, &c,, means a remission of so much temporal punishment, as would be expiated by the due performance of the Canonical Penance during so many days or years,

Whereas, a Plenary Indulgence (as now granted)

means a remission of the *whole debt* of temporal punishment due to *all* our sins.

II. THE CHURCH HAS POWER TO GRANT INDULGENCES :—Concerning Indulgences the Church teaches these two things:—1*st*, That she has received from Christ the power of granting them—and 2*ndly*, that the use of them is very salutary to Christian people.[29]

Proofs :—Christ said to St. Peter : "And I will give to thee *the keys* of the kingdom of heaven : and whatsoever THOU shalt bind upon earth, it shall be bound also in heaven ; and whatsoever thou shalt *loose* upon earth, it shall be *loosed* also in heaven."[30] "Amen I say to you, whatsoever *you* shall bind upon earth shall be bound also in heaven ; and whatsoever you shall loose upon earth, shall be loosed also in heaven."[31]

Here the power of *binding* contains the power of refusing absolution, when the case requires a refusal ; and also of imposing penances (when absolution is given), to satisfy the Divine justice ; the power of *loosing* contains the power of *absolving* the real penitent from *guilt* ; and also from TEMPORAL PUNISHMENT, for just reasons.

Such has always been the *doctrine* and *practice* of the Church from the time of the Apostles to the present day. We read in the New Testament, of St. Paul granting an Indulgence to one of the faithful at Corinth. That Corinthian had taken his father's wife ; and St. Paul exercised the power of *binding*, by inflicting a penance, and by excluding him from the assemblies of the faithful till he had performed it.[32] The Corinthian submitted with sincere and *fervent* repentance ; and the following year, St. Paul exercised also the power of *loosing*, by remitting the

(29) Conc. Trid. Sess. 25, de Reform. cap. 21, decr. de Indulgentis.
(30) Matt. xvi., 19.
(31) Matt. xviii., 18.
(32) 1 Cor. v,

remainder of the penance, "let such a one (he said) be swallowed up with over much sorrow."[33]

We know that it was the practice of the primitive Church, to impose very long penances: now, at the breaking out of a persecution, she granted indulgences to the *more fervent* of the Penitents, by abridging the duration of their penance, and admitting them to the Holy Communion; thus exercising, like St. Paul, that power of *binding* and *loosing*, which she has received from Christ. The Church, then, *has the power* of granting Indulgences.

And the very *nature* and *object* of Indulgences, (namely, to lessen, or remove, by remission, the debt of temporal punishment,) prove sufficiently their inestimable *advantages*, or, *that the use of them is very salutary to Christian people.*

III. Intention of the Church in granting Indulgences:—Is it the intention of the Church *to dispense*, by Indulgences, from the *obligation* of doing works of penance? No; "It never was the intention of the Church, (says Liebermann), to favour the slothful negligence of Christians, nor to exempt them from all obligation of doing penance, against that which is said: "*bring forth fruits worthy of penance.*" Hence, indulgences were anciently granted to such only as were *fervent* in doing works of penance. St. Cyprian (Tract. de Lapsis) very much blames those, who, at the recommendations of the martyrs, admitted penitents to reconciliation before they had done penance: 'Vain and false peace, (he says) dangerous to the givers, and of no advantage to the receivers.' "[34]

What, then, *is* the intention of the Church in granting Indulgences? Her intention is this:—

1. To assist penitents of *good will*, to discharge their

(33) 2 Cor. ii, 7.
(34) Liebermann, de Sacr. Pœnit., cap. 4, art. 3, § 3, quæs. 5.

debt of temporal punishment, by supplying, from the Treasury of the Church, their inability and insufficiency.

2. To excite the Faithful to greater piety and love of God. And indeed, for this purpose, certain acts of piety and religion are always prescribed and required, as *necessary* conditions.

IV. CONDITIONS for GAINING INDULGENCES:—What is necessary for gaining an Indulgence, especially a Plenary one?

1. It is necessary to be *in the state of Grace*—free from the *guilt* of mortal sin; at least, when the last condition is fulfilled. For, without this disposition, it is not possible to gain any Indulgence. We cannot obtain the *full* effect of a *Plenary* Indulgence, without being free from the guilt of *all* sin, both mortal and venial; and from all affection to any sin.

2. It is necessary to be in a disposition to satisfy the Divine justice; at least by performing the Sacramental penance, and the works enjoined in the grant of the Indulgence; and by offering to God the satisfactory merits of Christ, as an equivalent for the remission which is granted in the Indulgence.

But, whether it be necessary to be in the actual disposition to satisfy the Divine justice, as far as we can, by our *own penitential works*, is controverted among divines. Some assert that this disposition is necessary for gaining the effect of an Indulgence; whilst others teach the contrary. With regard to the opinion, which asserts that the actual disposition to satisfy, by our own penitential works, is necessary for gaining Indulgences, Bellarmine says, that it is salutary and pious, but *perhaps* not true; especially as it is opposed to the common teaching of divines. But, as Libermann says, "This is *certain*, that both the pious use of Indulgences, and also continual labour in doing works of penance and satisfaction, cannot be sufficiently recommended to the faithful. The business of salvation which we have to accomplish, is a most arduous and important work. He who is wise will choose the safer way. Now, undoubtedly, the safer way is this: to be so intent upon doing works of penance, as if no remedy were to be obtained from Indulgences; and to be so earnest in gaining Indulgences, as if nothing were to be expected from our own works. This is the surest way to salvation."35*

3. It is necessary to perform all the conditions prescribed, faithfully and devoutly, and with an intention of gaining the Indulgence; for some good works are always required, as conditions—as some compensation or satisfaction to the Divine justice, for the remission granted. (Such as prayers for some public and important purpose:—alms-deeds—visiting the sick, or other works of mercy—receiving the Sacraments of Penance and Communion, &c.)——No Indulgence can be gained, unless its conditions be *duly fulfilled* with an *intention* of gaining it. But it is not necessary that this intention be *actual;* for, a *virtual* intention is sufficient, i.e., one which has been actual, and which still continues virtually to exist. Hence, it would be a salutary, as well as pious practice, to form an actual intention every morning of gaining all the Indulgences which are attached to whatever devotions and good works we shall perform during the day: this intention (which may be made by way of oblation in our morning prayers) will continue *vir-*

(35) * "Certum est non posse Fidelibus satis commendari et pium indulgentiarum usum, et continuum in pœnitentiæ et satisfactionis operibus laborem. Gravissimum est quod nobis incumbit salutas negotium; qui sapit eliget quod tutius est. Est autem procul dubio tutius, pœnitentiæ laboribus ita incumbere, ac si nullum adesset ex Indulgentiis remedium, et ita studiose captare Indulgentias, ac si nihil esset ex propriis operibus sperandum. Certissima hæc est ad salutem via."—*De Sacr. Pœnit., cap.* 4, *art.* 3, *sec.* 3, *quæst.* 5.

tually and *validly* to exist, during the day; unless retracted by some contrary act or intention.

V. WHENCE DO INDULGENCES DERIVE THEIR EFFICACY in remitting the temporal punishment due to sin?—From the superabundant merits of Christ and his Saints. The merits of Christ, being infinite, are more than were necessary to purchase the Redemption of all mankind. Now, his superabundant merits, together with those of the Saints (the Blessed Virgin Mary, the Baptist, &c.), form a precious treasure, which Christ has left to his Church, with power to dispense it to the Faithful.

CONCLUSION:—How this concession commends the great goodness and bounty of God!—how it should influence our hearts with gratitude and love—and should stimulate us to fervour in doing penance! For, by living in the disposition and practice of penance, we shall be able to supply our weakness and insufficiency; because such disposition and practice will enable us to gain the Indulgences offered us by the Church; and thus, out of the treasure of the Church applied by Indulgences, we may discharge the whole of our debt of temporal punishment, and so be prepared for entering into heaven immediately after death

---

INSTRUCTION LXII.

EXTREME-UNCTION.

Extreme-Unction is a true Sacrament—its Effects—its Necessity—when, and by whom, it should be received—its Ceremonies—the Dispositions required.

What is Extreme-Unction?—Extreme-Unction is the anointing of the sick with holy oil, accompanied with prayer for the forgiveness of their sins.

When is the Sacrament given?—When we are in danger of death by sickness.

What authority is there in Scripture for the Sacrament of Extreme-Unction?—In the 5th Chapter of St. James, it is said: "Is any man sick among you, let him bring in the Priests of the Church; and let them pray over him, anointing him with oil, in the name of the Lord; and the prayer of faith shall save the sick man; and the Lord shall raise him up; and if he be in sins they shall be forgiven him."—*St. James* v., 14, 15.

Concerning the Sacrament of Extreme-Unction, the Council of Trent declares it to have been "regarded by the Fathers as being the completion, not only of penance, but also of the whole Christian life, which ought to be a perpetual penance." The Council, moreover, showing the goodness of our most gracious Redeemer towards his servants, declares and teaches that, "as, in the other Sacraments, He prepared the greatest aids, whereby, during life, Christians may preserve themselves whole from every more grievous spiritual evil; so did he guard the close of life, by the Sacrament of Extreme-Unction, as with a most firm defence. For, though our adversary seeks and seizes opportunities, *all our life long*, to be able in any way to devour our souls; yet is there no time wherein he strains more vehemently all the powers of his craft to ruin us utterly, and to make us fall, if he possibly can, even from trust in the mercy of God, than *when he perceives the end of our life to be at hand.*"[36]——All this shows the great advantages of receiving Extreme-Unction; and also the importance of being well-instructed concerning this Sacrament, that you may know how to receive it with greater benefit to your soul.

What, then, *is Extreme-Unction?*—Extreme-Unction is the anointing of the sick with holy oil, accompanied with prayer for the forgiveness of their sins.

(36) Conc. Trid., Sess. 14. Doctr. de Extr. Unc.

I. Extreme-Unction is a true Sacrament:—It has all that is necessary to constitute a Sacrament. For,

1. There is the "*outward Sign*" (or outward part performed by the Priest), namely, the anointing with *holy oil*, which is the *matter* of this Sacrament; and the accompanying prayers, which are its *form*.

2. There is the "*inward grace*" (or inward part performed by God), namely, strength against temptations—remission of sins—purifying the soul from the remains of sin—and the graces proper for making a due preparation for death.

The inward grace of Extreme-Unction is *signified* or represented by its outward part, which is therefore called a *sign*. For, as oil is often used to *soothe and cure wounds*, and *restore bodily strength* to parts that have been weakened; it is therefore very appropriately used to signify similar *spiritual* effects, produced in the soul by this last anointing; and the words or prayers which accompany the anointing, determine it to such a signification, by *expressing* the nature of the grace received.

3. There is the "*Institution of Christ*;" which we find intimated by St. Mark,[37] and described and promulgated by St. James, when he says: "Is any man sick among you? let him bring in the Priests of the Church, and let them pray over him, anointing him with oil, in the name of the Lord; and the prayer of faith shall save the sick man, and the Lord shall raise him up; and if he be in sins, they shall be forgiven him."[38] These words clearly show—

First, The *Divine Institution* of the Sacrament of Extreme-Unction; For it is evident that St. James only describes and promulgates what *Christ* had instituted; because the Apostles could not give to out-

(37) Mark vi., 13. (38) James v., 14 15.

ward acts and ceremonies the power of producing grace, pardon, or any other spiritual effect: only God can do this—He alone can give grace. Therefore, when the Apostle declares and promises these effects, it *is* and *must be* in consequence and in virtue of the *institution of Christ.* That it is a *Divine* institution, has been the constant doctrine of the Church; and been defined, moreover, by the Council of Trent.[39]

Secondly, The words of St. James show what Extreme-Unction is: that it is "the anointing of the sick with oil, accompanied with prayer, for the forgiveness of their sins."

Thirdly, They show who its Ministers are: "Let him bring in *the Priests* of the Church."

Fourthly, They point out who its subjects are: "Is any man *sick* among you?"

Fifthly, They specify its effects and advantages: "The prayer of faith shall save the sick man, and the Lord shall raise him up; and if he be in sins, they shall be forgiven him."

II. Effects of Extreme-Unction:--Most precious are the effects which this Sacrament produces in the soul of the worthy receiver; especially if we consider the critical time when those Effects are conferred, and how much they are then needed.

1. It strengthens the soul against the temptations of the enemy, which are more violent *then*, than at other times. Our adversary, the devil, is *always* going about, like a roaring lion, seeking to devour us; but, when he sees that our death is drawing near, he redoubles his efforts *then* to ruin us eternally, unless he be restrained by God, because he knows that *then* he either gains or loses us for ever: "Woe, to the earth, because the devil is come down to you, having great wrath, knowing that he hath but a short time."[40]

(39) Sess. 14, de Sacr, Extr. Unc. can. I. (40) Apoc. xii., 12.

"There are spirits that are created for vengeance; and, in the time of destruction, they shall pour out their force."[41]

Now, under these more violent attacks, how could the poor soul stand her ground? weakened, exhausted, and distracted by the pains and languor of expiring nature, and dismayed by the violence and continuance of temptations, she would fall an easy prey to the enemy, unless strengthened and supported by more powerful graces: now, Extreme-Unction was instituted to give these more powerful graces; and thus, the malicious efforts of the temper are counteracted.

2. It cleanses the soul from the *remains of sin*, and thus is "the completion of penance, and of the whole Christian life." After sin, even when remitted by penance, there remain in the soul spiritual weaknesses, stronger inclinations to evil, or an increased concupiscence, a sluggishness to good, pusillanimous fears, and other evil consequences. Now, so far as these are the effects or remains of our sins, they are remedied by Extreme-Unction; either wholly or in part, according to our disposition.—But,

3. As the remains of sin cannot be destroyed, so long as their *guilt* continues, it follows as a consequence, that this Sacrament removes that guilt, whenever it finds no obstacle in the way.

As to *venial sins:* it blots them out, provided they be repented of with *attrition;* and it does this as its own proper effect.

As to *mortal sins:* it also purifies the soul from *them*, when we cannot receive the Sacrament of Penance, if we remove the obstacle to grace by due repentance; as, for example, when the sick person, after absolution, fails into a mortal sin, and then repents of it with real attrition, and has the disposition or inten-

(41) Eccli. xxxix., 33, 34.

tion of confessing it; but before he can confess it, he quite forgets it, or becomes insensible; and the Priest, not knowing that there is any need of repeating the absolution, proceeds to administer Extreme-Unction. In this, and in all similar or equal cases, Extreme-Unction will restore the person to a state of grace; and will produce the other effects for which it was instituted, as if it had been received in the state of grace.[42*]

But when the sick person is *conscious*, at the time of receiving this Sacrament of being in mortal sin; he cannot, under such circumstances, *lawfully* receive it, without either obtaining absolution (if he can), *with attrition*; or else making such an act of sorrow for his sins, as he may prudently judge to be *Contrition*.[43†]

4. Extreme Unction gives calmness of mind—resignation to God's will—patience in bearing the last sickness—confidence in the Divine mercy.

5. It sometimes restores bodily health; i.e., it has this effect, if God foresees that it is expedient for our salvation.

III. Its Necessity:—Is it absolutely necessary to

(42) * *See* Note 15, pages 236, 237.

It should be observed, that, although the Note here referred to is true with regard to *all* the Sacraments *of the living*, yet it applies more directly to Extreme Unction than to the others; because *to remit sins* is one of the express objects of its institution: "And if he be in sins, they shall be forgiven him."

St. Alphonsus Liguori says: "Commune est inter Doctores per hoc Sacramentum remitti peccata tam venialia, quam *mortalia*, si hæc infirmus invincibiliter ignoret, habeatique *attritionem* qua auferatur obex peccati; Ita *S. Thomas*..... Sententia vero probabilior et communior dicit Extremam Unctionem remittere mortalia *per se*, et si consequentur. Ratio est, quia licet hæc Sacramentum sit vivorum, tamen *ex institutione* divina peccata remittit, ut patet ex verbis Apostoli."——*S. Alph. Lig.*, *Theol. Mor.*, *lib.* 6, *tract.* 5, *n.* 731.

(43) † "Ad Sacramentum hoc *cum fructu* recipiendum, in eo qui rationis est compos, et *conscius* peccatti mortalis, (si non confiteatur) requiritur contritio *saltem existimata.*"—*S. Alph. Lig.*, *Theol. Mor.*, *lib.* 6, *tract* 5, *n.* 716.

receive Extreme-Unction in our last sickness? No; but it cannot be *wilfully* neglected without some sin. Some Divines say that the sin would be mortal; and St. Alphonsus Liguori calls this a *probable opinion.*[44] To deprive one's self, through wilful neglect, of such powerful helps, when so much needed, would be exposing one's self to the danger of yielding to temptations, and of perishing eternally; and how can we *wilfully* expose ourselves to that danger, without sin?

IV. When, and by whom, is Extreme-Unction to be received? This Sacrament is to be received, "When we are in *danger of death by sickness;*" and we should not put off the reception of it till the last extremity; because we are not *then* able to receive it with so much spiritual profit; and also because we run great risk of putting it off till it be too late, and so being deprived of it altogether.

Persons who have lost the use of their senses are capable of receiving this sacrament: and they obtain its beneficial effects, if, at the time of being deprived of their senses, they were in requisite dispositions; i.e., if they had at least attrition.

Soldiers engaging in battle,—sailors in a storm—culprits about to be executed, &c., cannot receive Extreme-Unction; because, although they are in danger of death, yet their danger is not *by sickness*—Children also, before they have come to the use of reason,—idiots and insane persons who *never* had the use of reason, cannot receive this Sacrament; because, not having any *sin*, nor any *remains* of sin, and not being liable to any *temptations* to sin, they are incapable of experiencing its effects.

Can we receive Extreme-Unction more than once? Yes; as often as a sick person recovers from the danger of death, and then falls into it again; so often

(44) Theol. Mor., lib. 6, tract. 5, n. 733.

he can receive this Sacrament. But he cannot receive it a second time, while he continues in *that same* danger, wherein he was, when this Sacrament was administered to him.

V. ITS CEREMONIES:—How is Extreme-Unction administered? Confession having been made, and the Holy Viaticum received, the dying christian is fortified in his last struggles with the enemy, and enabled to perfect and complete his preparation for death, by this last holy anointing.——The Priest sprinkles the bed and the attendants with holy water, and then implores the blessings of heaven upon that house, and upon all who dwell therein. After this, the sick person (or some one in his name) repeats the "Confiteor;" and the Priest then prays for him, begging, in the name of the three Divine Persons, that, by the administration of this Sacrament, the whole power of the devil may be extinguished in him. Then follows the essential part of the Sacrament; namely, the Priest anoints, in the form of a Cross, the different senses of the body, i.e., the eyes, ears, nostrils, mouth, hands, and feet; saying at the same time: "By this holy anointing, and of his own most tender mercy, may the Lord forgive thee whatever thou hast committed *by thy sight*" ("......*by thy hearing*," &c., according to the particular sense which he is anointing). While the Priest is thus anointing the various senses, the sick person should unite with him in spirit, by craving that same pardon for himself.

The Priest concludes by imploring the Divine blessings for the sick person—the remission of his sins, the assistances of grace, spiritual consolation, and corporal relief.

VI. THE DISPOSITIONS REQUIRED.—What are the proper dispositions for receiving Extreme-Unction?

1. We should be in a *state of grace*, because this is a Sacrament *of the living*.——Yet, there are circum-

stances wherein it can be received lawfully, and with fruit, even by a person who is *not* in the state of grace: for, what was said just now with reference to the *effects* of Extreme-Unction, must be said also with reference to the *dispositions* of the Receiver; namely, that if he is in mortal sin of which he is *unconscious*, then attrition is a necessary and *sufficient* disposition; but if he is *conscious* of being in mortal sin, then such a repentance as he may prudently judge to be *contrition*, (supposing no absolution) is a disposition of soul *required*, under such circumstances, for receiving this Sacrament worthily.[45*]

2. We should have sincere repentance for *all* our sins, great or small, known or unknown; because even venial sins cannot be remitted without sincere repentance.

3. We should excite ourselves to great confidence in the Divine mercy, and in the merits of Christ; and endeavour to be completely resigned to God's will.

After receiving Extreme-Unction, we should return thanks to God for so great a blessing—cast one's-self on his mercy—and think only on him and eternity; bearing in mind, that, when we have but a short time to live, that time is very precious.

CONCLUSION:—I have now explained all that is necessary concerning this Sacrament. And how clearly do its Institution and Advantages show, 1*st*, The immense goodness and tender mercy of God towards us, and his sincere desire of our salvation; 2*ndly*, The great happiness of being members of that Church, in which alone this Sacrament can be received; 3*rdly*, How careful we should be to receive it in due time, while we are able to attend to its adminis-

(45) * "Notandum, quoad dispositionem animæ, quod si infirmus sit in peccato mortali, debet esse saltem contritus *putative*, ut hoc sacramento muniatur."—*S. Alph. Lig.*, *Hom. Apostol.*, *tract.* 17, *n.* 9.

See Note 43, page 352.

tration; and 4*thly*, How cautious we should be, during life, not to abuse God's graces by delaying repentance; lest, by a just judgment, we should be deprived of the graces of this Sacrament, at the time when they are so much needed; as there have been many striking examples.

INSTRUCTION LXIII.

HOLY ORDER.

Priesthood necessary to Religion; Order and Mission necessary to the Priesthood; Holy Order a true Sacrament; The different Orders; Dispositions for receiving Holy Orders; Celibacy.

What is Holy Order?—Holy Order is a Sacrament by which Bishops, Priests, and other Ministers of the Church are ordained; and receive power and grace to perform their sacred duties.

I. Priesthood necessary to Religion:—Although the Sacrament of Holy Order is received, comparatively, by *few* only of the Faithful; yet it concerns *all*, since it is necessary for the existence of the Church—for the administration of other Sacraments—for the celebration of the Holy Sacrifice, &c. Were the Faithful to be left without Pastors, they might perhaps persevere for a time; but how extremely rare would be the cases of any of them persevering long? What would become of children, without a parent or guardian? of the sick, without a physician? of a vessel, without some one to steer it? Therefore, what a terrible privation it is for any congregation to be left without a Pastor! How, then, we should lament the scarcity of Priests in this country; and implore our Lord to "send labourers into his harvest!"[46]—

(46) Luke x. 2

and how important and meritorious a duty it must be in the Faithful, to contribute to the support and extension of the Priesthood! For the Church, by the help of which they are to be saved, cannot subsist without Ministers.

The Priesthood, then, IS NECESSARY TO THE CHURCH—to the Faithful at large. Hence, Christ, in founding his Church, established in it an order of Ministers, whom he empowered and commissioned to offer Sacrifice—to administer the Sacraments—to instruct and guide the Faithful—and to govern the Church. The Apostles were the first to whom he gave *order*, and *mission* and *grace*, for the performance of these important functions. And, as his Church was to continue to the end of the world, he gave them, moreover, the power of communicating the same to their successors: "*As* the Father hath sent sent me, I also send you;"[47] i.e., as the Father hath sent me, his first Priest, with power to ordain and commission others: so I send you also, as Priests, with power to do *the same;* and your successors, having the same power as I have given you, can, in like manner, send others; and so on to the end of the world. Accordingly, the Apostles *did* ordain successors; and they instructed them *to ordain others after them:* for, the Apostles ordained Matthias, in place of Judas; [48] St. Paul ordained Timothy and Titus; and instructed them to appoint others; "Stir up the grace of God, which is in thee *by the imposition of my hands.*"[49] "And the things which thou hast heard of me by many witnesses, the same commend to faithful men, who shall be fit to teach others also."[50] "For this cause I left thee in Crete,......that thou shouldst ordain Priests in every city, as I also appointed thee."[51]

(47) John xx., 21.
(48) Acts i., 24, 25, 26; Acts xiv., 22.
(49) 2 Tim. i., 46.
(50) 2 Tim. ii., 2.
(51) Tit i., 5.

This succession of the Priesthood has continued, ever since, to be regularly handed down in the Church; and will so continue to the end of time.

II. ORDER AND MISSION NECESSARY TO THE PRIESTHOOD:—No one could ever lawfully exercise the functions of this ministry, unless duly ordained and commissioned by the Apostles or their lawful successors; and whoever, (knowing that he is not thus duly ordained and commissioned) presumes to exercise them, commits a grievous sin, and incurs the malediction of God: "Neither doth any man take this honour to himself, but *he* that is called by God, as Aaron was."[52] "How shall they preach unless they be sent?"[53] Such as are not *ordained* and *sent*, are not true pastors, but "hirelings;" they are "thieves and robbers, that enter not by the door into the sheepfold, but climb up another way;[54] they are those false prophets against whom our Lord cautions us, saying: "Beware of false prophets, who come to you in the clothing of sheep, but inwardly they are ravening wolves;"[55] "they are blind, and leaders of the blind, and if the blind lead the blind, both fall into the pit."[56] St. Peter foretold that there would be such: "There shall be among you lying teachers, who shall bring in *sects of perdition;*......bringing *upon themselves* swift destruction."[57]

God has shown the grievousness of this sacrilegious crime, by most terrible and visible judgments. (*Examples:* Ozias, King of Juda, presumed to exercise the functions of the priesthood—to offer incense; and the High Priest, Azarius, "withstood the king, and said: It doth not belong *to thee*, Ozias, to burn incense to the Lord; but *to the priests*, that is, the sons of Aaron, who are consecrated for this ministry." The

(52) Heb. v., 4.
(53) Rom. x., 15.
(54) John x., 1, 13, 13.
(55) Matt. vii., 15
(56) Matt. xv., 14.
(57) 2 Pet., ii., 1

king persisted; but God instantly struck him with leprosy, "and Ozias was a leper unto the day of his death."[58]——But a still more striking and terrible example has been given us, in the persons of Core, Dathan, and Abiron, who, with 250 leading men of the synagogue, assumed also the priestly office of offering incense to the Lord. For the earth broke asunder beneath the feet of Core, Dathan, and Abiron; and opening her mouth, swallowed them down alive into hell; and a fire coming out from the Lord, destroyed the 250 men that offered the incense; and when, on account of their death, the people murmured against Moses and Aaron, the Lord destroyed 14,700 more.[59]

Surely, all this is sufficient to prove, that no one has a right to "take this honour to himself, but he that is called by God, as Aaron was."[60] Therefore, in what a lamentable state, since the Reformation, is this country, where each successive *earthly Sovereign*, with the Government, assumes the functions of Peter, appointing bishops and parsons, who, for want of a Divine Commission, are as so many Cores, leading the people in the way of perdition! Or rather, the *temporal* power has assumed the very office of Christ, having established a religion and a priesthood of its own, in opposition to *His!* and it even proceeds to such a degree of religious folly, or rather impiety, as to give to any man, who applies for it, a written *licence* to be a preacher of any religion: thus giving an authorization to any one, to commit the grievous crime of Core, Dathan, and Abiron; and to expose his hearers, as well as himself, to the like spiritual ruin!!!

Of all such it may be literally said: "'I did not send them, yet they ran; I have not spoken to them, yet they prophesied:'[61] 'They have not entered by the

(58) 2 Par. xxvi., 16 to 21.
(59) Num. xvi.
(60) Heb. v., 4.
(61) Jer. xxiii., 21

door into the sheepfold, but have climbed up another way.'"[62] THEY only are "*sent*"—THEY only "*enter by the door*," who have received Order and Mission from the Apostles or their lawful successors. For the powers of the ministry, with grace for the due exercise of its functions, are conferred by the Sacrament of Holy Order, which our Blessed Lord has instituted for that purpose.

III. IS HOLY ORDER A TRUE SACRAMENT?—Yes; it has all that is necessary to constitute a Sacrament. For,

1. There is the "*outward Sign*" (or outward part performed by the Bishop), viz., the *imposition of hands*, and *prayer*, with the *delivery* of the instruments of that power which is communicated.

2. There is the "*inward grace*" (or inward part performed by God), viz., the *power* of the Order received, with an *indelible character* imprinted on the soul; and also *actual grace* for the due exercise of that Order, together with an increase of sanctifying grace."[63] But this Sacrament does not confer *mission*, because Ordination does not give jurisdiction

3. There is the "*Institution of Christ*." St. Paul declares, that this Sacrament confers grace, by prayer, with the imposition of hands: "Neglect not the grace that is in thee, which was given thee by prophecy, with imposition of the hands of the priesthood."[64] "I admonish thee that thou stir up the grace of God which is in thee by the imposition of my hands."[65] Now, it is evident, from these declarations of St. Paul, that Holy Order is a Divine Institution; because only God can give to outward acts the power of producing grace in the soul. When outward things, therefore, are made a certain and efficacious means of grace, it must be in virtue of a Divine Institution.

(62) John x., 1.
(63) *See* Note 15, pages 236 and
(64) 1 Tim. iv., 14.
(65) 2 Tim. i., 6

IV. The different Orders of Ministers:—No one can lawfully receive any Order, until he has first received the *Tonsure;* which is not an Order, but a preparation or disposition for Orders. The first four Orders that are received, are called *Minor Orders*: which are these: 1, The Order of Porter or Door-keeper; 2, Lector; 3, Exorcist; 4, Acolythe. The others are called the *Greater or Holy Orders*, namely, 5, Sub-deacon; 6, Deacon; 7, Priest; 8, Bishop. Bishops are the highest Order: they are properly *the Pastors* of the Church: Take heed to yourselves, and to the whole flock, wherein the Holy Ghost hath placed you Bishops, to rule the Church of God."[66] It belongs, of right, to *them only* to meet in Council and define what is of faith.——Ordination is the actual conferring of these Orders.

V. Dispositions for receiving Holy Orders:—What are the Dispositions necessary for receiving *Holy Orders?*

1. To be "called by God, as Aaron was:"[67]
2. To be in the state of grace:——
3. To have no canonical impediment—
4. To lead a good life—
5. To be single and chaste, with a fixed determination to continue so for life.

VI. Celibacy:—The practice of the Church, with regard to the Celibacy of the Clergy rests on very strong grounds.

1. The Scripture teaches that Celibacy is a more perfect state, and more acceptable before God, than that of Marriage:—

"I would that all men were as myself......I say to the unmarried, and to the widows: It is good for them if they so continue, even as I......Art thou loosed from a wife? seek not a wife......I would have

(66) Acts xx., 28. (67) Heb. v., 4.

you to be without solicitude: he that is without a wife, is solicitous for the things that belong to the Lord, how he may please God: but that he is with a wife, is solicitous for the things of the world, how he may please his wife; and he is divided. And the unmarried woman and the virgin thinketh on the things of the Lord, that she may be holy both in body and in spirit......And this I speak *for your profit:* not to cast a snare upon you, but for that which is decent, and which may *give you power to attend upon the Lord without impediment*......Therefore both he that giveth his virgin in marriage, doth well; and he that giveth her not, *doth better*."[68]

2. In accordance with this plain testimony of St. Paul, in favour of a life of Celibacy or Virginity, the Celibacy of the Clergy has been the practice of the Church *from the earliest ages*."[69]

Conclusion:—Thank the mercy and bounty of God for this sacred Institution, by means of which you receive *so many* and *so great* spiritual blessings—even all the blessings of Religion. For, by means of this Divine Institution, you receive the benefit of the Sacraments, and Sacrifice, whereby the merits of Redemption are efficaciously applied to your souls—you receive, moreover, authoritative instruction in faith and morality—counsel in your doubts—consolation in your heaviest troubles (those of conscience)—support in your greatest trials—secure guidance in the way of salvation—and (where most felt) comfort, consolation, and spiritual assistances, at that fearful time when you are about to stand before the judgment-seat of your God!

(68) 1 Cor. vii., 7, 8, 27, 32, 33, 34, 35, 38.

(69) See Challoner's Catholic Christian Instructed, chapter 17.

INSTRUCTION LXIV.

MATRIMONY.

Matrimony as a Contract—It is a true Sacrament—Indissoluble—Conditions required—Consent of Parents—Impediments.

What is Matrimony?—Matrimony is a Sacrament which gives grace to those who contract marriage with due dispositions, to enable them to bear the difficulties of their state, to love and be faithful to one another, and to bring up their children in the fear of God.

Only one Sacrament remains now to be explained, viz., *Matrimony*. In the Instructions on the preceding Sacraments, you cannot but have frequently ad mired the great mercy, goodness, and bounty of God, in having provided suitable and efficacious helps for every age and state of life, and for every condition in his Church."[70]

Married persons stand in need of special graces, adapted to their state; and our bountiful Redeemer has provided them in the Sacrament of Matrimony and what those graces are, I will proceed now to explain, after saying a few words on the nature and obligations of Marriage.

I. MARRIAGE AS A CONTRACT:—Marriage may be considered either as a mere *natural* contract, or as a *sacramental* contract.

1. *As a natural contract*, it is the union of a man and woman, till the death of one of them; with the view to be a mutual help to each other, and to have children who may love and serve God. This was instituted by God in the beginning: "And the Lord God said: It is not good for man to be alone; let us make him a help like unto himself. Then the Lord cast a deep sleep upon Adam: and when he was fast

(70) See INSTRUCTION XLIV., pages 233, 234, 235.

asleep, he took one of his ribs, and filled up flesh for it. And the Lord God built the rib, which he took from Adam, into a woman: and brought her to Adam. And Adam said: This is now bone of my bones, and flesh of my flesh. Wherefore a man shall leave father and mother, and shall cleave to his wife; and they shall be two in one flesh."[71]——Eve was made of a rib of Adam, to show, 1*st*, The close union that exists between man and wife;—2*ndly*, The subjection of the wife to her husband;—and 3*rdly*, That the husband should love his wife as a part of himself.

2. At the establishment of Christianity, this natural contract was raised to the dignity of being *sacramental;* and, as such, we are now to consider it.

II. Matrimony is a true Sacrament:—"If any one saith (says the Council of Trent) that Matrimony is not truly and properly one of the seven Sacraments of the Evangelic Law, instituted by Christ our Lord;......and that it does not confer grace; let him be Anathema."[72]

1. There is the "*outward sign*" (or outward part of this Sacrament,) viz., the mutual consent of the parties *expressed*, and the actual giving and taking of each other (under such conditions as God and his Church require.)

2. There is the "*inward grace*" (or inward part performed by God), viz., an increase of sanctifying grace; but principally *sacramental grace*, to enable the married couple to discharge the duties and obligations of their state in a proper manner.

3. There is the "*Institution of Christ.*" For our Blessed Lord says in the Gospel: "He who made man from the beginning, made them male and female;...... and they two shall be in one flesh: therefore now they are *not two*, but *one flesh.* What therefore God hath

(71) Gen ii., 18, 21, 22, 23. 24. (72) Sess. 24 de Matrim., can. I.

joined together, let not man put asunder."[73] The Council of Trent, quoting these words, says: "But the grace which might perfect that natural love, and confirm that indissoluble union, and sanctify the married, Christ himself, the Institutor and Perfecter of the venerable Sacraments, merited for us by his passion; as the Apostle Paul intimates, saying: *Husbands, love your wives, as Christ also loved the Church, and delivered himself up for it*; adding shortly after: "*This is a great Sacrament; but I speak in Christ and in the Church.*"[74]

III. INDISSOLUBLE:—Matrimony was instituted to be a perpetual bond...a union not to be dissolved, while *both* the parties live. They may, indeed, for *just reasons*, live separate; but they are still married persons: "whosoever shall put away his wife, and marry another, committeth adultery against her; and if the wife shall put away her husband, and be married to another, she committeth adultery......What, therefore, God hath joined together, let no man put asunder."[75]

IV. WHAT CONDITIONS ARE REQUIRED to render the celebration of marriage lawful:—

1. Proclamation of *banns;* where the decree for this is in force;—

2. To be celebrated before witnesses; and by their own proper Pastor, where the decree for this is received:—

3 To have no canonical impediment;—

4. To be in a state of grace.

V. CONSENT OF PARENTS:—The two parties should have the *consent of their Parents.* Parents may refuse their consent if they have just reasons, viz:

(73) Matt. xix., 4, 5, 6.
(74) Sess. 24, Doctrina de Sacr. Matrim....Eph. v., 25, 32.
(75) Mark x., 11, 12, 9.

1. If the Marriage would be a disgrace to, or disturb the peace of the family;

2. If it would prove highly detrimental to the child;

3. If it would endanger the loss of Religion.

But if the refusal be *unreasonable*, the parent sins; and if it be quite evidently so, then the child may marry, notwithstanding the Parent's refusal of consent.

VI. WHAT ARE IMPEDIMENTS? They are cases which are a hinderance to marriage, rendering it either *null* and *void*, or else *unlawful*.

First, Those impediments which render it *null*, (i.e., no marriage at all,) are these:—

1. A *solemn vow* of Chastity;—

2. *Consanguinity* to the fourth degree inclusively;

3. *Affinity*, by lawful marriage, to the fourth degree; by unlawful cohabitation, to the second degree; and also *the affinity* which arises from persons being sponsors in Baptism or Confirmation;—

4. Either party being *already married* to another;—

5. Either one, but only *one*, being unbaptized;—

6. Previous adultery, with a promise of marriage in case the innocent party should die;—

7. If the consent be *not free*, or be extorted by *great* fear.

Secondly, Those Impediments which render marriage *criminal*, though *valid*, are these:—

1. A *promise* of marriage to another person (that promise still existing);

2. A simple *vow* of Chastity;

3. *Solemnizing* the marriage in Advent or Lent.

I have yet to explain the *Dispositions* and *Preparation* necessary for receiving Matrimony worthily; and also the *Duties and Obligations* of married people, which the graces of this Sacrament enable them to fulfil. And the explanation of these shall be the subject of the next Instruction.

INSTRUCTION LXV.

MATRIMONY CONCLUDED.

The Dispositions for receiving the Sacrament of Matrimony—Duties and Obligations of Married People.

What is Matrimony?—Matrimony is a Sacrament which gives grace to those who contract marriage with due dispositions, to enable them to bear the difficulties of their state, to love and be faithful to one another, and to bring up their children in the fear of God.

Having explained the *Institution* and *Nature* of the Sacrament of Matrimony, and the *Conditions* necessary for rendering it valid and lawful; I have now to explain the *Dispositions and Preparation* necessary for receiving it worthily; and also the *Duties and Obligations* of married people.

I. WHAT, THEN, ARE THE DISPOSITIONS AND PREPARATION necessary for receiving this Sacrament worthily.

1. You should endeavour, in the first place, to *procure the favour and direction of Heaven*, by fervent prayer, by being attentive to all the duties of a good Christian, and by avoiding *dangerous* interviews; "A good wife is a good portion; she shall be given in the portion of them that fear God—to a man for his good deeds."[76]——Nothing is of greater importance, in entering into the married state, than to obtain the Divine blessing; and yet nothing is less attended to!

2. They who are about to get married should *con-*

(76) Eccli. xxvi, 3.

sult their Parents and Director; instead of allowing themselves to be hurried away by passion: "My son, do nothing without counsel, and thou shalt not repent when thou hast done."[77] "Children, hear the judgment of your father;"[78] and "seek counsel always of a wise man."[79]

3. They should have *a right intention*—such as God had in the institution of Marriage; viz., to be a mutual help to each other; to have children who may serve God; and to prevent incontinence. Their intention, then, should not be to gratify ambition, or avarice, or carnal desires: "The Angel Raphael said to Tobias: Hear me, and I will show thee who they are, over whom the devil can prevail. For they who in such manner receive Matrimony, as to shut out God from themselves and from their mind, and to give themselves to their lust, as the horse and the mule;......over them the devil hath power."[80]

4. They should be careful to *choose a proper person:* This is of very great importance! yet, to be of a *high family, rich, and beautiful*, seem to be made the *chief* considerations, by a great proportion of those who marry. These are very well as *secondary*, but should not be the *chief determining* motives.

The choice should fall on one of the *true Religion, and a good Christian:* your own peace and happiness; your own salvation, and that of your children, depend greatly upon it. Family, riches, and beauty, are but poor helps to happiness, if the temper be bad—the humour extravagant—or the passion violent: "It is better to dwell in a wilderness, than with a quarrelsome and passionate woman."[81] "Happy is the husband of a good wife, for the number of his years is doubled."[82]

(77) Eccli. xxxii., 24. (79) Tobias iv., 9. (81) Prov. xxi., 19.
(78) Eccli. iii., 2. (80) Tobias vi, 16, 17. (82. Eccli., xxvi 1.

What is the *more immediate Preparation?*

1. To get instructed in the nature of this Sacrament, and in the conditions and dispositions necessary for receiving it: and also in the duties and obligations of the married state—and to resolve to comply with them.

2. To be sufficiently instructed in Christian doctrine, on account of being able to teach the children.

3. To be in a state of grace: otherwise the marriage would be sacrilegious; and would tend to draw down the *curse* of God, instead of his *blessing*.[83]

4. To receive the Sacrament of Penance (if in a state of sin); and to spend some time in preparation and prayer.

II. I will now explain THE DUTIES AND OBLIGATIONS OF THE MARRIED STATE:—The duties of married people are most serious and important; because their *own* and their *children's* happiness, both here and hereafter, depend very much upon them. For the fulfilling of these duties, particular graces are necessary; and Faith teaches, that this Sacrament gives them. You will understand what these graces are, and the value of them, by learning those duties which they will enable you to fulfil.

What, then, are the *Duties and Obligations of the married state?*

1. The husband and wife must have a mutual love for each other:—The precept of Charity obliges married persons *most strictly:* "Husbands, love your wives *as Christ also loved the Church*......Men ought to love their wives, *as their own bodies:* he that loveth his wife, *loveth himself*."[84] Without this there will be no peace or happiness.

2. They must keep their love within proper bounds: For, they must love God more than they love each

(83) *See* Note 15, pages 236 and 237. (84) Eph. v., 25, 28.

other; and not act like Adam, who offended God by eating the forbidden fruit, rather than displease Eve.

3. They must give each other good Example; and pray for their mutual happiness and salvation: "So let your light shine before men, that they may see your good works, and glorify your Father who is in heaven."[85] How much more ought married persons to give edification to each other? St. Paul says: "I desire that prayers and supplications be made for *all men*."[86] How much more, then, ought husband and wife to pray for one another?

4. They must preserve inviolably the sanctity of the Marriage-bed:—(Let) marriage (be) honourable in all, and the bed undefiled: For fornicators and adulterers God will judge."[87] Adultery is *a most grievous crime*, being, 1*st*, The violation of a sacramental contract; 2*ndly*, the breach of a vow made before God and the Church; 3*rdly*, A great injustice to the innocent party.——If it should be discovered, (or suspected, which is frequently the case,) it then sows the seeds of perpetual discord.

5. The husband should exercise his authority *in a proper manner*, (with prudence, mildness, charity, &c.,) as God's law requires:—"The husband is head of the wife, *as Christ* is head of the Church."[88] Therefore, as Christ is solicitous for the good of his Church; so the husband, &c.

6. The wife should behave towards her husband with due *respect*, *obedience*, and *submission*:—"Let women be subject to their husbands, as to the Lord. ......As the Church is subject to Christ; so let wives be to their husbands in all things."[89]

If both parties would observe these duties, how happily they would live together! But, if *one* of

(85) Matt. v., 16. (86) 1 Tim. ii., 1. (87) Heb. xiii., 4. (88) Eph. v., 23. (89) Eph. v., 22, 24.

them should act contrary to them, what is the other to do? In such cases, they seldom act as they should. When, for instance, the wife offends, how frequently does the husband treat her with harshness; cursing, threatening, or striking her; and then pleading necessity in excuse for his conduct: "She has such a temper! (he says;) she is always out of humour, and for ever scolding and tormenting; so that I *must* be harsh."——When the husband offends, the wife uses reproaches; and will continue for hours together, uttering all kinds of spiteful expressions.——All this is the effect of impatience; and makes the matter much worse. When they disagree, there are generally faults on both sides, at least before they have done.——And when wives complain of harsh and violent treatment, although the husband may be faulty, yet they may generally thank themselves for the *ill usage* they receive: as St. Monica used to say to those who went to her with their complaints: "Lay the blame (she said) rather on yourselves and your tongues."[90]

7. There is another very important duty of married people, viz., to bring up their children religiously:—They must instruct their children; instil into them religious feelings; see to their prayers, confessions, and communions; watch over them; keep them from bad companions, and from occasions of sin; set them good example; and pray for them.——These duties towards children lay Parents under a heavy responsibility! and yet how generally are they neglected!!

These are the Duties and Obligations of the married state: they are important and difficult; and cannot be fulfilled *religiously*, without *particular graces*. These graces the Sacrament of Matrimony gives to such as receive it with proper dispositions. You see, then, how important it is to make a good preparation

(90) Butler's Lives of the Saints, Vol. 5, May.

for it! you see the great advantages of receiving it with proper dispositions! and how careful you should be afterwards not to lose, by sin, those special graces which it gives to those who receive it worthily.

EXPLANATION
OF
VIRTUES AND VICES.

INSTRUCTION LXVI.

THEOLOGICAL VIRTUE OF FAITH.

The Nature, Necessity, and Exercise of the Virtue of Faith—the Sins against Faith.

What is meant by the Theological Virtues?—Virtues that relate immediately to God.

How many, and what are the Theological Virtues?—Three; Faith, Hope, and Charity.

What does Faith help us to do?—It helps us to believe, without doubting, all that God has taught and the Church proposes.

I. Nature of Faith:—Faith is a supernatural and *Theological* Virtue, by which we firmly believe all the truths which God has revealed to his Church; and believe them, *because* He who has revealed them is Truth itself. It is called a *Theological* Virtue, because it has God himself for its immediate object, being a direct homage to His eternal Truth—to His Divine Veracity, which is one of His essential Attributes; and moreover, because it is not acquired by us, but *infused* into our souls by God: "Blessed art thou, Simon Bar-Jona; because flesh and blood hath not revealed it to thee, but my Father who is in heaven."[1]

(1) Matt. xvi., 17.

What we believe from the evidence of our senses, is not Faith, but *experience;* what we believe from arguments drawn from self-evident propositions, is *reason and demonstration;* what we believe from testimony, is FAITH, and it may be either *human* or *Divine.* It is *human* faith, when we believe anything on the authority of the word of *man* only: it is *Divine* Faith, when, on the authority of the word of *God*, we believe the truths which he has revealed, and which he proposes to us *as revealed*, by the teaching of his Church, "which (as St. Paul says) is the pillar and ground of the Truth."[2]

But the decisions of the Church, although infallible, are not *the motive* of our Faith; they are only *the sure means of knowing* the truths of Faith. The proper motive of Faith is the word of God—the Divine Veracity: we believe the truths of revelation precisely because God, who is Truth itself, has declared them; and we know with certainty that he has declared them by the infallible teaching of his Church. And the chief merit of Faith consists in believing, on the same authority--on the Divine Veracity, what we do not *see* or should not *otherwise know:* For "Faith is the substance of things to be hoped for—the evidence of things that appear not."[3]

This Divine Faith is the pure gift of God: "For by grace you are saved through Faith; and that not of yourselves, for it is the gift of God."[4]

II. NECESSITY OF FAITH.—The Virtue of Faith is of *strict obligation;* and is included in that homage of adoration, which is enjoined in the First Commandment. It is a most grievous insult to God, and mortally sinful, to refuse to believe his word: and hence Christ says: "He that believeth not, shall be con-

(2) 1 Tim. iii., 15. (3) Heb. xi., 1. (4) Eph. ii., 8.

demned;"[5] and St. Paul likewise assures us, that "without Faith it is impossible to please God."[6]

To satisfy this obligation, our Faith must have these two qualities, namely, it must be *firm*, without the least doubt or misgiving; and it must be *entire*, comprehending all revealed truths, either explicitly, or implicitly.——Our Faith is *explicit*, when, knowing that such or such a truth is revealed by God, we believe it *distinctly* or *in particular:* but it is *implicit*, when we believe all revealed truths *in general*, whether we know them or not; as, for instance, when we believe *all* that the Church believes and teaches.

There are some leading Truths which we must *know*, and *believe with an explicit* Faith; because an explicit belief of them is absolutely *necessary as a means of salvation* (*necessitate medii*). Thus, we must know, and explicitly believe, that there is a God, the Sovereign Lord of all things; and that he rewards those who love and serve him: "Without faith it is *impossible* to please God; for he that cometh to God, *must* believe that he is, and is a rewarder to them that seek him."[7] Therefore, when persons have come to the use of reason, there is no salvation for them, unless they believe *explicitly* in a God, whose Providence looks to our conduct; and in the existence of a future life, where each one will receive rewards or punishments according to his works.

Explicit Faith in the mysteries of the Adorable Trinity, and of the Incarnation and Passion of Jesus Christ, is also imperatively necessary for salvation; either because such explicit belief is an essential means of being saved, or, at least, because it is a Divine precept. [8]*

(5) Mark xvi., 16.
(6) Heb. xi., 6.
(7) Heb. xi., 6.
(8) * Divines are not unanimous, as to whether an *explicit* belief in these mysteries is necessary, as being an essential means of salvation (i.e., *necessi-*

By Divine precept (*necessitate præcepti*), we must also know and explicitly believe, at least in substance, the Apostles' Creed—the Lord's Prayer—the Commandments of God, and of the Church—the Sacraments which are more especially necessary, as Baptism, Penance, and the Holy Eucharist; and the others when we may have occasion to receive them.

By Ecclesiastical precept, we are still further obliged *to know by heart*, the Apostles' Creed, the Lord's Prayer, the Hail Mary, and how to make the Sign of the Cross.[9]

Those persons, therefore, are guilty of sin, 1*st*, who are ignorant of any of these, through their own wilful neglect; 2*ndly*, who wilfully, and without necessity, deprive themselves of the means or opportunity of knowing them; 3*rdly*, who neither instruct their children themselves, nor send them to be instructed, on these points; and 4*thly*, who in this respect hinder or neglect the servants or domestics who are under their charge.

III. Exercise of Faith:—We worship and honour God by the virtue of Faith, when we make *Acts* of this virtue; i.e., when we make protestations to God, that we do actually believe all the truths which he has revealed, and proposes to us, as revealed, by his Church; and that we believe them precisely because He, who is Truth itself, has revealed them. This is paying direct homage to God—it is an act of homage to His eternal Truth—it is the submission of

tate medii), or as being a Divine precept (i.e., *necessitate præcepti*): each opinion is probable; but the former is more common and more probable than the latter, and therefore we must act as if it were certain; because, *with regard to the essential means of salvation*, it is not lawful to adopt probable opinions and follow them in practice, merely because they are probable. The doubt is not as to the *obligation* of an explicit belief in these mysteries, but only as to the particular *ground* of the obligation.

(9) S. Alph. Lig. Theol. Mor., lib. 2, tract. 1, n. 3, *Resp.*, 2; et *Unde resolvitur* 2.

our fallible judgment to His infallible word.——These *Acts* serve to enliven and strengthen our Faith, to increase our attachment to Religion, and to confirm our resolution of practising what it teaches; and they should form a part of our daily prayer.

There are some circumstances, in which it is necessary that we should exercise our Faith, by making an outward and open profession of it; as, when God's honour, the cause of Religion, or our neighbour's salvation requires it. (*Example of the Martyrs*, who courageously made open profession of their Faith before persecuting tyrants, even when they knew it would cost them their life.)——It is never lawful to deny our Religion, or to be ashamed of it, before men: "He that shall deny me before men, I will also deny him before my Father who is in heaven"[10]

IV. Sins against the virtue of Faith:—The sins which are directly against the theological Virtue of Faith, are infidelity, apostacy, heresy, and doubts.

1. *Infidelity* comprehends Paganism, Judaism, and Mahometanism.——When infidelity is the effect of involuntary and invincible ignorance; as in those who have never heard of the Christian Religion, nor had the means of knowing it, it will not be imputed to them as a sin:[11] "If I had not come (says our Blessed Lord), and spoken to them, *they would not have sin;* but now they have no excuse for their sins."[12] "For whosoever have sinned (says St. Paul) without the law shall perish without the law; and whosoever have sinned in the law, shall be judged by the law."[13]—But, when the infidelity is voluntary, either directly or indirectly; i.e., either in itself or in its cause, it is grievously sinful: "But now (*after having heard the doctrines of Christ*) they are without excuse for

(10) Matt. x., 33.
(11) Gousset, Theol. Morale, Tom. 1, n. 33•.
(12) John xv., 22.
(13) Rom. ii., 12.

their sin."[14] "He that believeth not shall be condemned."[15]

2. *Apostacy* is the renouncing of Christianity—it is the entire abandonment of the Christian Faith: and it is a very grievous sin.

3. *Heresy* is a pertinacious adherence to such error, as is directly opposed to some Article of Faith—to some truth which the Church proposes to us, as having been revealed by God: it is refusing to believe what one *knows* to be declared by the Church of Christ, as a revealed truth—it is preferring one's own opinion to the infallible decisions of the Church. ——By apostacy *the whole* of Christianity is renounced; but by heresy *only some* of its truths are rejected. Heresy is a grievous mortal sin.

4. *Doubts* concerning any article of Faith, when they are voluntary, or wilfully consented to, are also grievously sinful. Whenever they arise in the mind, they should be rejected immediately as suggestions of the devil, without our stopping to reason them away: they should be opposed by *Acts of Faith*, and by *Prayer*.......If they proceed from ignorance it is necessary to get instructed; if from the enemies of our Religion, by giving ear to their irreligious conversation, or by reading their heretical books, then these must be avoided: for thus to expose one's Faith knowingly and unnecessarily, is a sin. True Faith is a most precious gift of God, for which we should daily thank him; and we should show our esteem for it, by using every means to preserve and practice it.

(14) John xv., 22. (15) Mark xvi., 16.

INSTRUCTION LXVII.

THEOLOGICAL VIRTUE OF HOPE.

The Nature,—Necessity,—Grounds,—Advantages,—and Exercise of the Virtue of Hope; the Sins against Hope

What is meant by the Theological Virtues?—Virtues that relate immediately to God.

How many and what are the Theological Virtues?—Three:—Faith, Hope, and Charity,

What does Hope help us to do?—It helps us to expect with confidence, that God will give us all things necessary for our salvation, if we do what he requires of us.

NATURE OF HOPE:—Hope is a supernatural and *Theological* Virtue, by which we confidently expect eternal life and the means of arriving at it; resting our confidence on the goodness, power, and promises of God, and on the infinite merits of Jesus Christ: it is a desire and expectation of salvation, with a firm confidence of obtaining it, through God's infinite goodness, and his promised mercy and assistance. It is called a *Theological* Virtue, because, like Faith, it has God himself for its immediate object, being a direct homage to his infinite goodness, Power, and fidelity to his promises; and because it is a virtue not acquired by us, but *infused* by God into our souls.

II. NECESSITY OF HOPE:—We may say of the virtue of Hope what St. Paul says of Faith, that, without it, it is impossible to please God: for it is absolutely necessary as a means of salvation (*necessitate medii*); and is included in that duty of adoration, which is required by the First Commandment. St. Paul says: "We are *saved* by Hope."[16] "Do not therefore lose your confidence, which *hath a great*

(16) Rom, viii., 24

reward."[17]——If we do not put our trust in God, but in ourselves, it is a sin: and, moreover, it is great folly: because of ourselves we could not take the least step towards heaven, but should fall into the very depth of vice: "We are not sufficient to think anything of ourselves, *as of ourselves;* but our sufficiency is *from God.*"[18] "Without me, you can *do nothing.*"[19] What folly, therefore, it is, and what presumption, to trust in ourselves!

III. Grounds of Hope:—Hope is grounded on God's infinite Goodness, Power, and Promises, through the infinite Merits of Christ. Notwithstanding our own weakness and inability to do good, notwithstanding even the number and grievousness of our sins, we have reason to place an entire confidence in God; and to trust that we shall receive from him all that is necessary both for this life and the next; not because we deserve any of his favours, but because He is good.——Hope has these two parts, viz., a complete *distrust in ourselves;* and an entire *confidence in God* With these dispositions, there is no blessing which we may not obtain: "*Because* he hath hoped in me, I will deliver him; I will protect him, *because* he hath known my name: he shall cry to me, and I will hear him; I will deliver him, and I will glorify him."[20]

IV. Advantages of Hope:—Hope brings to the soul that possesses it, many and very great Advantages:—

1. It gives us great courage and resolution in the service of God: "If God be for us, who is against us?......Who then shall separate us from the love of Christ? shall tribulation? or distress? or famine? or danger? or persecution? or the sword?......I am sure that neither death nor life,......nor powers, nor

(17) Heb, x., 35,
(18) 2 Cor. iii., 5.
(19) John xv., 5.
(20) Ps. xc., 14, 15.

things present, nor things to come,......nor any other creature shall be able to separate us from the love of God, which is in Christ Jesus our Lord."[21] "For though I should walk in the midst of the shadow of death, I will fear no evils, for thou (O God) art with me:"[22]

2. It enables us to triumph with ease and certainty over temptations: He that dwelleth in the aid of the Most High, shall abide *under the protection* of the God of Jacob...*Because* he hath hoped in me, I will *deliver him*; I will *protect* him, *because* he hath known my name."[23] "If armies in camp should stand together against me, my heart shall not fear: if a battle should rise up against me, in this will I be confident. The Lord is the protector of my life; of whom shall I be afraid?"[24]

3. It renders the greatest difficulties in God's service easy, and even agreeable to us. The practice of virtue is frequently represented as being difficult: it *is* so to those who are without hope; but when we possess this virtue, the difficulty vanishes; and hence, our Blessed Redeemer says: "Take up my yoke upon you, ...and you shall find rest to your souls; for my yoke is sweet, and my burden light."[25]

4. It sweetens all the pains and troubles of this life, by the certain prospect of future rewards: "The sufferings of this present time, which are momentary and light, work for us above measure, exceedingly, an eternal weight of glory."[26] "Blessed are ye, when men shall revile you, and persecute you, and speak all that is evil against you, untruly, for my sake; be glad and rejoice, for your reward is very great in heaven."[27]

V. Exercise of Hope:—We worship and honour

(21) Rom. viii., 31, 35, 38, 39 (24) Ps. xxvi., 3, 1. (26) 2 Cor. iv., 17.
(22) Ps. xxii., 4 (25) Mat. xi., 29, 30. (27) Mat. v. 11, 12.
(23) Ps. xc., 1, 14.

God by the practice of Hope, when we make *Acts* of this virtue: i.e., when, from our heart, we make protestations of God, that we place an entire and perfect confidence in him—that, relying on his goodness, power, and promises, we confidently hope for mercy, grace, and salvation from him, through the merits of Christ; accompanying these protestations with the determination or disposition of doing, on our part, what God requires from us. This is paying direct homage to his infinite Goodness and Mercy, to his Divine Power, and to his Fidelity to his promises; especially when we make these *Acts*, under difficult and trying circumstances; like Abraham, "who (as St. Paul says) *against hope believed in hope*; that he might be made the father of many nations, according to that which was said to him: *As the number of the stars, so shall thy seed be.*"[28] "Although he should kill me, I will trust in him."[29] These *Acts* of Hope, when they come from the heart, are very pleasing to God; and should form a part of our daily prayer: but they should be made with a real disposition to do, on our part, what God requires from us—to do what we can ourselves, confidently trusting that God will supply our insufficiency. Without this, our hope would be vain and presumptuous.

Exercise of hope in temporal things:—May we exercise Hope in temporal things, by praying for them with the hope of obtaining them? We not only *may*, but *ought:* because God directs us to do so, and promises that he will grant these things, as far as will be conducive to our real good: "When you pray, say: ......Give us this day our daily bread."[30] "Be not solicitous, saying: What shall we eat? or what shall we drink? or wherewith shall we be clothed? For your Father *knoweth* that you have *need* of all these

(28) Rom, iv., 18; and Gen. xxv., 5. (29) Job xiii., 15. (30) Luke xi., 3.

things. Seek ye therefore *first* the kingdom of God, and his justice; and *all these things* shall be added unto you."[31]

As to the *necessaries* of life, and the assistances we need for obtaining them: it is our duty to trust in God, with an entire resignation to his will; persuaded that he will bless our lawful endeavours, by sending us what he knows to be the best for us.——We should be thoroughly convinced of these two truths, viz.:—

1. Nothing that we undertake can succeed, without God's blessing, or against his will: "For "unless the Lord build the house, *they labour in vain* that build it; unless the Lord keep the city, he watcheth in vain that keepeth it."[32] In all things, therefore, we should have recourse to God; and should employ, on our part, such means only as are lawful; but we should *never* use *sinful* means; for, if we do, we cannot expect a blessing from God, but the contrary.

2. No malice of men, nor of devils, can hurt those who serve God, unless he permit it; and then, *only so far* as he shall permit. Therefore, when we meet with difficulties, or unjust opposition, we should never lose courage nor our confidence in God: "In God I have put my trust, I will not fear what flesh can do against me......In God have I hoped, I will not fear what man can do to me."[33] "If armies in camp should stand together against me, my heart shall not fear."[34] For, "if God be for us, who is against us?"[35]——Do nothing *sinful* to escape difficulties or dangers, but trust in God—look upon all trials as coming from his hand—and be resigned to his will in all things, "casting all your care upon him:" and then you need not fear what all the world can do against you.

VI. Sins against Hope:—The sins which are di-

(31) Matt. vi., 31, 32, 33. (33) Ps. lv., 5, 11. (35) Rom. viii., 31.
(32) Ps. cxxvi., 1. (34) Ps. xxvi., 3.

rectly opposed to the virtue of Hope, are despair and presumption.

1. *Despair* is a distrust of arriving at eternal happiness, or of obtaining the helps which are necessary for that purpose. It is a most pernicious and fatal crime; because it puts a stop to our endeavours, and opens the door to every kind of vice.

Those persons are guilty of it, who give up all hopes, 1, of salvation, on account of its difficulties—2, of pardon, on account of the number or grievousness of their sins—3, of amendment, on account of the violence of their evil inclinations, the force of their bad habits, or the experience which they have had of their weakness; 4, of obtaining what they ask for in prayer, because it is deferred—5, of receiving relief or support in distress or sickness; and so wish for death.

Remedies:—Prayer—Acts of Hope—Reflecting on the power, goodness, mercy, and promises of God—and on the merits of Christ.

2. *Presumption* is a vain expectation of salvation, and of the necessary helps, without performing the conditions required: It is in its own nature a grievous crime, because it makes the Divine goodness an encouragement to sin.

Those persons are guilty of presumption, 1, who continue in sin, with the intention of repenting before death; deferring their repentance because God is merciful—2, who trust their salvation, their repentance, or amendment, to their *own* strength and endeavours—3, who expose themselves, without necessity, to the immediate occasions of sin, depending on their own resolutions—4, who in temporal affairs, trust to their own power, prudence, or endeavours, independently of God.

Remedies:—Prayer—Acts of humility—Reflecting on the danger of living in sin.

God is infinitely *merciful;* therefore, do not despair: but he is also infinitely *just;* therefore, do not presume.

INSTRUCTION LXVIII

THEOLOGICAL VIRTUE OF CHARITY : ITS FIRST BRANCH.

The Love of God: Its Nature ;—Its Necessity ;—Grounds of its Obligation ;—Its Exercise ;—Its Effects ;—Means of obtaining and increasing it.

How many, and what are the Theological Virtues?—Three; Faith, Hope, and Charity.

What does Charity help us to do?—It helps us to love God above all things, and our neighbour as ourselves.

What are the two precepts of Charity?—1. Thou shalt love the Lord thy God with thy whole heart, with thy whole soul, with all thy strength, and with all thy mind 2. And thy neighbour as thyself.

I. Nature of the Love of God.—*Charity* is a supernatural and *Theological* Virtue, by which we love God above all things, for his own sake; and our neighbour as ourselves, for God's sake. "By one and the same charity, (says St. Augustin,) we love God and our neighbour: God indeed for his own sake; but ourselves and our neighbour for God's sake."[36*] This *Chaity* is the love of benevolence and of friendship, whereby we wish all good to God, on account of the infinite perfection of his Divine Nature. It is called a *Theological* Virtue, because, like Faith and Hope, it has God himself for its immediate object, being a direct homage to *all* his Divine Perfections, by which he is infinitely good in himself, and infi-

(36)* "Ex una cademque charitate, Deum proximumque diligimus; sed Deum propter Deum, nos autem et proximum propter Deum." *De Trinitate, lib, 8. cap. 8*

nitely deserving of our love; and also because it is a Virtue, not acquired, but *infused* by God into our souls: "For Charity is of God."[37] "The Charity of God is poured forth in our hearts by the Holy Ghost, who is given to us."[38]

All Love of God is not the love of *Charity:* for the Love of God may be either of that kind which is called *perfect*, or of that which is called *imperfect;* and the essential difference consists in the *motive* from which our love proceeds. *Perfect* Love is the love of *Charity*, by which we love God *for his own sake*, imperfect Love is the love of *Hope*, or of *Gratitude*, by which we do indeed love God, but on account of our own advantage, rather than purely for his sake, [39]*

Our Love of God is of that kind which is perfect, that is to say, it has the nature of perfect Charity,—

1. When, in loving God, we habitually fix our whole heart in Him; in such manner, that, for his sake, we will not allow ourselves any thought, or wish, which is contrary to his Divine love: This perfection (says St. Thomas) is common to all who possess the Virtue of *Charity*.[40]

2. When we desire to possess God; if we tend towards that possession rather for his glory, than for our own advantage. Thus, St. Paul made an act of perfect Charity, when he expressed his "desire to be dissolved and to be with Christ."[41] "Charity (says

(37) 1 John iv., 7.

(38) Rom. v., 5.

(39)* "Amor quidam est perfectus, quidam imperfectus, Perfectus quidem amor est quo aliquis secundum se amatur, ut puta cum aliquis secundum se vult alicui bonum; sicut homo amat amicum. Imperfectus amor est quo quis amat aliquid, non secundum ipsum, sed ut illud bonum sibi ipsi proveniat; sicut homo amat rem quam concupiscit. Primus autem amor pertinet ad Charitatem, quæ inhæret Deo secundum seipsum; sed spes pertinet ad secundum amorem, quia illo qui sperat, aliquid sibi obtinere intendit."—*S. Thom., Sum. p.* 2, 2 *q.* 17, *a.* 8.

(40) S. Thom., Sum. p. 2, 2 q. 24, a. 8.

(41) Philip. i., 23.

St. Alphonsus Liguori) tends to God as our last end; and therefore, the desire of possessing God, who is our last end; is a proper act of Charity, and indeed more perfect than others, for the possession of God is the consummation of Charity."[42]*

3. When we love God on account of his Divine Goodness, (which is one of his principal Perfections,) even inasmuch as it is advantageous to us, by assisting us to accomplish his will, and to obtain our last end; for this is to love God for his own sake.

But if we love God merely as the means of arriving at eternal life, or of avoiding eternal misery; our love is not that of *Charity*, but of *Hope*; neither is it the love of Charity, if we love God on account of the benefits which he confers upon us; for this is the love *Gratitude*. But, if we regard the favours and gifts of God as the effects of his Goodness, and love them for the sake of God—for the sake of his Goodness, rather than for our own sake; then our love is an act of Charity; for, in this case, it is not so much the favours or gifts themselves that we love, as the Divine Goodness—the source of all good and of every gift.

4. When we are in such disposition of soul, that we can truly say from our heart: *O my God! I love thee above all things, because thou art infinite Goodness*," or, *because thou art infinitely Good*."

Charity is the most excellent of the Theological Virtues: "And now there remain Faith, Hope, and Charity, these three; but the greater of these is Charity . . . . Charity never falleth away."[43]

II. Necessity of the Love of God:—The vir-

(42)* "Charitas tendit in Deum tanquam ultimum finem, et ideo desiderium possidendi Dei, qui est ultimus quidem noster finis, est proprius actus Charitatis, imo perfectior aliis; nam possessio Dei est Charitas consummata."——*Theol. Mor.*, *lib.* 2, *tract.* 3, *n.* 24, Hic dubitatur 1.

(43) 1 Cor. xiii., 13, 8.

ture of Charity is absolutely necessary, as an essential means of salvation (*necessitate medii*); it is included in that homage which is enjoined in the First Commandment; and it is declared, by our Blessed Redeemer, to be "the greatest and the first Commandment," on which "dependeth the whole law and the prophets."[44] It is that wedding garment," without which it will be said to us, when we appear before God to be judged: "Bind his hands and his feet, and cast him into the exterior darkness; there shall be weeping and gnashing of teeth."[45] The Virtue of Charity is so necessary, that St. Paul says of it: "If I speak with the tongues of men, and of angels, and have not Charity, I am become as sounding brass, or a tinkling cymbal . . . . And if I should have all faith, so that I could remove mountains, and have not Charity, I am nothing. And if I should distribute all my goods to feed the poor, and if I should deliver my body to be burned, and have not Charity, it profiteth me nothing."[46]

III. Grounds of the Obligation of Loving God:—Our obligation to love God is grounded on many and strong reasons, drawn from the excellency of his Divine nature. We are bound to love God,

1. Because he is infinitely good *in himself*—infinite in all perfections. Other virtues have some particular Attribute for their object, but this has *all*.

2. Because he is infinitely good also *to us*, both as to this world and the next.

3. Because he is our last end—to love him is the very end of our being: our happiness or misery depends upon it.

4. Because he (the Lord our God) commands us to love him: "Hear, O Israel: Thou shalt love the

(44) Matt. xxii., 38 40.
(45) Matt. xxii., 12, 13.
(46) 1 Cor. xiii., 1, 2, 3.

Lord thy God, with thy whole heart, and with thy whole soul, and with thy whole mind, and with thy whole strength."[47] Thus it is commanded in the strongest terms; for *all* our powers, and *the whole* of each, must be employed in loving God.

IV. Exercise of the Love of God:—The precept of Charity requires us to "love God with our whole heart, and soul, and mind, and strength."

1. To love God with our *whole heart*, we must actually give Him the preference in our affections—they must all centre in Him: we must be really and truly disposed to part with all things, rather than lose Him by sin: "Every one of you that doth not renounce all that he possesseth, (i.e., when the love of God requires him to make such a sacrifice,) he cannot be my disciple."[48] "He that loveth father or mother more than me, is not worthy of me; and he that loveth son or daughter more than me, is not worthy of me."[49] "Son, give me thy heart."[50]——This preference which we give to God, is loving him with our whole heart.

2. To love God with our *whole soul*, we must refer all that we do to God's honour and glory; performing everything *with a view* to please him: this should be our constant aim and intention: "Whether you eat or drink, or whatsoever else you do; do all to the glory of God."[51] Our will must be so fixed in God, as to make us habitually determined to suffer, endure, or sacrifice any thing rather than offend God by sin. (*Example of the Martyrs.*) Like the Apostles, we should be able to say: "Who shall separate us from the love of Christ? shall tribulation? or distress? or famine? or danger? or persecution? or the sword? ......I am sure that neither death, nor life, nor prin-

(47) Mark xii., 29, 30; Deut. vi., 4, 5.
(48) Luke xiv., 33.
(49) Matt. x., 37.
(50) Prov. xxiii., 26.
(51) 1 Cor. x., 31.

cipalities, nor powers, nor things present, nor things to come......nor any other creature, shall be able to separate us from the love of God, which is in Christ Jesus our Lord."[52]——This devotedness and determination of our will is loving God with our whole soul.

3. To love God with our *whole mind*, we must give him our thoughts: we must frequently *think* of Almighty God; meditate on his Divine Attributes or Perfections—on his infinite Goodness—on his Mercy, Bounty, and Love towards us—on the Necessity of loving and serving him—and on the means of doing so.——This is loving him with our whole mind.

4. To love God with our *whole strength*, we must *strive*, on all occasions, to act in accordance with his Law, and to do his will: we must *labour* for God—we must *do* what we can to promote his greater honour and glory. This is a natural consequence of the three former duties; for, a sincere affection of the heart, and entire devotedness of the will and the mind, naturally excite efficacious endeavours to please God in all our actions: "If you love me, keep my commandments."[53]——This is loving God with all our strength.

We worship and honour God by the exercise of this greatest of Virtues, when we make *Acts of Charity*, i.e., when we declare to God, *sincerely and truly*, that we do actually love him with our whole heart, above all things, on account of his infinite Goodness or Perfections: And if these declarations are joined with actual repentance for sin, they become also Acts of Contrition. When these Acts of Charity and Contrition are made *from the heart*, they are most pleasing to God, and should form part of our daily Prayer.

V. Effects of the Love of God:—This Divine

(52) Rom. viii., 35, 38, 39. (53) John xiv., 15; *Vide* S. Thomæ Sum. 2, 2 q. 24, a. 9.

Virtue produces the most happy *effects* in the souls of those who possess it.

1. An ardent *zeal* for God's honour and glory: for if we love him above all things, we shall be zealous and active in promoting his greater honour and glory.

2. A true *sorrow* for our sins. It will put the soul in those dispositions of repentance in which David was, when he said: "I know mine iniquity, and my sin is always before e......Lord, I am ready for scourges, and my sorrow is continually before me. ......I did eat ashes like bread, and mingled my drink with weeping."[54] (*Example of Peter*, when "going out, he wept biterly.")[55]

3. *Esteem* for God's graces, and for all his favours, and *thankfulness* for them. Nothing is considered little, that comes from those whom we really love.

4. *Respect* and *veneration* for whatever relates to God or to his service: for, love naturally extends itself to everything relating to the object of our love.

VI. MEANS OF OBTAINING AND INCREASING THE LOVE OF GOD:—How may we obtain this Divine Virtue, and increase it in the soul?

1. By Prayer: "Your heavenly Father will give the good spirit to them that ask him."[56] "Ask, and you shall receive."[57]

By mortifying and destroying our self-love; for thereby we remove our greatest obstacle to the love of God: "No man can serve two masters—you cannot serve God and mammon."[58]

2. By frequent meditation on the Divine Perfections, and on the great love of God towards us.

By a diligent performance of those duties, which the love of God requires from us.

(54) Ps. l., 5; xxxvii., 18; ci., 10.
(55) Luke xxii., 62.
(56) Luke xi., 13.
(57) John xvi., 24.
(58) Matt. vi., 24.

By frequent and fervent acts of the love of God, and of Contrition for the sins whereby we have offended him.

3 By rendering every thought, word, and deed an act of the Love of God, which is done by referring them all to his glory in order to please him.

And by that close union with God here, which proceeds from an habitual ardent desire of being inseparably united with him hereafter in eternal glory.

INSTRUCTION LXIX.

THEOLOGICAL VIRTUE OF CHARITY—ITS SECOND BRANCH.

Why we must Love our Neighbour—how we must Love him—We must Love even our Enemies.

What does Charity help us to do?—It helps us to love God above all things, and our neighbour as ourselves.

What are the two precepts of Charity?—1, Thou shalt love the Lord thy God, with thy whole heart, with thy whole soul, with all thy strength, and with all thy mind. 2, And thy neighbour as thyself.

The Theological Virtue of Charity has two branches. it helps us to love God above all things, for his own sake; and to love our neighbour as ourselves, for God's sake. "There are two precepts, (says St. Augustin,) but only one Charity;...because the Charity by which we love our neighbour, is no other than that by which we love God."[59]

The love of our neighbour, or fraternal Charity, is a Virtue by which we love *all* persons without exception, for God's sake, with a desire to procure their best interests, because such is the will of God.

(59) Serm: 265

I. WHY MUST WE LOVE OUR NEIGHBOUR?—We must love every neighbour.

1. Because the relation which he bears to God, requires us to do so. For we are all *children of God* both by creation, and by adoption; we are all *brothers* of Jesus Christ—*members* of his mystical body—and *coheirs* with him in eternal glory.

2. Because God *commands* us: "Thou shalt love thy neighbour as thyself."[60] "This is my commandment, that you love one another, as I have loved you."[61]

3. Because, in loving our neighbour, we love Jesus Christ, who assures us that what we do towards one another, he considers as done to himself; and who declares that fraternal Charity is the characteristic mark of his disciples—the very spirit of Christianity: "By this shall all men know that you are my disciples, if you have love one for another."[62]

4. Because the love of our neighbour is a most powerful and necessary means of obtaining mercy and blessing from God: "Above all things, have a constant mutual Charity among yourselves; for Charity covereth a multitude of sins."[63] "The love of our neighbour worketh no evil: love, therefore, is the fulfilment of the law."[64] "We know that we have passed from death to life, because we love the brethren: he that loveth not, abideth in death."[65]

II. HOW MUST WE LOVE OUR NEIGHBOUR?—The Scripture lays down for us two rules whereby we are to regulate our love for our neighbour; viz., AS *we love ourselves*; and AS *Christ has loved us*.

1. After having declared the Love of God to be "the greatest and first commandment," our Blessed Lord says: "And the second is like to this: "Thou shalt love thy neighbour *as thyself*. On these two

(60) Matt. xxii., 39. (61) John xv., 12. (62) John xiii., 35. (63) 1 Pet iv., 8. (64) Rom. xiii., 10. (65) 1 John iii., 14.

commandments dependeth the whole law and the prophets."[66]——Our Love of our neighbour should have the same characters or qualities, as our love of ourselves; i.e., we should love him from a sincere desire to promote his real happiness, both in this life and in the next; but chiefly *in the next.* Our love of one another should be such as is expressed in these two passages of Holy Scripture: 1*st*, "See thou never do to another what thou wouldst hate to have done to thee by another."[67] Therefore, *do no evil* to any one.—2*ndly*, "All things whatsoever you would that men should do to you, do you also to them."[68] Therefore *do good* to all men.

2. Our Blessed Lord says: "This is my commandment, that you love one another *as I have loved you.*"[69] Now *how* has Christ loved us? He has loved us, 1*st*, With a *gratuitous* love: "When as yet we were sinners, Christ died for us."[70]—2*ndly*, With a *universal* love: "He will have *all men* to be saved;" and so "gave himself a redemption *for all.*"[71]—3*rdly*, With a *constant* love: "Many waters cannot quench Charity, neither can the floods drown it."[72] "Having loved his own who were in the world, he loved them unto the end."[73] Such was the love of Christ: such, therefore, must be our love of one another.

We should love our neighbour in his adversity, as well as in his prosperity: "Bear ye one another's burdens; and so you shall fulfil the law of Christ."[74]——We should love him when he injures or ill-treats us, as well as when he is kind to us: "Do good to them that hate you."[75]

III. Must we, then, love our enemies?—

(66) Matt. xxii., 37 to 40.
(67) Tobias iv., 16.
(68) Matt. vii., 12.
(69) John xv., 12.
(70) Rom. v., 8, 9.
(71) 1 Tim. ii., 4, 6.
(72) Cant. viii., 7.
(73) John xiii., 1.
(74) Gal. vi., 2.
(75) Matt. v., 44.

Yes; we must love all persons, without exception, for God's sake. How must we love our enemies? 1*st*, We must lay aside all thoughts of revenge; .. 2*ndly*, We must forgive them from our hearts;—3*rdly*, We must return them good for evil. All this our Blessed Lord teaches us both by word and example: "Love your enemies, he says;) do good to them that hate you; bless them that curse you; pray for them that persecute and calumniate you."[76] Thus, although the Jews sought to kill him,[77] he did good to them;[78] to his enemy Malchus, he restored the ear which Peter had cut off;[79] he forgave and prayed for his very executioners, even at the very time when they were engaged in putting him to death.[80]

Our Blessed Lord and Model shows us the NECESSITY of imitating his example in this respect, (i.e., of *forgiving and loving* our enemies,) by making the fulfilment of this duty a condition for our obtaining pardon from our offended God: "If you forgive men their offences, your heavenly Father will forgive you also your offences."[81] Hence he teaches us to crave pardon from God on this condition: "Forgive us our trespasses, AS WE *forgive them that trespass against us.*"

You see, then, how you must forgive and love your enemies. You see also that this duty is of strict obligation.

IV. TWO COMMON DELUSIONS:—The duty of forgiving and loving our enemies is generally complained of, as being a most difficult duty; and very many Christians fail to comply with it. But the difficulty arises from two common delusions under which mankind generally labour.

(76) Matt. v., 44; Luke vi., 27, 28, 29. (77) John v., 13. (78) Matt. iv., 23, 24. (79) Luke xxii., 50, 51. (80) Luke xxiii., 34. (81) Matt. vi., 14.

1. Blinded by self-love, we have a great attachment to earthly goods and earthly enjoyments: in a great measure, we place our happiness in these things. Consequently, when prevented from obtaining them, or when deprived of them, we conceive an aversion against those persons who are the cause of this. Now, if you will lay aside this undue attachment to earthly things, and place your happiness in God alone, you will *then* find less difficulty in complying with the precept of forgiving and loving your enemies.

2. The other delusion is, that we look upon our neighbour, when he injures or offends us, as the real cause of what we suffer from him. We should correct this false notion, by considering what Faith teaches us on the subject, viz., that all crosses, &c. come to us from the hand of God; and that our neighbour, or enemy, is only a *mere instrument.* Then we shall find less difficulty in receiving injuries patiently, and in forgiving and loving those persons who are the immediate authors of them. Reflect, therefore, that all such trials are really ordained and sent by God for our greater good—that "good things and evil, life and death, poverty and riches, are from God."[82]——Our Blessed Lord teaches us, by his example, to act upon this reflection: "Put up thy sword into the scabbard; the chalice which *my Father* hath given me, shall I not drink it?"[83] Observe, he does not attribute his sufferings to the malice of the Jews, nor does he express any resentment against them, *as his enemies*; but he considers them only *as executing the appointments of heaven in his regard.* Let us imitate him in this; and then the difficulty of forgiving and loving our enemies will vanish.

(82) Eccli, xi., 14. (83) John xviii., 11.

INSTRUCTION LXX.

The four Cardinal Virtues.

How many are the Cardinal Virtues?—Four: 1, Prudence. 2, Justice. 3, Fortitude. 4, Temperance.

Of all the *moral* Virtues, these four, Prudence, Justice, Fortitude, and Temperance, are the most necessary for us in our journey through this world to our last end. They are called "*moral*" Virtues, because they regulate our *morals*, and our whole conduct, according to the Divine law: and they are called "*Cardinal*," (from the Latin word "*cardo*," which means a *hinge*,) because they are *as the hinges* whereon the whole Christian life must constantly move, and whereby it is necessarily supported.

1. PRUDENCE:—Prudence is a virtue which enlightens our mind, and leads us to take proper and effectual means for securing our salvation. This Virtue is required in every occurrence of life; in every undertaking, it is for Prudence to examine both sides, ...that we may not act *rashly*;—in doubts, it directs us to suspend our judgment, and, in the mean time, to seek information and advice: "My son, do nothing without counsel; and thou shalt not repent when thou hast done."[84]——Prudence tells us to consider our last End,—the advantages of obtaining it,—the consequences of losing it,—the proper means of arriving at it,—and to be earnest and diligent in employing those means;—it shows us the extreme folly of fixing our hearts on perishable riches,—and of yielding to forbidden pleasures, because "the end of them is death."[85]

II. JUSTICE:—In its limited sense, Justice is a

(84) Eccli. xxxii., 24. (85) Rom. vi., 2.

virtue whereby we give to every man his own; but, as a *Cardinal* virtue, it means much more--it includes all the duties which we owe both to *God* and *man:* "Render therefore to Cæsar the things that are Cæsar's; and to God, the things that are God's."[86] We render to Cæsar the things that are Cæsar's, or are just towards our neighbour, when we do no injury to him either in his goods, or in his honour, or in his person; and when, moreover, we fulfil towards him all those duties, which society and Religion give him a right to expect from us. And we render to God the things that are God's, and are therefore just towards *Him*, when we fulfil the whole of his Law, which is justice and truth: "All thy commandments are justice,..... and thy law is the truth."[87] If we transgress the Commandments of God, or neglect his service, we are then *unjust* towards God: "Unless your *justice* abound more than that of the Scribes and Pharisees, you shall not enter into the kingdom of heaven."[88] "Blessed are they that hunger and thirst after *justice;* for they shall have their fill."[89] "Seek ye therefore first the kingdom of God and his *justice*."[90]

III. Fortitude:—Fortitude is a Virtue which enables us to face any danger or difficulty, for the cause of justice and truth—to suffer anything, rather than act contrary to the fidelity which we owe to God; it is an invincible courage in the fulfilment of our duty, founded on the Goodness and Providence of God. And we have innumerable examples of it in the Martyrs, who endured the most excruciating torments, the most painful and lingering deaths, rather than do anything against either truth or morality. Such ought likewise to be *our* disposition.——We must not confound this virtue with *rashness:* Forti-

(86) Matt. xxii., 21. (88) Matt. v., 20. (90) Matt. vi., 33.
(87) Ps. cxviii. 172, 142. (89) Matt. v., 6.

tude is a *virtue;* but rashness is a *vice:* Fortitude springs from humility—from an humble confidence in God; but rashness from pride—from a presumptuous confidence in one's-self. Fortitude must be directed by Prudence: these two Cardinal virtues, acting in unison, will preserve us from exposing ourselves *rashly* or *unnecessarily* to danger; but they will lead us to brave any danger, when the Cardinal virtue of Justice, (i.e., when any duty which we *owe* to God or man) *requires* it from us. St. Paul possessed true Fortitude, and made an *Act* of this virtue, when he said: "Who shall separate us from the love of Christ? shall tribulation? or distress? or famine? or danger? or persecution? or the sword?......I am sure that neither death nor life, nor principalities, nor powers, nor things present, nor things to come,......nor any other creature, shall be able to separate us from the love of God, which is in Christ Jesus our Lord."[91] "If God be for us, who is against us?"[92]

IV. TEMPERANCE.—In its limited sense, Temperance means *moderation in eating and drinking;* but as a *Cardinal* virtue, it means *moderation in all things,* and enables us to restrain *every* desire of the heart, according to the dictates of reason and Religion. Even *virtues* may sometimes be injured by *excess,* as well as by deficiency; (as, for example, the virtue of mortification......)what would otherwise be a virtuous action, may, by intemperance in the performance of it, be rendered vicious. Our passions naturally incline us to run into excess: Temperance, therefore, is necessary for us; it is by means of this virtue that we are to restrain and subdue our passions, and to keep them in complete subjection to reason.

CONCLUSION:—From this short explanation of the Four Cardinal Virtues, you see how necessary they

(91) Rom. viii., 35, 38, 39. (92) Rom. viii., 31.

are for us,—how we have to practise them at all times, and on all occasions,—and with what reason it is, that they are called "*Cardinal;*" for you see how they contain the practice of every other moral virtue: how *Prudence*, by directing us to seek and secure our last end, leads us to esteem and employ the proper means of fulfilling our entire duty,—how Justice is the actual fulfilment of *every* obligation which we *owe* to God, to our neighbour, and to ourselves,—and how Fortitude and Temperance insure perseverance in our duty; for Fortitude secures us from being led away, by what is terrifying or painful to nature; and Temperance prevents us from incurring the like evil, by what is flattering to our inclinations or pleasing to the senses.

INSTRUCTION LXXI.

The Seven Gifts and Twelve Fruits of the Holy Ghost.

How many are the Gifts of the Holy Ghost?—Seven; 1, Wisdom. 2. Understanding. 3, Counsel. 4, Fortitude. 5, Knowledge. 6, Godliness. 7, Fear of the Lord.

How many are the Fruits of the Holy Ghost?—Twelve: 1, Charity. 2, Joy. 3, Peace. 4, Patience. 5, Benignity. 6, Goodness. 7, Longanimity. 8, Mildness. 9, Faith. 10, Modesty. 11, Continence. 12, Chastity.

1. THE SEVEN GIFTS OF THE HOLY GHOST:—Every soul, when in the state of sanctifying grace, is enriched more or less with these seven Gifts of the Holy Ghost: but it is in the Sacrament of Confirmation more particularly, that we receive the plenitude or fulness of them. These gifts are certain supernatural dispositions or habits of soul, conferred upon us by the Holy Spirit; leading us to act (whenever occasions require or opportunities offer) according to

the inspirations and motions of grace; and enabling us to fulfil the divine Law with readiness and ease, especially in difficult circumstances. They are called "*Gifts*," because we receive them from the pure bounty of God, without any merit or claim on our part. They are all mentioned by the Prophet Isaias, who speaks of the Holy Ghost as "the Spirit of Wisdom and of Understanding; the Spirit of Counsel, and of Fortitude; the Spirit of knowledge, and of Godliness ; and the Spirit of the Fear of the Lord."[93]

1. "*The Spirit of Wisdom*, is a Gift, which teaches us to set a right value on salvation, and on the means of obtaining it; and to undervalue all that is earthly and perishable; it leads us to despise the honours, riches, and pleasures of this short life,—to seek what is heavenly and eternal, and to employ our whole life in promoting God's honour, and in securing the possession of our last End.

2. *The Spirit of Understading*" is a Gift, which enables us to conceive the *truths* of Religion, and to penetrate the mysteries of Faith, as far as (according to God's particular designs in our regard) is necessary for us, or conducive to our good;—it fits us for meditating on the great truths of eternity; and for contemplating those mysteries of love mercy, humiliation, &c., which are manifested to us in the Incarnation, Life, Passion, and Death of our Blessed Redeemer.

3. "*The Spirit of Counsel*" is a Gift, which shows us the deceits of our spiritual enemies, directing us how to detect and escape their snares;—it discovers to us the true means of advancing in virtue;—and in doubts, it leads us to take the right side of the question: thus it helps very much to secure us in the path of salvation.

(93) Is. xi., 2, 3.

4. "*The Spirit of Fortitude*" is a Gift, which supports us in the trials of the Christian warfare, and makes us stand firm in the cause of truth and virtue, whatever difficulties, dangers, or persecutions we may have to encounter.

5. "*The Spirit of Knowledge*" is a Gift, which helps us to learn the *duties* of Religion; and leads us to prefer this learning, before any human science; it enables us to distinguish good from evil; and to avoid a false or blinded conscience, which is a source of so many sins and miseries.

6. "*The Spirit of Godliness*" is a Gift, which helps us to put the duties of Religion *in practice;* it leads us to keep the Commandments—to be regular and diligent in serving God—in prayer, meditation, public worship, confession, communion, acts of the theological virtues, and in general piety.

7. "*The Spirit of the Fear of the Lord*" is a Gift, which (being a filial fear) makes us dread incurring the anger of God, and so prevents us from offending him by sin; it sets before us the terrors of his judgments against sinners, and so makes us labour to avert them by leading a virtuous and penitential life: "The fear of the Lord hateth evil;" "it is a fountain of life, to decline from death."[94] "The fear of the Lord driveth out sin;" it is "the beginning of Wisdom;" it is even "fulness of wisdom." "The fear of God is the beginning of his love:" therefore, "blessed is the man to whom it is given to have the fear of God"[95]

From this explanation of the seven Gifts of the Holy Ghost, you see how truly rich are they upon whom they are bestowed! Were we possessed of these precious treasures, what advances should we daily make in virtue, and what a high degree of glory

(94) Prov. viii., 13; xiv., 27. (95) Eccli. i., 16, 20, 27; xxv., 15, 16

should we obtain hereafter! especially as our souls would be adorned, moreover, and enriched, with the Twelve Fruits of the Holy Ghost.

II. THE TWELVE FRUITS OF THE HOLY GHOST:—Oh! how *happy*, how supremely happy must *their* lives be, who, being possessed of the *Gifts* of the Holy Ghost, enjoy also the precious FRUITS which those Gifts never fail to produce in the soul!

These twelve *Fruits* are all enumerated by St. Paul, in his Epistle to the Galatians, where he says: "The *Fruit of the Spirit* is Charity, Joy, Peace, Patience, Benignity, Goodness, Longanimity, Mildness, Faith, Modesty, Continence, Chastity. Against such there is no law."[96]

1. *Charity*, by which we keep our eyes fixed on God, on his Divine Attributes or Perfections; and tend towards him incessantly, as the dearest object of our affections: "The Charity of God is poured forth in our hearts, by the Holy Ghost who is given to us."[97].

2. *Joy*, by which we serve God with cheerfulness, obey his will with alacrity, and taste those sweet consolations which are found only in the practice of virtue.

3. *Peace*, by which, amidst the storms of life, amidst sufferings and misfortunes, we preserve tranquillity of soul; and enjoy a perpetual calmness of conscience—that peace of God, which surpasseth all understanding."[98]

4. *Patience*, by which we endure the labours and troubles of life willingly, and with resignation to the Divine will; and even rejoice in sufferings, afflictions, and privations, as real goods.

5. *Benignity*, by which we conduct ourselves towards others with condescension and kindness; bearing with and compassionating their weaknesses.

(96) Gal. v., 22, 23. (97) Rom. v., 5. (98) Phil. iv., 7.

6. *Goodness*, by which we avoid doing any injury to others, and are always ready to render them whatever services we can, taking a pleasure in promoting their welfare.

7. *Longanimity*, by which we persevere steadfastly in our duty; and never desist or grow weary, whatever trials or difficulties we may have to endure, and however long those trials or difficulties may continue.

8. *Mildness*, by which we restrain the motions of anger, and preserve a perpetual gentleness of temper, which renders a person truly amiable, and beloved by all who know him, and also by God.

9. *Faith*, by which we keep to our engagements, and fulfil our promises.

10. *Modesty*, by which we are reserved in our comportment, and avoid self-commendation.

11. *Continence*, by which we restrain, and *effectually* resist, our carnal inclinations; and so force them into subjection to the Divine law.

12. *Chastity*, by which we have such a love and esteem for angelic purity, as preserves us effectually from every defilement of both body and mind, and entitles us to the fulfilment of the promise contained in this Beatitude: "Blessed are the clean of heart; for they shall see God."[99]

Between Continence and Chastity, St. Anselm makes this distinction: "Continence (he says) is in struggles, *in combat*; Chastity is *in peace*."[100] * Therefore, according to him, Continence is Chastity *militant* and *exercised by temptation*.

CONCLUSION:—These are the precious *Fruits* which arise from the Holy Ghost's abiding in the soul. If you possess them, happy are you! but, if you have lost them by sin, by banishing the Holy Ghost from your

(99) Matt. v., 8.

(100 * "Continentia in luctamine est, castitas in pace"

soul, endeavour to recover them immediately by sincere repentance. Whenever your conscience tells you that you are in mortal sin, hasten to the Sacrament of reconciliation, put yourselves in a state of grace, and employ the means which are necessary for enabling you to persevere in this state; and then you will enjoy these happy *Fruits* of the Holy Ghost, together with his *seven-fold Gifts.*——Pray fervently for these heavenly treasures—for the renewal of the graces of your Confirmation: recite, for this purpose, the "*Hymns to the Holy Ghost*," earnestly inviting him to come and impart to you his heavenly Gifts, and to produce his Fruits in your soul.

INSTRUCTION LXXII.

THE SEVEN CORPORAL WORKS OF MERCY.

Say the seven Corporal Works of Mercy.

1. To feed the hungry.
2. To give drink to the thirsty.
3. To clothe the naked.
4. To visit and ransom captives.
5. To harbour the harbourless.
6. To visit the sick.
7. To bury the dead.

In the *Second* of the two great Commandments of the Law, we are required to *love our neighbour as ourselves.* But as our love is not to be confined to mere *words only*, but must show itself in our *works*, the Catechism teaches us how we are to exercise charity towards our neighbour, in *all his wants*, both *corporal and spiritual.*

As to Corporal *works of Mercy*, we are strictly obliged to exercise them. The law of Nature requires that we should help the distressed. God has provided for the wants of the poor and destitute, by obliging those who are not poor, to relieve them by giving their superfluities: this he positively commands, saying: "There shall not be wanting poor in the land of thy habitation; therefore, I COMMAND *thee* to open thy hand to thy poor and needy brother"[1] "*Help* the poor, because of the Commandment; and send him not away empty-handed, because of his poverty."[2] "*Give* alms out of thy substance; and turn not away thy face from any poor person: for so it shall come to pass, that the face of the Lord shall not be turned away from thee."[3] "*Give*, and it shall be given to you; good measure, and pressed down, and shaken together, and running over."[4] ——God rewards those who comply with this command: for his Divine Word assures us, that, whilst "he that despiseth the entreaty of the poor, shall suffer indigence;[5] "he that hath mercy on the poor, lendeth to the Lord; and he will repay him."[6] "For the Lord maketh recompense, and will give thee seven times as much."[7] And to excite our confidence in these promises, the Almighty even says: "Try me in this: if I open not unto you the floodgates of Heaven, and pour you out a blessing even to abundance!"[8]

As there are seven kinds of *corporal miseries;* so there are seven corresponding *Corporal Works of Mercy:*—

1 *and* 2. TO FEED THE HUNGRY, *and* TO GIVE DRINK TO THE THIRSTY; i.e., to supply them with necessary food, or corporal nourishment: — How pitiable is the state of persons reduced to absolute want of food—perishing from hunger or thirst! How hard-hearted must he be, who can see them in this ex-

(1) Deut. xv., 11.
(2) Eccli. xxxix., 12.
(3) Tobias iv., 7.
(4) Luke vi., 38.
(5) Prov. xxviii., 27.
(6) Prov. xix., 17.
(7) Eccli. xxxv., 13.
(8) Mal. iii., 10.

tremity, and refuse relief! and how guilty must such a one be in the sight of God! With what hope can he beg the blessings of God, when he himself rejects the entreaties of his distressed neighbour? "Eat thy bread with the hungry, and the needy."[9] "Whosoever shall give to drink a cup of cold water only in the name of a disciple, amen I say to you, he shall not lose his reward."[10]

3. To Clothe the Naked:—When the poor are not only ill-*fed*, but ill-*clothed* also—covered only with a few tattered rags; their state becomes still more pitiable. The charitable Christian cannot see them in this destitute state, without melting into compassion; but what would be his feelings, if he could see the wretched condition of many poor, during the nights? if he were to behold both parents and children shivering with cold, under most scanty covering—exposed to the wind, which enters through broken panes, or through gaping cracks in the walls—perhaps also exposed to the rain, dropping upon them through the roof! What a charity it is, to relieve these miseries; and how meritorious!—If, instead of decorating themselves and their children with *useless* ornaments, people would save these expenses, in order to procure necessary comforts for the poor, how many human miseries would be thereby relieved! "When thou shalt see one naked, cover him."[11]

4. To visit and ransom captives:—By *Captives* are meant those who have been taken and confined unjustly, or through misfortune. To visit such, with a view to comfort them; and to endeavour to obtain their deliverance, are acts of great charity, and are highly meritorious. To afford poor prrsons the means of keeping out of the workhouse is a similar charity.

(9) Tobias iv., 17. (10) Matt. x., 42. (11) Is lviii, 7.

5. To harbour the Harbourless :—To lodge Strangers in one's house, in the present state of society, is neither safe nor prudent; so that, this Work of Mercy would be better exercised, by affording the *means* to those who stand in need, of procuring a sufficient lodging. In many cases, this is a great and necessary charity.

To visit the Sick ;—To attend the Sick, or to visit them, in order to afford consolation, is always considered a great work of mercy; it relieves their affliction, cheers their drooping spirits, and gives them comfort; and it is doing as we would be done by.

7. To bury the Dead :—To afford decent burial to the Dead, is the last act of charity we can perform for our neighbour, with regard to the *body*. It should be done from motives of charity. For this Work of Mercy, Tobias is highly commended in Scripture, and held out to others, as an example.[12]

Conclusion :—These Works of Mercy are of such *obligation* and *importance*, that, to the neglect or performance of them, our sentence at the last day will be attributed: "Then shall the King say to them that shall be on his right hand: Come, ye blessed of my Father, possess you the kingdom prepared for you from the foundation of the world. *For*, I was hungry, and you gave me to eat: I was thirsty, and you gave me to drink: I was a stranger, and you took me in; naked, and you covered me: sick, and you visited me: I was in prison, and you came to me. Then shall the just answer him, saying: Lord, when did we see thee hungry, and fed thee? thirsty, and gave thee drink? and when did we see thee a stranger, and took thee in? or naked, and covered thee? or when did we see thee sick or in prison, and came to thee? And the King answering, shall say to them :

(17) Tobias xii., 11, 12.

Amen I say to you, as long as you did it to one of these my least brethren, you did it to me.——Then shall he say to them also that shall be on his left-hand: Depart from me, ye cursed, into everlasting fire which was prepared for the devil and his angels. *For* I was hungry, and you gave me *not* to eat: I was thirsty, and you gave me *not* to drink: I was a stranger, and you took me not in: naked, and you covered me not: sick and in prison, and you did not visit me......Amen I say to you, as long as you did it not to one of these least, you did it not to me.——And these shall go into everlasting punishments; but the just, into life everlasting."[13]

What a powerful motive to induce us to practise these Corporal Works of Mercy! The performance, or neglect of them is to decide our lot for ever! Take care, therefore, not to neglect them.

INSTRUCTION LXXIII.

THE SEVEN SPIRITUAL WORKS OF MERCY.

Say the seven Spiritual Works of Mercy:

1. To convert the sinner.
2. To instruct the ignorant.
3. To counsel the doubtful.
4. To comfort the sorrowful.
5. To bear wrongs patiently.
6. To forgive injuries.
7. To pray for the living and the dead.

The exercise of fraternal Charity extends to the performance, not only of the *Corporal*, but also of the Spiritual *Works of Mercy:* and, indeed, these are

(13) Matt. xxv., 34 to 40. (14) Matt. xxv., 34 to 40.

of greater importance; because the welfare of the soul is of far more consequence, than that of the body. If, therefore, so great a reward is given to those who relieve the corporal wants of their neighbour;[14] what must be the reward given to those who relieve his *spiritual* wants? Certainly, they will be entitled to God's tenderest mercies, and most special graces, in this life; and to a higher degree of glory in the next: "For they that instruct many to justice, shall shine as stars for all eternity."[15] "He who causeth a sinner to be converted from the error of his way, shall save his soul from death, and shall cover a multitude of sins."[16]

I. To Convert the sinner:—The most necessary good that we can procure for any one who is living in habits of sin, is, to convert him from his evil ways: this is the greatest act of Charity we can exercise towards him.——To admonish sinners with a view to their amendment, though a delicate point, is often a strict duty; but it is a duty, in the performance of which great prudence is required. Neglect not to give charitable admonitions, when there is a prospect of doing good: "If a man be overtaken in any fault, you who are spiritual, instruct such a one in the spirit of meekness."[17]

2. To instruct the ignorant:—How many opportunities are there of performing this Work of Mercy? By embracing these opportunities, you both contribute to your neighbour's salvation, and also add very considerably to your own future glory: "They that instruct many to justice shall shine as stars for all eternity."[18]

3. To Counsel the doubtful:—When doubts are floating in a person's mind, with regard to Religion

(14) Matt. xxv., 34 to 40. (15) Dan. xii., 3. (16) James v., 20. (17) Gal. vi., 1. (18) Dan. xii., 3.

and duty; and when, with regard to these, he is in difficult circumstances; it is a great charity to give him suitable advice—to relieve his anxious waverings, by clearing up his doubts; thereby putting him in the way of salvation. St. James says: "That he who causeth a sinner to be converted from the error of his way, shall save his soul from death, and shall cover a multitude of sins."[19]

4. To COMFORT THE SORROWFUL:—When we soothe the afflicted heart with words of consolation; suggesting motives of patience, resignation, and penance; and when we show towards the distressed a compassionate and kind treatment; we then comply with these words of St. Paul: "Weep with them that weep."[20] And when this is done from pure motives, from the motives of Christian Charity, it is very meritorious in the sight of God.

5. To BEAR WRONGS PATIENTLY:—People's humours, ill-tempers, and other failings, and also their ingratitude for kindnesses received, are sometimes so tiresome and provoking, that it requires no little patience to bear with them. Yet we ought not to lose our patience; but to bear with these failings of our neighbour, considering our own, and encouraging ourselves by these words of St. Paul: "Bear ye one another's burdens; and so you shall fulfil the law of Christ."......"We that are stronger ought to bear the infirmities of the weak."[21]

6. To FORGIVE INJURIES:—If our enemy repent and ask pardon, Charity obliges us to forgive him; for, if we were in his place, we should wish to be forgiven: "If thy brother sin against thee, reprove him; and if he do penance, forgive him. And if he sin against thee, seven times in a day, and seven times in a day be converted unto thee, saying I repent; for-

(19) James v., 20.
(20) Rom. xii., 15.
(21) Gal. vi., 2; Rom. xv, 1.
(22) Luke xvii., 3, 4.

give him."[22] But, even if he do not ask pardon, still Charity requires us to forgive him, as Christ on the Cross forgave his executioners;[23] and as St. Stephen forgave those who were stoning him to death.[24]

7. TO PRAY FOR THE LIVING AND THE DEAD:—We should pray for *all mankind*—for both friends and enemies. The latter, indeed, have more need of prayers; and our praying for them shows a more disinterested charity: "Pray one for another, that you may have saved."[25] "Pray for them that persecute and calumniate you."[26]——We should pray also for the dead—for our deceased relatives, friends, and benefactors; and for *all* the faithful departed: this is the last act of charity that we can do for them: "It is a holy and wholesome thought to pray for the dead, that they may be loosed from sins."[27]

CONCLUSION:—Be diligent in exercising these Works of Mercy, both Corporal and Spiritual. For thereby you will be "laying up to yourselves treasures in heaven; where neither the rust nor the moth doth consume, and where thieves do not break through, nor steal."[28] You will, by these good works, "make sure your calling and election;"[29] and there will be "laid up for you a crown of justice, which (at your departure out of this world) the just Judge will render unto you."[30] Because then, instead of that "judgment without mercy;" which will be dealt out "to him that hath not done mercy;"[31] in *you* will be fulfilled this Beautitude, promised by your Redeemer: "Blessed are the merciful; for they shall obtain mercy."[32]

(23) Luke xxiii., 34.
(24) Acts vii., 59.
(25) James v., 16.
(26) Matt. v., 44.
(27) 2 Mac. xii., 46.
(28) Matt. vi., 20.
(29) 2 Pet. i., 10.
(30) 2 Tim. iv., 8.
(31) James ii., 13.
(22) Matt. v., 7.

INSTRUCTION LXXIV.

THE EIGHT BEATITUDES.

Say the Eight Beatitudes:

1. Blessed are the poor in spirit; for theirs is the kingdom of heaven.
2. Blessed are the meek; for they shall possess the land.
3. Blessed are they that mourn; for they shall be comforted.
4. Blessed are they that hunger and thirst after justice; they shall be filled.
5. Blessed are the merciful; for they shall find mercy.
6. Blessed are the clean of heart; for they shall see God.
7. Blessed are the peace-makers; for they shall be called the children of God.
8. Blessed are they that suffer persecution for justice' sake; for theirs is the kingdom of heaven.

In the Eight Beatitudes with which Christ commences his Sermon on the Mount,[33] he shows us wherein true happiness really consists, and by what means we are to arrive at it.——Man naturally and necessarily seeks happiness; but blinded and deluded by his passions—by his love of the honours, riches, and pleasures of this life, he seeks his happiness where it is not to be found. Our Blessed Lord directs our pursuit to proper objects: he lays down Eight Maxims, as the foundations of that sublime morality which he came to teach, and which are the sure way to a happy life here, and also to eternal happiness hereafter.

1. "*Blessed are the poor in spirit; for theirs is the*

(33) Matt. v., 3 to 10.

kingdom of heaven:—How consoling are these words to the poor and destitute! *Their* kingdom, their elevation is not of this world; but they are directed to look forward to that happy kingdom which is to be their everlasting inheritance. If, on earth, they have to endure labours, hardships, humiliations, contempt, privations, and destitution; after their short pilgrimage here, they will be exalted, enriched, and united with their God in the possession of eternal glory: "For theirs is the kingdom of heaven."

Yet this Beatitude regards such of the poor only, as are so "*in spirit*"—such as bear their privations in a spirit of patience, resignation, and humility: and are content with their condition.

It applies also to those among the *rich*, who are "*poor in spirit*"—who are detached in heart and affection from their possessions; and who employ their riches in doing good, by assisting the poor, and contributing to the support of Religion: "Blessed are the poor *in spirit;* for theirs is the kingdom of heaven."

2. "*Blessed are the meek: for they shall possess the land:*"—Meekness, mildness, and gentleness of temper, are amiable dispositions, and when manifested under insults, violence, oppressions, injuries, or any other ill-treatment, they show the *true Christian:* they make a person pleasing to God, and beloved by men; and promote his happiness both here and hereafter: "Do thy works in meekness, and thou shalt be beloved above the glory of men."[34] "Blessed are the meek; for they shall possess the land"—"the land of the living."[35]

3. "*Blessed are they that mourn; for they shall be comforted:*"—To mourn, to lament, and weep, seem to earthly-minded persons to indicate anything but happiness and comfort: they seek their comfort in

(34) Eccli. iii., 19. (35) Ps xxvi., 13.

earthly pleasures and festive enjoyments. But Christ tells us, that *they* only have *true* happiness or comfort who mourn—who, renouncing earthly and carnal pleasures, bewail their own and others" sins,—who sigh over the dangers, to which salvation is continually exposed,—and who look upon this life as a time of banishment "They who sow *in tears* shall reap in joy:"[36] and therefore, "Blessed are they that mourn; for they shall be comforted."

4. "*Blessed are they that hunger and thirst after justice; for they shall be filled:*"—By hungering and thirsting after justice, is meant, *desiring ardently* and *seeking earnestly* to become JUST; i.e., to become every day more and more virtuous. This disposition of soul is a very great grace, enabling us to advance rapidly, and with much facility, in the practice of virtue; and to arrive, in a short time, at a very high state of perfection: it is a constant source of abundant merit, and an effectual means of acquiring a greater degree of glory in heaven: therefore, "Blessed are they that hunger and thirst after justice; for they shall be filled.

5. "*Blessed are the merciful; for they shall find mercy:*" To show mercy to our brethren, is one condition for our obtaining mercy from God. What an encouragement in this Beatitude, to assist the poor and distressed! If their wants are regarding the *body*, we have to exercise the Corporal Works of Mercy: "Do good [even] to them that hate you; bless them that curse you; pray for them that persecute and calumniate you."[37] By thus showing mercy to others, we disarm the anger of God, and entitle ourselves to his mercy: "Blessed are the merciful; for they shall find mercy."

6. "*Blessed are the clean of heart; for they shall*

(36) Ps. cxxv., 5. (37) Matt. v., 44;—Luke vi., 27, 28.

see God:"—The clean of heart" are they who are free from earthly, carnal, and impure affections, which defile the heart in the sight of God. Our outward actions correspond with, and proceed from, our inward dispositions: Our Blessed Lord assures us, that, out of the heart come forth evil actions, as well as evil thoughts and desires.[38] Now, God sees the heart—he sees its affections and intentions; and, unless these be right, whatever our outward conduct may be, we cannot *see God;* it is only the upright of heart that can enjoy this blessing: "Blessed are the clean of heart; for they shall see God."

7. "*Blessed are the Peace-makers; for they shall be called the children of God:*"—Peace-makers are, in a special manner, the followers of Christ, whose title is "THE PRINCE OF PEACE;"[39] and who bequeathed his peace, as a legacy, to his followers.——We must first *make peace* in our own souls, by subduing our passions, &c.;—then we must endeavour to make and maintain peace with our neighbour: "If it be possible, as much as is in you, have peace with all men."[40] "*If it be possible,*" i.e., if we can have peace with them, without purchasing it at the expense of truth or virtue. We should endeavour to reconcile persons who are at variance, by making peace between them: "Blessed are the Peace-makers; for they shall be called the children of God."

8. "*Blessed are they that suffer persecution for justice sake; for theirs is the kingdom of God:*—To suffer persecution in the cause of truth and virtue is the last and highest degree of Beatitude: it is the most perfect sacrifice of ourselves which we can make to our Creator; and, consequently, it "works for us above measure, exceedingly, an eternal weight of

(38) Matt. xv., 19. (40) Rom. xii., 18.
(39) Is. ix., 6.

glory."[41] Convinced of this truth, the Apostles esteemed it as a great favour, when God permitted them to be persecuted: "They went from the presence of the Council, rejoicing that they were accounted worthy to suffer reproach for the name of Jesus."[42] "My brethren (says St. James), count it all joy, when you shall fall into divers temptations," (i.e., trials and persecutions); "knowing that the trying of your faith worketh patience, and patience hath a perfect work."[43] "All that will live godly in Christ Jesus, shall suffer persecution."[44] These considerations should console and encourage us, when we have anything to endure for the cause of truth, or for our duty to God: "Blessed are they that suffer persecution for justice sake; for theirs is the kingdom of heaven."

CONCLUSION:--Endeavour to become truly "*poor in spirit*," by disengaging your affections from all attachments to earthly possessions; to be "*meek*," mild, and patient under contradictions; to "*mourn*" over your own sins, and those of others, by making atonement for them; to be always longing and striving "*after justice*," or greater perfection; and to fulfil what is pointed out in the other Beatitudes: then will you be truly "*blessed*," for you will then be happy here, in the peace of a good conscience, and happy hereafter, in the eternal enjoyment of all that is promised in these Eight Beatitudes.

(41) 2 Cor. iv., 17.
(42) Acts v 41.
(43) James i., 2, 3 4.
(44) 2 Tim. iii., 12.

INSTRUCTION LXXV.

The Seven Deadly Sins; and the Contrary Virtues.

Say the Seven Deadly Sins.—	Contrary Virtues.—
Pride.	Humility.
Covetousness.	Liberality.
Lust.	Chastity.
Anger.	Meekness.
Gluttony.	Temperance.
Envy.	Brotherly love.
Sloth.	Diligence.

These seven Vices are called *deadly*, because they bring *death* to the soul that yields to them. They are also called the seven *capital* sins, because they are the *heads* from which all other sins proceed. On these Vices, there are, in the "*Garden of the Soul,*" some very excellent Instructions, entitled "*Remedies against Vices;*" which it would be well to read occasionally with attention.

In each person, there is (generally speaking) some one passion or vicious inclination, which is stronger than the rest, and which is called his *Predominant Passion.* This is the ruling passion of his heart, and the chief source of all the vices to which he may be enslaved. You should pay very special attention to your Predominant Passion, and also to its Contrary Virtue; that you may root out the one, and plant the other in its place: this is the warfare wherein you will have to be engaged as long as you live; and to succeed in it, should be your constant aim and endeavour: "To him that overcometh I will give the hidden manna......To him that shall overcome, I will give to sit with me in my throne."[45]

1. PRIDE is an inordinate love of one's own excel-

(45) Apoc. ii., 17:—iii., 21.

lence—an inordinate self-esteem. It is a most dangerous passion, because it is so natural, and subtle; and also because it branches out into so many other vices; for the proud become vain-glorious, or fond of the applause of men—ambitious, or in love with worldly honours, hypocritical, conceited, disdainful, obstinate, and contentious. Pride is essentially a *lie*, because it is founded on falsehood; it is essentially a *robbery*, because it is the taking to one's self what belongs to God; and it is the very *root* of all evil: "From pride all perdition took its beginning."[46]

HUMILITY, on the contrary, is the foundation of every virtue. It teaches us to look upon all good, as coming to us from God, without any merit on our part, "What hast thou, which thou hast not received? and if thou hast received, why dost thou glory as if thou hadst not received it?"[47] It leads us to believe, not only that we have *no merit*, but that we have much *de*merit—that, if we were to have our due, we should receive from God nothing but chastisements on account of our sins. Hence, the humble man debases himself below all others: happy disposition! because it is most pleasing to God, and draws down his favours and protection: "To the humble God giveth grace."[48]

2. COVETOUSNESS is an inordinate love of riches or earthly possessions. The more this love is gratified, the stronger and more insatiable it becomes: as the possessions of a covetous man increase, his *want* of still greater possessions also increases; and consequently, covetousness makes a man *wretchedly poor*, even in the midst of *plenty*; it renders him deaf to the cries of the destitute, unmercifully sparing to the wants of his poor relations, and even to his own individual necessities; and it leads to many other sins—to extortion, cheating, stealing, and lying. What with the

(46) Tobias iv., 14. (47) I Cor. iv., 7. (48) I Pet. v., 5.

desire of gaining, and the *fear* of losing, the covetous man is always restless and unhappy: "They that will become rich, fall into temptation, and into the snare of the devil, and into many unprofitable and hurtful desires, which draw men into destruction and perdition. For the desire of money is the root of all evils."[49]

LIBERALITY, which is opposite to covetousness, withdraws the affections from earthly possessions; and leads us to exercise Works of Mercy: it makes us look upon it as being "a more blessed thing *to give*, rather than receive;"[50] and it inclines us, therefore, to "bow down our ear *cheerfully* to the poor," and to open our hand *readily* for the relief of him that is in distress.[51]

3. LUST is an inordinate love or desire of carnal pleasures; and it comprises every kind of uncleanness in thought, word, and deed. This vice is so displeasing to God, and the crimes to which it leads are so hateful in his sight, that he speaks of them as being "*detestable things*,"—as "*abominations*," which draw down his vengeance: "Every soul that shall commit any of these abominations, shall perish from the midst of his people."[52] It enkindles his wrath to such a degree, that his severest and most extensive chastisements, executed upon mankind in this life, have been provoked by sins of the flesh; as, the universal Deluge;[53] the destruction of Sodom, and of the neighbouring cities;[54] and the four-and-twenty thousand Israelites, whom God ordered at once to be slain in the desert.[55] This vice, by blinding the understanding, and hardening the heart, leads to almost every kind of sin; and is most ruinous in its consequences, both to body and soul; as the last day will demonstrate, by showing us the vast multi-

(49) 1 Tim. vi., 9, 10.
(50) Acts xx., 35.
(51) Eccli. iv., 8, 3.
(52) Levit. xviii., 29
(53) Gen. vi., 1 to 13. (56) Matt. v., 8
(54) Gen. xviii, 20; xix., 24, 25.
(55) Num. xxv., 1, 3, 4, 9.

tudes of impenitent sinners who will owe their ruin to this fatal vice.

CHASTITY is the contrary Virtue, which is so pleasing to God, that it draws down upon us his choicest graces and blessings. It renders our souls the spouses of Jesus Christ; and makes us like angels on earth: it is therefore called *the Angelic Virtue*. In order to obtain and preserve it, be humble; because humility is the Mother and Guardian of Chastity: it is only to the humble that God gives the special grace of this virtue. Never expose your Chastity to danger, but preserve it with the greatest care, praying for it frequently and earnestly, and always cherishing a great love and esteem for it in your heart: "Blessed are the *clean of heart*; for they shall see God."[56]

4. ANGER is an inordinate desire of revenge. This vice is directly contrary to the Spirit of the Gospel, which breathes nothing more than meekness and patience. Anger hurries a person into many other sins; as contentions, enmities, hatred, revenge, and fighting; and how many oaths, curses, and blasphemies proceed from it? Therefore, "let all bitterness and anger......be put away from you."[57]

MEEKNESS is contrary to anger; and it shows itself in mildness of conduct, gentleness of temper, and patient forbearance: it is a most amiable Virtue, which not only corrects our own anger, but also disarms that of others; and it makes persons beloved both by God and man: Learn of me, because I am meek and humble of heart; and you shall find rest to your souls."[58]

5. GLUTTONY is an excess in the use of food, or an inordinate desire of eating or drinking. Food is given to us to be used for our support; and not to be abused by intemperance. They are guilty of this vice who take too much to the prejudice of their health--

(56) Matt. v., 8. (57) Eph. iv., 31. (58) Matt. xi., 29.

who are over-nice in what they take—or who are always hankering after eating and drinking. Such persons should reflect, that we do not live in order to eat and drink; but we eat and drink in order to live; and that, by perverting this order, they rank themselves with those of whom St. Paul says: "They are enemies of the Cross of Christ; whose God is their belly, and whose end is destruction."[59]

TEMPERANCE and sobriety are contrary to gluttony: and they are virtues necessary for us, not only as preservatives from that vice, and from many other sins; but also as means of practising that penance, mortification, and self-denial, so much insisted upon and enforced by Christ and his Apostles.

6. ENVY is a sadness or repining at another's good, because it seems to lessen one's own; and it is directly opposed to Christian Charity, which, as St. Paul says, "envieth not, but rejoiceth in good."[60] Envy destroys a person's peace of mind; and is the source of so many other sins, that St. James says: "Where envying and contention is, there is inconstancy, and *every evil work*."[61]

BROTHERLY LOVE, on the contrary, "rejoices with them that rejoice, and weeps with them that weep;"[62] —it is the very spirit and practice of Christianity: 'The love of our neighbour worketh no evil; love therefore is the fulfilling of the law;"[63]—it is also the characteristic mark of the true followers of Christ: "By this shall all men know that you are my disciples—if you have love one for another."[64]

7. SLOTH is a laziness of soul, by which persons neglect to begin, or to perform, such things as are necessary for salvation; for as one of the deadly sins, it means *spiritual* sloth. The more this sloth is in-

(59) Philip. iii., 18, 19. (61) James iii., 16. (63) Rom. xiii., 8 to 10.
(60) 1 Cor. xiii., 4, 6. (62) Rom. xii., 15. (64) John xiii., 35.

dulged, the more burdensome it becomes. The slothful Christian has indeed faith; but it is a dead faith, because he neglects to keep it alive by good works. We are sent into this world, not to live at our ease, but to *work* out our salvation; and to succeed in this work, me must not only be resolute in "declining from evil;" but diligent also in "doing good."[65] (*Example* of the five foolish Virgins; and also of the slothful servant.[66])

DILIGENCE or spiritual fervour is a virtue by which we are zealous in *labouring* for the service of God, and the salvation of our soul: it makes the duties of Religion apppear, not burdensome or tedious, but easy and agreeable; it keeps the lamp of our faith burning with the oil of good works; and so causes us to be *always ready*, like the five wise Virgins; and, having made us rich in good works, it will entitle us, at our entrance into eternity, to hear from our Lord these consoling words: "Well done, good and faithful servant; because thou hast been faithful over a few things, I will place thee over many things: enter thou into the joy of the Lord."[67]

INSTRUCTION LXXVI.

The Six Sins against the Holy Ghost—the Four Sins crying to Heaven for Vengeance—the Nine ways of being accessary to another Person's Sins.

Say the Sins against the Holy Ghost.—1, Presumption of God's mercy—2, Despair—3, Resisting the known truth—4, Envy at another's spiritual good—5, Obstinacy in Sin—6, Final impenitence.

Say the four sins crying to heaven for vengeance—1, Wilful murder—2, Sodomy.—3, Oppression of the Poor —4, Defrauding labourers of their wages.

(65) Ps. xxxvi., 27. (66) Mat. xxv., 1 to 30. (67) Matt. xxv., 21, 23.

Say the nine ways of being accessary to another persons sins—1, By counsel—2, By command—3, By consent—4, By provocation—5, By praise or flattery—6, By concealment—7, By partaking—8, By silence—9, By defence of the ill done.

I. THE SIX SINS AGAINST THE HOLY GHOST:—These are not sins of mere frailty or ignorance; but of real malice, or wickedness of heart. They are directly contrary to God's love and mercy—to the Divine Charity; and are therefore called "Sins against the Holy Ghost."

1. *Presumption of God's mercy*:—This Presumption is a rash confidence of obtaining mercy and eternal salvation, without taking the means that are necessary; and it is founded on the idea which some persons get, that God is too merciful to condemn them to everlasting misery. We should bear in mind, that, though God is infinitely merciful, he is also *infinitely just*.

2. *Despair*:—This sin against the Holy Ghost is committed, by giving up all hope of salvation, or of the amendment of our life; as if we were already numbered amongst the reprobate.

3. *Resisting the known truth*:—This sin consists in speaking or writing against the true Religion, at the same time knowing better; or in wilfully misrepresenting its doctrines and practices, or in refusing to embrace it, when convinced of its truth. How common in these days!

4. *Envy at another's spiritual good*:—How common also is this! for, how many are there, at the present day, who scoff at Religious Orders, celibacy, fasting, festival days, confession, and other practices of the Catholic Church, because they aim not at such devotion themselves? Our practices of religion are a reproach to them; and are therefore the objects of their misrepresentations, and of their invectives, sar-

casms, and abuse, of which they are not at all sparing.

5. *Obstinacy in sin:*—This crime is committed by those who go on in sin, *positively* resisting graces, admonitions, remorses, &c. This is a most dreadful state of soul! for it draws down the execution of that terrible judgment, which was denounced against the Jews: "Blind the heart of this people, and make their ears heavy, and shut their eyes; lest they see with their eyes, and hear with their ears, and understand with their heart, and be converted and I heal them."[68]

6. *Final impenitence:*—This consists in putting off one's repentance till death, and then dying *without* repentance.

"Therefore, I say to you: Every sin and blasphemy shall be forgiven men; but the blasphemy of the Spirit shall not be forgiven. And whosoever shall speak a word against the Son of Man, it shall be forgiven him, bu he that shall speak against the Holy Ghost, it shall not be forgiven him, neither in this world, nor in the world to come;"[69] i.e., it will be, very difficult for such a sinner to obtain the grace of true repentance. Fina impenitence, of course, *cannot possibly* be forgiven because, after death, repentance comes too late. T avoid this dreadful evil, begin your repentance *now*—put yourself *now* in the state of grace: Let your loin be girt, and lamps burning in your hands, and yo yourselves like to men who wait for their Lord,..... that when he cometh and knocketh, they may open to him immediately: Blessed are those servants, whom the Lord, when he cometh, shall find watching...... And if he shall come in the second watch, or if he shall come in the third watch, and find them so, blessed are those servants......Be *you* then also ready; for at what hour you think not, the Son of Man will

(68) Is. vi., 10. (69) Matt. xii., 31, 32.

come."[70] Comply with this advice of your Redeemer, and then, whatever your sins may have been, instead of dying impenitent, you will die the death of the just, and obtain the eternal happiness for which you were created.

II. THE FOUR SINS CRYING TO HEAVEN FOR VENGEANCE:—These are four very dreadful crimes, against which Almighty God expresses his anger in the strongest terms. The explanation of them belongs properly to the explanation of the Commandments: for, *Wilful Murder* is forbidden by the Fifth Commandment—*Sodomy* (which is an unnatural sin of impurity), by the Sixth—*Oppression of the poor*, and *defrauding labourers of their wages*, by the Seventh.

These four sins are said to "*cry to heaven for vengeance*," because we find them so represented in the sacred Scriptures:—

1. *Wilful Murder*:—The Lord said to Cain: "What hast thou done? the voice of thy brother's blood *crieth to me* from the earth."[71]

2. *Sodomy*:—"And the Lord said: *The cry* of Sodom and Gomorrha is multiplied, and their sin is become exceedingly grievous. I wil go down and see whether they have done according to *the cry that is come to me*."[72] And the Angels said to Lot: "We will destroy this place, because *their cry is grown loud before the Lord*, who has sent us to destroy them."[73]

3. *Oppression of the poor*:—"You shall not hurt a widow or an orphan. If you hurt them, they will *cry out to me, and I will hear their cry*."[74] "The Lord will not accept any person against a poor man, and *he will hear the prayer of him that is wronged*. He will not despise the prayers of the fatherless: nor the widow, when she poureth out her complaint. Do not

(70) Luke xii., 35 to 40.
(71) Gen. iv., 10.
(72) Gen. xviii 20, 21.
(73) Gen. xix., 13.
(74) Exod. xxii., 22 to 24.

the widow's tears run down the cheek, and *her cry* against him that causeth them to fall? For from the cheek *they go up even to heaven*, and the Lord that heareth will not be delighted with them."[75]

4. *Defrauding labourers of their wages:*—"Behold the hire of the labourers, who have reaped down your fields, which by fraud hath been kept back by you, *crieth*; and the cry of them hath entered into the ears of the Lord of Sabaoth."[76]

III. THE NINE WAYS OF BEING ACCESSORY TO ANOTHER PERSON'S SINS:—There are some persons, who concern themselves but very little about the sins which they *cause* their neighbour to commit; although they are as guilty before God, as if they committed the sinful acts themselves; and even more so. We may *cause* others to sin (and so be guilty ourselves), in these nine ways, viz.:—

1. *By counsel:* i.e., by advising or directing the commission of an evil;

2. *By command:* by forcing or obliging any one to it;

3. *By consent:* by permitting any of those who are under our control to commit it;

4. *By provocation:* by exciting any one to passion, to cursing, to lewedness, &c.;

5. *By praise or flattery:* by praising or flattering any person for the evil which he has done, and thereby causing him to do it again;

6. *By concealment:* By hiding the crime, or the criminal, or things that have been stolen; and thereby encouraging the evil to go on, or by harbouring thieves, or lewd persons, thereby favouring their criminal practices;

7. *By partaking:* by shar'ng in ill-gotten goods, or in any other fruits of wickedness, whereby we encourage the transgressions;

(75) Eccli. xxxv., 16 to 19 (76) James v., 4

8. *By silence:* by not speaking to prevent an evil, when we *should and could* have prevented it;

9. *By defence of the ill done:* by justifying the evil-doers, or their evil actions; and also by defending false Religions.

When an injury has been done to our neighbour by any of these sins; he who has *caused* the injury to be done, is bound to repair it, just as much as if he *had done it himself.*——Besides the sin of causing *injury to be done to others*, and the obligation of *repairing it;* there is also the *guilt of scandal*, i.e., of *leading* the person into sin who did the evil. Now, if the destroying of our neighbour's body is a crime which cries to heaven for vengeance:[77] how much more the destroying of his soul? "Woe to the world because of scandals!" Such indeed is the wickedness of man, that there will be scandals: "For it must needs be that scandals come: but, nevertheless woe to that man by whom the scandal cometh......He that shall scandalize one of these little ones that believe in me, it were better for him that a mill-stone should be hanged about his neck, and that he should be drowned in the depth of the sea."[78]

INSTRUCTION LXXVII.

The Three Eminent Good Works—the Evangelical Counsels—the Four Last things to be remembered.

Say the three eminent Good Works.—1, Prayer—2, Fasting—3, Alms-deeds.

Say the Evangelical Counsels.—1, Voluntary Poverty—2, Perpetual Chastity—3, Entire Obedience.

Say the four last things to be remembered.—1, Death—2, Judgment—3, Hell—4, Heaven.

(77) Gen iv 10 (78) Matt. xviii., 6, 7.

1. THE THREE EMINENT GOOD WORKS:—These three good works are called *Eminent*, because they are in a most especial manner pleasing to God: and because by them we devote to God all that we are, and all that we have. For, *by Prayer*, we make to God an offering of our soul, with all its powers; and of our heart with all its affections: employing them in Acts of Faith, Hope, Charity, Contrition, Adoration, Thanksgiving, and other virtues; — *By Fasting*, we devote to him our body, with all its senses; offering it to him perpetually as a living sacrifice;— *By Alms-deeds*, we dedicate to him our earthly possessions, with all our means of assisting others; using them *for him* in the persons of the poor, and of such as need our help.

1. *Prayer*, as an Eminent Good Work, comprises, not only petition, but acts of adoration, praise, and thanksgiving—acts of faith, hope, charity, and contrition; and also a good and regular use of the holy Sacraments and Sacrifice; and more especially the practice of daily meditation, and of frequently raising our minds and hearts to God.

2. *Fasting*, as an Eminent Good Work, extends, not only to a faithful observance of the fasts and abstinences commanded by the Church, but to every species of mortification and self-denial—so necessary for leading a *spiritual life*, which is a life of daily penance and of self-crucifixion.

3. *Alms-deeds*, in like manner, are to be taken in a comprehensive sense; for they are to be understood as including *all kinds of charities*, both corporal and spiritual, which we can render to our neighbour.

By these three Eminent Good Works, we offer to God, like the three Wise Men, our frankincense (prayer), our myrrh (fasting), and our gold (alms-deeds).[79]——Be regular, diligent, fervent, and gene-

(79) Matt. ii., 11

rous in the exercise of them: for, as the Archangel Raphael said to Tobias, " *Prayer* is good with *Fasting* and *Alms*, more that to lay up treasures of gold....... When thou didst *pray with tears*, and didst *leave thy dinner*, and didst *bury the dead;* I offered thy prayer to the Lord."[80]

II. THE THREE EVANGELICAL COUNSELS:— These are called *Counsels*, because they are not commanded, but recommended, as means of greater perfection; and they are called *Evangelical* Counsels, because they are recommended as such, in the Gospel.

1. *Voluntary poverty* is a leaving of all things, by our own free will, to follow Christ. The practise of this Counsel uproots a most *dangerous* passion. " For they that will become rich, fall into temptation, and into the snare of the devil, and into many unprofitable and hurtful desires, which drown men into destruction and perdition."[81] " There is not a more wicked thing than to love money; for such a one setteth even his own soul to sale."[82] And hence our Lord declares: " That a rich man shall hardly enter into the kingdom of heaven. It is easier for a camel to pass through the eye of a needle, than for a rich man to enter into the kingdom of heaven."[83] He also says: " Woe to you that are rich; for you have your consolation" in this world.[84] Now, these awful declarations lose their terrors, and the soul is put into the most secure way to perfection, by the practice of this Counsel: " And behold one came and said to him: Good Master, what good shall I do that I may have life everlasting? Who said to him:......If thou wilt enter into life, keep the commandment......The young man saith to him: All these have kept from my youth, what is yet wanting to me? Jesus saith to him: *If thou wilt be per-*

(80) Tobias xii., 8, 12. (82) Eccli. x., 10. (84) Luke vi., 24.
(81) 1 Tim. vi., 9. (83) Matt. xix., 23, 24.

fect go sell what thou hast, and give to the poor, and thou shalt have treasure in heaven ; and come, follow me."[85] "Peter answering, said to him: Behold, we have *left all things*, and have followed thee: what therefore shall we have? And Jesus said to them: Amen I say to you, that you, who have followed me, in the regeneration, when the Son of Man shall sit on the seat of his Majesty, you also shall sit on twelve seats judging the twelve tribes of Israel. And *every one* that hath left house, or brethren, or father, or mother, or lands, for my name sake, and for the Gospel, shall receive a hundred-fold, and shall possess life everlasting."[86] "Blessed are the poor in spirit; for theirs is the kingdom of heaven."[87]

2. *Perpetual Chastity* is a voluntary abstining from marriage, in order to dedicate one's self, in a more special manner, to the love and service of God, and to the great work of salvation. It is strongly recommended by our Blessed Lord, when he says: "He that *can* receive this word, *let him receive it*."[88] How forcibly also does St. Paul recommend it, in his First Epistle to the Corinthians, where he says: "I would have you to be without solicitude: he that is without a wife, is solicitous for the things that belong to the Lord, how may he please God: but he that is with a wife, is solicitous for the things of the world, how he may please his wife, and he is divided."[89] And the Revelation made to St. John, in the Apocalypse, represents those who have observed this Counsel, as singing in heaven a new Canticle, which none of the rest of the Blessed can sing; and as being privileged to "follow the Lamb whithersoever he goeth."[90]

(85) Matt. xix., 21. (86) Matt. xix., 29; Mark x., 29, 30. (87) Matt. v., 3. (88) Matt xix., 11, 12. (89) 1 Cor. vii., 32 to 35. (90) Apoc. xiv., 3, 4.

3 *Entire Obedience* is a total subjection of one's own will to that of lawful superiors, in all that is not sin. The life of Christ was one continued model of perfect obedience. From twelve to thirty years of age, all that we are told of him is, that he was obedient to those whom his heavenly Father had appointed to act as his superiors: "He went down with them to Nazareth, and *was subject to them*."[91] Thus, does he show the importance of Obedience. And, as to his Obedience to his heavenly Father, he says: "In the *head* of the book (i.e., in the beginning of his life) it is written of me, that I should do thy will: O my God, I have desired it, and thy law in the midst of my heart."[92] "My meat (he says) is to do the will of him that sent me, that I may perfect his work."[93] And in the *end* of the book or history of his life, it is also written of him, that "he became obedient unto death, even to the death of the Cross."[94] How important, then, is Obedience! It is a most effectual means of subduing *self-will* and *self-love*, which are our most fatal enemies: For, "if thou give to thy soul her desires, she will make thee a joy to thine enemies."[95] But, on the contrary, "the obedient man shall speak of victories;"[96] because Obedience draws down the most special and abundant graces; for, so pleasing is it to God, that he says of it: "Obedience is better than sacrifices."[97]

All those persons who enter Religious Orders, bind themselves (*voluntarily*) by vow, to observe these three Evangelical Counsels.

We frequently hear and read the most bitter invectives against Monks and Nuns, who devote themselves to observe these Counsels. But is there anything in these three Maxims of Perfection to call for invective

(91) Luke ii., 51.
(92) Heb. x., 7; Ps. xxxix., 8, 9.
(93) John iv., 34.
(94) Phil. ii., 8.
(95) Eccli. xviii., 31.
(95) Prov., xxi., 36.
(97) 1 Kings xv. 22

or sarcasm? They who utter or write such things, would do better to practise these Counsels themselves, rather than scoff, as they do, at what Christ recommends, because they find the observance thereof too difficult for them. Let them reflect before it be too late, upon those works of Holy Scripture, which, unless they repent in this life, are prophetic of their repentance in the next: The wicked, repenting and groaning for anguish of spirit, will say within themselves when they see the salvation of the just: "These are they, whom we had some time in derision, and for a parable of reproach. We fools esteemed their life madness, and their end without honour: behold how they are numbered among the children of God, and their lot is among the Saints! Therefore we have erred from the way of truth, and the light of justice hath not shined unto us, and the sun of understanding hath not risen upon us..... Such things as these the sinners said in hell."[98]

III. THE FOUR LAST THINGS TO BE REMEMBERED:—The Holy Scriptures recommend the remembrance of these four last things—Death, Judgment, Hell, and Heaven, as an effectual means for avoiding evil, and for leading a life of innocence and virtue "In all thy works remember thy last end; and thou shalt never sin."[99] By the word "*remember*," we are admonished to keep our last end always in mind.

1. DEATH: We *shall* die; therefore we must *prepare:* we shall die very *soon*, because life is short therefore we must prepare *soon:* we *may* die at *any moment:* therefore we must prepare *now*, and must keep ourselves *always ready*.

2. JUDGMENT: For immediately after Death, comes *Judgment:* our soul will be instantly placed before Jesus Christ, to render unto him a strict account of

(98) Wisd. v., 1 to 14. (99) Eccli. vii., 40

all that we have thought, said, and done, during life, whether good or evil: and to receive sentence from him accordingly.

3. HELL: If we shall be found to be in the guilt of mortal sin, that sentence will be followed by an ETERNITY of *extreme misery*, with the devils and condemned souls in everlasting flames.

4. HEAVEN: But, if we shall be found to be in the state of sanctifying grace, then it will be followed by an ETERNITY of *supreme happiness*, with God and his Saints, in the kingdom of heaven.

If we reflected *seriously* on these awful truths, how we should then *fear* the great evil of sin; and how carefully we should *avoid* it! how diligent we should be in making use of the *means* proper for obtaining God's grace, and for persevering in our duty to him! Reflect, therefore, fequently and seriously on these truths—on these four Last Things: keep them constantly in mind; and you will find them a powerful preservative against falling into sin, in time of temptation: "In all thy works, remember thy last end; and thou shalt never sin."[100]

EXPLANATION

OF THE

CHRISTIAN'S RULE OF LIFE.

INSTRUCTION LXXVIII.

The Founding of the Christian Religion—The Rule of Life which this Religion teaches, viz., to hate sin, to love God, and to love our neighbour.

Of what religion are you?—By the grace of God I am a Christian.

Who was the founder of the Christian Religion?—

(100) Eccli. vii., 40.

Jesus Christ, the Son of God, who came down from heaven to teach us the way to heaven.

What rule of life must we follow, if we hope to be saved? —We must follow the rule of life taught by Jesus Christ.

What are we bound to do by this Rule?—We are bound always to hate sin and to love God.

How must we hate sin?—Above all other evils; so as to be resolved never to commit a wilful sin, for the love or fear of anything whatsoever.

How must we love God?—Above all things, and with our whole heart.

How must we learn to love God?—We must beg of God to teach us, "O my God, teach me to love thee!"

What else must we do?—We must often think how good God is, often speak to him in our hearts, and always seek to please him.

And does not Jesus Christ teach us also to love one another?—Yes; he commands us to love all persons without exception for his sake.

In what manner are we to love one another?—In God and for God, so as to wish well to all, and pray for all; and never to allow ourselves any thought, word, or deed, to the prejudice of any one.

And are we also to love our enemies?—Yes, we are; not only by forgiving them from our hearts, but also by wishing them well, and praying for them.

I. Foundation of the Christian Religion:—Our Religion was founded by Jesus Christ: and being thus the work of God, it is unchangeable: it varies not with times and circumstances, like all human institutions: its doctrines of Faith and Morality are the very same now, as were taught by Christ and his Apostles. This constant uniformity is a standing proof of the divinity of our Religion; and raises it infinitely above all erroneous societies. These retain indeed the name of Christian; but when the Catechism here speaks of the "*Christian Religion*," it means *that* Religion of which Christ is the Founder—*that* Religion which is called, in the Apostles' Creed, "*The Holy Catholic Church*," and in the Nicene Creed, "*the One, Holy, Catholic, and Apostolic Church.*" And that Religion is essentially ONE.

That there would be men setting up their own opinions as revealed truths, and calling them the doctrines of Christ, was foretold. The founder of our holy Religion calls such men "strangers"; "thieves and robbers;"[1] "false prophets;" "ravening wolves;"[2] and both He and his Apostles caution us against them.[3] They are branches cut off and dead: the very date of their separation, or of their origin, stands against them; and destroys the force of every argument which they would urge in their favour. And hence, instead of attempting to prove their *own* doctrines to be true, they exert all their powers in misrepresenting ours, and then inveighing against them.

It may indeed be said, that, from the fall of Adam, there has been but ONE true Religion. Before the coming of Christ, all hope of salvation was through the merits of the promised Redeemer:[4] the Prophets all foretold him; Judaism prefigured him, and expressed the most ardent desires of his coming. And hence, the Christian Religion may be said to have existed from the beginning: yet Christ is its Founder, by fulfilling the prophecies, and substituting the *reality* in place of the ancient types and figures: "Do not think (he says) that I am come to destroy the law, or the prophets: I am not come to destroy, but to fulfil."[5]

After the lapse of more than 4,000 years, Jesus Christ lays the foundation of our Religion, by calling

(1) John x., 5, 8, 10, 12, 13.
(2) Matt. vii., 15.
(3) Matt. vii., 15; xxiv., 23 to 22; 2 Pet. ii., 1, 2, 3, 12.
(4) Acts iv., 12.
(5) Matt. v., 17.

his twelve Apostles,[6] of whom he makes St. Peter the head:[7] he teaches them the great mysteries of salvation, and the most sublime maxims of morality: and he confirms his teaching by miracles; for, at his word, "the blind see, the lame walk, lepers are cleansed, the deaf hear, and the dead rise again:"[8] all nature is obedient to his voice!

After his Death and Resurrection, he gives full power and commission to his Apostles to teach his doctrines to the whole world, and to establish his Church:[9] to enable them to accomplish this great work, he endues them with power from on high, by sending down upon them the Holy Spirit,[10] to abide with them:[11] and he promises to be himself perpetually with them.[12] Thus prepared and empowered, the Apostles enter upon their mission: they preach, and convert: whole nations profess the faith of Christ; and the Christian Religion increases, like the stone cut out of the mountain,[13] so as to fill the whole earth.[14] This Religion, against which the gates of hell could never prevail,[15] has continued ever since, the very same as the Apostles left it; and we ought to thank the Providence of God, for having provided *for us* the happiness of being members of it.

II. THE CHRISTIAN'S RULE OF LIFE:—This holy Religion teaches the *Rule of Life*, which is set down here in the Catechism.

1. The first thing we are bound to do by this Rule is, "*to hate sin above all other evils;*" so as to be resolved never to commit a wilful sin, for the love or fear of anything whatsoever." As an effectual means of exciting such a hatred, we should reflect on the

(6) Luke vi., 13 to 16.
(7) Matt. xvi., 18, 19; Luke xxii., 31, 32; John xxi., 15, 16, 17.
(8) Matt. xi., 3, 4, 5.
(9) Mark xvi., 15 to 20.
(10) Luke xxiv., 49; Acts ii., 1 to 4.
(11) John xiv., 16, 17.
(12) Matt. xxviii., 19, 20.
(13) Dan. ii., 34, 35, 44, 45.
(14) Col. i., 5, 6; Rom. i., 8.
(15) Matt. xvi., 18.

greatness of the evil of sin—we should consider how it is the greatest of all evils, because it is directly opposed to that infinite Goodness and Perfection, which we ought to love above all things: and also because the consequences of sin are infinitely worse than any other evil that can befal us; for nothing but sin can rob us of heaven, or condemn us to hell. We cannot, therefore, have too great a horror and hatred of sin.

2. The next thing we are required to do by the Christian's Rule of Life is, "*to love God above all things, and with our whole heart;*" i.e., to love him with a love of preference; we are required to prefer God's will before all things else—before our dearest friends, our interests, or pleasures, or even our very life. The want of this preference will condemn many Christians—those married persons, for instance, who prefer husband or wife before God—those parents, who love their children more than they love God—all those persons in every station who prefer the creature before the Creator.

How are we to excite in our hearts the love of God above all things? "We must earnestly beg it of God;" for, being his pure gift, it is to be sought by prayer: this is the first and most necessary means of obtaining it. But God will not grant this precious gift of his love, unless we show the sincerity and earnestness of our prayers, by using such means as are in our power to render our petitions effectual. Therefore, we must not only pray for the love of God, but we must strive to keep the Commandments: and, moreover, we must employ our minds in such reflections as are calculated to excite Divine love in our souls; and hence, we should frequently think on God's infinite perfections, which render him deserving of all our love; on his infinite Goodness towards us, as manifested in our Creation, Preservation, Redemption; in all the corporal and spiritual blessings conferred upon us in this life; and in the eternal glory prepared for us in the next. These are most powerful means of exciting the love of God in our souls.

3. To this love of God, we must join the *love of our neighbour:* "This commandment we have from God, that he who loveth God, love also his brother."[16] Our love of our neighbour must have the same qualities, as our love of ourselves, viz., we must wish him well from our hearts; we must act towards him with kindness, and render him assistance, when he needs it and we are able to render it, and never entertain thoughts, or cherish dispositions, to his prejudice.

The love which we owe to our neighbour, must extend even to our greatest enemies: we must love them for God's sake; so as to forgive sincerely all the injuries which they may have done against us; complying with this command of Christ: "I say to you: Love your enemies; do good to them that hate you; bless them that curse you; pray for them that persecute and calumniate you; that you may be the children of your Father who is in heaven, who maketh his sun to rise upon the good and bad, and raineth upon the just and the unjust."[17]

INSTRUCTION LXXIX.

The Christian's Rule of Life requires us also to deny ourselves—to take up our Cross—and to follow Christ.

What other rules does Jesus Christ give us?—"To deny ourselves, to take up our cross, and to follow him."—*St. Matt.* xvi., 24.

What is meant by denying ourselves?—The renouncing of our own will, and going against our own humours inclinations, and passions.

(16) 1 John iv., 21. (17) Matt. v., 44, 45.

Why are we bound to deny ourselves in this manner?—Because our natural inclinations are prone to evil from our very childhood; and, if not curbed and corrected by self-denial, will infallibly carry us to hell.

What is meant by taking up our cross?—Patiently submitting to, and willingly embracing, the labours and sufferings of this short life.

And what is meant by following Christ?—To follow Christ, is to walk in his footsteps, by an imitation of his virtues.

What are the virtues we are to learn of him?—To be meek and humble of heart, to be obedient unto death, and seek to do, in all things, the will of his Father.

1. To DENY OURSELVES:—The self-denial which the Christian's Rule of Life requires, consists in a general mortification of our natural inclinations and passions. In consequence of the fall of our first parents, such is our natural tendency to evil, that mortification is as necessary for preserving our souls from sin, as salt is for preventing meat from becoming tainted: "For, if you live according to the flesh, you shall die; but if, by the spirit, you *mortify* the deeds of the flesh, you shall live."[18]

Our practice of virtue, and all our spiritual progress, our perseverance and salvation, depend on our imitating the life of Christ: now, we do not and cannot imitate him, unless we renounce ourselves: "If any man will come after me, let him deny himself."[19] Christ's whole life was one of suffering and self-denial: He was "despised, and the most abject of men, a man of sorrows,.........and as one struck by God and afflicted:"[20] and St. Paul says, that "they that are Christ's have crucified the flesh with its vices and concupiscences."[21]

(18) Rom. viii., 13.
(19) Matt. xvi., 24.
(20) Is. liii., 3, 4.
(21) Gal. v., 24.

Adopt, therefore, *resolutely*, the practice of mortification: offer violence to self-love and self-will *with firmness:* a resolute will surmounts all difficulties: "The kingdom of heaven suffereth violence, and the violent bear it away."[22]

There are two kinds of mortification, viz., *external* or *of the senses*, and *internal* or *of the heart*. Internal mortification is far better than that which is merely external; and it consists in correcting and subduing our disorderly appetites and passions.

In order to succeed in the important work of correcting and subduing your disorderly appetites and passions, you must *begin* with outward mortification and self-denial: you must not only abstain from all sinful pleasures, but you should frequently deprive yourselves even of lawful gratifications: you will thus acquire habits of self-denial, and find less difficulty in overcoming temptations. For, as St. Gregory observes, we more easily refrain from forbidden pleasures, when we are accustomed to abstain from such as are permitted: but says St. Clement of Alexandria, "They who allow themselves to do everything that is lawful, will soon do things that are unlawful."[23*]

You must acquire a habit of moderating and repressing your desires: "Turn away from thy own will: if thou give to thy soul her desires, she will make thee a joy to thy enemies."[24]

Examine what passion or disorderly inclination troubles you most—what is the ruling passion of your heart; and, having discovered it, direct all your force against it, until you have completely subdued it; imposing a penance upon yourselves every time you yield to it: "If, by the spirit, you mortify the deeds of the flesh, you shall live."[25]

(22) Matt. xi., 12.

(23)* "Cito facient quæ non licent, qui faciunt omnia quæ licent." *Pædagog lib.*, c. 1.

(24) Eccli. xviii., 31.

(25) Rom. viii., 13.

A *constant* and *resolute perseverance* in these practices, if accompanied with continual *watchfulness* and *prayer*, will draw down upon you the Grace of God, and give you a complete victory over your passions.

If the practice of this *continual* mortification seem difficult to you, look up to heaven, and see the recompense prepared for them that persevere: encourage yourself with these words of St. Bernard: "If the labour terrifies, the reward invites;" and still more with the Divine promises: "To him that overcometh, I will give the hidden manna."[26] This hidden manna is a constant peace of soul, and the sweetness of heavenly consolations which a proper practice of mortification never fails to produce—it is "the peace of God which surpasseth all understanding."[27] And hence St. Bernard says of those who observe the life of the mortified Christian, and are discouraged: "They see the cross which he carries; but they do not see the unction which it brings to his soul."[28*]

II. To take up our Cross:—By taking up our Cross, as the Christian's Rule of Life requires, is meant "patiently submitting to, and willingly embracing, the labours and sufferings of this short life." The troubles and afflictions of this life—misfortunes, losses, the privations of poverty, tribulations, pains, sickness, &c., are all from God: whatever may be the immediate cause of them, they are sent by Him; and are designed to withdraw your affections from this world, and to afford you means of exercising patience, resignation, and penance. Receive them as such, and they will be to you a source of very great merit: "For that which is at present momentary and light of our tribulation, worketh for us above measure exceedingly an eternal weight of glory."[29]

(26) Apoc. ii., 17
(27) Philip. iv., 7.
(28)* "Crucem vident unctionem non vident."
(29) 2 Cor. iv., 17

Evidently, therefore, they are tokens of God's mercy, goodness, and love towards you: "My son, neglect not the discipline of the Lord; neither be thou wearied whilst thou art rebuked by him: for, whom the Lord loveth, he chastiseth; and he scourgeth every son whom he receiveth."[30]

III. To FOLLOW CHRIST:—"To follow Christ, is to walk in his footsteps, by an imitation of his virtues." The virtues which we are especially to learn of him, are, "to be meek and humble of heart; to be obedient unto death; and to seek to do in all things, the will of his Father." These virtues—meekness, humility, obedience, and conformity to the Divine will, were most conspicuous in the life of Christ; and the practice of them is most pleasing to God. But the practice of them supposes a life beset with trials, contradictions, and persecutions; with humiliations and contempt; with labours and difficulties. Such was the life of Christ; and such is also the life of his true followers: "For whom he foreknew (or called to be saints) he also predestinated to be made conformable to the image of his Son."[31] We must expect, therefore, to be exercised with trials, humiliations, difficulties, &c.: whenever God sends these, we should receive and suffer them, like Christ, in a spirit of meekness, humility, and obedience to God's will; encouraging and consoling ourselves by keeping his example before our eyes, and by looking forward to the promised reward: "For if we be dead with him, we shall live also with him; if we suffer, we shall also reign with him."[32]

(30) Heb. xii., 5 6 (31) Rom. viii., 28, 29 (32) 2 Tim. ii., 11, 12

INSTRUCTION LXXX.

The Enemies of our Salvation, viz., the Devil—the World—and the Flesh.

Which are the enemies the Christian must fight against all the days of his life?—The devil, the world, and the flesh.

What do you mean by the devil?—Satan and all his wicked angels, who are ever seeking to draw us into sin, that we may be damned with them.

Whom do you mean by the world?—All wicked company, and all such as love the vanities, riches, and pleasures of this world better than God.

Why do you number those amongst the enemies of the soul?—Because they are always seeking, by word or example, to carry us along with them in the broad road that leads to damnation.

And what do you mean by the flesh?—Our own corrupt inclinations and passions, which are the most dangerous of all our enemies.

What must we do to hinder these enemies from dragging us along with them to hell?—We must always watch, pray, and fight against all their suggestions and temptations.

Whom must we depend upon in this warfare?—Not upon ourselves, but upon God alone.

In following the Christian's Rule of Life, we must not expect to go on without opposition. Hence the Wise Man admonishes us to be prepared for combat: "Son, when thou comest to the service of God, stand in justice and in fear, and prepare thy soul for temptation."[33] In our way to heaven, we have enemies to contend with; their opposition is violent and persevering; it will not cease except with our life. Christ himself endured temptations; his Saints have passed through many and difficult temptations; and *we* can-

33) Eccli. ii., 1.

not hope to escape: "The life of man upon earth is a warfare."[34] Temptations are permitted by Almighty God, in order that we may have occasions of proving our fidelity to him.

I. THE DEVIL:—*The Devil* is permitted to tempt us: "For our wrestling (says St. Paul) is not against flesh and blood; but against principalities and powers, against the rulers of the world of this darkness, against the spirits of wickedness in high places."[35] "Your adversary the devil, as a roaring lion, goeth about seeking whom he may devour; whom resist ye, strong in faith."[36]

How does the devil tempt us? 1, He places before our imagination such representations as serve to darken and blind our understanding; 2, He endeavours to deceive us with promises of false happiness; 3, He avails himself of the assistance of our self-love, or our love of honours, riches, and pleasures. Lay aside these fatal attachments; eradicate them from your heart; and then you will have no difficulty in overcoming the temptations of the devil: for this is laying the axe effectually to the *root* of the evil.

II. THE WORLD:—*The World* also (another dangerous enemy) is permitted to tempt us. By the world, we mean that large portion of mankind, who follow their passions and concupiscences—who propagate the false maxims of self-love, or the seeking of honours, riches, and pleasures, as the chief objects of pursuit, who court the rich and powerful, whilst they despise the poor: who ridicule the pious and virtuous, as weak or superstitious; and who frequently make outward professions of kindness and friendship, when no corresponding feeling exists in the heart. Such is the world! "For all that is in the world, is the concupiscence of the flesh, the concupiscence of

(34) Job vii., 1 (35) Eph. vi., 12. (36) 1 Pet. v., 8.

the eyes, and the pride of life."[37] "The whole world is seated in wickedness."[38] And yet it is admired, loved, and courted! its approbation is sought after, and its censures are dread! What a general fear there is amongst men of what the world will think, or say, or do? how they dread the idea of being laughed at, or pointed at, by the world? It is this that renders the world so dangerous an enemy; because to be ridiculed, or laughed at, wounds self-love and pride.

If you would prevent this enemy from exercising dangerous influence over you, 1, Labour to destroy your attachment to the honours, riches, and pleasures of this life; be poor in spirit, and humble of heart; and then the world can make no impression upon you; 2, Do not conform to its dissipating and pernicious customs; 3, Never court its favour, nor fear its frowns: but despise its opinions: "To me it is a very small thing to be judged by you, or by man's day:......but he that judgeth me is the Lord;[39]—4, Glory in standing up for the cause of God and of virtue, bearing in mind the words of our blessed Redeemer: "Blessed are ye, when men shall revile you, and persecute you, and speak all that is evil against you, untruly, for my sake; be glad and rejoice, for your reward is very great in heaven. For so they persecuted the prophets that were before you."[40]

III. THE FLESH. *The flesh* is called the most dangerous of all our enemies; and with reason, because it is a domestic enemy, and because from it the other two derive their force. By the flesh is meant corrupt nature—self-love and its passions—our propensity to sensual gratifications.

God created us to serve him in a state of innocence; and man had no difficulty, so long as he preserved his

(37) 1 John ii., 16.
(38) 1 John v., 19.
(39) 1 Cor. iv., 3, 4.
(40) Matt v., 11, 12.

innocence, in complying with this duty, because his heart was upright before God. But, after sin, the heart of man became corrupted, and naturally bent upon evil: we are under the necessity of resisting this natural tendency to evil; and hence it is, that "the life of man upon earth is a warfare."[41]

Self-love and its passions lead to evil, by darkening the understanding—by perverting the reason and engaging it on their side—by filling the imagination with vain, sensual, and sinful ideas, and thereby corrupting the heart. When the understanding is thus darkened, the reason perverted, and the heart corrupted, the will easily yields; and the more it yields, the more it is in danger of yielding again. "God seeing that the wickedness of men was great on the earth, and that all the thought of their heart was bent upon evil at all times, it repented him that he had made man on the earth."[42]

In order to avoid being thus led away by self-love and its passions, that is to say, by the flesh, we must employ the proper means: 1, We must meditate on such truths as will convince us of the vanity and emptiness of the transitory enjoyments of this world, and the misery of indulging in such as are sinful: 2, We must keep a strict watch over our senses, lest they should be a cause of temptation and sin: 3, To our watching, we must join fervent petitions to God, imploring his help and protection: 4, Our watching and praying must be accompanied with the practice of mortification and self-denial; for we must necessarily "crucify the flesh with its vices and concupiscences;"[43] 5, Being thus armed, we are prepared for combat: with these necessary weapons we are to fight against all the suggestions and temptations, not only of the flesh, but also of the other enemies of our

(41) Job vii., 1. (42) Gen. vi., 5, 6. (43) Gal. v., 24.

salvation. But we must bear this truth constantly in mind, that all our watching, and praying, and practising mortification, and all our fighting against temptations, will not be sufficient to give us the victory, unless we avoid the *occasions* that lead to sin. The presence of the immediate occasion of any sin renders the temptation to that sin more vivid and violent. In the same manner, therefore, as a man cannot "hide fire in his bosom, and his garments not burn; nor "walk upon hot coals, and his feet not be burnt;"[44] so we cannot expose ourselves wilfully and unnecessarily to the immediate occasions of sin, without falling victims to temptation. For "he that loveth danger shall perish in it."[45] No matter what our resolutions may be: the immediate occasions of sin will upset them, if we will expose ourselves to those occasions without necessity.

Therefore, meditate frequently and seriously,—watch over yourselves continually,—pray without ceasing, and earnestly,—mortify your senses and your inclinations,—in every assault of your enemies, fight manfully,—and be careful to avoid the occasions of sin; and then you may depend upon God giving you a complete victory: for although it be necessary that we should employ these means, we are not to depend upon ourselves at all in this warfare, nor upon our own endeavours; but upon God alone: For, "unless the Lord keep the city, he watcheth in vain that keepeth it."[46]

(44) Prov. vi., 27, 28. (45) Eccli. iii., 27. (46) Ps. cxxvi., 1.

EXPLANATION
OF THE
CHRISTIAN'S DAILY EXERCISE.

INSTRUCTION LXXXI.

What we are to do in the Morning; and how we are to go through the Day.

What is the first thing you should do in the morning?—I should make the sign of the cross and offer my heart and soul to God.

What should you do next?—I should rise diligently, dress myself modestly, and entertain myself with good thoughts.

What are those good thoughts?—Such as thoughts on the goodness of God, who grants me this day to labour in it for the salvation of my soul; which day perhaps may be my last.

And what should you do after you have put on your clothes?—I should kneel down to my prayers, and perform my morning exercise.

How should you perform the first part of your morning exercise?—I should bow down my whole soul and body to adore my God; and offer myself to his divine service.

How should you perform the second part of your morning exercise?—I should give him thanks for his infinite goodness to me and to all his creatures; and desire to join with all the Angels and Saints in blessing and praising him.

How should you perform the third part of your morning exercise?—I should crave pardon, from my heart, for all my sins; and beg that I may rather die, than offend my God any more.

How should you perform the Fourth part of your morning exercise?—I should offer up to God all my thoughts, words, and actions of the day; and beg his blessing on them.

And what prayers should you say after this?—I should say the Our Father, the Hail Mary, and the Apostles' Creed; and make Acts of Faith, Hope, and Love of God.

Should you do anything else?—I should pray for my friends and for my enemies, for the living, and for the dead; and beg mercy, grace, and salvation for all. Then I should conclude by desiring our Blessed Lady to be a mother to me, and by recommending myself to my good angel, and to all the court of heaven.

Is this all a good Christian should do by way of morning exercise?—No; for he should also, if he has time and opportunity, meditate in the morning on his last end, or some other devout subject, and hear Mass with attention and devotion.

What should you do at the beginning of every work or employment?—I should offer it up to God's service, and think that I will do it, because it is his will, and in order to please him.

And what should you do as to your eating, drinking, sleeping, and diversion?—All these things I should use with moderation, and do them because such is the will of God, and with a good intention to please him.

By what other means should you sanctify your ordinary actions and employments of the day?—By often raising up my heart to God whilst I am about them, and saying some short prayer to him.

What should you do as often as you hear the clock strike?—I should turn myself to God, and say to him, "O my God, teach me to love thee in time and eternity."

What should you do as often as you receive any blessing from God?—I should endeavour immediately to make him a return of thanksgiving and love.

What should you do when you find yourself tempted to sin?—I should make the sign of the cross upon my heart, and call upon God as earnestly as I can, saying "Lord, save me, or I perish."

And what if you have fallen into sin?—I should cast

myself in spirit at the feet of Christ, and humbly beg his pardon, saying, "Lord, be merciful to me a sinner."

What should you do when God sends you any cross, or suffering, or sickness, or pain?—I should say, "Lord, thy will be done; I take this for my sins."

And what other little prayers should you say to yourself, from time to time in the day?—Lord, what wilt thou have me to do? O teach me to do thy holy will in all things. Lord, keep me from sin. Come, my dear Jesus, and take full possession of my soul. Glory be to the Father, and to the Son, and to the Holy Ghost. As it was in the beginning, is now, and ever shall be, world without end. Amen.

This "*Christian's Daily Exercise*" is a very beautiful and useful part of the Catechism: it teaches us how we are to reduce to practice all the rest, by describing for us the method of introducing Religion into all the common actions of life: it descends to particulars, and leads us through the various occupations of each day, showing us how to render them virtuous and meritorious.

I. In the Morning, the first thing you should do, when you awake, is to make the Sign of the Cross, and immediately to offer your heart and soul to God: thus you will consecrate to him the first fruits of the day. In all our works a good beginning is of great importance: it will draw down the grace and blessing of heaven upon what remains to be done; so that, if we begin well, we are in a fair way of ending well.

When the proper time arrives for rising, rise immediately, without giving way to slothful indulgence. Observe due modesty in dressing, bearing in mind that you are in the presence of God and his Angels; and, as you must be thinking of something, strive to acquire the habit of occupying yourself with good thoughts; and more particularly to call to mind the subject which you have chosen for your Meditation.

[*Parents should be careful to prevent their children from appearing before each other without being sufficiently dressed, to the injury of their morals.*]

Being dressed, kneel down to say your Morning Prayers: let nothing but *real necessity* prevent you from doing so. In performing this duty, begin by placing yourselves in the presence of God, and imploring his assistance. Then, bowing down your whole soul and body, adore God as your Sovereign Lord and Creator, offering yourselves to his love and service; thank him for all his benefits, begging a continuance of them; crave pardon for all your sins, resolving to avoid them in future; and offer up to God all your thoughts, words, and actions of the day, begging his blessing upon them. All this may be done according to the following form:—

Behold me, O Lord, prostrate in thy holy presence, in order to bless and praise thine infinite Goodness, and to supplicate thy Mercy? oh: give me grace to pray as I ought.

Bowing down my whole soul and body, I adore thee as my Sovereign Lord and Creator, as my first Beginning and last end, on whom I depend for everything that I have or can hope for.

With sincere gratitude, I acknowledge the many and great blessings which I have received from thy Bounty; and I thank thee for them; vouchsafe to grant me a continuance of them.

I acknowledge also, with heart-felt sorrow, my past ingratitude—my many grievous sins committed against thee; and I implore thy forgiveness; resolved with the help of thy grace, never more to offend thee.

I offer up to thee all my thoughts, words, actions, and sufferings of this day, and of my whole life, and beg thy blessing on them; and I give myself wholly to thy love and service—henceforth I will live for thee, and for thee only: my sole intention shall be, during the remainder of my life, to please thee, by complying in all things with thy holy will.——And knowing that I owe a heavy debt of punishment for my past sins, I desire to make full satisfaction to thy justice while I am in this world; and therefore, by all the devotions and good works which I shall perform this day, I intend to gain all the indulgences attached to them; and, with this view, I offer them to thee now for the required intentions.

Then, in these dispositions and intentions, say the *Our Father*, *Hail Mary*, *Apostles' Creed*, and *Confiteor;* and make *Acts of Faith*, *Hope*, *Charity*, and *Contrition*. To these may be added such other prayers as shall be suitable to your time and devotion. Neglect not to pray for your friends and enemies, both living and dead; and to implore the graces and blessings of heaven for all the world. And never conclude your morning prayers without begging the intercession and protection of the Blessed Virgin, of your Angel Guardian, of your Patron Saint, and of the whole court of heaven.

Set apart a proper time, in the morning, for your *Meditation:* and be regular and diligent in this important exercise. [And never let a day pass without reading some portion of a spiritual Book, either in the morning, or some other part of the day.]

It is a very devout practice to *hear Mass* also, in the morning, whenever time and opportunity permit: hearing Mass is a most powerful means of grace, and of drawing down the Divine blessings upon yourselves and your families.

In this manner you should *begin* the day.

II. During the Day: or after you have finished your Morning Exercise, until the evening; you will be employed in the various occupations of your state of life; and perhaps you will have but little time to spend in prayer Still, we are admonished by our

Blessed Redeemer "that we ought *always* to pray."[47] How can you *pray always*? By living and acting in the spirit of prayer; i.e., by keeping yourselves in the Divine presence; and by performing all your actions *well*, for the love of God; offering them to him; and saying some short prayer to him from time to time, whilst you are performing them. By this means, *all* your actions, even the most trivial—your very eating, drinking, sleeping, and diversions, will be a kind of prayer; for, being done with the pure intention of pleasing God, and sanctified by your manner of performing them, they will be a means of drawing down graces and blessings upon you.

At the beginning, then, of every employment, offer it up to God: "O my God, I offer up to thee this ......: be pleased to give it thy blessing." If the employment be one of long continuance, offer it up again occasionally. By this means, you will walk in the presence of God, and lay up a rich store of merits for eternity.

In the course of the day, there are other occasions on which you ought to think of your Maker. For, as the Catechism teaches, you ought to make him a return of thanksgiving and love, whenever you receive any blessing from him; such as preservation from some danger, comfort in distress, victory over your passions, or over any temptation, &c. Never neglect to make this grateful return; for, gratitude for blessings received is the surest way of obtaining a continuance of them.

Again, if assaulted with temptations, think on your weakness—on the fatal consequences of yielding—and, remembering that in God alone is your help and safety, cry to him with perfect confidence: "Lord save me, or I perish!"[48] This will give vigour to your soul, and strengthen your resolution against sin.

(47) Luke xviii., 1. (48) Matt. viii., 25.

But if, unhappily, you have fallen into some sin, oh! think then on the uncertainty of human life—that you may die suddenly, when you least expect it; think on the happiness which you have lost, and the miserable eternity into which you are in danger of falling—think also on the GOOD GOD whom you have ungratefully offended, and, with a heart full of sorrow, exclaim: "'O God, be merciful to me, a sinner!'[49] For the sake of thy Sovereign Goodness, which I love above all things, I am sorry from my heart for having offended thee: oh! forgive me for thy mercy's sake!"——"Delay not to be converted to the Lord, and defer it not from day to day: for his wrath shall come on a sudden, and in the time of vengeance he will destroy thee."[50]

Again, if you feel the hardships of labour, the inclemency of the weather, the privations of poverty, pains, sickness, &c., endeavour to make a merit of these sufferings; consider them as coming from the hand of God for your good—to wean your affections from the love of this world, and to afford you opportunities of patience, resignation, and atonement. Receive them, therefore, in this spirit; saying from your heart: "Lord, thy will be done; I take this for my sins. 'Not my will, but thine be done.'"[51]

If you will spend your days in the manner just described, they will be to you *full days:* you will thus, "by good works, make sure your calling and election; for, doing these things, you shall not sin at any time: for so an entrance shall be ministered to you abundantly into the everlasting kingdom of our Lord and Saviour Jesus Christ."[52] For, you will be entitled to hear, after death, that consoling sentence. "Well done, good and faithful servant; because thou

(49) Luke xvii., 13.
(50) Eccli. v., 8, 9.
(51) Matt vi., 10; Luke xxii., 42.
(52) 2 Peter i., 10, 11.

hast been faithful over a few things, I will place thee over many things; enter thou into the joy of thy Lord."[53]

INSTRUCTION LXXXII.

Further directions how we should go through the day;—how we should finish the day.

How should you perform your evening exercises?—I should say the Our Father, the Hail Mary, and Belief, together with the acts of Faith, Hope, and the Love of God, &c., as I did in the morning.

And should you not also join with the family in saying the Litanies and other evening prayers, which are usually said in Catholic Families?—Yes; as also in the daily examination of conscience.

How should you prepare for your evening examination of conscience?—I should place myself in the presence of God, as I usually do at the beginning of all my prayers, and beg his light and help to know my sins, and to be sorry for them.

How should you make your examination of conscience?—I should consider how I have spent the day from morning till night; in what manner I have performed my prayers and all other duties; what blessings I have received from God; and what offences I have been guilty of against him, by commission or omission.

What acts should you perform after your examination of conscience?—I should give thanks to God for all his blessings, and beg pardon for all my sins, endeavouring to make a hearty act of contrition for them.

How should you conclude this evening exercise?—I should recommend my soul into the hands of God, with the best dispositions I can of love and conformity to his blessed will, as if I were to die that night.

How should you finish the day?—I should observe due modesty in going to bed; entertain myself with the

(53) Matt. xxv., 21.

thoughts of death; and endeavour to compose myself to rest at the foot of the cross, and to give my last thoughts to my crucified Saviour.

How do you make an Act of Faith?—O Eternal Truth who hast revealed thyself to men, one God in three Persons, Father, Son, and Holy Ghost, I believe in thee. O Jesus Christ, the Son of God, my Saviour and Redeemer, who hast died for us all, I believe in thee: I believe all the Divine truths which thou, my God, hast taught us by thy word and by the Church, because thou hast taught them, who art the Sovereign Truth; and I had rather die than call in question any of these truths.

How do you make an Act of Hope?—O my God, who art infinitely powerful and infinitely good, and merciful, who hast made me for thyself, and redeemed me by the blood of thy Son, and promised all good through him; I firmly hope for mercy, grace, and salvation from thee, through the same Jesus Christ my Saviour, ; resolving, on my part, to do all that thou requirest of me.

How do you make an Act of the Love of God?—O my God and my All, infinitely good in thyself, and infinitely good to me, I desire to praise thee, bless thee, and glorify thee for ever. O take possession of my whole soul, and make me for ever a servant of thy love.

How do you make an Act of the love of your Neighbour?—O my God, thou hast commanded me to love every neighbour as myself, for thy sake: O give me grace to fulfil this commandment. I desire to love every neighbour, whether friend or enemy, in thee and for thee. I renounce every thought, word, and deed, that is contrary to this love. I forgive all that have in any way offended me, and I beg thy mercy, grace, and salvation for all the world.

How do you make an Act of Contrition or your sins?—O my God, who art infinitely good, and always hatest sin, I beg pardon from the bottom of my heart for all my offences against thee; I detest them all and am heartily sorry for them, because they offend thy infinite goodness, and I beg I may rather die than be guilty of them any more.

The last Instruction shows, how you should *begin the day*, by offering your whole heart and soul to God; and by the due performance of your *Morning Exercise;* How you should *go through the day*, by doing all your actions *for God*—with the view to please him; How you should act when you receive any blessing from God; and also when he sends you crosses, afflictions, &c.;—How you should have immediate recourse to him for assistance and protection, when you are tempted to sin; and for mercy and pardon, whenever you have been so unhappy as to offend him.

I. PIOUS THOUGHTS AND EJACULATIONS DURING THE DAY:—But, besides these, there are many other occasions which will naturally direct your thoughts to God; as, for example, when you hear the clock strike, it should remind you how quickly time passes away: Reflect that you are then an hour nearer death, judgment, eternity! resolve to spend the time that remains in loving and serving God; and beg that he would enable you to do so: "O my God! teach me to love thee in time and eternity."—— When you see a large fire, think on the fire of hell, exclaiming with the Prophet Isaias: "Who can dwell with devouring fire? who shall dwell with everlasting burnings?"[54]——When you see a person dying, or dead, or hear the funeral bell from a neighbouring church, or hear of sudden death, or pass through a church-yard, say to yourself: "My turn may be next; resolve to prepare immediately for your last hour, and to keep yourself always ready; praying in the words of the Church: From sudden and unprovided death, deliver me, O Lord."[55]—— When you wash yourself, think of the state of your soul—how frequently it has been defiled with sin;

(54) Is. xxxiii., 14. (55) Lit of the Saints.

and make fervent *acts of Contrition*, saying, with the Penitent David: "Wash me yet more from mine iniquity and cleanse me from my sin."[56]——Thunder and lightning will remind you of the awful Majesty of God, and also of the day of judgment; and will suggest to you a variety of useful reflections, and, amongst the rest, this question: "Am I prepared to stand before the Divine Tribunal?"——When you behold the beauties of nature, direct your thoughts to heaven, saying with St. Augustin: "If thy magnificence, O Lord, be so illustriously displayed in this our dungeon; how resplendently shall it blaze forth in the palace of thy glory!......If this prison afford so many comforts, oh! what enjoyments are prepared for thy servants in their true and everlasting country?"[57]—Sincere genuine piety will suggest to you good thoughts, on many other occasions during the day.

II. HOW TO FINISH THE DAY:—Having described how you should *begin*, and *go through* the day; I have now to explain how you should *end* it. When you have finished your worldly employments, you are not to consider that all the duties of the day are completed; for you have yet to perform your *Evening Exercise.*

Never neglect your evening devotions, as too many do, who lie down to rest at night, like the beast of the field, without thinking of their Creator. Do not imitate them; but, before you retire to rest, say your *Night Prayers*, and endeavour to say them well. [Heads of Families should assemble their domestics, for the purpose of saying these prayers in common.] Night prayers should consist of the *Our Father*,—*Hail Mary*,—*Apostles' Creed*,—*Confiteor*,—and the *Acts;* with some other prayers according to

(56) Ps. l., 4. (57) Solil. cap. 21.

your devotion, or according to the forms which you find in your Prayer-Books.

Your Daily Examination of Conscience should never be omitted; but should form a part of your Evening Exercises; and it may be made in this manner:—First call to mind the benefits which you have received from God, and thank him for them, imploring a continuance of them: and then examine what sins you have committed during the day; make fervent *acts of Contrition* for them; resolving to avoid them in future, and also the occasions of them; and begging God's grace for this purpose. Endeavour, every night, to put yourself into such dispositions, as you would wish to be in at the moment of your death.

Never conclude your Evening Exercise, without recommending yourself to the intercession of the Blessed Virgin Mary, and all the saints and Angels; and begging your good Angel to guard and preserve you during the night.——When undressing yourself, remember that God and his holy Angels see you. And when you get into bed, say: "In the name of our Lord Jesus Christ, I lie down to rest. Lord, I offer my sleep to thee: preserve me, this night, from all evils of soul and body." Thus, even your sleep will be sanctified.

Begin and spend the next day according to the same plan; and so on, as long as you live; and then your life will be a life of virtue, and will entitle you hereafter to the possession of your God in a happy eternity.

Besides the daily examination of your Conscience, every night on your conduct during the day; you would do well to examine yourself every Sunday, on your conduct during the week; and to compare one week with another, humbling yourself at the sight of your sins, and resolving to spend the next week better. You must, of course, examine yourself again, when you prepare for Confession or Communion, on your conduct since your last Confession. Make it a point to approach frequently to the holy Communion; or, at least, as often as your spiritual director shall advise. At those times, renew your fervour in God's service, and form plans for the amendment of your life. By means of these self-examinations, and the graces of the Holy Communion, you will be enabled to keep yourself always ready for appearing before your God, whenever he shall be pleased to call you out of this life into eternity.

CONCLUSION:—Be always striving to practise this "Christian's Daily Exercise," which the Catechism recommends: persevere in this method, which is pointed out to you. Then you will "be perfect, as also your heavenly Father is perfect."[58] You will be "laying up to yourself treasures in heaven," which no one can take from you.[59] You will be "like the wise man who built his house upon a rock;"[60] for you will be firmly established on the rock of solid virtue, which no temptation will be able to shake. You will enjoy true contentment of heart, and peace of conscience, here during life; and the sight and possession of God, for all eternity, in the kingdom of heaven.

(58) Matt. v., 48. (59) Matt. vi., 19, 20. (60) Matt. vii., 24, 25.

THE END.